TORT LAW DEFENCES

The law of torts recognises many defences to liability. While some of these defences have been explored in detail, scant attention has been given to the theoretical foundations of defences generally. In particular, no serious attempt has been made to explain how defences relate to each other or to the torts to which they pertain. The goal of this book is to reduce the size of this substantial gap in our understanding of tort law. The principal way in which it attempts to do so is by developing a taxonomy of defences. The book shows that much can be learned ... ven defence from the way in which it is classified.

T '- **Volume 8 in the series Hart Studies in Private Law**

Tort Law Defences

James Goudkamp

·HART·
PUBLISHING
OXFORD AND PORTLAND, OREGON
2016

Hart Publishing

An imprint of Bloomsbury Publishing Plc

Hart Publishing Ltd
Kemp House
Chawley Park
Cumnor Hill
Oxford OX2 9PH
UK

Bloomsbury Publishing Plc
50 Bedford Square
London
WC1B 3DP
UK

www.hartpub.co.uk
www.bloomsbury.com

Published in North America (US and Canada) by
Hart Publishing
c/o International Specialized Book Services
920 NE 58th Avenue, Suite 300
Portland, OR 97213-3786
USA

www.isbs.com

HART PUBLISHING, the Hart/Stag logo, BLOOMSBURY and the
Diana logo are trademarks of Bloomsbury Publishing Plc

First published in hardback in 2013

British Library Cataloguing-in-Publication Data

A catalogue record for this book is available from the British Library.

ISBN: 978-1-84946-291-4 (hardback)
ISBN: 978-1-50990-502-7 (paperback)

Typeset by Hope Services, Abingdon
Printed and bound in Great Britain by
Lightning Source UK Ltd

To find out more about our authors and books visit www.hartpublishing.co.uk. Here you will
find extracts, author information, details of forthcoming events and the option to sign up for our
newsletters.

For my mother and father

PREFACE TO
THE PAPERBACK EDITION*

I am delighted that Hart Publishing agreed to publish *Tort Law Defences* ('*TLD*') in paperback. Publication in this format enables me to record publicly my debt of thanks to everyone who has engaged with the book. I refer to many of the published responses to it in this preface. However, I am equally grateful to the numerous people who have corresponded with me privately in relation to the arguments offered. I owe a particular debt of gratitude in this regard to Andrew Dyson, Charles Mitchell, John Murphy, Donal Nolan, Robert Stevens and Frederick Wilmot-Smith. I am also fortunate to have had the opportunity to receive feedback on *TLD* from participants in seminars held at City University, the University of Cambridge, the University of Edinburgh, the University of Oxford and the University of Western Australia. These valuable discussions enabled me to see fresh ways of looking at problems in the law of tort defences.

Save for correcting some typographical, grammatical and cognate errors and updating all of the citations where a better citation subsequently became available, the main text of *TLD* has been left unaltered. (The team at Hart Publishing has been able to ensure that the pagination of the main text is identical as between the hardback and paperback editions.) There are two main reasons why I resisted the urge to amend the text. First, the core claims made in *TLD* are not, in my view, affected by changes in the law, and certainly not by relatively minor changes. Suppose, for example, that a given doctrine that presently operates as a defence is modified so that it functions instead as a negative element of a cause of action. Such a change would not require any of the key propositions advanced in *TLD* to be reworked. The doctrine in question simply would be expelled from the taxonomy of defences articulated in *TLD*. If, conversely, a certain rule that currently functions by attacking an element of a cause of action is converted into a defence, the rule in question would be allocated to the appropriate category within the taxonomy. Accordingly, *TLD* continues, I think, to be relevant regardless of developments in the law. Readers who are interested in how the material substantive law in the United Kingdom has evolved since the hardback edition was published can find my thoughts (for what they are worth) in this regard elsewhere.[1]

---

* Frederick Wilmot-Smith provided me with insightful comments on an early draft of this preface. Needless to say, he bears no responsibility for the remaining mistakes.

[1] See, eg, E Peel and J Goudkamp, *Winfield & Jolowicz: Tort*, 19th edn (London, Sweet & Maxwell, 2014); J Goudkamp, 'A Long, Hard Look at *Gray v Thames Trains Ltd*' in P Davies and J Pila (eds), *The Jurisprudence of Lord Hoffmann: A Festschrift in Honour of Lord Leonard Hoffmann* (Oxford, Hart

Second, by leaving the main text unchanged, the published responses to *TLD* easily can be read alongside it.

Reply to Critics

Scholars have offered a wide range of responses to the arguments advanced in *TLD*. This section engages with certain of these responses. (It has been necessary to be selective due to space restrictions.) It is assumed for the purposes of this preface that the reader is familiar with *TLD*. In a nutshell, however, the claims made in *TLD* reduce to the following central propositions: (1) the entirety of that part of tort law that specifies when liability arises separates into the elements of torts (causes of action) and defences, where defences are understood as rules that prevent liability from arising even if all of the elements of the tort in which the claimant sues are present; (2) the law consequently distinguishes between pleas that deny that an element of the tort in which the claimant sues is present ('denials') and defences; (3) defences also differ from rules that merely diminish the extent of the claimant's recovery where the claimant is able to establish liability; (4) where the elements of a tort are satisfied, the defendant is a wrongdoer even if a defence applies; (5) all defences fall into two and only two categories, these being justificatory defences and public policy defences, with the former being defences the application of which depends on the reasonableness of the defendant's conduct and the latter being defences the application of which is not so dependent. When I refer in this preface to the taxonomy, I am referring to the classificatory system mentioned in point (5).

(i) Developments in tort law

Paul Mitchell argues:[2]

> To put it baldly, the logic of taxonomy insists that each specimen must be placed in one category or another; but where the specimen is a legal doctrine, that can lead to difficulties. There is no way to account for legal development in the course of which a doctrine has moved from one category to another . . .

Mitchell doubts whether the taxonomy can account for developments in the law. One possible reply to him ('R1') is that it is not the taxonomy's purpose to cap-

---

Publishing, 2015); J Goudkamp, 'The Doctrine of Illegality: A Private Law Hydra' (2015) 6 *United Kingdom Supreme Court Yearbook* 254; J Goudkamp, 'A Revolution in Duty of Care?' (2015) 131 *Law Quarterly Review* 519; J Goudkamp and M Ihuoma, 'A Tour of the Action in Negligence' (2016) *Professional Negligence* (forthcoming).

[2] P Mitchell, 'Tort Law Defences' (2014) 36 *Sydney Law Review* 185, 186–87. Consider also AM Frøseth, 'Book Review' (2015) 6 *Journal of European Tort Law* 102, 105. Frøseth writes: '[t]here is a risk . . . that the model proposed by Goudkamp will be too "simple" and lacking in nuance for it to facilitate the optimal dynamic development of the dichotomy between torts and defences . . .'.

ture systems of tort law that might exist in the future; it only seeks to organise the law as it presently stands. It might be said, accordingly, that Mitchell seeks unfairly to hold the taxonomy to a standard that it does not endeavour to meet. The taxonomy, understood according to R1, merely aims to explain how the law of tort defences crystallised as at the current day should be arranged. I am reluctant to embrace R1. This is because R1 is essentially a confession that the taxonomy has a short shelf life where such confession is not required. The better reply to Mitchell is that, contrary to what he contends, the taxonomy is in fact capable of accounting for developments in tort law ('R2'). Illustrations have already been offered of the taxonomy's capacity to accommodate change.[3] The simple point made by these illustrations is that when tort law undergoes a development to which the taxonomy is sensitive, the rule concerned is added to the appropriate category within the taxonomy, shifted from one category within the taxonomy to the other, or expelled from the taxonomy, as the case requires. Mitchell might retort that R2 is unconvincing precisely because it admits of the need to *reclassify* the law of tort defences following a relevant change. Reclassification, he might say, involves casting the taxonomy aside and installing a new taxonomy in its place. However, such a retort would lose sight of what is really happening. Changes to tort law (except perhaps for revolutionary shifts) do not require that any changes be made to the *categories* that constitute the taxonomy. Rather, changes demand only that the *contents* of the categories be refreshed. Updating the contents of the categories is not the same thing as installing a new taxonomy.

(ii) Composite rules

Paul Mitchell argues that the taxonomy cannot:[4]

> reflect the composite nature of a doctrine. Thus, the decision to treat *Gray v Thames Trains Ltd* as a denial of causation rather than a defence can be made with confidence only if one focuses exclusively on the speech of Lord Hoffmann . . . Lord Rodger's view was subtly different. For him, the illegality doctrine was essentially about causation, but the causation principles were being modified for public policy reasons to have a more restrictive effect than might otherwise have been the case. The most accurate way to characterise Lord Rodger's speech would be to put it mostly in denials, but also partly in public policy defences; unfortunately the taxonomical approach does not permit that kind of compromise.

Mitchell argues that certain rules might have features that require them to be placed into more than one category within the taxonomy (or might possess features that demand that they be placed both inside and outside the taxonomy). Such 'composite' rules, Mitchell says, defy attempts at classification. He offers the illegality doctrine as an example of a composite rule. Mitchell considers that according to the

---

[3] See the text accompanying n 1 above.
[4] Mitchell (n 2) 187.

way in which Lord Rodger understood it in *Gray v Thames Trains Ltd*,[5] the doctrine should be treated both as a denial of the causation element of the tort of negligence and as a public policy defence. It is tempting to respond to Mitchell by suggesting that Lord Rodger's speech did not reflect the *ratio decidendi* of *Gray*.[6] However, even if this were true, such a response obviously would not answer Mitchell's more general point. It would merely cast doubt on the adequacy of his example.

It is important in this regard to review the definitions of several key concepts in *TLD*. A public policy defence is a defence that is insensitive to the rational defensibility of the defendant's conduct. So defined, public policy defences cannot overlap with justificatory defences, the latter being defences that are concerned with the rational defensibility of what the defendant did. Neither can either type of defence overlap with denials. This is because whereas denials attack an element of the tort in which the claimant sues, defences preclude liability from arising only if all of the elements of the tort in question are satisfied. All three concepts – denials, justificatory defences and public policy defences – are mutually exclusive. The fact that no overlap exists between them means that it is impossible for 'composite' rules to exist. A given rule, in the context of any given action, can be only a denial, a justificatory defence or a public policy defence.

Mitchell thinks that rules can be 'composite' only because he uses the terminology of 'public policy' differently from the way in which it is used in *TLD*. By speaking of 'public policy' Mitchell appears to refer to the reasons for recognising a given rule. (He refers in the quoted passage to 'public policy reasons'.) It is readily accepted that all rules are (or should be) underpinned by public policy in the sense that their existence should be justified. When the words 'public policy' are used in this way, *every* rule is based on public policy. But this does not mean that rules can be part denial and part public policy defence. Denials and public policy defences, as defined in *TLD*, are mutually exclusive. So the overlap between denials and public policy defences perceived by Mitchell is merely imagined. In *TLD* I sought to stave off precisely the mistake made by Mitchell.[7] In retrospect, I probably should have opted for different terminology given the multiple meanings borne by the words 'public policy'.

---

[5] [2009] UKHL 33; [2009] 1 AC 1339. Subsequent developments arguably have overtaken the decision in *Gray* (consider *Hounga v Allen* [2014] UKSC 47; [2014] ICR 847; *Les Laboratoires Servier v Apotex Inc* [2014] UKSC 55; [2015] AC 430; *Bilta (UK) Ltd (in liq) v Nazir* [2015] UKSC 23; [2015] 2 WLR 1168). But this fact does not affect the gist of Mitchell's point.

[6] Certainly, subsequent judicial treatment of *Gray* has been fixated on Lord Hoffmann's speech: Goudkamp, 'A Long, Hard Look at *Gray v Thames Trains Ltd*' (n 1) 34–37.

[7] *TLD* 104. The same error is made by G Virgo, 'Book Review' (2015) 74 *Cambridge Law Journal* 160, 162. Virgo writes: 'the boundary between justificatory and public policy defences might not always be as clear as Goudkamp suggests. For example, he characterises the defence of public necessity as a justification because the defendant's conduct must be reasonable for the defence to be engaged, but the rationale of the defence depends on public policy objectives.' Virgo is quite right to say that the defence of public necessity is (or should be) based on public policy. But he is wrong to think that it follows that that defence is somehow partially a public policy defence. It is clear that Virgo means something very different when he speaks of 'public policy defences' from the way in which that concept is invoked in *TLD*, as evinced by his emphasis on the 'rationale' and 'objectives' of public policy defences.

There is a closely related misunderstanding that I am eager to forestall and which is consequently convenient to address here. That misunderstanding is that the taxonomy is somehow defective because a given rule can sometimes function in the context of one tort as a defence *and* as a denial in the context of another. Consider, again, the doctrine of illegality. That doctrine can attack the existence of an element of the tort in which the claimant sues.[8] When it operates in this way, it is a denial. However, the doctrine also can prevent liability from arising when all of the elements of the claimant's cause of action are present. Here, the doctrine is a (public policy) defence.[9] None of this presents the slightest difficulty for the taxonomy. There is no inconsistency in saying that a rule is a denial in the setting of one tort and a defence in another (and, importantly, this does not mean that the illegality doctrine is 'composite' rule in the sense meant by Mitchell for it is not functioning as both a denial and a public policy defence *simultaneously*). Far from the existence of rules that operate as a denial in relation to one tort and as a defence in connection with another somehow presenting a problem for the taxonomy, they confirm the taxonomy's importance. This is because they illustrate how the taxonomy can enrich understanding of tort law. The taxonomy reveals that certain rules function in different ways in relation to different causes of action in circumstances where such differences are otherwise likely to go unnoticed.

(iii) Uncertainty in the law

Eric Descheemaeker writes:[10]

> It will be recalled that, if we accept [Goudkamp's] argument, what is going to tell us what is a tort (and therefore what is defence) is not the allocation of onus of proof but whether we can find good reason for inaction, ie for the law prima facie to prohibit the conduct in question. The question thus immediately arises: where are we going to find these reasons? Two possible answers, between which the author does not choose, would be common morality and the oracles of the law (which, on this view, are meant to apply or translate pre-existing 'philosophical' judgments). In other words, the answer can come from the law itself, by looking at how it defines the cause of action – in a substantive, not procedural way – or it can come from outside the law, the assumption being that the two sets of rules will not conflict. This might answer the question in theory; but in practice it does not look like either source, or even their combination, is going to get us even close to answering the question with a sufficient degree of clarity. Given that, [for Goudkamp], knowing whether a particular rule belongs to the side of torts or that of defences is the most foundational question – determining in particular whether it belongs in the law of torts in the first place – this is an extremely significant problem.

---

[8] *TLD* 61, 71.

[9] *Ibid*, 126–27.

[10] E Descheemaeker, 'Tort Law Defences: A Defence of Conventionalism' (2014) 77 *Modern Law Review* 493, 501 (footnote omitted).

TLD does in fact commit explicitly to what Descheemaeker calls the 'oracles of the law' view.[11] But what should be made of Descheemaeker's point that it is often uncertain whether a given rule is part of the claimant's cause of action or a defence? Descheemaeker uses the doctrine of truth compellingly to illustrate just how severe the uncertainty can be. He observes (correctly) that it is most unclear whether that doctrine is a denial of an element of the tort of defamation or a defence.[12] So, it is true that it is sometimes obscure how a given rule should be allocated within the taxonomy (and whether a rule is part of the definitional elements of a tort, and hence falls outside the taxonomy, or a defence, and thus inside the taxonomy). But that only is because lawmakers sometimes fail to describe rules with sufficient precision. No problem with the taxonomy is uncovered. An analogy may assist. Early in Australia's colonial history, little information initially was available to British scientists about the platypus.[13] It was incompletely described (by way of rough sketches) by explorers who encountered it. As a result, significant debate broke out as to how it should be classified. However, the mere fact that the platypus was described inadequately for a time was not an indictment of existing systems of classification. The difficulty lay, instead, with an incomplete understanding of the platypus. Because of an initial lack of information about the monotreme, it was impossible to classify it with justified confidence. So it is with many legal doctrines, which are often incompletely specified, truth being a prime example. Indeed, far from revealing a problem with the taxonomy, Descheemaeker has merely alighted upon one reason why certainty in the law of tort defences is desirable. If sufficient detail is given as to a rule, and provided that one has a sound taxonomy of tort defences, it is possible for it to be organised properly. Uncertainty as to the state of the law gives us no more reason to discard a legal taxonomy than uncertainty as to the characteristics of an animal should cause us to abandon a system of biological classification.

(iv) Exclusions from the taxonomy

Several writers have queried whether the taxonomy is satisfactory given that it excludes from its net many rules. Erika Chamberlain, for instance, argues that the taxonomy lacks utility because it 'exclude[s] a number of defence-like doctrines,

---

[11] '[I]t is necessary to say a few words about how one can determine whether a given plea is a denial or a defence. Sometimes, *the courts or the legislature* state explicitly how a particular plea operates ...' (*TLD* 47 (footnote omitted) (emphasis added)); 'When the law of torts recognises particular conduct as tortious, *it* creates a duty not to engage in the conduct in question' (*ibid*, 39 (footnote omitted) (emphasis added)); 'not every reason that a defendant might be able to cite in an attempt to explain why he committed a tort forms the basis of a defence, *irrespective of the strength of the reason in question outside of the law*. Tort law is highly selective ... in choosing which reasons for committing a tort will furnish the defendant with a defence' (*ibid*, 82 (emphasis added)).

[12] For discussion, see *ibid*, 62–65.

[13] The story is told in BK Hall, 'The Paradoxical Platypus' (1999) 49 *BioScience* 211.

such as contributory negligence, consent and illegality.'[14] The first thing to observe is that consent[15] and illegality[16] can both function as defences and so, in fact, are not excluded from the taxonomy (although they are sometimes also denials of an element of certain causes of action,[17] and when they so function they fall outside the taxonomy). Having moved this point out of the way, what should be made of Chamberlain's query?[18] It is clear that myriad rules, some of which are of great practical significance, fall outside the taxonomy. The statutory provision for damages to be apportioned for contributory negligence[19] is a good example. However, the apportionment provision (and rules that belong to the same family, such as the mitigation of damage doctrine) is distinct from defences (and hence excluded from the taxonomy) for the reason that, unlike defences, it does not prevent liability from arising but merely reduces the amount of relief to which a claimant who has established liability is entitled. It is a remedy-restricting rule.[20] There is a fundamental difference between such rules and defences, this being the difference between that part of private law that determines when liability arises (of which defences form an important part) and that part that specifies which remedies are available.[21] This cleavage is as basic to private law as that between liability rules and sentencing rules in the criminal law. It follows that the suggestion that the taxonomy is inadequate because it does not capture rules such as the apportionment provision is misplaced. Indeed, the fact that remedy-restricting rules are placed outside the taxonomy is a virtue rather than a weakness of the taxonomy as it means that the taxonomy tracks and highlights the fundamental difference between liability-defeating rules and remedy-restricting rules.

(v) A distinction without a difference?

Luís Duarte d'Almeida has embarked on a highly sophisticated examination of the concept of exceptions from a jurisprudential perspective.[22] As a small part of his wider work, Duarte d'Almeida attacks my contention that defences (as that

---

[14] E Chamberlain, 'Classifying Tort Law Defences: Why Does it Matter?' (2015) 56 *Canadian Business Law Journal* 314, 314. Chamberlain amplifies this criticism at 315–16, 320–21.

[15] *TLD* 113–14.

[16] *Ibid*, 126–27.

[17] *Ibid*, 65–68, 113–14 (in relation to consent) and 61–62, 71 (in relation to illegality).

[18] For similar doubts about the taxonomy, see D Ryan, 'Tort Law Defences' (2014) 34 *Legal Studies* 743, 743–4. Ryan writes: 'Many may disagree with Goudkamp's decision to confine his focus exclusively to "confession and avoidance" pleas. In particular, the consequence this has of deeming contributory negligence to be outside the scope of the ambit of a study of defences may provoke criticism that Goudkamp's thesis pursues elegant taxonomical purity at the expense of practical inclusiveness.'

[19] Law Reform (Contributory Negligence) Act 1945 (UK), s 1.

[20] *TLD* 3.

[21] Chamberlain actually seems to acknowledge the significance of this distinction. She does not state in the passage quoted at the start of this section that the apportionment provision provides for a defence but a 'defence-*like* doctrine' (emphasis added).

[22] See, esp, L Duarte d'Almeida, *Allowing for Exceptions: A Theory of Defences and Defeasibility in Law* (Oxford, Oxford University Press, 2015). For a learned review, see F Wilmot-Smith, 'Allowing for Exceptions: A Theory of Defences and Defeasibility in Law' (2015) 131 *Law Quarterly Review* 681.

term is defined in *TLD*) are separate from the elements of torts.[23] He concludes that I offer no convincing basis for distinguishing between these concepts, with the result that I implicitly embrace 'incorporationism', Duarte d'Almeida's term for the thesis that denials and defences 'are just different *names* for two subsets of circumstances whose function is precisely the same.'[24] For example, Duarte d'Almeida writes:[25]

> Goudkamp is convinced that there *is* a 'fundamental difference' between the ingredients of torts . . . and the absence of valid defences . . . He thinks that to deny an element of the tort in which the claimant is suing is something significantly distinct from invoking a defence . . . But then he owes us an explanation of what, precisely, that difference is. For what the simple incorporationist model seems to show is precisely that there is *no* difference – no formal or structural or logical difference at any rate. A defendant who denies an element of the tort in which the claimant sues . . . seems to be doing exactly the same as a defendant who invokes a defence . . . Both are seeking to establish the *absence* of an element on which the claimant's success depends. So – asks the incorporationist – where is the difference?

Duarte d'Almeida doubts that I give a satisfactory answer (or, indeed, any answer) to this question.

While there is undoubtedly much of value to be learned from Duarte d'Almeida's analysis, most of it falls by the wayside *qua* criticism of *TLD*. This is because it is not, in fact, argued in *TLD* that there is any 'formal, or structural or logical difference' between denials and defences. *TLD*, unambitiously, simply makes the trite observation that lawmakers draw a distinction between torts and defences.[26] What is made, in other words, is a claim about the positive law. True, as Duarte d'Almeida notes, it is said in *TLD* that the distinction is, for example, 'fundamental'.[27] But by this I meant only that it is regarded as fundamental in the law's eyes. The distinction 'is one of the most basic organising devices *in tort law*.'[28] It 'is one of the most recognisable features *of the law of torts*.'[29] *TLD* specifically avoids committing as to whether the distinction upon which lawmakers have alighted is meaningful or is a distinction without a difference.[30] Undoubtedly, I did not explain myself as clearly as I should have. Nevertheless, numerous other theorists have made a particular point of the fact that I remain deliberately agnostic on the propositions to which Duarte d'Almeida's reads me as being committed.[31]

---

[23] L Duarte d'Almeida, 'Defining "Defences"' in A Dyson, J Goudkamp and F Wilmot-Smith (eds), *Defences in Tort* (Oxford, Hart Publishing, 2015)

[24] *Ibid*, 52 (emphasis in original).

[25] *Ibid*, 40 (emphasis in original) (footnotes omitted).

[26] *Ibid*, 1–3.

[27] *Ibid*, 6.

[28] *Ibid*, 5 (emphasis added).

[29] *Ibid*, 45 (emphasis added).

[30] *Ibid*, 40–41.

[31] See, eg, J Plunkett, 'Tort Law Defences' (2014) 88 *Australian Law Journal* 214, 214 ('Goudkamp . . . queries whether there is an intrinsically significant distinction between torts and defences, but does not commit either way'); Ryan (n 18) 744 ('ch 2 of [*TLD*] . . . does not arrive at any particularly firm conclusions on the intrinsic significance of the tort/defence distinction . . .').

It is only near the end of his relevant contribution that Duarte d'Almeida grapples with the material claim made in *TLD*, that is, that tort law treats as fundamental the distinction between elements of torts and defences. He disputes the accuracy of that claim. Duarte d'Almeida writes that I am:[32]

> wrong that *that* is the distinction that constitutes 'one of the basic organising devices in tort law'. The distinction that is indeed uniformly 'recognised . . . throughout the law of obligations', and comparable to the 'corresponding distinction [the offence/defence distinction, which] is also a central feature of the criminal law', is a different one. It is a distinction drawn within the universe of the circumstances that bear on the merits of an action in tort.

Duarte d'Almeida contrasts rules that 'bear on the merits of an action in tort' with 'procedural requisites.'[33] He may well be right that this distinction is recognised as important (however, even if correct, that would not mean that tort law does not also recognise the distinction between denials and defences). Nevertheless, it is beyond serious argument that tort law (and, indeed, private law generally) is sensitive to the difference between the elements of actions and defences. The divide between the elements of actions and defences is thoroughly engrained in tort law's vocabulary. Our entire system of pleadings, to give one example, is premised on the distinction (it being for claimants to plead in their statement of case facts which satisfy the elements of the action that they assert exist, and for defendants to plead, inter alia, facts that raise rules that are external to the cause of action on which the claimant relies, including defences).[34] Standing in the way of Duarte d'Almeida's claim, made in the first sentence in the last quoted passage, which is *a claim about the state of tort law*, is a hurdle of authority that is so toweringly high that Duarte d'Almeida cannot possibly surmount it. He does not even confront it.

(vi) The relevance of the criminal law?

Graham Virgo and Kumaralingam Amirthalingam take issue with the use that is made in *TLD* of scholarship regarding criminal law defences.[35] Virgo writes: 'Whilst it is important to have regard to what happens on the other side of the tort/crime divide, this must always be conducted carefully with regard to the aims and responses of the two systems.'[36] Amirthalingam states: '[Goudkamp] appears to assume that criminal law theory provides a good base on which to build the theory of tort law defences, despite alluding to the fundamental difference

---

[32] Duarte d'Almeida (n 23) 49 (footnote omitted).

[33] *Ibid*, 48.

[34] *TLD* 33, 138.

[35] Cf Frøseth (n 2) 104–05 who seems to think that there is insufficient cross-fertilisation between tort law and the criminal law in *TLD*. She writes: 'there should be a scope for their operation to fertilise and influence the development of each other after careful consideration in specific areas.' Frøseth is critical of scholars who understand tort law and the criminal law as being fundamentally separate institutions.

[36] Virgo (n 7) 162.

between the functions of criminal law and tort law . . . This review questions that assumption.'[37] Virgo and Amirthalingam's points are effectively the same. They doubt whether it legitimate for *TLD* to have had recourse to criminal law concepts and literature given the differences between tort and crime.[38]

I have not denied even for a moment that there are numerous fundamental differences between tort law and the criminal law.[39] However, the existence of such differences is not to the point. *TLD* relies upon only a handful of basic distinctions drawn by the criminal law. The relevant distinctions are principally those between, first, offences and defences and, second, denials, justifications, excuses and denials of basic responsibility. Neither Virgo nor Amirthalingam seem to dispute that tort law recognises parallel distinctions. Accordingly, nothing that Virgo or Amirthalingam say about the separation between tort law and the criminal law has caused me to doubt that tort law and the criminal law are cast in the same mould in the respects that matter for the purposes of the claims that are made in *TLD*. The very sophisticated criminal law literature regarding the distinctions in question consequently casts considerable light on tort law defences.

(vii) Affirmative answers to defences

Descheemaeker contends that the existence of affirmative answers to defences stands in the way of the idea that defences are separate from the elements of torts.[40] It is necessary to explain some of the terminology here. It is argued in *TLD* that tort law distinguishes between the elements of torts and defences. It is suggested in *TLD* that it would be possible to have a more complex system, such as a tripartite arrangement in which a further set of rules exists. Such a further set of rules – affirmative answers to defences – would fall to be considered only if and when it is determined that a defence applies. When an affirmative answer to a defence is established, the defence concerned does not prevent liability from arising even though facts necessary to enliven it exist.[41] No position is taken in *TLD* as to whether affirmative answers to defences are recognised by tort law.[42] However, Descheemaeker contends that they are indeed recognised. He says that[43]

---

[37] K Amirthalingam, 'Tort Law Defences' [2014] *Singapore Journal of Legal Studies* 443, 443.

[38] It is slightly odd that Virgo presses this point given that he has argued (compellingly) that tort law and the criminal law interact, and should interact, at a deep level: G Virgo, '"We do this in the Criminal Law and that in the Law of Tort": A New Fusion Debate' in SGA Pitel, JW Neyers and E Chamberlain (eds), *Tort Law: Challenging Orthodoxy* (Oxford, Hart Publishing, 2013). See also G Virgo, 'Justifying Necessity as a Defence in Tort Law' in A Dyson, J Goudkamp and F Wilmot-Smith (eds), *Defences in Tort* (Oxford, Hart Publishing, 2015).

[39] 'It is of course undeniable that there are very significant differences between the criminal law and tort law' (*TLD* 26 (footnote omitted)).

[40] Descheemaeker (n 10) 503–04. See also E Descheemaeker, 'Mapping Defamation Defences' (2015) 78 *Modern Law Review* 641, 644, 647

[41] *TLD* 31–34.

[42] *Ibid*, 34.

[43] Descheemaeker (n 10) 503.

it is very clear that English law knows affirmative answers to defences. The best example is probably to be found in the law of defamation with malice and qualified privilege: by establishing the defendant's malice . . . the claimant "qualifies" the privilege . . .

Descheemaeker considers that the existence of affirmative answers to defences reveals that the definition of a 'defence' embraced in *TLD* is inadequate. A defence, according to *TLD*, is a rule that prevents liability from arising even though all of the elements of the cause of action in which the claimant sues are present. Descheemaeker is correct to point out that a difficulty arises in this regard if affirmative answers to defences exist. In his words, pursuant to the definition of a 'defence' adopted in *TLD*:[44]

> we need [if affirmative answers to defences are found in tort law] to accept that (i) the defendant has committed a tort; (ii) the defendant has a defence; (iii) the defendant is liable. Thus, it is possible to have a defence yet be liable.

All that this uncovers, however, is that the definition of a 'defence' needs to be spelled out more fully if affirmative answers to defences exist (work that is not done in *TLD* because it remains agnostic regarding the existence of affirmative answers to defences). It would be a simple matter to expand the definition of a defence, if required. An expanded definition might be as follows: a defence is a rule that prevents liability from arising although all of the elements of the claimant's cause of action are present, unless a further rule applies that prevents liability from arising even though a defence has been engaged.

Contrary to what Descheemaeker thinks (and, as far as I can see, he does not explain his reasons for holding this view), expanding the definition of a defence would have no implications for the claim made in *TLD* that tort law recognises a separation between the elements of torts and defences. The existence of that distinction would be unaffected by the recognition of a further distinction between defences and affirmative answers to defences.

(viii) Actionable breaches of duty

Descheemaeker observes that *TLD*, in distinguishing between the elements of torts and defences, separates breaches of duty from actionable breaches of duty. It is possible, according to *TLD*, for there to be a breach of duty without, due to the application of a defence, that breach being actionable. Descheemaeker considers this to be problematic and, consequently, as casting doubt on the correctness of the idea that the elements of torts are separate from defences. He writes:[45]

> the moment we draw a distinction between breach of duty and actionability, we find ourselves with an enormous practical problem: how are we going to distinguish between a wrong and a non-wrong, in other words, between an unactionable breach of duty and a non-breach . . .?

[44] *Ibid*, 504.
[45] *Ibid*, 505.

The objection is puzzling. The distinction between actionable wrongs and wrongs that are not actionable is deeply entrenched in private law. It has been recognised at least since the origins of Roman law. Many rules depend very visibly upon the distinction, such as limitation bars and immunities. Such rules leave a breach of duty intact and merely prevent it from being actionable. The answer to Descheemaeker's question is as follows: a wrong is committed as soon as the elements of the cause of action in which the claimant sues are satisfied; wrongs, however, are not actionable if a defence applies. It is unclear why this understanding presents the 'enormous practical problem[s]' to which Descheemaeker alludes. Descheemaeker hints that the feared problems would arise because the courts do not 'perform works of supererogation by addressing the question whether a duty was breached over and above the separate question whether the defendant is liable.'[46] This, however, is manifestly false. It is entirely conventional for judges to consider, first, whether the elements of the tort in which the claimant sues are satisfied (and hence if a breach was committed) before considering, usually under a separate heading, whether a defence applies.[47] There is nothing problematic, either in theory or in practice, in the concept of a duty a breach of which cannot be redressed.

(ix) Jurisdictional divergence in the law

Virgo argues that the attempt made in *TLD* to apply the taxonomy to a range of legal systems fails (or is at least deeply problematic) because there are often major divergences in the law between jurisdictions.[48] This criticism is misplaced. It is of course true that there are significant differences between the various legal systems that are treated in *TLD*.[49] The existence of these divergences, however, is irrelevant to the success of the taxonomy. This is because no matter in which legal system one is operating, the taxonomy developed in *TLD* can be applied to its tort defences regime. It is true that a given rule might be classified in one way within the taxonomy in relation to a given legal system and differently with regards to another system. However, that fact does not strike at the taxonomy's foundations. It simply shows that the contents of the taxonomy's categories might differ depending on the legal system with which one is concerned.

---

[46] *Ibid.*

[47] *TLD* 13–14.

[48] Virgo (n 7) 162.

[49] For discussion stressing the scale of the divergences, see J Goudkamp and J Murphy, 'Divergent Evolution in the Law of Torts: Jurisdictional Isolation, Jurisprudential Divergence and Explanatory Theories' in A Robertson and M Tilbury (eds), *The Common Law of Obligations: Divergence and Unity* (Oxford, Hart Publishing, 2016).

Intractable Problems

Finally, I want to sketch several persistent problems in the law governing tort defences. None of these problems has been satisfactory resolved, and in respect of most of them very little learning exists. They are ripe for future consideration.

(i) Three questions about excuses

Perhaps the main difficulty that any attempt to organise tort law defences confronts concerns excuses. There are at least three important debates that need to be had in this regard. The first is what an excuse is. The second is whether tort law provides for excuses. The third is whether tort law should recognise excuses. The experience in relation to the criminal law strongly suggests that none of these questions admits of a straightforward answer. It is regrettable, however, that tort lawyers have not, for the most part, attempted to offer even tentative answers to them.[50] Readers of *TLD* who are looking for engagement with these questions will be disappointed. Little is said about the concept of an excuse.[51] *TLD* hints that there are no excuses in tort law, although all that is shown is that certain rules that might be thought to be excuses turn out, on closer examination, not to be excuses.[52] Next to nothing is said about whether excuses should be welcomed into tort law. I engaged with that issue in a subsequent contribution.[53] That treatment, however, is merely nascent.

(ii) Justified wrongs?

Another problem of vast proportions is whether wrongs can be justified or whether talk of justified wrongdoing is contradictory. The resolution of this issue has implications for the satisfactoriness of the taxonomy that is promoted in *TLD*. If justified conduct is not wrong, it would seem to be tricky to separate denials from justificatory defences, since both concepts simply would go to whether the claimant committed a wrong. The position taken in *TLD*, following seminal scholarship in the criminal law context, is that justified conduct is wrongful.[54] Whether or not this position is correct is highly controversial.

---

[50] Although see JCP Goldberg, 'Inexcusable Wrongs' (2015) 103 *California Law Review* 467.

[51] *TLD* 83–86.

[52] *Ibid*, 83–101.

[53] J Goudkamp, 'Defences in Tort and Crime' in M Dyson (ed), *Unravelling Tort and Crime* (Cambridge, Cambridge University Press, 2014) 224–31.

[54] *TLD* 76–80.

(iii) Why defences?

A question that has received virtually no attention (in both private law and criminal law scholarship) is why defences exist. Why are certain rules hived off and treated separately from the elements of torts (or offences)? Why, instead, has the law not opted to treat all rules that are presently understood as defences as negative definitional elements? Unless there is a compelling reason for continuing to embrace the current more complex bipartite structure, a unitary system should be embraced given that it is simpler. *TLD* offers some possible lines of argument in support of the current system but stops short of accepting any of them as being sufficient to justify the separation between the elements of torts and defences.[55] The question 'why defences?' is one of the most basic things that can be asked about the structure of both private law and the criminal law.

James Goudkamp
Keble College, Oxford
20 March 2016

---

[55] *Ibid*, ch 2.

PREFACE TO
THE HARDBACK EDITION

Defences to liability in tort are fascinating. Because they add an extra dimension to determinations of responsibility in tort law, they immediately reveal tort law's richness and complexity. Nevertheless, they are a part of tort law to which theorists have largely failed to attend. Thus, this book is an effort to address this failure. It attempts to deal with it by explaining how tort defences operate as a system and how they are integrated within the law of torts. It is argued that, in the great mass of cases and statutes, patterns in the law of tort defences can be identified. By paying attention to these patterns, much can be learned about individual defences and, indeed, about tort law generally.

This book is a distant descendant of a doctoral thesis that I completed at the University of Oxford. My gratitude is due first and foremost to my supervisors, Andrew Ashworth and Roderick Bagshaw. I could not have hoped for better people to guide me in my work. Their comments were invariably penetrating and insightful. Through gentle questioning, they persuaded me to moderate or to abandon some of my more ill-conceived ideas. Although I wanted to work with Andrew because I felt (and still believe) that tort lawyers can learn many valuable lessons from the criminal law literature, I quickly discovered that he knew an immense amount about tort law, and I am grateful to him for saving me from many bad mistakes regarding points of substantive tort law. My examiners, John Gardner and Ken Oliphant, also provided me with many thoughtful remarks and reactions that proved to be invaluable in the process of making the transition from thesis to book.

A large amount of the work on this book was completed during the course of a visiting position that I held at Harvard Law School. I am particularly grateful to John Goldberg and Henry Smith for the warm welcome that they extended to me and for inviting me to present my thinking regarding tort defences to the Harvard Private Law Group. The intense and sustained questioning to which I was subjected by the members of that Group provoked me to change quite radically my position on some key points. I also benefited greatly from a similar experience at a research forum at Melbourne Law School, which was generously organised by Andrew Robertson.

I have incurred several other large debts of gratitude while writing this book. Many friends and colleagues gave me their reactions to several chapters or to the entire book, including Simon Douglas, Peter Mirfield, John Murphy, Jason Neyers, Keith Rewell and Benjamin Spagnolo. I profited from wide-ranging discussions about the ideas that I promote in the book with Peter Cane, Jeremy Horder, Nicholas Southwood, Jane Stapleton and Robert Stevens. Special thanks are due to James Edelman, Charles Mitchell and Donal Nolan. It is without any exaggeration that I say that this book would not exist but for their encouragement and support over several years. My indefatigable research assistant, Jodi Gardner, played a large role in helping me to bring this book to fruition. Mimi Zou and Inês Veloso also provided me with valuable assistance with certain chapters.

I have been privileged to have had intellectually rich environments in which to work at Oxford. While a student at Madgalen College, I learned a great deal not only from my supervisor, Roderick Bagshaw, but also from Katharine Grevling, Roger Smith and Colin Tapper. As a Lecturer at St Hilda's College, I had the privilege of working with Katja Ziegler. While a Junior Research Fellow at Jesus College, I benefited greatly from having Peter Mirfield as a colleague. At Balliol College, I have been most fortunate to have had the opportunity to work with Timothy Endicott, Leslie Green and Grant Lamond.

Unfortunately, it was not possible for me to deal comprehensively with the Defamation Act 2013 (UK), which was enacted in the final stages of the production of this book (and is not yet in force). However, I was able to add some scattered references to it.

James Goudkamp
Balliol College, Oxford
25 May 2013

ACKNOWLEDGEMENTS

A highly condensed version of chapters 3, 5 and 6 appears as James Goudkamp, 'A Taxonomy of Tort Law Defences' in Simone Degeling, James Edelman and James Goudkamp (eds), *Torts in Commercial Law* (Sydney, Thomson Reuters, 2011). This material is reprinted with the kind permission of Thomson Reuters.

Chapter 8 appeared, in a rather different form, as James Goudkamp, 'Insanity as a Tort Defence' (2012) 31 *Oxford Journal of Legal Studies* 727. It is reprinted with the kind permission of the Oxford Journal of Legal Studies.

SUMMARY OF CONTENTS

CONTENTS

TABLE OF CASES

Australia

Table of Cases

Canada

European Court of Human Rights

Ireland

New Zealand

South Africa

United Kingdom

United States of America

TABLE OF STATUTES

Netherlands

Poland

Switzerland

United Kingdom

TABLE OF DELEGATED LEGISLATION

TABLE OF CONVENTIONS

TABLE OF MODEL CODES
AND RESTATEMENTS

1

Introduction

1.1. Tort Law Defences

In morality, a person who is accused of committing a wrong may be able to offer an answer to the allegation made against him. Answers to allegations of wrongdoing can have a bearing on one's moral responsibility. Analogous remarks can be made about the law of torts. A defendant whose conduct falls within the definition of a tort may be able to offer a defence. If accepted, the defence will have a bearing on his responsibility within the law of torts. Defences are the subject of this book. Its concern is not, for the most part, to identify the rationales for specific defences (or lack thereof). Neither is it to determine when individual defences are enlivened (or should be enlivened). These are matters of significant importance about which a great deal could be usefully said. But they are not the agenda of this book. Rather, the overarching aims of this book are to explain how defences operate as a system and to learn how they are woven into the tapestry that is tort law. Although defences are an important part of tort law (there are numerous defences available to every tort) and have existed since its inception, an analysis of this kind – a systematic study of the law of defences as an independent field – has never before been undertaken. This introductory chapter lays the foundations of the argument that follows.

1.2. What is a 'Defence'?

1.2.1. Multiple Meanings

The word 'defence' bears numerous meanings in the tort law context, and a considerable amount of confusion has been spawned by the widespread failure of legal scholars, judges and legislators to indicate what they mean by the word. This situation is a significant impediment to clear thinking in relation to tort law generally. Accordingly, it is essential to begin the analysis by distinguishing the several senses in which the word 'defence' is used in the tort law context and specifying clearly how it will be used in this book.

1.2.1.1. To include denials of elements of the tort in which the claimant sues

First, the word 'defence' is sometimes used to refer to any argument made by the defendant with the aim of persuading the court to hold that he is not liable.[1] So understood, the word 'defence' encompasses denials by the defendant of one or more of the elements of the tort in which the claimant sues.[2] Examples of denials include pleas by a defendant in proceedings in negligence that he did not owe the claimant a duty of care, that he acted reasonably or that the claimant did not suffer any damage. These pleas merely attack matters that constitute the claimant's cause of action. They do not introduce into the proceedings any issue that the claimant will not have already put into contention.

1.2.1.2. Liability-defeating rules that are external to the elements of the claimant's action

In a second and stricter sense, the word 'defence' refers only to rules that, when enlivened, result in a verdict for the defendant even though all of the ingredients of the tort in which the claimant sues are present. A defendant invokes a defence within this meaning of the word when he argues along the following lines: 'Even if I committed a tort, judgment should nevertheless be entered in my favour because of rule so and so.' Denials of elements of the tort in which the claimant sues do not qualify as defences when the word 'defence' is used in this way. Only rules such as limitation bars, public necessity and self-defence qualify. A defendant who relies on any of these rules seeks to avoid liability not by denying the claimant's allegations but by going around them.

Defences in the second sense of the word used to be known as pleas in 'confession and avoidance'. This terminology, which is occasionally still used,[3] is revealing.[4] It brought out clearly the fact that defences on the second meaning of that word are rules that are external to the elements of the claimant's action. Offering a defence involved a defendant 'confessing' that the facts narrated by the claimant in his pleadings amounted to a tort and alleging further facts that, if true, would

---

[1] It was so used by Brennan CJ and McHugh J in *Chakravarti v Advertiser Newspapers Ltd* [1998] HCA 37; (1998) 193 CLR 519, 527 [8], when they said that 'defences are either by way of denial or confession and avoidance'.

[2] Blackstone thought that the word 'defence' was properly confined to denials. He wrote: 'Defence, in it's [*sic*] true legal sense, signifies not a justification, protection, or guard, which is now it's [*sic*] popular signification; but merely an *opposing* or *denial* (from the French verb *defender* [*sic*]) of the truth or validity of the complaint. It is the *contestatio litis* of the civilians: a general assertion that the plaintiff hath no ground of action, which assertion is afterwards extended and maintained in his plea. For it would be ridiculous to suppose that the defendant comes and *defends* (or, in the vulgar acceptation, justifies) the force and injury, in one line, and pleads that he is *not guilty* of the trespass complained of, in the next': W Blackstone, *Commentaries on the Laws of England*, vol 3 (Oxford, Clarendon Press, 1768) 296–97 (emphasis in original).

[3] Eg, *Bryanston Finance Ltd v de Vries* [1975] QB 703, 734 (CA); *Chakravarti v Advertiser Newspapers Ltd* [1998] HCA 37; (1998) 193 CLR 519, 527 [8].

[4] See further JH Baker, *An Introduction to English Legal History*, 4th edn (London, Butterworths, 2002) 77–78.

enable the usual legal effect of the facts pleaded by the claimant to be 'avoided'. The terminology of confession and avoidance fell into disuse, however, because of its association with the long since abandoned rule that those defendants who wished to dispute liability had to choose between offering a denial and advancing a defence. The word 'confession' marked the fact that defendants could not, in earlier times, offer a denial and a defence. Today, defendants do not need to elect between these pleas.[5] They can simultaneously deny the claimant's allegations and appeal to a rule that circumvents their legal effect. One downside of this change is that it removed an incentive to distinguish rigorously between denials and defences in the second sense of the word.

1.2.1.3. Principles that diminish the claimant's relief

Thirdly, the word 'defence' is used to refer to principles in the law of remedies that restrict the relief available to claimants who succeed in establishing liability. One of the main situations where the word 'defence' is deployed in this sense concerns contributory negligence. It is commonplace for the provision for apportionment for contributory negligence[6] to be described as a defence.[7] Other remedial principles that are routinely described as defences include the doctrine of mitigation of damage[8] and the doctrine of illegality (which is part of the law of remedies in so far as it operates to diminish recovery under particular heads of damages[9]). This third meaning of the word 'defence' is distinct from the first and second meanings. It refers to rules that diminish the claimant's relief, whereas the former meanings refer to pleas that negate liability.

1.2.1.4. Rules in respect of which the defendant carries the onus of proof

Fourthly, a defence is sometimes said to be a rule the applicability of which is for the defendant to prove. Tony Weir used the word 'defence' in this way when he wrote: 'Contributory negligence is unquestionably a defence . . . [since] it is for the defendant to plead and prove it.'[10] So did the current editor of *Winfield & Jolowicz* when he said that arrest and certain other pleas that may be raised in the context of false imprisonment 'are defences in the true sense, that is to say, it is for the defendant to raise and to establish them'.[11]

---

[5] For discussion, see JH Friedenthal, MK Kane and AR Miller, *Civil Procedure*, 4th edn (St Paul, Minn, Thomson West, 2005) 301ff; D Dow, 'The Right to Plead Inconsistent Defenses' (1948) 28 *Nebraska Law Review* 29.

[6] Law Reform (Contributory Negligence) Act 1945 (UK), s 1.

[7] Among countless examples see *Reeves v Commissioner of Police of the Metropolis* [2000] 1 AC 360, 371 (HL); *Corr v IBC Vehicles Ltd* [2008] UKHL 13; [2008] 1 AC 884, 905 [19]; P Cane, *The Anatomy of Tort Law* (Oxford, Hart Publishing, 1997) 58.

[8] Eg, *Halifax plc v Gould* [1998] 3 EGLR 177, 182 (CA).

[9] As in *Gray v Thames Trains Ltd* [2009] UKHL 33; [2009] AC 1339 (damages denied in respect of the consequences of the imposition of a criminal sanction).

[10] T Weir, *An Introduction to Tort Law*, 2nd edn (Oxford, Clarendon Press, 2006) 129.

[11] WVH Rogers (ed), *Winfield & Jolowicz on Tort*, 18th edn (London, Sweet & Maxwell, 2010) 120 [4.19] (footnote omitted).

One who gives the word 'defence' this meaning uses it in a way that is distinct from the senses previously mentioned. It is obviously different from the first meaning of the word. The first sense in which the word 'defence' is used encompasses denials of elements of the claimant's cause of action, and it normally falls to the claimant to prove the elements of his action.[12] In contrast, a defence in the fourth sense of the word is a rule that the defendant bears the onus of establishing.

The distinction between the second and fourth meanings of the word 'defence' is harder to spot and many torts scholars have failed to notice it. Consider the following passage in John Goldberg and Benjamin Zipursky's *The Oxford Introductions to US Law: Torts*:[13]

> Affirmative defenses are legally recognized grounds for defeating liability even when a legal wrong has been committed. To treat these grounds as affirmative defenses is to say that it is the defendant's burden, rather than the plaintiff's, to raise them in court pleadings and to prove them.

Confusingly, Goldberg and Zipursky use the word 'defence' in different ways in this passage. The first sentence adopts the second meaning of the word 'defence', while the second sentence embraces the fourth meaning. It is possible to illuminate the difference between the second and fourth senses in which the word 'defence' is used by considering limitation bars. A limitation bar is a defence in the second identified sense (it is a rule that defeats liability that is external to the elements of the claimant's action) but it is not (at least in England) a defence on the fourth meaning of the word. It is not a defence in the fourth sense of the word because, rightly or wrongly, once a limitation bar is put in issue by the defendant, the claimant bears the onus of showing that the action was brought in time. In the words of the English Law Commission, 'the claimant has the burden of disproving a limitation defence where the defendant has pleaded one'.[14] This reveals the difference between the second and fourth definitions of the word 'defence'. The difference exists because rules that are defences in the second sense of the word do not always need to be established by the defendant.

The fourth meaning of the word 'defence' is also distinct from its third identified meaning. Consider the provision for apportionment for contributory negligence. That provision is a defence in the third sense, as has been noted. It is also a defence in the fourth sense as the defendant bears the onus of showing that it applies.[15] But this does not mean that there is no difference between the third and

---

[12] See the text accompanying n 66 below and 6.4.

[13] JCP Goldberg and BC Zipursky, *The Oxford Introductions to US Law: Torts* (Oxford, Oxford University Press, 2010) 110. See also at 183: 'Affirmative defenses must be pleaded and proved by the defendant. Where applicable, they defeat the plaintiff's claim even though the defendant acted tortiously toward the plaintiff.'

[14] Law Commission, *Limitation of Actions* (Law Com No 270, 2001) 195 [5.29]. See also Law Commission *Limitation of Actions* (Law Com CP No 151, 1998) 170–71 [9.23]–[9.25]; *Lloyds Bank plc v Crosse & Crosse* [2001] EWCA Civ 366; [2001] PNLR 34, 839 [41]; *Fiona Trust & Holding Corp v Privalov* [2010] EWHC 3199 (Comm) [315].

[15] *Flower v Ebbw Vale Steel, Iron and Coal Co Ltd* [1936] AC 206, 216 (HL); *Joslyn v Berryman* [2003] HCA 34; (2003) 214 CLR 552, 559 [18].

fourth meanings of the word 'defence'. Suppose that the legislature enacts a statute that provides that the claimant must prove that he took reasonable care for his own safety in order to avoid having his damages apportioned.[16] Were such a statute passed, the apportionment provision would cease to be a 'defence' in the fourth sense of the word. But it would remain a defence on the third sense.

1.2.1.5. The final element of the claimant's cause of action

It is sometimes asserted that the absence of defences is the final element of certain torts or of all torts. John Fleming used the word 'defence' in this way. He asserted that the action in negligence consists in five elements, the fifth of which was the absence of any defences.[17] In a similar vein, the Restatement (Second) of Torts organises the action in negligence into four elements, the last of which is the inapplicability of any defences.[18] Perhaps the most striking usage of the term 'defence' in this sense is found in the writings of John Wigmore.[19] Wigmore argued that all torts have three elements: a damage element, a responsibility element and a defences or 'excuse or justification' element.

This usage gives a distinct meaning to the word 'defence'. Unlike the fourth meaning, this meaning, by internalising defences within the definition of the relevant tort, would require claimants to disprove defences. Unlike the third meaning, this meaning of the word 'defence' directs attention to liability rules rather than to remedial rules. Unlike the second meaning, it does not regard defences as rules that stand outside of the elements of the tort in which the claimant sues. And unlike the first meaning, it would produce the result that the only denials that qualify as defences are those that target the supposed 'no defences element'.

1.2.2. The Meaning Given to the Word 'Defence' in this Book

The word 'defence' should not be used in the first-mentioned sense. Describing any argument made by the defendant that he should not be held liable as a defence suppresses the difference between the claimant's cause of action and liability-defeating rules that are external to the elements of the claimant's action. Obscuring this distinction is undesirable. This is because it is one of the most basic organising devices in tort law. A sense of its significance may be gleaned from the fact that it is recognised not only in tort law but throughout the law of obligations. A corresponding distinction is also a central feature of the criminal law.

---

[16] As has been done in many Australian jurisdictions in certain settings: see, eg, Civil Liability Act 2002 (NSW), s 50(3); Motor Accidents Compensation Act 1999 (NSW), s 138.

[17] JG Fleming, *The Law of Torts*, 9th edn (Sydney, Law Book Co, 1998) 115–16. This understanding is preserved in the 10th edition of Fleming's book: C Sappideen and P Vines (eds), *Fleming's The Law of Torts*, 10th edn (Sydney, Lawbook Co, 2011) 122 [6.20].

[18] § 281 defines the action in negligence. The word 'defence' does not actually feature in § 281. But the final clause of § 281, clause (d), incorporates §§ 463–496 by reference. These sections encompass defences.

[19] JH Wigmore, 'The Tripartite Division of Torts' (1894) 8 *Harvard Law Review* 200; JH Wigmore, 'A General Analysis of Tort-Relations' (1895) 8 *Harvard Law Review* 377.

The third meaning of the word 'defence' is also unhelpful. If one uses the word 'defence' to include principles in the law of remedies, one conflates liability rules and remedial rules. These are fundamentally different types of rules and the one term should not be used to refer to them indiscriminately. It is routine for tort law textbooks to discuss rules that merely diminish the remedy to which a successful claimant is entitled (such as the apportionment provision for contributory negligence) alongside rules that prevent liability from arising.[20] This is a significant error in classification induced by the careless use of the word 'defence'. The slipshod use of this term has also led to the frequent commission of the converse and equally bad error, which is to include analyses of rules that preclude findings of liability (such as the doctrine of abatement[21]) in discussions of remedies.[22]

It is difficult to support using the word 'defence' in the fourth identified way. A major problem with saying that defences are rules in respect of which the defendant carries the burden of proof is that it draws within its net many rules that no one would intentionally count as defences. Foreign matter that is identified as defences on this meaning of the word includes the very many procedural rules the applicability of which must be established by the defendant. Such rules encompass the provisions that enable defendants to obtain security for their costs,[23] to obtain accelerated service of a claim form[24] and to amend their pleadings after service.[25] To apply the term 'defence' to any of these rules would be a gross distortion of language.

The fifth meaning of the word 'defence' is downright bizarre. It is doubtful whether those who use the word in this way really intended to do so. The idea that the absence of defences constitutes the final *element* of actions in tort (as opposed to the final *question* to be asked in deciding whether liability should be imposed) simply does not enjoy support in the case law.[26] It is notable that those who claim that the absence of defences is the final element of torts do not cite any authorities that endorse this position. The fifth meaning of the word 'defence' should be assiduously avoided.

In contrast with the other definitions of the word 'defence', the second meaning of the word facilitates clear thinking about tort law. This definition, unlike all of the others, brings into focus the fundamental difference between rules that

[20] Eg, Sappideen and Vines (n 17) ch 12; Rogers (n 11) ch 6; C Witting (ed), *Street on Torts*, 14th edn (Oxford, Oxford University Press, 2015) ch 7.

[21] Abatement is discussed in 5.2.1.3.

[22] Eg, Rogers (n 11) 1069–70 [22.47]; Sappideen and Vines (n 17) 524 [21.280]; WP Keeton, DB Dobbs, RE Keeton and DG Owen (eds), *Prosser and Keeton on Torts*, 5th edn (St Paul, Minn, West Publishing Co, 1984) 641–43. For discussion of this error see R Zakrzewski, *Remedies Reclassified* (Oxford, Oxford University Press, 2005) 47–48.

[23] CPR 25.12.

[24] CPR 7.7

[25] CPR 17.1.

[26] In relation to the tort of negligence, see DG Owen, 'The Five Elements of Negligence' (2007) 35 *Hofstra Law Review* 1671. Owen observes that the courts have enumerated the elements of negligence in many different ways. However, despite his thorough review of the case law, Owen did not uncover any cases in which the absence of defences is regarded as an ingredient of that tort.

define torts and rules that release from liability a defendant whose conduct constitutes a tort. This is a conceptually sound way of organising that part of the law of torts that is concerned with specifying when liability arises. It also gives the concept of 'defence' sensible boundaries (it does not, for instance, encompass procedural rules that no one would count as defences). For these reasons, the second definition of the word 'defence' will be adopted in this book. Thus, a defence will be regarded as a rule that relieves the defendant of liability even though all of the elements of the tort in which the claimant sues are present.

Some readers will doubtlessly find this meaning of the word 'defence' to be rather odd. It excludes from the category of defences the provision for apportionment for contributory negligence. That provision is, as has been observed,[27] widely referred to as a defence. Some might consider it to be the most important defence in the modern law of torts in terms of practical relevance. However, if confusion is to be avoided, basic distinctions, such as that between liability rules and remedial rules, should be reflected in the language that is used to discuss the law of torts. Principles that comprise the law of remedies should not be referred to as defences.

1.3. The Neglect of Defences

One of the most striking features of the tort law literature is the neglect of defences. At every turn, the impression is given that they are a peripheral part of tort law that is undeserving of serious consideration. Defences are not mentioned in some introductory books on tort law.[28] No extant defence forms the subject matter of a monograph.[29] Collections of essays on tort law rarely contain contributions concerned with defences.[30] No tort law textbook inspects more than a small selection of defences, and those defences that are treated are typically mentioned cursorily. The authors of some tort law textbooks downplay the significance of defences by

---

[27] See the text accompanying n 7 above.

[28] Eg, G Williams and BA Hepple, *Foundations of the Law of Tort*, 2nd edn (London, Butterworths, 1984).

[29] However, Glanville Williams wrote a magisterial book that is concerned, in part, with the extinct defence of contributory negligence: GL Williams, *Joint Torts and Contributory Negligence: A Study of Concurrent Fault in Great Britain, Ireland and the Common-Law Dominions* (London, Stevens & Sons, 1951).

[30] Eg, none of the following collections includes an essay on defences: PD Finn (ed), *Essays on Torts* (Sydney, Law Book Co, 1989); NJ Mullany (ed), *Torts in the Nineties* (Sydney, LBC Information Services, 1997); P Cane and J Stapleton (eds), *The Law of Obligations: Essays in Celebration of John Fleming* (Oxford, Clarendon Press, 1998); NJ Mullany and AM Linden (eds), *Torts Tomorrow: A Tribute to John Fleming* (Sydney, LBC Information Services 1998); GJ Postema (ed), *Philosophy and the Law of Torts* (Cambridge, Cambridge University Press, 2001); MS Madden (ed), *Exploring Tort Law* (Cambridge, Cambridge University Press, 2005); JW Neyers, E Chamberlain and SGA Pitel (eds), *Emerging Issues in Tort Law* (Oxford, Hart Publishing, 2007); D Nolan and A Robertson (eds), *Rights and Private Law* (Oxford, Hart Publishing, 2012).

combining their examination of defences with other parts of tort law, such as remedies for torts.[31] Several treatises on comparative tort law ignore almost completely defences in the system of tort law with which they are concerned.[32] Some books about specific torts or particular families of torts barely mention defences to liability arising in the torts under examination.[33]

The lack of interest in defences has left numerous substantial gaps in our understanding of them. The size of these gaps may be put into perspective by comparing our learning regarding torts with what we know about defences. Consider, first, the fact that while concerted efforts have been made to explain what a tort is,[34] no detailed definition of a defence has been developed. Secondly, although comprehensive catalogues of torts have been drawn up,[35] no one has attempted to itemise defences. Thirdly, theorists have suggested systems for classifying torts[36] but no fully articulated taxonomy of defences has been constructed.[37] Fourthly, although many attempts have been made to justify tort law, these attempts tend to leave defences out of the picture.[38] Fifthly, analyses of the differences between the law of torts and other branches of the law virtually never consider how tort law is distinctive in terms of its defence regime. For instance, although we have many 'maps' of the law of obligations that purport to describe the unique topography of tort law,[39] they are all seriously incomplete as they fail to reveal how tort law stands apart from the other parts of the law of obligations in terms of its system of defences.

Why have defences failed to attract more attention? The lack of interest can arguably be chalked up to the gradual decline in the number and potency of

---

[31] Eg, S Deakin, A Johnston and B Markesinis, *Markesinis and Deakin's Tort Law*, 7th edn (Oxford, Clarendon Press, 2013) pt VIII.

[32] Eg, BS Markesinis and H Unberath, *The German Law of Torts: A Comparative Treatise*, 4th edn (Oxford, Hart Publishing, 2002).

[33] Eg, H Carty, *An Analysis of the Economic Torts* (Oxford, Oxford University Press, 2001); S Douglas, *Liability for Wrongful Interferences with Chattels* (Oxford, Hart Publishing, 2011); T Weir, *Economic Torts* (Oxford, Clarendon Press, 1997). A refreshing exception is J Murphy, *The Law of Nuisance* (Oxford, Oxford University Press, 2010) ch 5.

[34] Eg, P Birks, 'The Concept of a Civil Wrong' in DG Owen (ed), *Philosophical Foundations of Tort Law* (Oxford, Oxford University Press, 1995).

[35] Eg, B Rudden, 'Torticles' (1991–1992) 6/7 *Tulane Civil Law Forum* 105.

[36] Eg, R Stevens, *Torts and Rights* (Oxford, Oxford University Press, 2007) ch 13.

[37] While no comprehensive taxonomy of tort defences has been developed, it is true that vague suggestions can be found in the literature as to ways in which defences might be organised. These suggestions are the subject of ch 7.

[38] This was noted in JL Coleman, *Risks and Wrongs* (Oxford, Oxford University Press, 1992) 216. Coleman wrote that 'few theorists have analyzed the role of . . . defenses in the theory of liability' (footnote omitted). A good illustration of the tendency of theorists to gloss over defences is EJ Weinrib, *The Idea of Private Law* (Cambridge, Mass, Harvard University Press, 1995). After setting out his claim that tort law is an exercise in corrective justice, Weinrib selects the tort of negligence to test this hypothesis. While he discusses the main features of this tort, his treatment of defences to liability in negligence is limited to a single footnote (at 169, n 53). Another example is Robert Stevens's *Torts and Rights* (n 36), which is almost completely silent on the subject of defences.

[39] Eg, P Birks, 'Definition and Division: A Meditation on the *Institutions* 3.13' in P Birks (ed), *The Classification of Obligations* (Oxford, Clarendon Press, 1997); Cane (n 7) ch 6; Stevens (n 36) 284–90.

defences over the second half of the nineteenth century and the twentieth century. During this period, many defences were killed off or emasculated.[40] Defences that have been cast out of tort law include common employment,[41] contributory negligence (which was replaced by the apportionment regime), the inter-spousal immunity,[42] the immunity of highway authorities for nonfeasance,[43] the immunities of advocates[44] and expert witnesses,[45] and the charities' immunity.[46] An excellent example of a defence that was previously of considerable importance but which has been deprived of much of its power is the immunity of the Crown.[47] It is conceivable that the shrinking stock of defences combined with the enfeeblement of some that remain prompted scholars generally to conclude that defences are on the way out and are not a research priority.

A second explanation for the lacuna of theorising regarding defences lies in the preoccupation of many torts scholars with the tort of negligence. This preoccupation is significant because there are fewer defences to negligence than to many other torts. In particular, it has no justificatory defences. Much more will be said about this important type of defence later.[48] For the moment, it suffices to say that justificatory defences are defences the application of which depends upon the defendant acting reasonably in committing a tort. There is no logical space for any justificatory defences to negligence because negligence can be committed only if one acted unreasonably, which is simply another way of saying that one acted without justification.[49] The relatively small number of defences available to the tort of negligence may have contributed to defences generally failing to attract the interest of theorists.

A third explanation for the general neglect by scholars of tort law defences relates to the fact that many defences to liability arising in tort are not specific to tort law. Many tort law defences are available throughout the law of obligations. Examples of such defences include abuse of process, illegality,[50] limitation bars,

---

[40] See further J Goudkamp, 'Statutes and Defences' in TT Arvind and J Steele (eds), *Tort Law and the Legislature: Common Law, Statute and the Dynamics of Legal Change* (Oxford, Hart Publishing, 2013).

[41] Law Reform (Personal Injuries) Act 1948 (UK), s 1(1).

[42] See 5.3.1.12.

[43] *Ibid.*

[44] *Ibid.*

[45] See ch 5, n 133.

[46] See 5.3.1.12.

[47] See 5.3.1.8.

[48] See 4.3.1–4.3.2.

[49] For an argument that to act reasonably means to act with justification see J Gardner, 'The Mysterious Case of the Reasonable Person' (2001) 51 *University of Toronto Law Journal* 273.

[50] 'We do not consider that the public policy that the court will not lend its aid to a litigant who relies on his own criminal or immoral act is confined to particular causes of action': *Clunis v Camden and Islington Health Authority* [1998] QB 978, 987 (CA); '[the defence] applies across the board': *Vellino v Chief Constable of Greater Manchester* [2001] EWCA Civ 1249; [2002] 3 All ER 78, 87 [44]; [2002] 1 WLR 218, 228. The defence has defeated proceedings in trespass to the person (*Cross v Kirkby* The Times, 5 April 2000 (CA)), trespass to land (*Brown v Dunsmuir* [1994] 3 NZLR 485 (HC)), negligence (*Delaney v Pickett* [2011] EWCA Civ 1532; [2012] 1 WLR 2149, conversion (*Thackwell v Barclays Bank plc* [1986] 1 All ER 676 (QBD)), detinue (*Thomas Brown and Sons Ltd v Fazal Deen*

release and *res judicata*. The fact that numerous tort law defences are defences to liability arising in other branches of the law of obligations has led some writers to conclude that tort lawyers do not need to concern themselves with many tort law defences. This thinking is visible in, for instance, Robert Stevens's *Torts and Rights*. Stevens argues that tort law theorists do not need to dwell on defences such as illegality because it is a defence not only to liability in tort but to 'a claim based upon the assertion of any other right'.[51] Stevens then says:[52]

> All rights, whether they are based upon contract or unjust enrichment, found in law or equity, or *in rem* or *in personam* are subject to the principle of *ex turpi causa non oritur actio* (a base cause does not give rise to an action). Consequently, it is better considered in relation to all rights, rather than specifically in relation to the law of torts.

This thinking overlooks the fact that defences that are not specific to tort law often assume a distinctive shape in the tort context. The very example that Stevens gives – the defence of illegality – exemplifies this situation. The law governing that defence as it applies in the tort law setting is quite different from the law that controls the defence as it operates in other departments of the law of obligations.

A fourth reason why defences may have been largely ignored by legal writers is the fact that they are rules that, generally speaking, enunciate exceptional situations when liability will not arise.[53] The fact that many defences are engaged only relatively infrequently might have led to the perception that defences are a sideshow and that the elements of torts are the 'main event' in tort law, both in practical and theoretical terms. In other words, defences might be considered to be part of the periphery and something with which it is unnecessary to come to grips in order to understand tort law.

A fifth explanation for the relative lack of interest in defences concerns the fact that defences are second-tier questions.[54] The first major question that a court trying a tort action needs to consider is whether all of the elements of the tort in which the claimant sues are present. A court should ask whether a defence applies only if it decides that all of the elements of the relevant tort exist. The fact that the question 'Does a defence apply?' is a subsidiary one may have contributed to defences being largely ignored by legal writers.

A sixth and final reason for the general neglect of defences may have to do with their institutional origins. The law that specifies the elements of torts remains overwhelmingly judge-made. Consider, for example, the building blocks of the action in negligence, namely, a duty of care, a breach of that duty and non-remote damage caused by the breach of duty. The principles that govern these elements are located almost exclusively in the common law, not in acts of Parliament.

(1962) 108 CLR 391 (HCA)), and malicious prosecution and misfeasance in a public office (*Emanuele v Hedley* (1997) 137 FLR 339 (ACTSC)).

[51] Stevens (n 36) 304.
[52] *Ibid*, 304–05.
[53] See further 2.3.3.
[54] See further 1.5.

Although we live in the 'age of statutes',[55] they have escaped legislative intervention essentially unscathed. The same can be said of the elements of many other torts, including all of the varieties of trespass, private and public nuisance, the tort recognised in *Rylands v Fletcher*[56] and all of the economic torts. In contrast, a much greater proportion of the law of defences is born of statute.[57] For example, the English legislature has intervened extensively in relation to defences to defamation[58] and trespass.[59] The entire system of limitation of actions[60] is an invention of the legislature. The fact that there is more statutory law in the field of defences than in that which controls the elements of torts is significant for present purposes since, as is well known, lawyers are generally profoundly uninterested in legislation, despite the fact that it is formally superior to the common law as a source of law. As Justice Harlan Stone memorably put it, statutes have usually been perceived by lawyers as 'an alien intruder in the house of the common law'.[61] This is certainly an accurate description of the attitude of most tort lawyers.[62] The greater volume of statutory law in the defence context might have played a role in the relative neglect of defences by scholars.

1.4. Why are Defences Worth Investigating?

There are at least two reasons why defences are of such general theoretical significance that they deserve considerably more attention than they have received to date. The first reason is that they make a significant contribution to tort law's correlative structure,[63] that is to say, the fact that tort law is notionally concerned

[55] G Calabresi, *A Common Law for the Age of Statutes* (Cambridge, Mass, Harvard University Press, 1982).

[56] (1866) LR 1 Exch 265 (Exch Ch).

[57] The details are given in Goudkamp (n 40). Possible reasons for the legislature's concentration on defences when legislating with respect to tort law are given in 9.1.2.

[58] Eg, Defamation Act 1952 (UK); Defamation Act 1996 (UK); Defamation Act 2013 (UK).

[59] Eg, Mental Health Act 1983 (UK); Police and Criminal Evidence Act 1984 (UK), pts 1–2; Mental Capacity Act 2005 (UK); Criminal Justice and Police Act 2001 (UK), pt 2.

[60] Limitation Act 1980 (UK).

[61] HF Stone, 'The Common Law in the United States' (1936) 50 *Harvard Law Review* 4, 15. Similarly, Jack Beatson observed that lawyers see 'statutes as evil devices marring the symmetry of the common law': J Beatson, 'Has the Common Law a Future?' (1997) 56 *Cambridge Law Journal* 291, 299. Likewise, Andrew Burrows writes that 'those with a deep love of the common law, and working in an area such a contract or tort or unjust enrichment, have tended to regard statutes as an unwelcome visitor into a territory dominated by case law': A Burrows, 'The Relationship between Common Law and Statute in the Law of Obligations' (2012) 128 *Law Quarterly Review* 232, 232.

[62] TT Arvind and J Steele complain that 'there has been a relative lack of scholarly attention devoted to legislation in the law of tort' and that 'legislation tends to be left at the periphery of the subject, either unconsciously, or deliberately': TT Arvind and J Steele, 'Introduction: Legislation and the Shape of Tort Law' in TT Arvind and J Steele (eds), *Tort Law and the Legislature: Common Law, Statute and the Dynamics of Legal Change* (Oxford, Hart Publishing, 2013) 1–2.

[63] In relation to defences to liability in negligence, see A Beever, *Rediscovering the Law of Negligence* (Oxford, Hart Publishing, 2007) ch 10.

with both parties equally.[64] Consider the focus of torts and defences respectively. Generally speaking, the issues listed under the 'tort' heading are concerned primarily with the defendant's behaviour. Take, for example, the tort of negligence. That tort directs attention mainly to the defendant's conduct. Did the defendant act reasonably? Should he have foreseen that the claimant might be injured by his conduct? The same is true of most other torts. Conversely, issues that fall under the 'defence' heading tend to centre attention on the claimant. A good example is the defence of illegality. That defence is claimant-orientated. It is concerned with whether the claimant was injured while acting illegally. The defendant's conduct features only in modest ways in relation to it. Defences, therefore, play a central role in counterbalancing the disproportionate attention that the elements of torts place on the defendant's conduct. Unless due attention is given to them, the correlative nature of the law of torts cannot be fully understood.

Defences contribute to the correlative structure of tort law not only by compensating for the tendency of the elements of torts to centre on the defendant's behaviour. They also further tort law's bilateral nature via the rules governing the onus of proof.[65] It is a general and well-established rule that the claimant bears the onus of proving facts that satisfy the elements of the tort in which he sues, while it is for the defendant to establish facts that enliven any defences.[66] Because of this principle, defences have a role in tort law's placing both parties under a burden of proof. If defences did not exist, as the rules concerning the assignment of the onus of proof presently stand, only claimants would be obliged to prove anything in relation to liability. This would be incompatible with tort law's correlative structure. Tort law would not treat the parties equally in terms of procedure if only claimants were put under a burden of proof.[67]

The second reason why defences deserve much more scholarly interest than they have received concerns the fact that they are avenues by which responsibility in tort law can be avoided. As mentioned at the very beginning of this chapter, outside the law, a person who is accused of wrongdoing may be able to give an answer to the allegation. An account of a person's moral responsibility that ignored answers would be seriously incomplete. The same is true in relation to the law of torts. Any theory of a person's responsibility in the law of tort that could not account for defences would be manifestly deficient. As Peter Cane remarked, 'No account of criteria of legal liability . . . is complete without reference to answers. Answers are an integral part of judgments of responsibility.'[68]

It is worth observing that it cannot be plausibly said that the law governing defences does not deserve greater attention than it has received because it is less

---

[64] Regarding the correlative structure of tort law, see generally Weinrib (n 38) ch 5.

[65] For further discussion see A Porat and A Stein, *Tort Liability under Uncertainty* (Oxford, Oxford University Press, 2001) 37–42; Beever (n 63) 446–47. See also 2.3.4, 6.4.

[66] *Hall v Hebert* [1993] 2 SCR 159, 184; *Marcic v Thames Water Utilities Ltd* [2001] EWCA Civ 64; [2002] QB 929, 994–95 [86]; *Grant v Torstar Corp* [2009] SCC 61; (2009) 3 SCR 640, 658 [28]–[29].

[67] See further 2.3.4.

[68] P Cane, *Responsibility in Law and Morality* (Oxford, Hart Publishing, 2002) 90–91 (footnote omitted).

complicated or less bulky than the law that specifies the elements of torts. The law controlling defences is at least as complex and as extensive as the law that controls the elements of torts. Defences to some torts are very numerous. Consider, for instance, the tort of trespass to the person. There are a bewildering number of defences available to liability arising in this tort. The same may be said in relation to the tort of defamation. (It seems likely that this state of affairs is a result of attempts to offset the fact that it is very easy to commit the torts of trespass or defamation. As a general rule, the fewer the matters that comprise the claimant's action, the greater the number of defences that are available.)

1.5. The Temporal Logic of Tort Law

An important but under-appreciated feature of tort law is its temporal logic. Tort law is structured so that trial judges should deal with certain issues in a prescribed sequence.[69] It is necessary to grasp this logic in order to understand how defences fit into tort law's framework. The first matter with which a trial court should deal is whether a tort has been committed. If no tort has been committed, judgment should be entered for the defendant. No other substantive issues arise for consideration. If, however, all of the elements of a tort are in place, the court should ask whether a defence is applicable.[70] If a defence is engaged, the court should rule in favour of the defendant. All other substantive issues fall away. Conversely, if no defence is enlivened, the court ought to find in favour of the claimant and consider the remedy that he should be granted.

Although express support can be found in the case law for analysing torts, defences and remedies in this sequence,[71] many tort law theorists seem to believe that torts, defences and remedies should be dealt with in a different order. For instance, Robert Stevens argues in *Torts and Rights* under a heading that reads 'How to Write a Torts Textbook' that a properly structured textbook on tort law would put remedies before defences.[72] Stevens offers no rationale for treating remedies as an anterior matter. It addition to defying the temporal logic approved by the authorities, that structure is unhelpful, since the issue of remedies needs to be addressed if and only if no defence is applicable. If the defendant has a defence, the claimant has no entitlement to a remedy. Were a court to deal with the issue of relief before defences, it might well be wasting its time. The structures of some other books on tort law imply that consideration of defences should precede

---

[69] Some parts of tort law may be temporally inert. It is unnecessary to explore this possibility here.

[70] 'Affirmative defenses are relevant only if the plaintiff has made a prima facie case by providing testimony to show all the required elements and if the jury believes that testimony': DB Dobbs, *The Law of Torts* (St Paul, Minn, West Group, 2000) 37.

[71] Eg, *Perrett v Sydney Harbour Foreshore Authority* [2009] NSWSC 1026 [39]–[40]; *Boehmke v Grant* [2010] BCSC 682 [151].

[72] Stevens (n 36) 303–04. Textbooks that adopt this structure include C Sappideen and P Vines (eds), *Fleming's The Law of Torts*, 10th edn (Sydney, Lawbook Co, 2011) pt 3; Rogers (n 11) chs 22, 25.

enquiries into whether the defendant committed a tort.[73] This structure is also flawed. This is so partly because it is often impossible to talk sensibly about defences until it is determined whether a tort has been committed. For example, it is nonsensical to discuss the issue of whether the defendant acted in self-defence before ascertaining whether the defendant acted in a way that satisfies the elements of the action in battery.

It is true that trial judges sometimes proceed in a sequence other than that which has just been described. For example, defences may be raised in a strike-out application and hence dealt with first. It might be suggested that this demonstrates that there is no temporal logic to tort law or that tort law is temporally ordered other than has been claimed. Such a suggestion should be rejected. When a defence is dealt with in a strike-out application, the court asks whether the defence relied upon by the defendant renders it a foregone conclusion that the claimant will fail. Consequently, the court proceeds *on the footing* that the facts alleged by the claimant are true (ie, that all of the elements of a tort are present).[74] Instances where the courts consider defences first in strike-out applications do not, therefore, disprove the existence of the temporal structure described above. On the contrary, they paradoxically affirm it.[75]

1.6. Labels in Tort Law

This section considers the role that labels play in tort law. It is worth thinking about labels in their own right. However, the primary purpose of turning attention to labels here is that doing so is a prelude to the argument in the next section in relation to the concept of a partial defence.[76] Lawyers have devised labels to

---

[73] Eg, AM Dugdale and MA Jones (eds), *Clerk & Lindsell on Torts*, 21st edn (London, Sweet & Maxwell, 2014).

[74] *Hill v Chief Constable of West Yorkshire* [1989] AC 53, 58 (HL); *Malik v Bank of Credit and Commerce International SA* [1998] AC 20, 33 (HL).

[75] What about appeals? Is it not the case that appellate courts, when dealing with appeals that raise both the issue of whether a tort was committed and whether a defence applies, sometimes deal fist with the ground of appeal that concerns the defence? Indeed it is (for a recent example see *Pegasus Management Holdings SCA v Ernst & Young* [2010] EWCA Civ 181; [2010] 3 All ER 297 (addressing a limitation bar defence before a plea of 'no duty of care')). However, this does not undermine the claim that consideration of the question whether a tort was committed should precede analysis as to whether a defence applies. To see why this is so, some basic differences in the procedure that governs trials and appeals must be kept in mind. Trial judges must address *all* of the issues on which the parties are in dispute. They cannot cherry-pick issues that they will consider. Even if they reach a decision on a given issue that is fatal to one party's case, they must decide all of the outstanding issues in contention. This is to avoid the need for retrials in the event of errors that are subsequently corrected on appeal (see *Kuru v New South Wales* [2008] HCA 26; (2008) 236 CLR 1, 6 [12]). The procedure that guides appellate judges is quite different. Appellate judges can be selective in considering the grounds of appeal. This is because, in order to reach the conclusion that an appeal should be allowed, only one of the grounds of appeal needs to be accepted as valid. Given that appellate courts can be selective in dealing with the grounds of appeal, the fact that they do not respect the temporal logic of tort law is immaterial.

[76] See 1.7.

refer to many torts. For example, when lawyers speak of the 'tort of slander' they mean to refer to the intentional or negligent publication of a statement in transient form that tends to lower the defendant in the estimation of others with the result being that the defendant suffers special damage. Similarly, 'the tort of private nuisance' refers to a state of affairs for which the defendant is responsible that interferes unreasonably with the claimant's right to the quiet enjoyment of his land. Lawyers also use labels to refer to defences. For instance, when spelt out in full, the phrase the 'defence of self-defence' means the application of proportionate defensive force in circumstances where it was objectively necessary to use defensive force.

1.6.1. The Purpose of Labels

Labels are used in tort law merely for convenience. They are a form of shorthand. They have no legal significance.[77] The following three facts bear this point out. First, as a matter of civil procedure, labels do not need to be mentioned in pleadings.[78] A claimant does not need to identify the tort that he alleges was committed against him in his statement of case. It is sufficient for him to set out the facts on which he relies.[79] The same is true of defences. A defendant who wishes to rely on a defence does not need to mention the defence concerned in his statement of defence. It is enough for him to describe facts which, if true, would enliven a defence.[80]

Secondly, not all torts have been assigned a label.[81] The classic example of an innominate tort is that committed in *Wilkinson v Downton*.[82] The defendant in that case, in the course of what he considered to be a practical joke, falsely told the claimant that her husband had been seriously injured in an accident. His statement caused the claimant to suffer psychiatric injury. The trial judge, Wright J,

---

[77] There are some minor and presently irrelevant exceptions to this position. For example, the label may matter from the point of view of an insurance contract. An insurer may have contracted to insure a tortfeasor for liability in, say, negligence but not in trespass to the person.

[78] Interestingly, the situation in the criminal law is different. Allegations in informations or counts in indictments should name the offence with which the defendant is accused of committing: CrPR 7.3(1), 14.2(1).

[79] CPR 16.2(1)(a); *Vandervell (No 2)* [1974] Ch 269, 321–22 (CA).

[80] CPR 16.5.

[81] 'There is no necessity whatever that a tort have a name. New and nameless torts are being recognized constantly . . .': Keeton *et al* (n 22) 3 (footnote omitted); '[T]ortious liability is constantly expanding and there is ample evidence that a plaintiff's claim is not necessarily prejudiced because the plaintiff is unable to find a specific label for the wrong of which he complains. New and innominate torts have been constantly emerging . . .': Sappideen and Vines (n 17) 7 [1.30]; 'Most wrongs have no special names': HT Terry, 'The Arrangement of the Law. II' (1917) 17 *Columbia Law Review* 365, 380; '[T]he various kinds of torts which have received specific names do not include all the wrongs which courts are accustomed to recognize as coming under the general head of torts. Hence the admission that, besides wrongs with particular names, there are "wrongs without names" ("innominate grievances,") which are subjects of action, and for which damages are recoverable': J Smith, 'Torts without Particular Names' (1921) 69 *University of Pennsylvania Law Review* 91, 93 (footnote omitted).

[82] [1897] 2 QB 57 (QBD).

held that the claimant had a good cause of action. His lordship reached this conclusion despite the fact that no label for the defendant's conduct existed (the
labels of 'battery' and 'assault' were inapplicable since, among other reasons, there
was no physical contact or fear thereof respectively). Just as there are innominate
torts, there is no requirement that defences have a name.[83]

Thirdly, labels in tort law are not really used to draw morally salient distinctions between litigants.[84] They tend to lump litigants of widely varying degrees of
culpability within a single category.[85] A good example is the tort of battery.
Tortious batteries range from the slightest and most innocuous touching[86] to bru-
tal beatings, rape and murder. Another illustration is the defence of truth to liability in defamation. This defence is available to all defendants whose defamatory
imputations are factually accurate. It is equally open to defendants who did not
think and had no reason to suspect that their statement was defamatory[87] and to
defendants who knew of the defamatory character of their statement and published it solely in order to humiliate the claimant. In this respect, tort law differs
radically from the criminal law. Labels in the criminal law are, on the whole, considerably more refined. There are, for instance, many different types of offences
against the person, and many of these offences are subdivided to reflect, among
other things, the status of the victim, the extent and type of harm caused, and the
species of fault exhibited by the defendant.[88]

1.6.2. On What Basis are Labels Selected?

Although labels in tort law have no legal significance, it is worth saying a few words
about how they are chosen. Most torts have been named by reference to the right
that they protect. Obvious examples include defamation, false imprisonment and

---

[83] 'Many privileges are well-established; many are called by commonly used names. But there is no
closed master list of privileges any more than there is a closed list of claims': Dobbs (n 70) 155.

[84] Although in *Ashley v Chief Constable of Sussex Police* [2008] UKHL 25; [2008] 1 AC 962 the House
of Lords seemed to think that the label attached to a litigant might not be unimportant in this regard.
In this case, the defendant admitted liability in negligence for the death of a man but denied liability in
assault and battery. Before the House, the defendant argued that since it had admitted liability in negligence, the proceedings in assault and battery should be stayed. This argument was rejected. It is
unnecessary to go into the House's reasons in detail here. It suffices to say that the House thought that
it was important for the claimants to have the opportunity to pursue the assault and battery actions for
vindicatory purposes (see especially at 975–77 [22]–[23], 985–89 [56]–[72]).

[85] But note that tort law attaches different labels to defendants who utter false statements that are
detrimentally relied upon depending on the type of fault exhibited by the defendant. Fraudulent misrepresentations attract the label 'deceit'. Negligent misrepresentations are referred to as 'negligent mis-
statements'.

[86] 'It has long been established that any touching of another person, however slight, may amount to a
battery': *Collins v Wilcock* [1984] 3 All ER 374, 378; [1984] 1 WLR 1172, 1177 (QBD) (Robert Goff LJ).

[87] *Maisel v Financial Times Ltd* [1915] 3 KB 336 (CA); *Pamplin v Express Newspapers Ltd (No 2)*
[1988] 1 All ER 282; [1988] 1 WLR 116n (CA).

[88] See A Ashworth, *Principles of Criminal Law*, 6th edn (Oxford, Oxford University Press, 2009)
297–324.

private nuisance. The main exception to this trend is the tort of negligence. This tort has been branded in accordance with the type of fault that the defendant must exhibit in order to be held liable for it.[89] While the labels assigned to torts have, for the most part, been chosen by reference to the right that they protect, the titles of defences have been bestowed haphazardly. The names of some defences describe conduct on the part of the defendant. Examples include innocent dissemination, honest comment and responsible journalism. Others are derived from behaviour on the part of the claimant, such as illegality. Several defences, such as self-defence and discipline, allude to behaviour on the part of both parties.

1.7. Complete Defences and Partial Defences

A distinction is often drawn between 'complete defences' and 'partial defences' to liability in tort.[90] Those who draw this distinction consider a 'complete defence' to be a rule that prevents liability from arising and a 'partial defence' to be a rule that reduces the damages to which a successful claimant is entitled. The provision for apportionment for contributory negligence is typically given as an example of a partial defence. The problem with this understanding is that, as has been seen,[91] it elides the law governing liability with the remedial law. Principles in the law of remedies should not be called defences at all. They should not, accordingly, be described as partial defences. This description serves only to confuse.

Criminal lawyers also speak of complete and partial defences. However, the meaning that they ascribe to the term 'partial defence' is quite different from that given to it in the tort law domain. Criminal lawyers do not count rules that mitigate the sentence imposed on the defendant – the criminal law equivalent of rules that diminish the remedy to which a claimant who establishes liability is entitled – as partial defences. Rather, for criminal lawyers, a partial defence is a rule that, when applicable, results in the defendant being convicted of a lesser offence than that with which he was charged.[92] The most important partial defences to criminal liability are diminished responsibility[93] and provocation (in the United Kingdom, loss of control[94]), both of which reduce liability from murder to manslaughter.

---

[89] For criticism of this aberration see Birks (n 34) 23; Stevens (n 36) 291; A Burrows, *Understanding the Law of Obligations: Essays on Contract, Tort and Restitution* (Oxford, Hart Publishing, 1998) 5–6.

[90] Eg, *Imperial Chemical Industries Ltd v Shatwell* [1965] AC 656, 672–73 (HL) (Lord Reid); A Burrows, *Remedies for Torts and Breach of Contract*, 3rd edn (Oxford, Oxford University Press, 2004) 129; Weir (n 10) 129.

[91] See 1.2.2.

[92] For discussion of the concept of a partial defence to criminal liability, see M Wasik, 'Partial Excuses in the Criminal Law' (1982) 45 *Modern Law Review* 516; S Uniacke, 'What are Partial Excuses to Murder?' in SMH Yeo (ed), *Partial Excuses to Murder* (Sydney, Federation Press, 1990); J Horder, *Excusing Crime* (Oxford, Oxford University Press, 2004) 143–52; D Husak, *The Philosophy of Criminal Law: Selected Essays* (Oxford, Oxford University Press, 2010) ch 12.

[93] Homicide Act 1957 (UK), s 2.

[94] Coroners and Justice Act 2009 (UK), ss 54, 56(1).

Partial defences to criminal liability really are defences since they block liability for the more serious offence.

Unlike the criminal law, tort law does not recognise any rules that answer to the description of a 'partial defence' as this concept is properly understood. There are no rules that relieve the defendant of liability for one tort and result in his being held liable for a 'lesser tort'. Why do tort law and the criminal law differ in this regard? The answer to this question is found in the principle of fair labelling. That principle holds that wrongs should be labelled so as to describe accurately what their commission entails.[95] The criminal law embraces this principle for several reasons, the most important of which is that it would be unfair to offenders to misdescribe the nature of their wrongdoing. Defendants in the criminal sphere do not care only about whether they are convicted. The label that is applied to them on conviction is also significant. Partial defences promote the principle of fair labelling as they result in different labels being applied to different offenders on the basis of their culpability. This is a large part of the story of why the criminal law provides for partial defences. Unlike the criminal law, however, tort law does not embrace the principle of fair labelling. As has been seen, the label that is applied to a tortfeasor upon being found liable is of no real consequence.[96] This explains why there are no partial defences in tort law.

1.8. Who Can Raise Defences?

Who can raise defences? The answer to this question may seem to be obvious. It might be replied quickly that it falls to the defendant to decide whether to rely on a defence. To an extent, this is true. However, matters are not quite so simple.

1.8.1. Insurers

Defendants to tort actions are typically insured.[97] Consequently, it is normally the defendant's insurer rather than the defendant who has the power to make decisions concerning defences (as with all tactical matters).[98] Thus, even though a defendant

---

[95] The principle of fair labelling was first articulated in A Ashworth, 'The Elasticity of Mens Rea' in CFH Tapper (ed), *Crime, Proof and Punishment: Essays in Memory of Sir Rupert Cross* (London, Butterworths, 1981). For further discussion of it, see G Williams, 'Convictions and Fair Labelling' (1983) 42 *Cambridge Law Journal* 85; J Chalmers and F Leverick, 'Fair Labelling in Criminal Law' (2008) 71 *Modern Law Review* 217; V Tadros, 'Fair Labelling and Social Solidarity' in L Zedner and JV Roberts, *Principles and Values in Criminal Law and Criminal Justice: Essays in Honour of Andrew Ashworth* (Oxford, Oxford University Press, 2012) 67; Ashworth (n 88) 78–80.

[96] See 1.6.1.

[97] Statistics are provided in P Cane, *Atiyah's Accidents, Compensation and the Law*, 7th edn (Cambridge, Cambridge University Press, 2006) 233.

[98] Insurers invariably enjoy the ability to determine how the case for the defendant will be conducted under the terms of the insurance policy. For discussion, see *Beacon Insurance Co Ltd v Langdale* [1939] 4 All ER 204 (CA); *Groom v Crocker* [1939] 1 KB 194 (CA).

may wish to admit liability,[99] his insurer can invoke a defence. Similarly, even if a defendant would like to rely on a certain defence, the insurer is for the most part free to admit liability or present a different defence.[100] The insurer does not usually even have to consult with or notify the defendant of the course it will take.[101]

1.8.2. The Court

Can the court raise defences that are open on the facts?[102] As a general principle, it cannot.[103] It is a basic rule that the courts only have jurisdiction to decide matters that are in dispute between the parties.[104] Rightly or wrongly, however, there are some exceptions to this situation. For example, the court can raise the defence of illegality *proprio motu.*[105] Courts are compelled by statute to invoke certain defences. Consider section 1(1) of the State Immunity Act 1978 (UK), which confers a general immunity on foreign States. Section 1(2) obliges the courts 'to give effect to this immunity even though the [defendant State] does not appear in the proceedings in question'. This provision therefore requires the court to raise the defence in section 1(1) on its own motion.[106]

1.9. Multiple Defences

Just as a single set of facts can generate liability in multiple torts, so too can several defences arise in a given case. In other words, defences may overlap. Indeed, certain

---

[99] An obvious situation where a defendant may want liability to be admitted is where the claimant and defendant are domestic partners.

[100] Regarding limits of the power of the insurer to determine the tactical posture adopted, see *Groom v Crocker* [1939] 1 KB 194, 201–04, 223–24, 227–28 (CA).

[101] Of course, if the defendant wishes, he can release his insurer from its contractual obligations and take control of the proceedings: *ibid*, 227–28.

[102] See further 6.9.

[103] Consider the decision in *Dann v Hamilton* [1939] 1 KB 509 (KBD). In that case, the court felt that it could not consider a defence (*viz*, contributory negligence, which was a defence at the time) that was plainly open on the facts because it had not been raised by the defendant.

[104] *Khiaban v Beard* [2003] EWCA Civ 358; [2003] 3 All ER 362, 366 [13]–[14]; [2003] 1 WLR 1626, 1630; *Island Maritime Ltd v Filipowski* [2006] HCA 30; (2006) 226 CLR 328, 355 [81]; A Zuckerman, *Zuckerman on Civil Procedure: Principles of Practice*, 2nd edn (London, Sweet & Maxwell, 2006) 397–403 [10.8]–[10.24]. This principle is discussed further in 6.9, 8.5.1.2.

[105] *Cross v Kirkby* The Times, 5 April 2000 (CA); Law Commission, *The Illegality Defence: A Consultative Report* (Law Com Consultation Paper 189, 2009) 133 [7.22]. Consider also the contract law cases of *Lipton v Powell* [1921] 2 KB 51 (Div Ct); *Ferguson v John Dawson & Partners (Contractors) Ltd* [1976] 3 All ER 817, 821; [1976] 1 WLR 1213, 1218 (CA); *Pickering v Deacon* [2003] EWCA Civ 554; The Times, 19 April 2003. The position in Australia is apparently different. Illegality must be pleaded by the defendant: see, eg, Uniform Civil Procedure Rules 2005 (NSW), r 14.14(3); *Corliss v Gibbings-Johns* [2010] QCA 233.

[106] *NML Capital Ltd v Republic of Argentina* [2010] EWCA Civ 41; [2011] QB 8, 21 [49] (not doubted on appeal to the Supreme Court: *NML Capital Ltd v Republic of Argentina* [2011] UKSC 31; [2011] 2 AC 495).

defences tend to be triggered in tandem. A good example of this tendency concerns the defences of self-defence and illegality.[107] In proceedings in battery, these pleas are often raised together.[108] If C attacks D and D exercises defensive force that causes injury to C, D may be able to succeed on the defence of self-defence and the defence of illegality.

Two things that are connected with the fact that defences can overlap are worth observing. First, where multiple defences are potentially applicable, the defendant can escape from liability if he proceeds in a way that enlivens only a single defence. For example, if an intruder threatens D's life and D's property, D may be able to avoid liability on the basis of the defence of self-defence if he kills the intruder, even though the defence of property defence is inapplicable because it was excessive to use such force to protect property.[109] Secondly, the defendant does not stand to gain much in practical terms from the fact that more than one defence is available to him.[110] One defence is just as good as ten offences in terms of preventing liability from arising.

1.10. Scope of the Book

1.10.1. Tort Law

This is a book about tort law defences. It is not a book about defences to liability arising in the law of obligations, or about defences in the law generally. Setting the scope of this book in this way requires thought to be given to which actions are actions in tort. In particular, attention needs to be paid to how actions in tort differ from actions in equitable wrongs and for breaches of contract. Some brief remarks will be made in this connection in a moment. Fortunately, however, it is unnecessary to go into much detail in this regard. This is because it is inessential for present purposes to distinguish tort law rigorously from the other branches of the law of obligations. There are two main reasons why this is so. The first reason is that theorists broadly agree which actions are actions in tort. This is

---

[107] The connection between the defences of self-defence and illegality is explored in J Goudkamp, 'Self-Defence and Illegality Under the *Civil Liability Act* 2002 (NSW)' (2010) 18 *Torts Law Journal* 61.

[108] Eg, *Cross v Kirkby* The Times, 5 April 2000 (CA).

[109] This example is taken from PH Robinson, *Criminal Law Defenses*, vol 2 (St Paul, Minn, West Publishing Co, 1984) 11. The defence of defence of one's property probably does not permit lethal force to be used: see 5.2.1.2.

[110] However, defendants may have reason to prefer one defence over another nevertheless. This possibility is explored in 8.6.2.

not, of course, to deny the existence of points of controversy in this regard. No definition of a tort has been developed that commands anything approaching universal support.[111] But, plainly, there is a generally accepted understanding which actions are actions in tort. If no such understanding existed it would be impossible to have meaningful discussions about tort law, and this is self-evidently not the case.

The second reason why it is possible for this book largely to avoid the debate about how tort law differs from other departments of the law of obligations is that a certain amount of the analysis that will be offered is capable of being applied, *mutatis mutandis*, to the law of obligations generally.[112] It is obvious that the defence regimes of all of the branches of the law of obligations have a great deal in common. Many defences to liability in tort are defences to liability arising out of events that are not torts.[113] However, this book does not attempt to prove that that which holds true in relation to tort law defences goes also for defences to liability arising in the law of obligations generally.

1.10.2. Equitable Wrongs

Wrongs recognised in equity include breach of trust, knowing receipt of trust property, breach of confidence and breach of fiduciary duty. Although some of these wrongs are sometimes referred to as torts,[114] the conventional view is that they are not torts. The traditional understanding is epitomised by Gleeson CJ, McHugh, Gummow, Hayne and Heydon JJ's claim in *Tanwar Enterprises Pty Ltd v Cauchi* that there are no 'equitable torts'.[115] James Edelman rejects the conventional view.[116] He contends that all equitable wrongs are torts. If he is right, defences to such wrongs would need to be included in the analysis offered in this book. Edelman offers two arguments in support of his position. His first

---

[111] '[A] really satisfactory definition of a tort is yet to be found': Keeton *et al* (n 22) 1; 'Tort is what is in the tort books, and the only thing holding it together is their binding': Weir (n 10) ix; 'a satisfactory definition of tort remains somewhat elusive': Witting (n 20) 3; 'Numerous attempts have been made to define a "tort" or "tortious liability", with varying degrees of lack of success': Rogers (n 11) 1 [1.1].

[112] Indeed, it is hoped that the framework for thinking about tort law defences promoted in this book can be adapted to serve as a model for understanding defences to all civil wrongs: see 9.4.

[113] See the text accompanying nn 50–52 above.

[114] Eg, breach of confidence is described as a tort in *Re A Local Authority (Inquiry: Restraint on Publication)* [2003] EWHC 2746 (Fam); [2004] Fam 96, 111–12 [55]; *Campbell v MGN Ltd* [2004] UKHL 22; [2004] 2 AC 457, 464–65 [14]–[15]; *Hosking v Runting* [2004] NZCA 34; [2005] 1 NZLR 1, 15 [42], 16 [47], 30 [109]; *McKennitt v Ash* [2006] EWCA Civ 1714; [2008] QB 73, 80 [8]; *HRH Prince of Wales v Associated Newspapers Ltd* [2006] EWCA Civ 1776; [2008] Ch 57, 123–24 [64]–[65]; cf *Kitechnology BV v Unicor GmbH Plastmaschinen* [1995] FSR 765, 777 (CA); *Douglas v Hello! Ltd* [2005] EWCA Civ 595; [2006] QB 125, 160 [96].

[115] [2003] HCA 57; (2003) 217 CLR 315, 325 [24].

[116] J Edelman, 'Equitable Torts' (2002) 10 *Torts Law Journal* 64.

argument is that equitable wrongs are torts because both equitable wrongs and torts are breaches of duties. Although Edelman is obviously correct in saying that both torts and equitable wrongs are breaches of legal duties, this argument does not work.[117] Merely because one legal concept has a characteristic (or, indeed, several characteristics) in common with another concept does not mean that they are one and the same thing. The hearsay rule and the bad character rule are both exclusionary rules of evidence, but it would be a mistake to say that the hearsay rule is the bad character rule or vice versa. It simply does not follow from the fact that equitable wrongs, like torts, are breaches of duties that equitable wrongs are torts. Edelman's second argument is that equitable wrongs are torts because the courts respond to equitable wrongs in the same way as they do to torts. This argument rests on the same fallacy as the first. It is incorrect to say that because two wrongs are met by an identical legal response they are the same type of wrong. As Nicholas McBride and Roderick Bagshaw point out, 'We would not say that rape is murder even if the law responded to a rape in exactly the same way as it does to someone's committing murder'.[118]

John Gardner recently attempted to distinguish torts from equitable wrongs. Gardner argues that torts and equitable wrongs differ in terms of the reasons for their existence. He contends:[119]

> The main reason why the defendant has duties to the plaintiff in the law of torts is to protect the plaintiff from losses, and the main mode of recourse that a plaintiff has against the defendant in a tort case is therefore recourse in respect of his losses. This contrasts with the position in equity, where the main reason for the defendant's duties is to secure that the defendant's dealings are conducted for the plaintiff's advantage, and not for the defendant's own. So the emphasis in equity is on the diversion of advantage – in the form of assets or profits – as opposed to the causation of loss, which is tort law's first concern.

There are various difficulties with Gardner's argument.[120] A central problem with it is that many of the wrongs that Gardner counts as equitable wrongs do not exist, at least not primarily, in order to ensure that the defendant promotes the claimant's interests rather than his own. Consider the action for breach of trust. Suppose that a trustee who is empowered to buy shares under the trust instrument sells his own shares to the trust and makes an enormous profit in the process. This does not constitute a breach of trust. It is quite immaterial for the purposes of determining the liability of the trustee *qua* trustee that the trustee acted to advance his own

---

[117] Some of what follows here is based on penetrating remarks made in NJ McBride and R Bagshaw, *Tort Law*, 3rd edn (Harlow, Pearson Longman, 2008) 8, n 19. These remarks have been omitted from later editions of this book, although the position adopted by McBride and Bagshaw in this regard was clearly unchanged as of the fourth edition of their text: see NJ McBride and R Bagshaw, *Tort Law*, 4th edn (Harlow, Pearson, 2012) 20–21.

[118] McBride and Bagshaw (2008) (n 117) 9, n 19.

[119] J Gardner, 'Torts and Other Wrongs' (2012) 39 *Florida State University Law Review* 43, 51 (footnote omitted).

[120] Several weaknesses are pointed out in N McBride, 'Thinking About Tort Law – Where Do We Go From Here?' (unpublished article).

interests.[121] The fact that there is no breach of trust in this scenario suggests that, contrary to Gardner's claim, the action in breach of trust is not concerned, at least not mainly, with ensuring that the defendant acts to promote the claimant's interests rather than his own. Note also that the action in breach of trust may be available even if the defendant has not acted for his own benefit. Suppose, this time, that a trustee, attempting to discharge his obligations *qua* trustee, conveyed trust property to a fraudster because he reasonably believed that the fraudster was the beneficiary. The trustee is liable for breach of trust (since liability for breach of trust is strict) even though he was trying to advance only the beneficiary's interests.

The easiest way to separate equitable wrongs from torts is on the basis of their separate historical development. Whereas torts are wrongs that were developed by the common law courts, equitable wrongs were created by the chancery courts. This is not to deny that there may be additional ways in which torts are distinct from equitable wrongs. But it is unnecessary to explore this possibility here. The important point to note is that dividing torts from equitable wrongs on the basis of their different histories is a sound, albeit conceptually uninteresting, basis for distinguishing between them. Defences to equitable wrongs that are not also tort defences can, therefore, be left to one side for this book's purposes.

1.10.3. Breach of Contract

It is widely thought that breaches of contract and torts are separate wrongs. Peter Birks rebelled against this view. He argued that breaches of contract are torts, since both torts and breaches of contract involve a breach of duty. As he put it, 'the common law . . . [i]n effect . . . adds breach of contractual duty to the list of torts'.[122] The main difficulty with this argument is that merely because a breach of contract and a tort can both be described as a breach of a duty, does not mean that breaches of contract are torts. This is same fallacious reasoning to which Edelman subscribes.[123] Manslaughter by criminal negligence involves a breach of duty, but no one thinks that this wrong should be counted as a tort rather than as a crime. Birks's argument should be rejected.

This is not the place to look comprehensively at respects in which torts and breaches of contract are distinct.[124] To do so would consume much more space than is available. However, the most promising way of separating torts from breaches of contract would seem to be by reference to the different sources of tortious duties and contractual duties. A breach of contract is a breach of a duty the

---

[121] It is true that the trustee commits a breach of fiduciary duty, but that fact is irrelevant for that is a separate wrong.

[122] Birks (n 34) 51.

[123] See the text accompanying n 117 above.

[124] For a small sampling of the literature on this point, see PS Atiyah, *Essays on Contract* (Oxford, Clarendon Press, 1986) 40–42; C Bridgeman and JCP Goldberg, 'Do Promises Distinguish Contract from Tort?' (2012) 45 *Suffolk University Law Review* 873; Burrows (n 89) 8–14; Cane (n 7) 183–86; PH Winfield, *The Province of the Law of Tort* (Cambridge, Cambridge University Press, 1931) ch 6.

existence and content of which is determined predominately by the parties' agreement. In contrast, the existence and content of tortious duties are specified primarily by the law. It is of course true that the law indicates when an agreement will give rise to a contractual duty. It is also true that agreements between the parties' can play a role in the recognition and scope of a tortious duty. But when due weight is given to the claim that contractual duties spring *mainly* from the parties' agreement whereas tortious duties arise *primarily* by the law, it is possible to distinguish between torts and breaches of contract, at least in a rough-and-ready way. It is for this reason that defences to liability arising in breach of contract that are not also tort law defences will not be discussed in this book.

1.10.4. Conclusion

Some very brief remarks have been made about how torts differ from equitable wrongs and breaches of contract. However, for the reasons given at the start of this section, it has not been necessary to explore in any detail here the distinctiveness of tort law in this regard. There is a general agreement about which wrongs are torts, and this book is a book about defences to those wrongs. Defences to liability arising in respect of equitable wrongdoing and breaches of contract are not discussed, and no attempt is made to extend the claims that will be made about tort law defences to defences to these other wrongs.

1.11. Jurisdictions

The analysis offered in this book is not specific to any jurisdiction. It is intended to be relevant to all legal systems that are based on the common law. Although reference is made to legal materials in Australia, Canada, the United Kingdom and the United States more frequently than to sources in other jurisdictions, the overall message of the book would be the same were illustrations drawn from elsewhere in the common law world. In not confining the analysis to a single jurisdiction it is not, of course, being suggested that law governing defences to liability in tort in one jurisdiction is the same as in another. Different approaches are certainly taken in relation to specific defences in different jurisdictions. These differences are sometimes significant. Nevertheless, typically, the variation that exists is usually unimportant for the purposes of this book. It is possible to identify broad themes regarding tort defences that unite common law jurisdictions. It is with such broad themes that this book is concerned.

1.12. Methodology

1.12.1. Taxonomic Analysis

Some brief remarks need to be made about the general methodological approach adopted in this book. There are several things that this book does not seek to do. As was explained at the beginning of this chapter,[125] it does not attempt to describe the law controlling individual defences. It does not, in other words, attempt to determine the circumstances in which particular defences are enlivened. Neither is this book concerned, on the whole, with the reasons (or lack of reasons) underpinning specific defences or with when specific defences should (or should not) be enlivened. Rather, the main aim of this book is to suggest how the law governing tort defences as a whole should be conceptualised. Expressed differently, it is largely a classificatory enterprise.

Why is this type of analysis offered? There are three main reasons. The first is that no serious attempt has previously been made to construct a detailed map of the entirety of this area of the law. Secondly, as this book will show, much can be discovered about the law of tort defences by thinking about how defences should be classified. The third reason is that the classificatory treatment offered here may feed into any attempt to work out what the law of tort law defences ought to be. Put differently, the manner in which the law of tort defences is conceptualised might impact upon whether a given defence should have its scope expanded or contracted, whether new defences should be created and whether existing defences should be abolished. There is a case, therefore, for beginning with a taxonomic analysis of the law of tort defences before talking about the appropriate ambit of specific defences.

1.12.2. Criminal Law Theorising Regarding Defences

In sharp contrast with the lack of interest shown by tort lawyers in tort law defences,[126] criminal law theorists have generated a voluminous and highly sophisticated literature concerning criminal law defences. In particular, criminal law scholars have spent a very substantial amount of time thinking about the organisation of criminal law defences.[127] This book draws in places on relevant criminal

---

[125] See 1.1.

[126] See 1.3.

[127] Eg, GP Fletcher, *Rethinking Criminal Law* (Boston, Little, Brown & Co, 1978) chs 7, 9–10; Robinson (n 109) (two volumes); DN Husak, *Philosophy of Criminal Law* (Totowa, Rowman & Littlefield, 1987) ch 7; JC Smith, *Justification and Excuse in the Criminal Law* (London, Stevens & Sons, 1989); Horder (n 92) esp ch 3; J Chalmers and F Leverick, *Criminal Defences and Pleas in Bar of Trial* (Edinburgh, W. Green & Son Ltd, 2006); RA Duff, *Answering for Crime: Responsibility and Liability in the Criminal Law* (Oxford, Hart Publishing, 2007) esp chs 9 and 11; J Gardner, *Offences and Defences: Selected Essays in the Philosophy of Criminal Law* (Oxford, Oxford University Press, 2007) esp chs 4–9.

law writing. It might be thought that this is ill-advised. Traditional learning has it that tort law and the criminal law are so different that there is little scope for cross-fertilisation. Jules Coleman embraced this view when he said that 'The differences between torts and the criminal law are so fundamental that the net result of applying one's understanding of the criminal law to torts is bad philosophy and total confusion.'[128] It is of course undeniable that there are very significant differences between the criminal law and tort law.[129] Consequently, learning in one context should not be applied automatically to the other. But it does not follow that tort lawyers cannot profitably have recourse to criminal law scholarship.[130]

It is important not to lose sight of the many fundamental similarities between tort law and the criminal law in so far as their defence regimes are concerned.[131] Two general parallels are particularly noteworthy for present purposes. First, many defences to criminal liability are also defences in tort law. Examples include arrest, discipline, lawful authority, limitation, necessity and self-defence. The principles that govern the criminal and tort versions of these defences are remarkably similar.[132] In considering the scope of the tort versions of these defences judges routinely consult the authorities that control their criminal law counterparts[133] and vice versa. Likewise, the writers of books about tort law usually have little compunction in citing criminal law cases as authorities regarding the scope of tort law defences.[134] Indeed, the authors of one casebook, in their discussion of self-defence, go so far as to say that 'The privilege of self-defense is covered in Criminal Law, and detailed discussion must be left to that course.'[135] The writers

---

[128] Coleman (n 38) 222.

[129] Regarding the relationship between tort and crime generally, see Winfield (n 124) ch 8; J Hall, 'Interrelations of Criminal Law and Torts' (1943) 43 *Columbia Law Review* 753 and 967; RA Epstein, 'The Tort/Crime Distinction: A Generation Later' (1996) 76 *Boston University Law Review* 1; A Ripstein, *Equality, Responsibility, and the Law* (Cambridge, Cambridge University Press, 1999) ch 5; G Virgo, '"We do this in the Criminal Law and that in Tort Law": A New Fusion Debate' in SGA Pitel, JW Neyers and E Chamberlain (eds), *Tort Law: Challenging Orthodoxy* (Oxford, Hart Publishing, 2013).

[130] 'It is appropriate for those working on different sides of the frontier to have regard to what is being done on the other side': Virgo (n 129) 117.

[131] Criminal law defences and tort law defences are compared and contrasted in J Goudkamp, 'Defences in Tort and Crime' in M Dyson (ed), *Unravelling Tort and Crime* (Cambridge, Cambridge University Press, 2014).

[132] There are admittedly sometimes differences in the detail. Consider, for example, the remarks in *Ashley v Chief Constable of Sussex Police* [2008] UKHL 25; [2008] 1 AC 962 in relation to self-defence. This case is discussed in some detail in 9.3.4.

[133] Eg, *Presidential Security Services of Australia Pty Ltd v Brilley* [2008] NSWCA 204; (2008) 73 NSWLR 241, 262 [122], 264 [134]–[135] (self-defence); *Watkins v State of Victoria* [2010] VSCA 138; (2010) 27 VR 543, 560–61 [70]–[75] (self-defence); *XA v YA* [2010] EWHC 1983 (QB) [103]–[106] (discipline); *Sidaway v Board of Governors of the Bethlem Royal Hospital and the Maudsley Hospital* [1984] QB 493, 511, 515 (CA) (consent).

[134] Eg, Tony Weir in his *A Casebook on Tort* extracted several criminal law cases in the course of describing tort law defences: T Weir, *A Casebook on Tort*, 10th edn (London, Sweet & Maxwell, 2004) 402–03 (*Townley v Rushworth* (1963) 62 LGR 95 (Div Ct) (prosecution for assault raising the issue of self-defence)), 406–07 (*Whatford v Carty* The Times, 29 October 1960 (Div Ct) (prosecution for assault presenting the issue of defence of property)).

[135] VE Schwartz, K Kelly and DF Partlett, *Prosser, Wade and Schwartz's Torts: Cases and Materials*, 12th edn (New York, Foundation Press, 2010) 104.

of criminal law textbooks also have recourse to authorities regarding tort defences,[136] albeit probably to a lesser extent. The obvious parallels between many criminal law and tort law defences prompted Graham Virgo to claim that 'defences are generally defined in the same way, regardless of whether they are being deployed in the criminal or civil law'.[137] Secondly, criminal law and tort law defences often depend on the same basic concepts. For example, the concept of justification is of fundamental importance to defences in both contexts.

The foregoing considerations lie behind this book's reliance on theorising regarding criminal law defences. This learning is a rich vein that is well worth mining.[138]

1.13. Outline of the Argument

It may be helpful to provide an outline of the argument that will be presented in the following chapters. The primary goal of chapter two is to explore the distinction between torts and tort defences. Two main questions are considered. First, should the distinction be retained? Secondly, in the event that the distinction should be kept, what determines the allocation of issues relevant to liability as between the tort and defence camps? Few concrete conclusions are reached in relation to either of these questions. This is because they represent terrain that tort theorists have left essentially unexplored. The analysis simply puts forward various ideas that may point the way towards correct answers to these questions.

In order to understand defences, it is necessary to purge from the category of defences extraneous matter. Denials by the defendant that one or more of the elements of the tort that the claimant alleges was committed against him are mistaken for defences with alarming regularity. Unless they are corrected, such mistakes will seriously compromise efforts to come to grips with defences. Accordingly, chapter three identifies a large number of pleas that are denials rather than defences.

Chapter four is the conceptual core of the book. It develops a taxonomy of tort law defences. It is argued that all tort defences can be separated into just two categories: justification defences and public policy defences. These categories are derived from the story that the defences that constitute these categories tell about the quality of the defendant's practical reasoning. Justification defences reveal that the defendant acted reasonably in committing a wrong. Public policy defences are silent on the justifiability of the defendant's wrongful act. Attention is given to

---

[136] Eg, J Herring, *Criminal Law: Text, Cases, and Materials*, 5th edn (Oxford, Oxford University Press, 2012) 656 includes extracts from the reasons given in *Southwark London Borough Council v Williams* [1971] 1 Ch 734 (CA), a tort case concerned with the defence of necessity.

[137] Virgo (n 129) 104.

[138] It is interesting to observe that although criminal law scholarship is, on the whole, considerably more advanced than tort law theory, tort lawyers have not generally looked to this scholarship for guidance. Instead the tendency has been to attempt to find insights from writing about other branches of private law, especially the law of contract.

whether tort law recognises other types of defences, in particular excuses and defences that are enlivened by a lack of 'basic responsibility'[139] on the part of the defendant, that is to say, a lack of the capacity to be guided by reasons. It is concluded that no additional defences exist in tort law.

Chapters five, six and seven build upon the analysis presented in chapter four. Chapter five applies the twofold taxonomy. It suggests how a large selection of tort law defences should be classified. Chapter six discusses several implications that might be derived from the taxonomy. It shows that the bipartite taxonomy is pregnant with important practical ramifications. Chapter seven looks at several alternative ways in which tort defences might be organised. It concludes that these rival methods of division are all inferior to the twofold taxonomy.

Chapter eight is concerned with defences that are engaged by a lack of basic responsibility. The criminal law provides for several such defences, most notably insanity, infancy and unfitness to plead. Denial of basic responsibility defences are not recognised by tort law. It is argued that this position is unsatisfactory. Insanity and infancy (but not unfitness to plead) should join the ranks of defences to liability in tort. If these defences were to be welcomed into tort law, it would be necessary to add an extra category to the taxonomy of tort defences developed in chapter four in which to house them.

Chapter nine concludes the book by considering a selection of issues that are important to the future of tort defences. It begins by discussing the consequences of the 'statutorification' of the law of tort defences. It then addresses how the reform of the law governing tort defences ought to proceed. Next, it considers a range of ways in which the law of tort defences interacts with other parts of the law. Lastly, it calls for the analysis presented in this book to be extended to the other departments of the law of obligations. A map of defences to civil wrongs generally is needed to complement the advances that have been made in recent decades regarding the classification of those wrongs.

---

[139] The terminology is taken from Gardner (n 127) ch 9.

2

Torts and Defences

2.1. Introduction

The law of torts, like all areas of the law, is built upon a collection of fundamental distinctions. One of the oldest and most basic of these distinctions is that between torts and defences. Unfortunately, this distinction is one of the many casualties of the general neglect of defences by scholars.[1] No comprehensive account of it has been offered. As a result, relatively little is known about it. It is not known, for instance, whether the distinction is defensible. Neither is it known what determines whether a given issue is listed under the 'tort' heading or the 'defence' heading. These matters, which are about as basic as any in tort law, have been almost completely ignored by theorists. The aim of this chapter is to reduce the size of this very substantial gap in our understanding of tort law. Because this area of tort law is essentially untouched by scholars, the analysis is predominantly exploratory in nature. It does not offer many concrete conclusions. Its purpose is to identify relevant issues and to put forward some tentative ideas.

2.2. Is the Distinction Exhaustive?

Before directly confronting the distinction between torts and defences, it is worth asking whether it captures the entirety of the law of torts. Can every issue that is relevant to the circumstances in which liability in tort arises be arranged into torts and defences? This is an important question. If the rules that constitute tort law cannot be sorted into just these categories, it would be necessary to explain not only the separation between torts and defences but also the relationships of those categories to whatever other additional categories exist. Two challenges to the exhaustiveness of the separation of tort law into torts and defences are considered in this section.

---

[1] Regarding this neglect, see 1.3.

2.2.1. Standing Rules

Standing rules are rules that determine whether a given claimant is the type of person who can maintain judicial proceedings. They are distinct from torts and defences. Conventional wisdom holds that there are no standing rules in tort law or, indeed, in the law of obligations generally.[2] Standing rules, according to this view, are found only in public law. This traditional learning may or may not be accurate. Standing rules might exist in the law of torts (and elsewhere in the law of obligations[3]). If they exist, it would be inadequate to organise tort law merely into torts and defences.

A possible example of a standing rule in the law of torts is the rule that estops a claimant from maintaining an action in tort if he has made a legally-binding promise not to sue the defendant. Arguably, a promise not to sue renders the claimant a type of person whom the court will not hear, to the extent that hearing him would permit him to escape from the obligation created by his promise. However, this is not the only way in which the operation of a promise not to sue can be understood. Perhaps the absence of such a promise is an implicit element of all actions in tort. Another possibility is that the existence of such a promise furnishes the defendant with a defence. Unfortunately, the cases simply do not tell us how, precisely, a legally-binding promise not to sue prevents the claimant from establishing liability.

The doctrine of illegality bears some resemblance to a standing rule, at least in some of the cases in which it has been considered. Lord Mansfield's famous description of the doctrine of illegality in *Holman v Johnson* is framed in language that is consistent with presenting the doctrine as a standing rule. Lord Mansfield wrote:[4]

> No Court will lend its aid to a man who founds his cause of action upon an immoral or an illegal act. If, from the plaintiff's own stating or otherwise, the cause of action appears to arise ex turpi causa, or the transgression of a positive law of this country, there the Court says that he has no right to be assisted. It is upon that ground the Court goes; not for the sake of the defendant, but because they will not lend their aid to such a plaintiff.

---

[2] P Cane, *Administrative Law*, 5th edn (Oxford, Clarendon Press, 2011) 281–82: 'Standing is not normally a requirement for bringing a "private-law claim" . . . There are certain private-law concepts that resemble rules of standing: for example, duty of care in the tort of negligence, the principle that breach of a statutory duty will be actionable in tort only if the duty is owed to the claimant as an individual (as opposed to the public generally), and the doctrine of privity of contract. However, these are not seen as separate from the rules that define the relevant wrong, but as part of the definition of the wrong.' Cf K Schiemann, 'Locus Standi' [1990] *Public Law* 342, 342–43.

[3] Judges often ask whether claimants have standing to bring private law actions: see, eg, *Burns v Shuttlehurst Ltd* [1999] 2 All ER 27, 36 [34]; [1999] 1 WLR 1449, 1458 (CA); *Peer International Corp v Termidor Music Publishers Ltd* [2006] EWHC 2883 [31] (Ch); *Pope v Energem Mining (IOM) Ltd* [2011] EWCA Civ 1043 [8] (contract); *Re Denley's Trust Deed* [1969] 1 Ch 373, 382 (Ch D); *Hollis v Rolfe* [2008] EWHC 1747 (Ch) [134]; *Walker v Stones* [2000] All ER (D) 1003 (CA) (trusts); *Stein v Blake* [1998] 1 All ER 724, 726 (CA) (directors' duties); *Chocosuisse Union des Fabricants Suisses de Chocolat v Cadbury Ltd* [1999] RPC 826 (CA) (passing off).

[4] (1775) 1 Cowp 341, 343; 98 ER 1120, 1121.

Lord Mansfield's references to the court's refusal to 'lend its aid' to a claimant whose action arises from an illegal act, and his assertion that such a claimant has no 'right to be assisted', are telling. Lord Mansfield can be plausibly read as saying that the court will shut its doors to the wrongdoing claimant even if he has a valid cause of action. This suggests that the doctrine of illegality is a standing rule. However, it is far from clear that this is how the doctrine of illegality operates in the modern world, despite judges' ritualistic incantation of Lord Mansfield's words. Since Lord Mansfield's time, the courts have stressed that offenders are not persons from whom the law automatically withholds all relief.[5] The judicial *Zeitgeist* is opposed to construing the doctrine of illegality as a standing rule.

Lastly, consider the action in public nuisance. A private citizen can sue in public nuisance only if he suffers 'special damage'.[6] This requirement is routinely described as a standing rule.[7] However, even if this description is warranted, it does not necessarily follow that tort law recognises standing rules. This is due to doubts regarding the status of the action in public nuisance. Several writers argue forcefully that public nuisance is not a tort.[8] Reasons given in this connection typically relate to the fact that public nuisance protects public rights rather than private rights.

In summary, it is arguable that tort law provides for standing rules. Several instances where it might do so have been outlined. But it is far from clear that such rules exist in tort law.

2.2.2. Affirmative Answers to Defences

If the claimant succeeds in establishing that all of the elements of the tort in which he sues are present, all is not lost from the defendant's point of view. He may be able

---

[5] 'The door of a court is not barred because the plaintiff has committed a crime. The confirmed criminal is as much entitled to redress as his most virtuous fellow citizen; no record of crime, however long, makes one an outlaw': *Olmstead v United States* 277 US 438, 484 (1928) (Brandeis J); 'The medieval concept of outlawry is unacceptable in modern society. An outlaw forfeited the protection of the law. He could not invoke the assistance of the court to enforce non-existent rights. In the United Kingdom today there are no outlaws. However abhorrent the crime, whatever the subsequent conviction, the protection of the law extends to the criminal who enjoys rights not only in theory but enforceable in practice': *Cross v Kirkby* The Times, 5 April 2000 (CA) (Judge LJ).

[6] *Wallasey Local Board v Gracey* (1887) 36 Ch D 593, 597 (Ch D); *Jan de Nul (UK) Ltd v AXA Royale Belge SA* [2002] EWCA 209; [2002] 1 Lloyd's Rep 583, 591–92 [60]. The choice of the label 'special damage' is unfortunate. It suggests that the claimant must suffer a specific type of damage, or damage that attracts an award of special damages. This is not the case. As Prosser observed, what is required is not a specific type of damage but 'damage of any kind individual to the plaintiff, as distinguished from that which he shares with the rest of the public': WL Prosser, 'Private Action for Public Nuisance' (1966) 52 *Virginia Law Review* 997, 997.

[7] Eg, *Nuneaton Local Board v General Sewage Co* (1875) LR 20 Eq 127, 131 (Ch D); *Gravesham Borough Council v British Railways Board* [1978] Ch 379, 397–99 (Ch D); *Wallace v Powell* [2000] NSWSC 406 [33].

[8] See, especially, TW Merrill, 'Is Public Nuisance a Tort?' (2011) 4 *Journal of Tort Law* 4. See also R Stevens, *Torts and Rights* (Oxford, Oxford University Press, 2007) 186–88; NJ McBride and R Bagshaw, *Tort Law*, 5th edn (Harlow, Pearson, 2014) 658–59.

to rely on a defence. If the defendant invokes a defence, the claimant will be given an opportunity to cast doubt on whether the facts needed to enliven it exist. What happens, however, if a defence bites? Is that the end of the road for the claimant? Or can the claimant circumvent a defence by way of another rule?[9] Such rules will be called 'affirmative answers to defences'. To be clear, a rule is an affirmative answer to a defence if pleading it is consistent with accepting that the defendant's defence applies and if it stops that defence from preventing liability from arising.

It is unclear whether tort law recognises affirmative answers to defences. Suppose that D strikes C. C is injured and sues D in trespass. D pleads that he acted in self-defence. C concedes that D acted in self-defence but maintains that he used excessive force. It is clear that D will be liable if he used excessive force.[10] But how, exactly, is this result achieved? It is arguable that the plea of 'excessive force' is an affirmative answer to the defence of self-defence. This interpretation is, perhaps, arguably reinforced by cases in which it was held that the claimant bears the onus of proving that the force used was disproportionate.[11] But, unfortunately, the authorities do not put the matter beyond doubt. It might be the case that the defence of self-defence includes as one of its elements a requirement that the defensive force be reasonable.[12]

Consider, also, the defence of qualified privilege. A defendant who published a defamatory statement maliciously will not be able to avoid liability on the basis of qualified privilege. But how, precisely, does the 'no malice' rule work? Is the absence of malice an element of the defence of qualified privilege? Or is the fact that the defendant acted maliciously an affirmative answer to the defence of qualified privilege? In support of the latter interpretation, it might be pointed out that where the defence of qualified privilege is in issue, the burden rests on the claimant to show that the defendant acted maliciously in publishing the statement concerned.[13] Regrettably, however, the authorities give no clear indication as to how tort law accommodates the issue of malice. Judges often speak of malice 'destroying'[14] or 'defeating'[15] qualified privilege, or of qualified privilege being 'defeasible'[16] on proof of malice, but these labels are ambiguous in relation to the crucial issue of how the 'no malice' rule functions.

---

[9] For a brilliant argument that there should be no limit on the number of rounds of defences, see RA Epstein, 'Pleadings and Presumptions' (1973) 40 *University of Chicago Law Review* 556, esp 568–71. Epstein develops this analysis in RA Epstein, 'The Not So Minimum Content of Natural Law' (2005) 25 *Oxford Journal of Legal Studies* 219, 233–43.

[10] *Sofola v Coles* [2000] EWCA Civ 392 [15]; *Miska v Sivec* [1959] OR 144, 148 (CA).

[11] *McClelland v Symons* [1951] VLR 157, 166 (Full Ct); *Green v Costello* [1961] NZLR 1010, 1012 (SC); cf *Mann v Balaban* [1970] SCR 74, 87; *Watkins v State of Victoria* [2010] VSCA 138; (2010) 27 VR 543, 548 [74].

[12] This seems to have been the view of Morden JA in *Miska v Sivec* [1959] OR 144, 148 (CA), who said 'Self-defence is an answer to a claim for assault but only when the force used was not unreasonable in the circumstances. *The reasonableness of the force is an integral part of the defence*' (emphasis added).

[13] *Horrocks v Lowe* [1975] AC 135, 149–51 (HL).

[14] Eg, *ibid*, 149–53.

[15] Eg, *Reynolds v Times Newspapers Ltd* [2001] 2 AC 127, 194 (HL).

[16] Eg, *Seray-Wurie v The Charity Commission of England and Wales* [2009] EWCA Civ 153 [5].

Parallel observations can be made in relation to the defence of public necessity. Suppose that D is the captain of an oil tanker. Due to his negligence, the tanker is beached on a sand bar and is at risk of being lost with all hands. D jettisons the tanker's load in order to increase its buoyancy. The tanker and its crew are saved, but the discharged oil pollutes a waterfront property owned by C. C sues D in private nuisance. D invokes the defence of public necessity. C, in response, relies on the fact that D negligently caused the emergency. It is arguable that this plea (if it is a good one[17]) is an affirmative answer to D's defence of public necessity. But equally, the absence of fault on the part of D might be an element of the defence. The authorities simply do not address this issue.

A hint that tort law might provide for affirmative answers to defences can be found in the English rules of civil procedure. To appreciate why this is the case, it is necessary to say some brief words about pleadings. An action is commenced when the claimant files his statement of case and serves it on the defendant.[18] In his statement of case, the claimant should allege facts that constitute a tort. The statement of case should not anticipate and respond to defences that the defendant might raise.[19] The defendant, once he has been served with the statement of case, then has the opportunity to file a statement of defence.[20] In his statement of defence, the defendant can deny the existence of the facts alleged by the claimant. He can also offer a defence. The claimant, if he wishes to do so, may respond to the defendant's statement of defence by filing a reply.[21] The mere fact that the claimant can file a reply does not reveal the existence of affirmative answers to defences. The fact that claimants are able to file replies shows only that claimants can deny facts that would, if true, enliven a defence pleaded by the defendant. The next pleading in the sequence is a rejoinder. If defendants can file rejoinders it follows that one of the purposes of replies must be to permit the claimant to present affirmative answers to defences. This is because rejoinders would serve no purpose if affirmative answers to defences could not be pleaded in replies. The issue, then, is whether it is possible for claimants to file rejoinders. The law in this connection is stated in rule 15.9 of the Civil Procedure Rules ('CPR'). This rule provides:[22]

> A party may not file or serve any statement of case after a reply without the permission of the court.

[17] Devlin J thought that it was in *Southport Corporation v Esso Petroleum Co Ltd* [1953] 2 All ER 1204, 1209–10; [1953] 3 WLR 773, 779 (QBD). Devlin J's decision was affirmed in *Esso Petroleum Co Ltd v Southport Corporation* [1956] AC 218 (HL) but the House did not discuss this issue. See also *Rigby v Chief Constable of Northamptonshire* [1985] 2 All ER 985, 994; [1985] 1 WLR 1242, 1253 (QBD).

[18] CPR 7.2(1).

[19] 'It is no part of the statement of claim to anticipate the defence, and to state what the Plaintiff would have to say in answer to it': *Hall v Eve* (1876) 4 Ch D 341, 345 (CA).

[20] CPR 15.2.

[21] CPR 15.8.

[22] CPR 15.9 is inconsistent with the recommendations of Lord Woolf from which they were born. Lord Woolf expressly recommended that pleading after a reply should not be permitted: Lord Woolf, *Access to Justice: Final Report to the Lord Chancellor on the Civil Justice System in England and Wales* (London, HMSO, 1996) [17]. That position is taken in the Federal Rules of Civil Procedure r 7(a)(7). For discussion of that provision, see JH Friedenthal, MK Kane and AR Miller, *Civil Procedure*, 4th edn (St Paul, Minn, Thomson West, 2005) 311–12.

Because the CPR apply to civil litigation generally, by making provision for rejoinders to be filed and served, CPR 15.9 contemplates only that affirmative answers to defences might exist somewhere in the civil law. It does not show that they exist in tort law.[23] Unfortunately, therefore, CPR 15.9 does not show conclusively that affirmative answers to defences are recognised by the law of torts. At the very most, it hints at their existence.

2.2.3. Conclusion

This section asked whether the whole of tort law can be split only into torts and defences. It was considered whether two additional types of rules – standing rules and affirmative answers to defences – exist. Tort law may well recognise such rules. But the evidence is inconclusive. Since it is unclear whether these or any other types of rules exist, this chapter will proceed on the assumption that the law of torts can be organised into torts and defences.

2.3. Defending Defences

Some issues that are relevant to liability constitute elements of torts. Others are treated as defences. It is important to note that, generally speaking, any issue could be placed on either side of the equation. Elements of torts could be converted into defences, and defences could be assimilated within the definitions of torts. In short, issues relevant to liability are transposable. To give some concrete examples, the damage element of the action in negligence could be extracted from the definition of that action and turned into a defence, the defence of self-defence to liability in trespass could be inserted into the definition of the tort of battery and so on.

The fact that issues are transposable has important implications. One such ramification is that the distinction between torts and defences could be dissolved. It would be possible to assimilate *all* issues that are relevant to liability within the definitions of torts. Were this done, what will be termed a 'unitary system of tort law' would be created. This part of the chapter considers whether a unitary system of tort law would be preferable to the current bipartite arrangement. A unitary system would have the significant advantage of simplicity. A compelling argument is therefore needed to justify the retention of the present system.

---

[23] The fact that CPR 15.9 requires the defendant to obtain the court's leave before he can file a rejoinder is hard to understand. If affirmative answers to defences exist, defendants should be entitled to file rejoinders as of right as they must, surely, be allowed to contest the asserted facts underpinning any affirmative answers raised by the claimant.

2.3.1. Mere Assertions

Some theorists who support the division of tort law into torts and defences have merely offered assertions in support of the division. It is important not to mistake these assertions for arguments. For example, Richard Epstein writes:[24]

> Assume, for the moment, that the plaintiff's allegation, 'the defendant unlawfully struck the plaintiff,' states a prima facie case. What argument can the defendant make that admits the allegation in the complaint, yet supports the contention that he should not be held liable? Clearly, there is none. Once he has admitted that his conduct is 'unlawful,' it is no longer possible to find an excuse or justification appropriate to a plea in avoidance. The problem with this form of allegation, therefore, is not that it is too weak, but rather that it is too strong. The plaintiff's prima facie case should erect a presumption that shifts the burden of explanation to the other party; it should not foreclose all possibility of explanation.

This passage is riddled with problems. Epstein's claim that there are 'clearly' no responses available to a defendant who admits the allegation 'the defendant unlawfully struck the plaintiff' is transparently false. Epstein appears to have forgotten about the existence of rules such as immunities, the doctrine of illegality and limitation bars. Such rules do not challenge the 'unlawfulness' of the defendant's behaviour and yet, when applicable, they exempt the defendant from liability. Another problem is that Epstein does not rigorously separate defences from rules the applicability of which it falls to the defendant to prove.[25] He talks of arguments that the defendant can make that 'admit' the allegations against him but which nevertheless enable the defendant to avoid being held liable, and of 'pleas in avoidance'. Here, Epstein has defences in mind. But, confusingly, Epstein also refers to the '[shifting of] the burden of explanation' to the defendant. At this point, Epstein slips from defences to rules in respect of which the defendant carries the onus of proof. But most significantly, for present purposes, although Epstein seems to support the distinction between torts and defences, he offers no reason for his readers to agree with him. The final sentence in the quoted passage, in which Epstein apparently defends the separation between torts and defences, is simply a bald assertion.

2.3.2. An Inadequate Rationale

One rationale for retaining the distinction between torts and defences can be quickly cast aside. It might be suggested that defences exist in order to keep the net of liability in tort from being cast too widely. If defences did not exist, the courts may be inundated with claims, with dire consequences for the administration of justice (the 'floodgates' concern), defendants may be would be saddled

---

[24] Epstein (n 9) 561.
[25] Regarding the distinction between these concepts, see 1.2.1.4.

with liability that is disproportionate to their fault and freedom of action may be unacceptably diminished. This argument clearly does not do the trick. This is because it is not an argument for the existence of defences specifically. Rather, it is an argument for limiting the circumstances in which liability in tort arises generally. It does nothing to show that liability should not be delimited instead by adding elements to the definitions of torts, or by making it more difficult to establish existing elements.

2.3.3. The Efficient Administration of Justice

The distinction between torts and defences promotes the efficient administration of justice by preventing the wastage that would occur if claimants had to prove or disprove every fact relevant to liability.[26] Because claimants bear the onus of proving the elements of torts,[27] were all of the defences to liability in tort drawn within the definitions of torts, the number of facts that claimants would need to prove to establish liability would be greatly increased. Every fact that would enliven a rule that is currently a defence would need to be disproved by every claimant. For example, every claimant would need to show that the defendant did not act in self-defence, that the defendant was not immune from liability, that the doctrine of *res judicata* is inapplicable, that the defendant's conduct in question was not authorised by a statute, that the relevant limitation period had not expired and so on. To require claimants to prove such matters would be a waste of resources. As Richard Posner puts it, 'It would be particularly inefficient to require the plaintiff to anticipate and produce evidence contravening the indefinite number of defenses that a defendant might plead in a given case.'[28] Likewise William Prosser and Page Keeton said that 'It would . . . [be] manifestly unsound and impractical to require a plaintiff to negative at the outset all possible excuses or justifications.'[29] The main reason why this is so is that, in most cases, it is unlikely that facts capable of enlivening many rules that are presently cast as defences will exist.

2.3.4. Procedural Justice

The distinction between torts and defences can also be defended on the basis that it promotes procedural justice. Again, because of the principles that govern the allocation of the onus of proof,[30] the separation between torts and defences means

---

[26] A more elaborate analysis of the division between torts and defences from the standpoint of efficiency is offered in TR Lee, 'Pleading and Proof: The Economics of Legal Burdens' [1997] *Brigham Young University Law Review* 1.

[27] See the text accompanying n 66 in ch 1 and 6.4.

[28] RA Posner, *Economic Analysis of Law*, 7th edn (New York, Aspen Publishers, 2007) 647.

[29] WP Keeton, DB Dobbs, RE Keeton and DG Owen (eds), *Prosser and Keeton on Torts*, 5th edn (St Paul, Minn, West Publishing Co, 1984) 108.

[30] See the text accompanying n 66 in ch 1 and 6.4.

that both parties are responsible for establishing certain facts. Were the distinction between torts and defences collapsed, the claimant would be the only party placed under a burden of proof. This would be contrary to a fundamental tenet of procedural justice. It is a basic principle of law that litigants in the civil sphere must be treated as even-handedly in terms of procedure as is reasonably possible.[31] The distinction between torts and defences therefore plays a role in advancing procedural justice.

This argument might be taken one step further. Certain facts will, as a general rule, be significantly easier for claimants to prove or disprove than for defendants and vice versa. This may be because some facts may tend to be peculiarly within the knowledge of one party. Or it may be because requiring one party to establish a certain fact would involve calling on that party to prove a negative.[32] The distinction between torts and defences can be used to ensure that litigants generally are treated fairly in terms of what they are called upon to establish.[33] For example, if a particular fact is normally much easier for claimants to prove than for defendants, it might be procedurally fairer to allocate that issue to the tort category so that claimants will be called upon to establish it.[34]

2.3.5. Relative Value of the Parties' Interests

Peter Cane sketches an argument that seems to be aimed at supporting the division between torts and defences.[35] He claims:[36]

> The interests of the party to whom the onus of proof on any particular issue is allocated are less well protected by the law than those of the party who enjoys the benefit of this allocation because in the face of uncertainty that cannot be resolved on the available evidence, the latter's interests will be preferred by the law to those of the former. Allocation of the onus of proof provides a technique by which the law can express and give effect to value judgments about the strength of the various interests to which responsibility judgments relate.

---

[31] This principle is discussed in A Zuckerman, *Zuckerman on Civil Procedure: Principles of Practice*, 2nd edn (London, Sweet & Maxwell, 2006) 104–10 [2.132]–[2.146], and in relation to the onus of proof specifically at 755–56 [21.39]–[21.42]. At 755–56 Zuckerman writes: 'Precisely because both parties are entitled to equal protection from the risk of error it makes sense to hold that while one party runs a higher risk on one issue, the opponent should bear the risk on another issue.'

[32] Cf KW Saunders, 'The Mythic Difficulty in Proving a Negative' (1985) 15 *Seton Hall Law Review* 276.

[33] Cf Epstein (n 9) 579–80. Epstein argues that it is better to handle the potential for unfairness created by disparities in access to the evidence by way of rules concerning disclosure rather than via the distinction between torts and defences (at 580): '[W]henever the question of access [to evidence] is crucial, there are better techniques available for handling it. . . . [D]iscovery procedures can largely eliminate the problem of unequal access.'

[34] Judges often place weight on the difficulty of proving particular facts in deciding how the onus of proof should be allocated in respect of the fact in question: see, eg, *Salter v Purchell* (1841) 1 QB 209, 219–20 (Ex Ch); *Morton v West Lothian Council* 2006 Rep LR 7, 11–12 [70] (OH); *Non-Marine Underwriters, Lloyd's London v Scalera* [2000] SCC 24; [2000] 1 SCR 551, 575 [33].

[35] P Cane, *Responsibility in Law and Morality* (Oxford, Hart Publishing, 2002) 90–92.

[36] *Ibid*, 91.

Cane elaborates upon his thinking in this regard with reference to the concept of contributory negligence, and the different ways in which it applies to the tort of negligence and to the tort of negligent misstatement. He writes:[37]

> Contributory negligence is a defence available in cases, for instance, of negligently inflicted personal injury. The onus of proving contributory negligence rests on the person whose negligence allegedly inflicted the personal injury . . . The result of a successful plea of contributory negligence is reduction of the compensation that would otherwise be payable by the person whose negligence allegedly caused the injury . . .
>
> In the case of liability for negligent misstatement, . . . [the fact that the victim's reliance on the defendant's misstatement must be reasonable], coupled with the imposition on the victim of the onus of proof on this issue, gives expression to a judgment that in respect of the risk of suffering financial loss as a result of relying on false statements, people should take more care to protect their own interests than is required in cases in which contributory negligence is available as a defence.

Because the distinction between torts and defences is the mechanism by which the onus of proof is distributed between the parties, Cane's logic, if sound, seems to go some way towards supporting the distinction. Cane is confused about the state of the law in so far as he suggests that contributory negligence is unavailable in the context of negligent misrepresentation,[38] but this error is unimportant for present purposes. Cane commits a different and more serious error in claiming that the allocation of the issue of contributory negligence to the tort category in the case of the tort of negligent misstatement means that claimants should take more care to protect their financial interests than would be the case were contributory negligence a matter of defence to liability arising in this tort. The tort of negligent misstatement, like all torts, tells defendants how they should conduct themselves, not claimants. But Cane is on to something in so far as he says that the way in which issues relevant to liability are allocated as between the 'tort' and 'defence' headings is one way in which the law gives expression to the relative strength of the parties' interests. By assigning an issue to the 'tort' category, the law gives greater weight to the defendant's interests in being able to do what he wishes, whereas allocating an issue to the 'defence' category affords heightened protection to the interests protected by the cause of action in question. Judges have sometimes referred to this consideration in deciding whether issues relevant to liability should be cast as part of a cause of action or as a defence.[39]

---

[37] *Ibid.*
[38] See 3.6.6.
[39] A plum example is *Non-Marine Underwriters, Lloyd's London v Scalera* [2000] SCC 24; [2000] 1 SCR 551 (reasons of McLachlin J).

2.3.6. The Rule of Law: Duties and Privileges

When the law of torts recognises particular conduct as tortious, it creates a duty not to engage in the conduct in question.[40] For example, the tort of defamation creates a duty not to defame people, the tort of private nuisance creates a duty not interfere unreasonably with occupiers' enjoyment of their land, the tort of false imprisonment creates a duty not to impair a person's freedom of movement and so on. Defences are quite different from torts in this regard. Unlike torts, defences do not create duties. Rather, defences identify situations where the duties created by torts may be disregarded. So, for example, whereas the tort of battery creates a duty not to strike other people without their consent, the defence of self-defence merely affords a person who has been attacked or threatened with an attack a privilege to exercise defensive force.[41] The existence of the defence of self-defence does not oblige a person entitled to it to do anything. In particular, the fact that the defence of self-defence would enable a person to strike another individual without incurring liability in tort does not require that person to use defensive force. A person entitled to the defence of self-defence is at liberty to allow himself to be pummelled by an aggressor.[42] This fundamental difference between torts and defences may point the way to a reason for retaining the present bipartite arrangement of tort law. It is conceivable that, by separating torts from defences, tort law is better positioned to comply with the rule of law than would be the case if defences did not exist. Arguably, the rule of law places greater demands on duties than on privileges in terms of the precision with which they need to be stated. If this is correct, more malleable and open-textured rules (which tort law must retain in order to be able to respond with sufficient flexibility to the diverse situations that life presents) can be cast as defences in order to bring tort law into increased compliance with the rule of law.

2.3.7. Promoting Rationality in Judicial Reasoning

It is arguable that the distinction between torts and defences should be maintained because it promotes rationality in judges' reasoning processes. Organising

---

[40] The argument here has been influenced by John Gardner and George Fletcher: J Gardner, *Offences and Defences: Selected Essays in the Philosophy of Criminal Law* (Oxford, Oxford University Press, 2007) 116–18; GP Fletcher, 'The Nature of Justification' in S Shute, J Gardner and J Horder (eds), *Action and Value in Criminal Law* (Oxford, Clarendon Press, 1993) 180–81.

[41] The classic treatment of the distinction between duties and privileges is WN Hohfeld, 'Some Fundamental Legal Conceptions as Applied in Judicial Reasoning' (1913) 23 *Yale Law Journal* 16, 30–44.

[42] Of course, a person may simultaneously be privileged in performing a particular act and, pursuant to a separate rule, be under a duty to perform it: see *ibid*, 32–33. For example, a police officer who sees a member of the public being attacked is under a legal duty to intervene (*Haynes v Harwood* [1935] 1 KB 146, 161–62 (CA)) and is privileged to use force to disable and arrest the attacker. Similarly, a person may have a legal duty to publish a defamatory statement concerning another individual and be privileged to publish the statement in question.

rules that determine the scope of tortious liability into torts and defences may help judges to keep their thoughts straight in at least three distinct ways. First, it increases the visibility of both connections between rules that fall within the same category and distinctions between rules that belong to different groups. This increased visibility guards against the risk that judges will overlook links between related rules or conflate discrete rules. Secondly, by arranging the process of determining liability in a tort stage and a defence stage, judges may be more likely systematically to address all of the relevant liability rules rather than arbitrarily to determine whether liability should be imposed. Thirdly, the distinction may help to prevent judges from dealing with rules in an illogical sequence. As discussed in chapter one,[43] it is a principle of tort law that judges should ascertain whether the claimant's cause of action is complete before investigating the applicability of any defences. The distinction between torts and defences can therefore be used to minimise the risk that judges will deal with rules in a nonsensical order. Rules that logically arise for consideration as anterior matters can be treated as part of a tort, whereas rules that ought to be considered only after other rules have been addressed can be cast as defences.

2.3.8. Harmonisation with Other Departments of the Law of Obligations

It is arguable that the fact that all of the other areas of the law of obligations embrace the distinction between actions and defences gives some reason for the law of torts to follow suit. This may make things more straightforward when a claimant sues in tort and in another department of the law of obligations.[44] Suppose, for example, that proceedings are brought in respect of a tort, a breach of contract and a breach of trust, and the defendant pleads the doctrine of illegality in relation to all of these causes of action. Because illegality is treated as a defence to liability for breach of contract and breach of trust, if tort law did not distinguish between torts and defences, the plea of illegality would be treated as a denial by the defendant that the claimant's cause of action is complete. This situation might be confusing, both for the parties (who might be perplexed about who needs to plead and prove facts relevant to the issue of illegality) and for judges.

2.3.9. Discussion

This part of the chapter considered whether the distinction between torts and defences is justified. This is not a task that has been attempted previously by theorists. This being the case, the goal has been relatively modest. It has merely been to

---

[43] See 1.5.
[44] This logic is visible in *Hall v Hebert* [1993] 2 SCR 159, 185.

put some rationales for recognising defences on the table rather than to reach firm conclusions. It might be that some of the rationales offered ought, on closer inspection, to be rejected. Several general points about the analysis will now be made.

2.3.9.1. Arguments that depend upon the allocation of the onus of proof

Three of the arguments put forward depend for their strength on the fact that the onus of proof is allocated by reference to the division between torts and defences. These arguments are those based on the efficient administration of justice,[45] procedural justice[46] and the relative value placed by the law on the parties' interests.[47] There are two reasons for thinking that these arguments, although they cannot be dismissed out of hand, are relatively weak. The first is that were the way in which the onus of proof is distributed in respect of the various facts in issue changed (it could obviously be allocated according to a different criterion), these arguments would lose their force. They only make sense given the way in which the onus of proof is presently distributed. Secondly, the benefits that flow from distinguishing between torts and defences that these arguments identify could be obtained even in a unitary system of tort law. Hence, they merely show that the distinction between torts and defences is useful, as opposed to indispensable. Take, for example, the efficient administration of justice argument. For the reasons that have already been given, there is an interest in requiring the defendant to prove facts that are relevant to liability that do not often exist. But the onus of proof in respect of such facts could be allocated to the defendant even in a unitary system. The legislature could, for instance, identify the facts concerned and provide that the defendant bears the onus of establishing them. Indeed, it is entirely possible to convert to a unitary system of tort law without changing the way in which the burden of proof is allocated in respect of a single issue.

2.3.9.2. Is the distinction between torts and defences intrinsically significant?

Is the distinction between torts and defences intrinsically significant? Many judges and commentators believe that it is not. The law reports and the writings of scholars are littered with assertions that it is morally unimportant whether liability is withheld on the basis that an element of the tort in which the claimant sues is absent, or on the ground that the defendant has a defence.[48] Given the dearth of theorising as to the rationales for the distinction between torts and defences, it is surprising that such claims have been made so freely. This is because their validity

---

[45] See 2.3.3.

[46] See 2.3.4.

[47] See 2.3.5.

[48] Eg, *Smith v Jenkins* (1970) 119 CLR 397, 422 (HCA); *Jackson v Harrison* (1978) 138 CLR 438, 464 (HCA); *Condon v Basi* [1985] 2 All ER 453, 454; [1985] 1 WLR 866, 868 (CA); *Vellino v Chief Constable of the Greater Manchester Police* [2001] EWCA Civ 1249; [2002] 1 WLR 218, 226 [35], 233–34 [62]; *D'Orta-Ekenaike v Victoria Legal Aid* [2005] HCA 12; (2005) 223 CLR 1, 33–34 [95]. See also S Hedley, *Tort*, 6th edn (Oxford, Oxford University Press, 2008) 324.

depends on the reason or reasons for the existence of the distinction between torts and defences. If the separation between torts and defences exists merely, for example, in order to facilitate the efficient administration of justice or to promote rationality in judicial reasoning, then this separation would indeed be of no moral consequence. But matters would be otherwise if the distinction can be justified on certain of the other grounds discussed in this part of the chapter, such as on the basis that it guides defendants in their conduct by stating clearly when defendants are under a duty to act in a particular way and when they have a privilege to commit torts.[49]

While one should reach a definite conclusion as to the purpose of the distinction between torts and defences before saying with conviction whether it is morally salient, it is nevertheless worth observing that the suggestion that the distinction is not inherently significant looks decidedly implausible. Is it really the case that it is not inherently significant whether, for example, a sexual battery is defined to include the absence of consent or whether consent is treated as a defence to liability arising in respect of a sexual battery? It is unlikely that there is no morally important difference between these alternatives. Similar remarks can be made about many other torts. Can it seriously be thought that the way in which the issue of truth is allocated in the setting of defamation serves only instrumental ends?

Before leaving this issue, it is worth mentioning that criminal law theorists have debated at great length whether the distinction between offences and defences is morally significant. Interestingly, the prevailing view in this regard is the opposite of that which obtains in relation to tort law. The minority view is that the distinction between offences and defences is of only instrumental utility. This position was famously championed by Glanville Williams. In his words,[50]

> there is no intrinsic difference between the elements of an offence and an exception (or defence) to that offence. . . . [A]ll the exceptions (defences) can be stated in negative form as part of offences, instead of as something outside the offences.

---

[49] See 2.3.6.

[50] G Williams, 'The Logic of Exceptions' (1988) 47 *Cambridge Law Journal* 261, 277. See also G Williams, 'Offences and Defences' (1982) 2 *Legal Studies* 233. Williams's position is endorsed in JC Jeffries and PB Stephan, 'Defenses, Presumptions, and Burden of Proof in the Criminal Law' (1979) 88 *Yale Law Journal* 1325, 1331–33 and J Quigley, 'The Common Law's Theory of Criminal Liability: A Challenge from across the Atlantic' (1989) 11 *Whittier Law Review* 479, 497–500. A small number of theorists independently reached the same conclusion as Williams. For instance, Heidi Hurd claims, '[t]hat the law has distributed the criteria for nonculpable right actions between the prima facie case and the defenses is of no moral concern': HM Hurd, 'Justification and Excuse, Wrongdoing and Culpability' (1999) 74 *Notre Dame Law Review* 1551, 1567. Gabriel Chin asserts that 'it is arbitrary whether the existence or non-existence of a fact is made an element of an offense, or denominated a defense': GJ Chin, 'Unjustified: The Practical Irrelevance of the Justification/Excuse Distinction' (2009) 43 *University of Michigan Journal of Law Reform* 79, 86, n 24. Frederick Schauer argues that 'there is nothing special or inexorable about the line between an exception and what it is an exception to': F Schauer, 'Exceptions' (1991) 58 *University of Chicago Law Review* 871, 893.

The majority of criminal law philosophers who have considered the issue have subjected Williams's analysis to spirited attacks.[51] The leading contribution in this regard is by Kenneth Campbell.[52] Campbell argues that the distinction between offences and defences descends from the difference between reasons for and against action. According to this contention, which will be called the 'practical conflicts thesis', offence definitions describe acts that one has a *prima facie* reason not to perform. By '*prima facie* reason', Campbell does not mean something that merely appears to be a reason. Rather, by describing a reason as *prima facie* he means a reason that may be, but is not necessarily, conclusive as to how one should act.[53] It is a reason that may be defeated by a countervailing reason. This is where defences enter the picture. Defences, according to the practical conflicts thesis, specify circumstances in which the *prima facie* reasons against engaging in the behaviour described in the offence definition are outweighed by opposing reasons. Campbell brilliantly unites these strands of thought to explain why the criminal law counts the absence of consent as an element of the offence of rape as opposed to treating consent as a defence. Were consent a defence to rape, that would imply that there is a *prima facie* reason to refrain from sexual intercourse *tout court*. Because there is no such reason,[54] at least according to our sexual morality, this is why the criminal law builds non-consent into the definition of rape.

It is crucial to realise that, according to the practical conflicts thesis, an act that falls within an offence definition constitutes a wrong even if it attracts a defence. This is due to the continued existence of the relevant *prima facie* reasons. Campbell explained this clearly:[55]

> Suppose someone kills a terrorist who is about to detonate a bomb which will certainly kill dozens of people. His action is certainly permissible, and probably more than just that. So long, however, as the law takes the view that the life, even of that terrorist, was something of value then it recognises the existence of some reason against the action, albeit one which was clearly overridden.

---

[51] Eg, K Campbell, 'Offence and Defence' in IH Dennis (ed), *Criminal Law and Justice: Essays from the W.G. Hart Workshop, 1986* (London, Sweet & Maxwell, 1987); DN Husak, *Philosophy of Criminal Law* (Totowa, Rowman & Littlefield, 1987) 188; CO Finkelstein, 'When the Rule Swallows the Exception' in L Meyer (ed), *Rules and Reasoning: Essays in Honour of Fred Schauer* (Oxford, Hart Publishing, 1999); J Horder, *Excusing Crime* (Oxford, Oxford University Press, 2004) 254–57; V Tadros, *Criminal Responsibility* (Oxford, Oxford University Press, 2005) 103–15; RA Duff, *Answering for Crime: Responsibility and Liability in the Criminal Law* (Oxford, Hart Publishing, 2007) 208–28; Gardner (n 40) ch 7; A Ashworth, *Principles of Criminal Law*, 6th edn (Oxford, Oxford University Press, 2009) 308.

[52] Campbell (n 51).

[53] Regarding the difference between *prima facie* reasons and conclusive reasons, see J Raz, *Practical Reason and Norms* (Oxford, Oxford University Press, 1999) 27–28.

[54] Cf MM Dempsey and J Herring, 'Why Sexual Penetration Requires Justification' (2007) 27 *Oxford Journal of Legal Studies* 467; GP Fletcher, *Rethinking Criminal Law* (Boston, Mass, Little, Brown & Co, 1978) 707.

[55] Campbell (n 51) 83.

As this passage indicates, the *prima facie* reasons not to kill the terrorist are merely defeated in the contest with the reasons in favour of killing the terrorist. They are not cancelled.[56] They do not cease to exist. They are still valid reasons. Hence killing the terrorist is a wrong, albeit a justified one.

It is arguable that the practical conflicts thesis also finds some traction in the law of torts. There is no real difficulty with the suggestion that torts generally specify acts that one has *prima facie* reasons not to commit.[57] Likewise, many defences seem to articulate circumstances where the *prima facie* reasons not to commit torts are outweighed by countervailing reasons. That the practical conflicts thesis might apply also to tort law should come as no surprise given that many crimes are torts and that the defences that are applicable to many torts are broadly similar to the defences that are available to many crimes.[58]

2.3.9.3. *Allocation of issues*

If the distinction between torts and defences is justifiable, the rationale or rationales that support it will govern how the issues relevant to liability should be classified as between the 'tort' and 'defence' headings. For example, if one is persuaded by the efficient administration of justice argument[59] then one should conclude that issues which are infrequently relevant should be presented as defences to ensure that the court needs to spend resources investigating them only if they are put in issue by the defendant.[60] Similarly, if the harmonisation argument[61] is found to be convincing, one should reason that issues should be allocated in a manner that is consistent with the allocation of cognate issues in other branches of the law of obligations.[62]

Certain other rationales do not supply similar guidance as to how individual issues should be cast. Consider, for instance, the procedural justice argument.[63] This argument is concerned with how the totality of issues that are relevant to liability is treated rather than with the classification of any single issue. The difficulty experienced by claimants in discharging the burden resting on them to establish that all of the elements of an action are present should be roughly com-

---

[56] Regarding the difference between reasons being cancelled and reasons being overridden, see Raz (n 53) 27.

[57] The most serious challenge to this understanding is presented by torts that are based on negligence. This because such torts do not identify acts in respect of which there are *prima facie* reasons not to commit. Rather, because the absence of justification is part and parcel of these torts (see the text accompanying nn 48–49 in ch 1), they specify acts that, all things considered, one ought not to commit. For an argument that, despite appearances, negligence-based torts actually specify acts that are *prima facie* wrong, see J Gardner, 'What is Tort Law For? Part 1. The Place of Corrective Justice' (2011) 30 *Law and Philosophy* 1, 42–43.

[58] See 1.12.2.

[59] See 2.3.3.

[60] For discussion see Epstein (n 9) 581; Lee (n 26) 7.

[61] See 2.3.8.

[62] If there are multiple sufficient principles by which issues relevant to liability should be allocated, it would need to be determined how to resolve conflicts between those principles.

[63] See 2.3.4.

mensurate to the task that defendants face in proving that defences apply. This argument is uninterested, therefore, in how a given issue, taken in isolation, is classified as between the action and defence categories.

It is worth observing that issues relevant to liability should be allocated only on the basis of reasons for the existence of the distinction between torts and defences (whatever those reasons may be). A criterion of allocation that does not flow from a reason for distinguishing between torts and defences is a flawed criterion. This point has often been overlooked. Judges and legal theorists routinely nominate criteria of allocation that are not derived from a convincing rationale for separating torts and defences, and without even pausing to ask why torts are separated from defences. Consider, for example, the suggestion that certain rules that have fallen from favour or are thought to be unjustified should be treated as defences in order to marginalise them.[64] Allocating rules on the basis of this criterion is illogical since this consideration does not descend from a convincing rationale for distinguishing between torts and defences. It does not make sense to say that the reason for recognising defences is to marginalise unjustified rules. Unjustified rules should be abolished, not merely side-lined.[65]

2.4. Conclusion

The distinction between torts and defences is one of the most recognisable features of the law of torts. Yet it has been all but ignored by theorists. No serious attempt has previously been made to explain why it exists. This chapter has offered several possible rationales for the distinction. Specifically, it has been argued that it might be justified on the ground that it:

(1) facilitates the efficient administration of justice;
(2) promotes procedural justice;
(3) is a device for giving expression to the relative value of the parties' interests;
(4) allows tort law to give clearer guidance to defendants as to how they should conduct themselves than would be the case if the distinction did not exist;
(5) promotes rationality in judicial reasoning; and
(6) enables tort law to be harmonised with other departments of the law of obligations, and to diminish the risk that litigants and judges will be confused about the law.

---

[64] McLachlin J, in an otherwise cogent opinion in *Hall v Hebert* [1993] 2 SCR 159, seemed to make this suggestion in relation to the doctrine of illegality: at 184.
[65] This point is Richard Epstein's: Epstein (n 9) 579.

3

Denials

A legal concept cannot be fully understood unless it is clearly differentiated from others in its field, and the exercise of differentiation remains impossible as long as a concept is studied in isolation.[1]

3.1. Introduction

This book explores tort law defences. In order to understand defences, it is crucial to separate them rigorously from other concepts in tort law. If foreign matter is allowed to intrude into the category of defences, attempts to come to grips with the role that defences play within tort law will be jeopardised. One of the most serious threats in this regard comes from denials. Denials, recall, are pleas by the defendant that one or more of the elements of the tort in which the claimant sues is missing.[2] Many denials are frequently mistaken for defences. The purpose of this chapter, therefore, is to identify a wide selection of denials so that the field of defences can be kept pure. It is convenient to organise denials into the following five categories:

(1) denials of the act element;
(2) denials of a fault element;
(3) denials of the causation element;
(4) denials of the damage element; and
(5) denials of other elements.

For the avoidance of doubt, it is stressed that the examination here is concerned only with identifying those pleas that are in fact denials. The goal, in other words, is to populate a partial list of denials according to the law as it presently exists. It is not contended that the law of torts should be altered so as to convert pleas that are currently denials into defences or vice versa. Neither is any argument presented to the effect that the status quo should be retained in this regard. This is not to deny the existence of a need for theorising in this connection. On the contrary, pre-

---

[1] P Birks, 'The Concept of a Civil Wrong' in DG Owen (ed), *Philosophical Foundations of Tort Law* (Oxford, Oxford University Press, 1995) 33.
[2] See 1.2.1.1.

cious little has been said about whether given issues should be conceptualised as falling into the tort or the defence category, presumably as a result of the widely-held assumption that the manner in which issues are allocated is unimportant.[3] But it is not the aim of this chapter to provide such analysis.

Before the discussion can get underway, it is necessary to say a few words about how one can determine whether a given plea is a denial or a defence. Sometimes, the courts or the legislature state explicitly how a particular plea operates.[4] Where such statements exist, the task of classification is usually straightforward.[5] But unfortunately, such express statements are relatively uncommon. Where there is no explicit guidance as to how a particular plea operates, the best technique for determining how it functions is as follows. First, it is necessary to obtain as clear a picture as is possible of the definitional elements of the tort to which the plea concerned relates. It should then be asked whether the plea in issue is inconsistent with accepting that all of the elements of the tort in which the claimant sues are satisfied. If such inconsistency exists, the plea must be a denial. Conversely, if there is no inconsistency, the plea must be a defence. This technique often makes it possible to tell, with a reasonable degree of certainty, whether a given plea is a denial or a defence. But this is not always the case. Regrettably, the way in which certain pleas operate is profoundly ambiguous because of uncertainty as to the elements of the tort to which they relate.

The manner in which the onuses of pleading and proof are allocated in respect of a particular issue is not a particularly good guide when it comes to determining whether that issue forms part of a tort or is a defence. It is true that the burdens of pleading and proof are normally allocated by reference to the distinction between torts and defences,[6] but this practice is not universally followed.[7] Consequently, one who looks to the onuses of pleading and proof for guidance in determining whether a given issue is part of a tort or is a defence is liable to be led astray. This was noted long ago by John Wigmore in an article that has not received the attention it deserves. It is worth setting out Wigmore's warning:[8]

> As a rule certain principles of pleading are based on the distinction between [elements of torts], throwing on the defendant the business of making out the existence and the application of [defences]. For instance, justifications for a battery and privileges for

---

[3] This assumption is discussed in 2.3.9.2.

[4] Examples of explicit judicial statements are given throughout in this chapter and ch 5. An example of an explicit legislative statement is s 329 of the Criminal Justice Act 2003 (UK). This provision is discussed in 5.3.1.11.

[5] The qualification 'usually' is needed here because, among other reasons, contradictory statements are sometimes made as to how a given plea functions.

[6] See the text accompanying n 66 in ch 1 and 6.4.

[7] Eg, the doctrine of illegality can function as a denial of a duty of care for the purposes of the tort of negligence (see 3.6.5), but it falls to the defendant to establish that it is applicable: *Gala v Preston* (1991) 172 CLR 243, 254 (HCA); *Reeves v Commissioner of Police of the Metropolis* [1999] QB 169, 186 (CA); *Brown v Harding* [2008] NSWCA 51 [40]; *Wills v Bell* [2002] QCA 419; [2004] 1 Qd R 296, 304 [12]. See further J Goudkamp, 'The Defence of Joint Illegal Enterprise' (2010) 34 *Melbourne University Law Review* 425, 434–35.

[8] JH Wigmore, 'The Tripartite Division of Torts' (1894) 8 *Harvard Law Review* 200, 207.

defamation are left to the defendant to urge. Sometimes, however, the principles of pleading cannot be relied upon to show in this way the line of distinction.

3.2. Denials of the Act Element

3.2.1. Involuntariness

As is the case with many criminal offences, some torts incorporate an act element. This element requires that the defendant be the author of his impugned bodily movement. The most prominent example of a tort that contains an act element is that of battery. This tort will be established only if it is proved that there was an act committed by the defendant.[9] Because the law does not (rightly or wrongly) regard involuntary movements as acts,[10] a defendant who pleads involuntariness in proceedings in battery denies the act element of that tort. He does not offer a defence. The other varieties of trespass to the person – assault and false imprisonment – probably also contain act elements.[11] If this is the case, the plea of involuntariness is therefore a denial of that element of those torts as well.

It appears that the tort of trespass to land incorporates an act element too.[12] Consequently, involuntariness negates this ingredient of the action. D commits no act, and hence no trespass to land, if he was thrown onto C's land by a third party,[13] entered C's land while 'in an effective state of automatism'[14] or was blown onto C's land by a violent gust of wind.[15] The view that involuntariness is a denial

---

[9] 'To make the actor liable for a battery, the harmful bodily contact must be caused by an act done by the person whose liability is in question': Restatement (Second) of Torts, § 14.

[10] 'There cannot be an act without volition': *ibid*, § 2, cmt a. The understanding that only voluntary movements qualify as acts enjoys significant support. For instance, Prosser and Keeton wrote that 'it is tautological to speak of a "voluntary act," and self-contradictory to speak of an "involuntary act," since every act is voluntary': WP Keeton, DB Dobbs, RE Keeton and DG Owen (eds), *Prosser and Keeton on Torts*, 5th edn (St Paul, Minn, West Publishing Co, 1984) 35. Similarly, Austin maintained that '[a] voluntary movement of my body, or a movement which follows a volition, is an *act*. The *involuntary* movements which are the consequences of certain diseases are *not* acts': J Austin, *Lectures on Jurisprudence*, vol 1, 3rd edn (London, John Murray, 1869) 427 (emphasis in original). But the contrary view has also been vigorously defended. According to Fletcher, 'there are enormous differences between the criteria of action and of voluntariness': GP Fletcher, *The Grammar of Criminal Law: American, Comparative, and International*, vol 1 (Oxford, Oxford University Press, 2007) 286. See also HLA Hart, *Punishment and Responsibility: Essays in the Philosophy of Law*, 2nd edn (Oxford, Oxford University Press, 2008) 109; P Cane, *The Anatomy of Tort Law* (Oxford, Hart Publishing, 1997) 29; PH Robinson, *Structure and Function in Criminal Law* (Oxford, Clarendon Press, 1997) 31–38, 164–69.

[11] This is the view adopted in the Restatement (Second) of Torts: see § 21(1)(a) (assault) and § 35(1)(a) (false imprisonment).

[12] 'One whose presence on the land is not caused by any act of his own or by a failure on his part to perform a duty is not a trespasser': *ibid*, § 158, cmt f.

[13] *Network Rail Infrastructure Ltd v Conarken Group Ltd* [2010] EWHC 1852 (TCC) [65]. The third party may be liable for trespass to land: *Smith v Stone* (1647) Style 65; 82 ER 533.

[14] *Network Rail Infrastructure Ltd v Conarken Group Ltd* [2010] EWHC 1852 (TCC) [65].

[15] Restatement (Second) of Torts: see § 158, cmt f, illustration 2.

in the context of trespass to land was challenged by some of the judges in *Public Transport Commission (NSW) v Perry*. Barwick CJ treated involuntariness as a defence. His Honour said that a 'defendant may have a defence in the involuntary nature of the action which is said to be the trespass',[16] asserted that an 'actionable trespass requires volition on the part of the trespasser'[17] and spoke of an 'involuntary trespasser'.[18] Gibbs J was apparently of the same opinion. His Honour doubted 'whether it is right to say that a person can never be regarded as a trespasser . . . if his presence on the premises came about involuntarily'.[19] It is unclear whether the views of Barwick CJ and Gibbs J represent the law in Australia on this point.

3.3. Denials of a Fault Element

3.3.1. Involuntariness

It has just been explained why the plea of involuntariness is a denial of the act element of torts that incorporate such an element. But it is doubtful whether all torts contain act elements. For instance, the action in negligence is not regarded as encompassing an act element.[20] Consequently, the plea of involuntariness cannot be a denial of an act element in proceedings in negligence. But it does not follow that involuntariness is a defence to that tort. Rather, the plea is analysed by the courts as negating the requirement of fault.[21] A defendant whose movements are involuntary does not act carelessly, subject to the doctrine of prior fault.[22] Thus, motorists whose behaviour was involuntary because they spontaneously lost consciousness,[23] because

---

[16] (1977) 137 CLR 107, 126 (HCA).

[17] *Ibid.*

[18] *Ibid.*

[19] *Ibid*, 133.

[20] Leading descriptions of the tort of negligence do not mention an act element: eg, Keeton *et al* (n 10) 164–65; DG Owen, 'The Five Elements of Negligence' (2007) 35 *Hofstra Law Review* 1671; C Sappideen and P Vines (eds), *Fleming's The Law of Torts*, 10th edn (Sydney, Lawbook Co, 2011) 122 [6.20]; JCP Goldberg and BC Zipursky, *The Oxford Introductions to US Law: Torts* (Oxford, Oxford University Press, 2010) 72.

[21] Eg, Restatement (Third) of Torts, § 11(b).

[22] This doctrine prevents a defendant from taking refuge in the fact that his impugned bodily movements were involuntary if he negligently failed to minimise the risk that such movements would occur, or unreasonably omitted to institute precautions against the risk that he would cause harm to the claimant through such movements. See, eg, *Kay v Butterworth* (1945) 110 JP 75 (CA) (driver who fell asleep held negligent), *Derdiarian v Felix Contracting Corp* 51 NY 2d 308; 414 NE 2d 666 (1980) (driver who failed to take medication for epilepsy held liable); *Seals v Morris* 410 So 2d 715 (1981) (driver distracted by a snake slithering over his shoulder held liable because he negligently left his vehicle's windows open while parked in an area infested by snakes) and *C (a child) v Burcombe* [2003] CLY 3030 (CC) (driver who ignored doctor's advice and suffered heart attack held liable).

[23] *Robinson v Glover* [1952] NZLR 669 (SC); *Dessaint v Carriere* [1958] OWN 481; [1958] 17 DLR (2d) 222 (CA); *Jones v Dennison* [1971] RTR 174 (CA).

they suffered a seizure[24] or a heart attack,[25] or because they were stung by a swarm of bees,[26] have been absolved of liability in negligence on the basis that they were not at fault.

3.3.2. Infancy

A defendant who relies on the fact that he was an infant at the relevant time may be denying the fault element of the tort in which he is sued.[27] Consider, for example, torts that require proof of negligence. As infants are only required to achieve the standard of the reasonable child of the same age[28] rather than that of the reasonable adult,[29] it is ordinarily more difficult for a claimant to establish negligence on the part of an infant than an adult. It may be reasonable for an infant to commit acts that would be negligent if performed by an adult. For example, it is not negligent for a boy aged 13¾ years to run backwards in a school corridor,[30] for a girl aged 15 years to engage in a fencing match with another girl using a plastic ruler,[31] for a 15-year-old boy to fling twigs and pieces of bark at a classmate,[32] for a 12-year-old boy to throw a metal dart in the direction of a girl[33] or for a child aged eight years to play with matches in a barn.[34] It is, presumably, negligent for an adult to do all of these things. Hence, an infant defendant in proceedings in negligence may place weight on his immaturity in the hope that doing so will prevent the claimant from establishing a lack of reasonable care on his part. If the defendant is so young that the reasonable child of the same age would lack the capacity to foresee risks, a finding of negligence could never be made.[35] This is because it would be

---

[24] *Gootson v R* [1947] 4 DLR 568 (Ex).

[25] *Waugh v James K Allan Ltd* [1964] SC (HL) 102; *Ryan v Youngs* [1938] 1 All ER 522 (CA); *Sheldon v Gray* (1994) 75 OAC 350 (CA).

[26] *Scholz v Standish* [1961] SASR 123 (SC).

[27] It seems to have been said in *Tillander v Gosselin* [1967] 1 OR 203, 210; (1966) 60 DLR (2d) 18, 25 (HC) that the conduct of very young infants is not voluntary: '[One cannot] describe the act of a normal three-year-old child in doing injury to the . . . plaintiff in this case as a voluntary act on his part.' An appeal against this decision was dismissed without reasons being published: *Tillander v Gosselin* (1967) 61 DLR (2d) 192n (Ont CA). On this analysis, infancy may open the door to a denial of the act element.

[28] *McHale v Watson* (1966) 115 CLR 199 (HCA); *Mullin v Richards* [1998] 1 All ER 920; [1998] 1 WLR 1305 (CA); *O v L* [2009] EWCA Civ 295; The Times, 14 April 2009; Restatement (Third) of Torts, § 10(a).

[29] An infant defendant is required to meet the standard set by the reasonable adult where he is engaged in a 'dangerous activity that is characteristically undertaken by adults': Restatement (Third) of Torts, § 10(c). There is no accepted definition of a dangerous adult activity. However, such activities have been held to include driving a motor vehicle (*Tucker v Tucker* [1956] SASR 297 (SC)), using a motorboat (*Dellwo v Pearson* 259 Minn 452; 107 NW 2d 859 (1961)) and riding a trail bike (*McErlean v Sarel* (1987) 61 OR (2d) 396 (CA)).

[30] *O v L* [2009] EWCA Civ 295; The Times, 14 April 2009.

[31] *Mullin v Richards* [1998] 1 All ER 920; [1998] 1 WLR 1305 (CA).

[32] *Blake v Galloway* [2004] EWCA Civ 814; [2004] 3 All ER 315; [2004] 1 WLR 2844.

[33] *McHale v Watson* (1966) 115 CLR 199 (HCA).

[34] *Yorkton Agricultural & Industrial Exhibition Association v Morley* (1967) 66 DLR (2d) 37 (Sask CA).

[35] *Cotton v Commissioner for Road Transport and Tramways* (1942) 43 SR (NSW) 66, 70 (Full Ct).

impossible for such a defendant to sink below the standard of the reasonable child. No bright line exists as to the age below which it is impossible to find negligence. However, it was accepted as axiomatic in *Tillander v Gosselin*[36] that a child aged just shy of three years was incapable of acting negligently.

Just as the fact that the defendant was an infant can undermine an allegation of negligence, it may also incline the court to find that the defendant was not subjectively at fault and hence prevent torts that require proof of such fault from being constituted. For example, if a defendant in proceedings in respect of the tort recognised in *Wilkinson v Downton*[37] was an infant at the relevant time, the court might be less likely to infer that he intended to cause the claimant to suffer emotional distress. Age is plainly a relevant factor to consider in this connection.[38] Thus, an infant defendant in an action in the tort in *Wilkinson v Downton* who relies on the fact that he is of tender years may be doing so in the hope of prompting the court to find that the fault element of the tort is not established.

3.3.3. Insanity

The fact that a defendant was insane[39] at the relevant time may pave the way to a denial of certain species of fault.[40] For instance, if it is alleged that the defendant committed the tort of deceit, the fact that he was insane at the relevant time may reduce the probability that the court will conclude that he was seized of a fraudulent intent.[41] Unless the existence of such an intention is established, the action in deceit will not be constituted.[42] Hence, a defendant who pleads insanity in the

---

[36] [1967] 1 OR 203; (1966) 60 DLR (2d) 18 (HC), affd *Tillander v Gosselin* (1967) 61 DLR (2d) 192n (Ont CA).

[37] [1897] 2 QB 57 (QBD).

[38] '[W]hether [an infant defendant possessed the requisite intention] . . . is a factual question where the child's age, experience and knowledge may . . . be taken into consideration': *Cleveland Park Club v Perry* 165 A 2d 485, 488 (DC Mun Ct App 1960) (footnote omitted).

[39] It is necessary to make a brief terminological remark. Many criminal lawyers now avoid describing persons as 'insane' and prefer to use a different label, such as 'mentally disordered' individuals. This shift was motivated primarily by the fact that the word 'insane' has a 19th-century ring to it. While there are certainly downsides to using the word 'insane' in a legal context, it is nevertheless employed in this book because of its familiarity.

[40] A small amount of authority also suggests that insanity can undermine the act element: see *Wilson v Zeron* [1941] OWN 353, 354; [1941] 4 DLR 510, 512 (HCJ) (affd on other grounds in [1942] OWN 195; [1942] 2 DLR 580 (CA)); *Morriss v Marsden* [1952] 1 All ER 925, 927 (QBD); *Breunig v American Family Insurance Co* 45 Wis 2d 536; 173 NW 2d 619 (1970); K Barker, P Cane, M Lunney and FA Trindade, *The Law of Torts in Australia*, 5th edn (Oxford, Oxford University Press, 2006) 64 ('If, by reason of insanity, a person is incapable of appreciating the nature and quality of his or her acts, insanity would be available as a defence [to the action in trespass to the person] on the ground that the act could not be described as voluntary' (footnote omitted)). This is a minority view. The dominant opinion is that the behaviour of insane defendants is voluntary. The relationship between involuntariness and insanity is helpfully discussed in DN Husak, *Philosophy of Criminal Law* (Totowa, Rowman & Littlefield, 1987) 203. Although Husak is concerned with the criminal law, his thinking is nevertheless instructive for tort lawyers.

[41] *Becker v Becker* 138 NYS 2d 397 (Sup Ct 1954).

[42] *Derry v Peek* (1889) 14 App Cas 337 (HL).

context of proceedings in deceit may be offering a denial of fault.[43] However, in contrast with the position where the defendant is an infant, the fact that the defendant was insane will not render it easier for him negate the fault element of the action in negligence than if he was of sound mind. This is because the reasonable person is not, according to established principle, attributed with mental disabilities suffered by the defendant.[44] Mental disabilities are among those idiosyncrasies that the objective standard eliminates from consideration.[45]

3.3.4. Intoxication

Voluntary intoxication will not assist a defendant to counter an allegation of negligence. It is firmly established that a drunk or drugged defendant who is sued in negligence will be held to the standard of the reasonable sober person.[46] Hence, a plea of intoxication by such a defendant cannot provide the foundation for a successful denial of negligence. Conversely, involuntarily intoxicated defendants are judged by reference to the standard of the reasonable person who is equally intoxicated,[47] with the result being that it will be harder to establish negligence on the part of an involuntarily intoxicated defendant than a sober defendant, all other things being equal. It follows that the plea of involuntary intoxication may be made with a view to attacking a claimant's assertion that the defendant fell below the requisite standard of care. In other words, the plea of involuntary intoxication in the context of proceedings in negligence is a denial of fault. There is a paucity of authority on the relevance of the defendant's intoxication in the context of torts that require proof of subjective fault. Presumably, however, the fact that the defendant was intoxicated at the relevant time may cast light on whether he possessed the required state of mind[48] and hence open the door to a denial that the relevant mental state was present.

---

[43] Consider, also, *Lawson v Wellesley Hospital* (1975) 9 OR (2d) 677; (1975) 61 DLR (3d) 445) (CA) (insanity preventing fault element of the action in battery from being satisfied).

[44] *Vaughan v Menlove* (1837) 3 Bing NC 468; 132 ER 490; *Sforza v Green Bus Lines, Inc* 268 NYS 446 (Mun Ct 1934); *Creasy v Rusk* 730 NE 2d 659 (Ind 2000); *Carrier v Bonham* [2001] QCA 234; [2002] 1 Qd R 474; *Ramey v Knorr* 130 Wash App 672; 124 P 3d 314 (2005); *Town of Port Hedland v Hodder (No 2)* [2012] WASCA 212; (2012) 294 ALR 315, 376 [277]. The Restatement (Third) of Torts, § 11(c) provides: 'An actor's mental or emotional disability is not considered in determining whether conduct is negligent . . .'.

[45] *Mansfield v Weetabix Ltd* [1998] 1 WLR 1263 (CA) is inconsistent with this proposition. In that case the defendant truck driver failed to control his vehicle. As a result, it ran off of the road and into the claimants' shop. The loss of control occurred because the defendant's brain was not functioning properly owing to a glucose deficiency. The defendant was unaware of his severely reduced level of consciousness. The Court of Appeal held that he should be judged against the standard of care that would have been achieved by 'a reasonably competent driver unaware that he is or may be suffering from a condition that impairs his ability to drive' (at 1268). It is submitted that this holding is anomalous and incorrect.

[46] Restatement (Third) of Torts, § 12, cmt c.

[47] *Ibid*, § 12, cmt c; *Davies v Butler* 95 Nev 763; 602 P 2d 605 (1979).

[48] The criminal law solution to the problem of intoxication in the context of offences that require subjective fault is discussed in A Ashworth, *Principles of Criminal Law*, 6th edn (Oxford, Oxford University Press, 2009) 197–205.

3.3.5. Inevitable Accident

The plea of inevitable accident (which is also known as unavoidable accident[49]) is advanced periodically in actions in trespass and negligence. It is convenient to consider the role that it plays in the trespass context first. For most of its history, liability in trespass was strict. In order to make out his side of the case, the claimant needed to show only that the defendant made direct non-consensual contact with his person or property. However, this harsh regime was tempered by various defences.[50] One of these defences was that of inevitable accident, which was available when contact with the claimant or his property could not have been avoided by taking reasonable care.[51] This system of liability underwent a radical reversal in the second half of the nineteenth century when the courts declared that no action in trespass would lie in the absence of fault.[52] This change had the effect of converting inevitable accident from a defence into a denial of the newly-minted fault element[53] since a defendant will not be at fault for failing to prevent an accident that is inevitable. Thus, where the defendant in an action in trespass asserts that the physical contact with claimant's person or property was due to an inevitable accident, he merely calls into question whether all of the elements of the action are present.

A plea of inevitable accident is also advanced from time to time in proceedings in the tort of negligence.[54] In the negligence setting, the plea often operates as a denial of the fault element. Consider the decision in *Sik v Lajos*.[55] The claimant passenger in this case was injured when the car in which he was being driven ran off the road and collided with two poles. The driver lost control over the vehicle because the steering mechanism spontaneously and unforeseeably failed. The court found for the defendant on the ground that the accident was 'inevitable'.[56] However, all that the court meant by this label was that the defendant was not

---

[49] 'Inevitable means unavoidable': *The Merchant Prince* [1892] P 179, 188 (CA) (Lord Esher MR).

[50] See PH Winfield, 'The Myth of Absolute Liability' (1926) 42 *Law Quarterly Review* 37; DJ Ibbetson, *A Historical Introduction to the Law of Obligations* (Oxford, Oxford University Press, 1999) 61–62.

[51] *Weaver v Ward* (1616) Hobart 135; 80 ER 284 (KB). Cf SG Gilles, 'Inevitable Accident in Classical English Tort Law' (1994) 43 *Emory Law Journal* 575, who argues that the defence of inevitable accident could not be satisfied merely by proof that the defendant was not negligent and required that the defendant did everything that was realistically possible to avoid the harm.

[52] *Brown v Kendall* 60 Mass 292 (1850); *Holmes v Mather* (1875) LR 10 Ex 261 (Exch); *Stanley v Powell* [1891] 1 QB 86 (QBD).

[53] Initially, the defendant bore the onus of disproving fault. It was not until *Fowler v Lanning* [1959] 1 QB 426 (QBD) was decided that the claimant was required to establish fault.

[54] It was pleaded in, eg, *M'Kerrow v Niven* 1922 SLT 95 (Sh Ct); *Latour v St Anne des Plaines* [1935] 3 DLR 609 (SCC); *Gootson v R* [1947] DLR 568 (Exch); *Dessaint v Carriere* [1958] OWN 481; [1958] 17 DLR 2(d) 222 (CA); *Smith v Lord* [1962] SASR 88 (SC); *Geelong Harbour Trust Commissioners v Gibbs, Bright & Co* (1970) 122 CLR 504 (HCA); *Sheldon v Gray* (1994) 75 OAC 350 (CA).

[55] [1962] SASR 146 (Full Ct).

[56] *Ibid*, 148.

negligent. In the court's words, 'it seems to us that it has not been established that the [driver] failed to act with due care'.[57]

3.3.6. Act of God[58]

Passages can be found in the law reports that suggest that the plea of act of God is a defence to proceedings in negligence.[59] It is tolerably clear, however, that the fact that the damage suffered by the claimant was caused by an act of God cannot be a defence to this tort. This is because if the damage about which the claimant complains was caused by an act of God, which has been defined by the courts as 'an irresistible and unsearchable Providence nullifying all human effort',[60] one or more of the elements of the action in negligence will be absent. The plea of act of God, when advanced in proceedings in negligence, is, therefore, a denial. Very often, it is the fault element that is attacked. For example, defendants have been held to have acted reasonably in failing to prevent damage resulting from an exceptional frost,[61] an unusually heavy snowfall,[62] an extraordinarily violent gale[63] and an unforeseeable heart attack,[64] on the ground that the damage was due to an act of God.

---

[57] *Ibid*, 150. Consider, also, the following statements in which the phrase 'inevitable accident' was equated with the absence of negligence: 'I do not find myself assisted by considering the meaning of the phrase "inevitable accident." I prefer to put the problem in a more simple way, namely, has it been established that the driver of the car was guilty of negligence?': *Browne v De Luxe Car Services* [1941] 1 KB 549, 552 (CA) (Sir Wilfrid Greene MR); 'In the modern negligence action the plaintiff must prove that the injury complained of was proximately caused by the defendant's negligence, and the defendant under a general denial may show any circumstance which militates against his negligence or its causal effect. The so-called defense of inevitable accident is nothing more than a denial by the defendant of negligence, or a contention that his negligence, if any, was not the proximate cause of the injury': *Butigan v Yellow Cab Co* 49 Cal 2d 652, 658–59; 320 P 2d 500, 504 (1958) (Gibson CJ). The Restatement (Third) of Torts, § 6, cmt g, states that a plea of inevitable accident in negligence cases 'is merely a repetition of the general rule that an actor is not liable for harm unless the harm was caused by the actor's failure to exercise reasonable care.' Cf *Smith v Lord* [1962] SASR 88, 89–90 (SC), in which the plea of inevitable accident is presented not as a denial of fault but as a defence to an action in negligence.

[58] See generally CG Hall, 'An Unsearchable Providence: The Lawyer's Concept of Act of God' (1993) 13 *Oxford Journal of Legal Studies* 227.

[59] Eg, the plea is described as an 'affirmative defence' in *Sky Aviation Corporation v Colt* 475 P 2d 301, 304 (Wyo 1970); *Kaminsky v Hertz Corporation* 94 Mich App 356; 288 NW 2d 426, 429 (Ct App 1980); *Lanz v Pearson* 475 NW 2d 601, 602 (Iowa 1991).

[60] *The Mostyn* [1928] AC 57, 105 (HL). See also *Greenock Corporation v Caledonian Railway Co* [1917] AC 556, 571–72, 580–81 (HL).

[61] *Blyth v Birmingham Waterworks Co* (1856) 11 Ex 781; 156 ER 1047 (Exch).

[62] *Briddon v The Great Northern Railway Co* (1858) 28 LJ Ex 51 (Exch); *Slater v Worthington's Cash Stores (1930) Ltd* [1941] 1 All ER 245 (CA).

[63] *Hudson v Bray* [1917] 1 KB 520 (Div Ct); *Radley v London Passenger Transport Board* [1942] 1 All ER 433, 434 (KBD); cf *Keogh v Electricity Supply Board* [2005] IEHC 286; [2005] 3 IR 77.

[64] *Ryan v Youngs* [1938] 1 All ER 522, 525 (CA). See also *Hill v Baxter* [1958] 1 QB 277, 283 (Div Ct).

3.3.7. Mistake

Where the claimant sues in a tort that contains a fault element, a plea of mistake by the defendant may be a denial of that element. Three examples will be given. Take, first, the tort of deceit. In order to establish liability in that tort, the claimant must prove, among other things, that the defendant knew that his misrepresentation of fact was false, or that he did not care whether it was true or false.[65] A plea by the defendant that he made an honest mistake in relation to this tort is therefore a denial of this requirement. Consider, secondly, the action in negligence. If a defendant who is sued in this tort contends that the damage suffered by the claimant was due to a reasonable mistake on his part, he is merely contesting the breach element of the negligence action. The final example concerns defamation. This tort is often described as one of strict liability.[66] It is true that the action does not require that the defendant realised that his statement is defamatory[67] or that it referred to the claimant.[68] But such descriptions overlook the fact that the action will not be constituted without proof that the defendant intentionally or negligently published the defamatory statement to a third party.[69] A plea of mistake can attack this element.[70] Suppose, for example, that D utters defamatory remarks about C while arguing with him, and that D's remarks were overheard by T. It is open to D to plead that he reasonably but mistakenly believed that no one was in earshot. Such a plea is a denial of the requirement that the defamatory statement be intentionally or negligently published to a third party.

3.3.8. Voluntary Assumption of Risk

The task of determining how, precisely, the doctrine of voluntary assumption of risk prevents liability from arising is challenging. Significant problems arise in this connection on account of the use of imprecise language and a widespread failure to keep the distinction between torts and defences in view. Consider the following passage in Glanville Williams' *Joint Torts and Contributory Negligence*:[71]

> [I]t may be said that no question of *volens* arises until the plaintiff has proved that a presumptive tort has been committed. For example, if the plaintiff alleges the tort of

---

[65] *Derry v Peek* (1889) 14 App Cas 337 (HL).

[66] Eg, *Grant v Torstar Corp* [2009] SCC 61; (2009) 3 SCR 640, 658 [28]; R Stevens, *Torts and Rights* (Oxford, Oxford University Press, 2007) 101.

[67] *Newstead v London Express Newspaper Ltd* [1940] 1 KB 377, 389 (CA).

[68] *E Hulton & Co v Jones* [1910] AC 20 (HL); *Newstead v London Express Newspaper Ltd* [1940] 1 KB 377 (CA); *Dwek v Macmillan Publishers Ltd* [1999] EWCA Civ 2002; [2000] EMLR 284; cf *O'Shea v MGN Ltd* [2001] EMLR 943 (QBD).

[69] *Huth v Huth* [1915] 3 KB 32 (CA); *Powell v Gelston* [1916] 2 KB 615 (KBD); *Theaker v Richardson* [1962] 1 All ER 229; [1962] 1 WLR 151 (CA).

[70] *White v J & F Stone (Lighting and Radio) Ltd* [1939] 2 KB 827, 836 (CA).

[71] GL Williams, *Joint Torts and Contributory Negligence: A Study of Concurrent Fault in Great Britain, Ireland and the Common-Law Dominions* (London, Stevens & Sons Ltd, 1951) 295.

negligence, he must show a duty of care, a presumptive breach of that duty, and damage not too remote in consequence. It is only then that the defendant is called upon to defend himself by proving, if he can, that the plaintiff was *volens*. This point is sometimes overlooked, the question of *volens* being gone into although the defendant has not been proved to have been negligent or otherwise presumptively liable in tort, or although the damages claimed are too remote.

It is unclear from this confused passage how Williams thought that the doctrine of voluntary assumption of risk operates. Portions of it suggest that Williams believed that it denies the breach element of the action in negligence. He speaks of a 'presumptive breach'. It is not clear what he means by this, but this language arguably implies that the doctrine, when applicable, shows that, despite initial appearances, there was in fact no breach of a duty of care. On the other hand, in stressing that the doctrine should be 'gone into' only after the defendant has 'been proved to have been negligent', Williams presents the doctrine as a defence. In short, Williams, within the space of a handful of words, accepted interpretations of the doctrine that are diametrically opposed. This elementary error is symptomatic of a failure to pay sufficient attention to the difference between torts and defences.

Although most discussions of the voluntary assumption of risk principle are ambiguous as to how it should be classified, a clear stance on this point has occasionally been adopted. In *Smith v Baker & Sons*, Lord Halsbury LC said that the point of law under consideration by the House of Lords in that case was 'whether [the claimant] consented to undergo [the] particular risk [that materialised], and so disentitled himself to recover when a stone was negligently slung over his head or negligently permitted to fall on him and do him injury'.[72] In the same case, Lord Herschell wrote that 'if there had been no breach of duty it would not have been necessary to inquire whether the maxim, "Volenti non fit injuria," accorded a defence'.[73] Both of these quotations construe the voluntary assumption of risk principle as a defence. The doctrine is characterised as a rule that prevents liability from arising even though the defendant is negligent. This interpretation seems to be supported by John Goldberg and Benjamin Zipursky. They contend 'that assumption of risk is . . . a genuine affirmative defense',[74] although some doubt exists as to what they mean here on account of their omission to indicate clearly what they mean by an 'affirmative defense'.[75]

Conceptualising the voluntary assumption of risk principle as a defence can be supported on the basis that the test that governs it turns attention to matters that

---

[72] [1891] AC 325, 335–36 (HL).

[73] *Ibid*, 366.

[74] Eg, JCP Goldberg and BC Zipursky, 'Shielding Duty: How Attending to Assumption of Risk, Attractive Nuisance, and other "Quaint" Doctrines can Improve Decisionmaking in Negligence Cases' (2006) 79 *Southern California Law Review* 329, 340.

[75] The imprecise way in which Goldberg and Zipursky speak of an 'affirmative defense' is discussed in ch 1 at the text accompanying n 13.

are external to the definition of the action of negligence. A claimant will be *volens* to the risk of injury when he:[76]

(1) freely accepted the risk;
(2) with full knowledge of it.

These matters are not ingredients of the tort of negligence. Because pleading the principle does not appear to be inconsistent with accepting the truth of the allegations of a claimant who sues in negligence, the principle seems to be a defence.

However, a significant problem with categorising the principle of voluntary assumption of risk as a defence is the fact that when judges hold that the principle applies, it is difficult to escape from the conclusion that they are actually reaching their decisions on the ground that one or more of the elements of the action in negligence is absent. In other words, it appears that, in practice, the plea of voluntary assumption of risk is a denial.[77] There is little doubt that many of the cases in which it was held that the claimant voluntarily assumed the risk of injury are in fact no-breach cases. The decision in *Murray v Harringay Arena Ltd*[78] is a good illustration. The claimant in this case, who was six years old at the time, was injured by an errant puck while watching an ice-hockey match. Singleton LJ, on behalf of the Court of Appeal, held that the claimant could not recover damages from the owner of the rink because he voluntarily assumed the risk of injury by attending the match. Significantly, however, in the course of reaching this conclusion, Singleton LJ focused on matters pertinent to the issue of fault. His Lordship mentioned the same factors that were decisive in the classic case of *Bolton v Stone*:[79] the low incidence with which pucks are hit out of rinks, the small risk that they will cause significant harm when they escape and the (apparent) impracticality of taking precautions to prevent pucks from escaping.

Another example of a no-breach case that was dressed up in the language of voluntary assumption of risk is *Proctor v Young*.[80] The claimant in this matter suffered injury when she fell from a racehorse that she was exercising on a beach. The fall occurred because the horse stumbled in a depression in the sand. The claimant failed in her bid to recover compensation from her employer and the occupier of the beach. The judge based his decision on the voluntary assumption of risk doctrine.[81] However, his reasons centred on factors relevant to the breach issue, especially the impracticality of taking preventative measures. This is perfectly understandable, since the reasonable person would not have attempted the impossible task of eliminating all variations in the beach's surface.

---

[76] *Bowater v Rowley Regis Corp* [1944] KB 476, 479 (CA).

[77] This idea is powerfully developed in SD Sugarman, 'Assumption of Risk' (1997) 31 *Valparaiso University Law Review* 883. The fact that the plea of voluntary assumption of risk strikes at elements of the action in negligence is one of the factors that led the Reporters of the Restatement (Third) of Torts: Apportionment of Liability to argue for the plea's abolition: see § 2, cmt I and the Reporters' note thereto.

[78] [1951] 2 KB 529 (CA).

[79] [1951] AC 850 (HL).

[80] [2009] NIQB 56.

[81] *Ibid* [35].

As a final illustration, consider the decision in *Geary v JD Wetherspoon plc*.[82] The claimant in this case, a patron in the defendant's pub, climbed onto and attempted to slide down a banister (she was seeking to emulate Mary Poppins). She toppled over the banister and suffered serious injury when she struck the floor. An action in negligence failed on the ground that the claimant voluntarily assumed the risk of injury.[83] But the judge's reasons on this point focused on the absence of fault on the part of the defendant. Coulson J wrote that 'there was nothing unsafe about these premises, and no danger attributable to their structure ... [T]he banister was not defective.'[84] In short, the plea of voluntary assumption of risk in this case functioned as a denial of fault.

In summary, the doctrine of voluntary assumption of risk might appear at first glance to be a defence, but it is reasonably clear that when judges profess to be deciding a case on the basis of the doctrine, they are frequently holding that there is no negligence on the part of the defendant. Hence, the plea of voluntary assumption of risk is, very often, a denial of the fault element of the tort of negligence.

3.4. Denials of the Causation Element

3.4.1. Inevitable Accident

It has already been observed that a defendant who pleads inevitable accident is often denying the fault element of the tort in which he is sued.[85] The plea may also be a denial of the causation element. Suppose that a hooligan is driving his car at 100 mph in a 40 mph zone. An infant emerges spontaneously from between two parked vehicles and is struck by the defendant's car. Expert evidence indicates that the accident would have occurred even if the driver had been travelling at 20 mph and kept a proper lookout. The driver was clearly negligent. He was driving much too fast. However, he nevertheless can avoid liability on the ground that the accident was inevitable, in the sense that it would have happened even if he had been driving his car at a reasonable speed. Thus, in a situation such as this, the plea of inevitable accident is a denial of causation.

3.4.2. Act of God

As has already been noted, when a defendant pleads act of God, he may deny the fault element of the tort that the claimant alleges he committed.[86] Sometimes,

---

[82] [2011] EWHC 1506 (QB).
[83] *Ibid* [56].
[84] *Ibid* [59].
[85] See 3.3.5.
[86] See 3.3.6.

however, the defendant, when he relies on this plea, denies the causation element. The defendant may, for instance, concede that he was negligent but contend that, even if he had taken reasonable care, the damage about which the claimant complains would still have resulted because it was brought about by an act of God. Assume that the following occurs. The defendant occupier omits to bring a dangerously unstable fence on his property into repair and, during a storm, it collapses onto and damages the claimant's house. The claimant sues the defendant in negligence. The defendant pleads act of God and adduces unchallenged expert evidence that the storm was so fierce that even a properly-maintained fence would have given way. In pleading act of God, the defendant is not denying that he was at fault. He is denying that his fault caused the claimant's damage.[87]

3.4.3. Act of Third Party

The plea of act of third party (which is also known as 'act of stranger') features primarily in private nuisances cases.[88] In the context of such cases, it is a denial of causation.[89] In order to establish liability in private nuisance, the claimant must show (relevantly) that his right to enjoy his land was unreasonably interfered with and that the defendant was responsible for the interference. The defendant can prevent the claimant from establishing that the defendant was responsible for the interference by demonstrating that it was caused by a third party.[90] For example, defendants have been absolved of liability in private nuisance in respect of interferences consisting in falling roof tiles,[91] seeping oil[92] and flooding,[93] on the basis that these interferences were caused by third parties. Because the plea of act of third party attacks the causation element of private nuisance, it is a denial and not a defence.

---

[87] This example was inspired by *Duboue v CBS Outdoor, Inc* 996 So 2d 561 (LA App 4 Cir, 2008) (hurricane blowing advertising board into building).

[88] The plea is not confined to the setting of private nuisance. It also lies, for instance, in actions under the rule in *Rylands v Fletcher: Dominion Natural Gas Co Ltd v Collins* [1909] AC 640, 646 (PC); *Rickards v Lothian* [1913] AC 263, 278 (PC).

[89] 'What is referred to as the "chain of causation" may be broken and the most common example of a break in the chain is the intervening act of a third person': *Lamb v Camden London Borough Council* [1981] QB 625, 640 (CA) (Lord Denning MR).

[90] *Sedleigh-Denfield v O'Callaghan* [1940] AC 880 (HL). In this case the defendant was held liable for a private nuisance that had been created on his land by a trespasser because he had adopted and continued it. However, but for such adoption, it is clear that the result would have been different. As Lord Atkin said, '[t]he occupier . . . is not an insurer; there must be something more than the mere harm done to the neighbour's property to make the party responsible . . . some degree of personal responsibility is required' (at 897).

[91] *Cushing v Peter Walker & Son (Warrington & Burton) Ltd* [1941] 2 All ER 693 (Liverpool Assizes).

[92] *Smith v Great Western Rail Co* (1926) 135 LT 112 (KBD).

[93] *Box v Jubb* (1879) 4 Ex D 76 (Div Ct).

3.4.4. Claimant Default

In the context of certain torts that impose strict liability, it is sometimes said that 'claimant default' is an answer to liability. For example, in *Rylands v Fletcher* Blackburn J said that a defendant could 'excuse himself [of liability in the tort recognised in this case] by shewing that the escape [of the dangerous object that caused the damage] was owing to the plaintiff's default'.[94] Because the action in *Rylands v Fletcher* is complete only if the defendant is causally responsible for the escape of the dangerous object, the plea of claimant default in the context of this tort is inconsistent with accepting that all of its definitional elements are satisfied. Consequently, the plea is not a defence. It is a denial of causation.[95]

3.4.5. Voluntary Assumption of Risk

It has already been demonstrated that when the courts use the language of voluntary assumption of risk, they are often describing a failure of the claimant to show that the defendant was negligent.[96] In other words, the plea of voluntary assumption of risk is frequently a denial of the fault element of the action in negligence. But the phrase 'voluntary assumption of risk' is also used to denote the absence of a causal connection between the defendant's breach of duty and the claimant's damage.[97] An excellent example of this usage can be found in the decision of the House of Lords in *Reeves v Commissioner of Police of the Metropolis*.[98] That case arose out of the suicide of a man while in police custody that the police negligently failed to prevent. The defendant pleaded voluntary assumption of risk. Lord Hoffmann, who delivered the principal speech, said that the defendant, in entering this plea, was simply contesting causation.[99] His Lordship wrote:[100]

> In the present case, volenti non fit in injuria can only mean that [the deceased] voluntarily caused his own death to the exclusion of any causal effect on the part of what was done by the police. So I think it all comes to the same thing: was the breach of duty by the police a cause of the death?

---

[94] (1866) LR 1 Ex 265, 279–80 (Exch Ch). The plea of claimant default is also a denial in proceedings in respect of trespassing livestock and dangerous animals: Animals Act 1971 (UK), s 5(1).

[95] See further D Nolan, 'The Distinctiveness of *Rylands v Fletcher*' (2005) 121 *Law Quarterly Review* 421, 430.

[96] See 3.3.8.

[97] See further Sugarman (n 77) 869–70.

[98] [2000] 1 AC 360 (HL).

[99] The House rejected the defendant's contention on this point on the facts.

[100] [2000] 1 AC 360, 367 (HL). Consider also *Imperial Chemical Industries Ltd v Shatwell* [1965] AC 656, 672–73 (HL). In this matter, Lord Reid remarked where the claimant's act is the sole cause of his injury, his failure to recover compensation may be described as a voluntary assumption of risk.

3.4.6. Illegality

In England, the leading decision regarding the common law doctrine of illegality in the setting of the tort of negligence is that of the House of Lords in *Gray v Thames Trains Ltd.*[101] The principal speech in this matter was given by Lord Hoffmann. His Lordship said that the doctrine has two manifestations. He explained these manifestations in the following highly-influential passage:[102]

> In its wider form, [the doctrine holds] that you cannot recover compensation for loss which you have suffered in consequence of your own criminal act. In its narrower and more specific form, it is that you cannot recover for damage which flows from loss of liberty, a fine or other punishment lawfully imposed upon you in consequence of your own unlawful act. In such a case it is the law which, as a matter of penal policy, causes the damage and it would be inconsistent for the law to require you to be compensated for that damage.

This text suggests that, in England, to plead the common law doctrine of illegality in proceedings in negligence is to attack the causation element of the action in negligence, and therefore to offer a denial. When the defendant appeals to the wide version of the doctrine, he contends that it was the claimant's illegal act, rather than any conduct for which the defendant was responsible, that brought about the claimant's damage. When the narrow version of the doctrine is invoked, the defendant asserts that it was the criminal justice system that was the immediate cause of the claimant's damage rather than any behaviour in which the defendant engaged.

It should be noted that *Gray* was not a case in which the parties were engaged in a joint illegal enterprise. The defendant in *Gray* was not implicated in the claimant's illegal act. Accordingly, it was unclear at the time that *Gray* was decided whether Lord Hoffmann's description of the doctrine of illegality (which broke with the previous authorities[103] in important respects) applied to joint illegal enterprise cases. These doubts have been dispelled: Lord Hoffmann's statement of the doctrine has been regarded as authoritative in the context of such cases.[104]

The common law concerning the doctrine of illegality in England is, largely as a consequence of the decision in *Gray*, rather different from that in certain other jurisdictions. In some legal systems the doctrine is a denial, but not of the

---

[101] [2009] UKHL 33; [2009] AC 1339, noted in J Goudkamp 'The Defence of Illegality: *Gray v Thames Trains Ltd*' (2009) 17 *Torts Law Journal* 205.

[102] [2009] UKHL 33; [2009] AC 1339, 1370 [29].

[103] Consider, for example, the very different approach to the doctrine of illegality adopted in *Pitts v Hunt* [1991] 1 QB 24 (CA).

[104] *Delaney v Pickett* [2011] EWCA Civ 1532, [2012] 1 WLR 2149; *Joyce v O'Brien* [2012] EWHC 1324 (QB); [2012] Lloyd's Rep IR 553; *Clarke v Clarke* [2012] EWHC 2118 (QB). The decisions in *Delaney* and *Joyce* are noted in J Goudkamp, 'The Defence of Illegality in Tort Law: Wither the Rule in *Pitts v Hunt*?' (2012) 71 *Cambridge Law Journal* 481.

causation element. In others, it is a defence. The way in which the doctrine prevents liability from arising in selected other legal systems is discussed later.[105]

3.4.7. *Novus Actus Interveniens*

The maxim *novus actus interveniens* has often been described as a defence.[106] However, it is clear that a defendant who relies on this maxim to resist the imposition of liability[107] is offering a denial of the causation element of the tort in question. The denial is based on the claim that a *novus actus* (rather than the defendant's conduct) was the cause of the claimant's loss. The maxim is not a defence.

3.5. Denials of the Damage Element

3.5.1. Truth

It is an ancient rule that liability will not arise in defamation if the defendant's impugned statement is true.[108] But is the plea of truth (or justification, as it is sometimes unhelpfully called[109]) a denial or a defence? Most discussions of truth are hopelessly ambiguous on this score. Problems arise in this regard primarily because of a failure of most writers to specify what they mean by the word 'defence'. Although it is frequently said that truth is a defence, such assertions usually provide no guidance on the issue of classification, since it is rarely indicated what the word 'defence' means.

Exceptionally, however, a clear stance is taken on how the plea of truth should be conceptualised. For instance, the present editor of *Street on Torts* writes:[110]

It is no part of the claimant's case to establish that the defendant's statement was untrue:

---

[105] See 3.6.5, 5.3.1.10.

[106] Eg, *Huddart Parker Ltd v Cotter* (1942) 66 CLR 624, 636 (HCA); *Stone & Rolls Ltd v Moore Stephens* [2009] UKHL 39; [2009] 1 AC 1391, 1425 [77].

[107] The maxim is not invoked only by a defendant who seeks to avoid liability. It is also raised to insulate defendants who are liable from having to pay damages for particular losses.

[108] The statement need not be true in every detail: *Alexander v North Eastern Railway Co* (1865) 6 B & S 340; 122 ER 1211; *Turcu v News Group Newspapers Ltd* [2005] EWHC 799 (QB) [108]; Defamation Act 2013 (UK), s 2(1). Substantial accuracy is sufficient.

[109] The practice of referring to the plea of truth as 'justification' has been rightly condemned as grossly misleading. The editors of *Gatley on Libel and Slander* properly complain that 'the name [justification] . . . may convey to lay people the idea that there must be some good reason for the publication, whereas in fact . . . it is not actionable as defamation maliciously to publish the truth': R Parkes, A Mullis and G Busuttil (eds), *Gatley on Libel and Slander*, 12th edn (London, Sweet & Maxwell, 2015) [11.1] (footnotes omitted). To similar effect see Committee on Defamation, *Report of the Committee on Defamation* (Cmnd 5909, 1975) 33 [129].

[110] C Witting (ed), *Street on Torts*, 14th edn (Oxford, Oxford University Press, 2015) 551.

the claimant has merely to prove the publication of a statement defamatory of him. If, however, the defendant can prove that his statement was true, he has a complete defence . . .

This presents truth as a defence. This characterisation seems to be preferred in *Gatley on Libel and Slander*[111] and in *Fleming's the Law of Torts*.[112] While none of the authors of these works cite any evidence to support their view that truth is a defence, such evidence can, with a little digging, be found. For example, in *Browne v Murray*, Lord Abbott CJ said that 'the plaintiff may, if he thinks fit, content himself with proof of the libel, and leave it to the defendant to make out his justification'.[113] This statement implies that the cause of action in defamation can be established without having regard to the issue of the truth. If this is right, truth must be a defence. Consider also the following statement of McLachlin CJ in *Grant v Torstar Corp*:[114]

A plaintiff in a defamation action is required to prove three things to obtain judgment and an award of damages: (1) that the impugned words were defamatory, in the sense that they would tend to lower the plaintiff's reputation in the eyes of a reasonable person; (2) that the words in fact referred to the plaintiff; and (3) that the words were published, meaning that they were communicated to at least one person other than the plaintiff. If these elements are established on a balance of probabilities, falsity and damage are presumed.

McLachlin CJ speaks here of matters that must be proved rather than elements of actions and defences. This passage does not show conclusively, therefore, that falsity of the impugned statement is not among the building blocks of the action in defamation. But this is arguably implicit in what the Chief Justice says. If this is the case, this passage supports the claim that truth is a defence.

But firm evidence that truth is a defence is quite difficult to come by and, notwithstanding the foregoing, good grounds exist for thinking that a defendant who pleads truth is in fact offering a denial. Recall that damage is an element of slander.[115] It is strongly arguable that damage is an element of libel too.[116] Were damage not an element of libel, there would be no need for it to be presumed. If it is accepted that damage is an element of both slander and libel, it can forcefully be contended that a plea of truth is a denial in proceedings in defamation generally. Reading the plea of truth as a denial of the damage element is supported by the numerous authoritative statements to the effect that claimants about whom true

[111] Parkes, Mullis and Busuttil (n 109) [10.1]–[10.2]. Cf the previous edition of this work, P Milmo and WVH Rogers (eds), *Gatley on Libel and Slander*, 11th edn (London, Sweet & Maxwell, 2008) [1.6], where the plea of truth seems to have been presented as a denial: 'Defamation is committed when the defendant publishes to a third person words or matter containing an untrue imputation against the reputation of the claimant' (footnotes omitted).

[112] Sappideen and Vines (n 20) 644 [25.160].

[113] (1825) Ry & Mood 254, 254; 171 ER 1012, 1012.

[114] *Grant v Torstar Corp* [2009] SCC 61; (2009) 3 SCR 640, 658 [28].

[115] *Stanhope v Blith* (1585) 4 Co Rep 15a; 76 ER 891.

[116] Cf Sappideen and Vines (n 20) 632–33 [25.140]: 'Actual injury, whether material or to reputation, is not an essential element of actionable libel'.

defamatory statements are made, while they might suffer factual loss, suffer no loss in the eyes of the law. For example, Blackstone wrote that[117]

> in the remedy by action on the case, which is to repair the *party* in damages for the injury done him, the defendant may . . . justify the truth of the facts, and shew that the plaintiff has received no injury at all.

In *Rofe v Smith's Newspapers Ltd*, Street ACJ said that 'no wrong is done to [a claimant] by telling the truth about him'.[118] In *Lonrho Plc v Fayed (No 5)*, Stuart-Smith LJ claimed that 'no one has a right to a reputation which is unmerited. Accordingly one can only suffer an injury to reputation if what is said is false.'[119] Such passages suggest that a defendant who pleads that his impugned statement is true denies that the claimant suffered damage. Whereas a claimant who is defamed by a true statement might suffer a factual loss, such loss does not qualify as damage.[120]

The proposition that the plea of truth is a denial of the damage element is not without difficulty. Recall that the Court of Appeal held in *Dow Jones & Co Inc v Jameel*[121] that the presumption of damage that applies in the case of libel is irrebutable. The defendant in that case was in the unusual position of being able to show that its libellous statement regarding the claimant had been read by hardly anyone. But the Court held that it was, nevertheless, not open to the defendant to adduce such evidence with a view to showing that the claimant had not been damaged. This holding presents a problem for the claim that a plea of truth is a denial of the damage element. This is because it is inconsistent to say (1) that damage is conclusively presumed to have been sustained in the case of libel and (2) that defendants can avoid liability in libel by demonstrating that no damage was suffered, by adducing evidence that their libellous statement was true. A possible means of explaining away this inconsistency is to view the decision in *Jameel* as establishing only that the presumption of damage cannot be rebutted by evidence that the libellous statement had few recipients, and not as holding that this presumption cannot be overcome by evidence that what the defendant said was true.

In summary, it is difficult to determine how the plea of truth prevents liability in defamation from arising. Problems arise in this connection primarily because the courts have not specified the definitional elements of the action with sufficient precision. The dominant view among scholars seems to be that truth is a defence; but because of the slapdash way in which the word 'defence' is generally used, it is

---

[117] W Blackstone, *Commentaries on the Laws of England*, vol 3 (Oxford, Clarendon Press, 1768) 126 (emphasis in original) (footnote omitted).

[118] (1924) 25 SR (NSW) 4, 21 (SC).

[119] [1994] 1 All ER 188, 202; [1993] 1 WLR 1489, 1502 (CA).

[120] This seems to be the conclusion reached by Eric Descheemaeker in his important recent article regarding the plea of truth: E Descheemaeker, '"Veritas non est defamatio"? Truth as a defence in the law of defamation' (2011) 31 *Legal Studies* 1. Unfortunately, it is impossible to know for certain if this is Descheemaeker's view because it is unclear what he means by the word 'defence'.

[121] [2005] EWCA Civ 75; [2005] QB 946.

impossible to be certain what most commentators believe in this regard. It is suggested, however, that the superior view is that a plea of truth is a denial of the damage element of the action in defamation. A claimant who is defamed suffers no damage if the defamatory statement is true.

3.6. Denials of Other Elements

3.6.1. Consent[122]

One of the most important contexts in which the plea of consent falls to be considered is that of trespass to the person. Unfortunately, it is unclear how it should be classified in this setting. In *Freeman v Home Office (No 2)*, which is generally regarded as the leading English case in this area, McCowan J asserted that 'the burden of providing absence of consent is on the plaintiff'.[123] This statement is inconclusive as to how the plea of consent functions. It is one thing to stipulate how the onus of proof is allocated in relation to a particular issue, and quite another to say whether that issue is an ingredient of the claimant's cause of action or a defence.[124] In *Marion's Case*, which is the main Australian authority on the issue of consent in the context of proceedings in trespass to the person, McHugh J wrote that 'Notwithstanding the English view, . . . the onus is on the defendant to prove consent.'[125] As with the decision in *Freeman*, this gives no real instruction as to how the issue of consent ought to be classified. Nothing express is said on this crucial point. Leading authorities in Canada[126] and New Zealand[127] are equally unhelpful.

The academic commentary is not, on the whole, much more sophisticated. The present editor of *Winfield & Jolowicz* writes that 'Where there is consent to the contact there is no battery . . .'.[128] This sentence is ambiguous. It is unclear whether the editor means to say that consent is a denial (which would mean that non-consent is an element of the tort of battery) or a defence. The uncertainty exists because the editor does not say whether he believes that there is still a battery if the elements of battery are satisfied but the defendant has a defence.[129] If the editor

---

[122] See generally FH Bohlen, 'Consent as Affecting Civil Liability for Breaches of the Peace' (1924) 24 *Columbia Law Review* 819.

[123] [1984] QB 524, 539 (QBD). The case went to the Court of Appeal ([1984] QB 524, 548) but the Court did not offer any relevant remarks. Cf *Ashley v Chief Constable of Sussex Police* [2006] EWCA Civ 1085; [2007] 1 WLR 398, 410 [31].

[124] See 1.2.1.4.

[125] *Marion's Case* (1992) 175 CLR 218, 310–11 (HCA).

[126] *Non-Marine Underwriters, Lloyd's of London v Scalera* [2000] SCC 24; [2000] 1 SCR 551.

[127] *H v R* [1996] 1 NZLR 299, 305 (HC).

[128] WVH Rogers (ed), *Winfield & Jolowicz on Tort*, 18th edn (London, Sweet & Maxwell, 2010) 108 [4.8].

[129] The issue of whether a defendant who enjoys a defence commits a tort is considered in 4.3.1.1.

thinks that there is still a battery, he would be committed to the proposition that consent is a defence. If, however, he thinks that there is no battery, it is impossible to say whether he believes that non-consent is part of the tort of battery or a defence.

The Restatement (Second) of Torts is also obscure. It does not mention consent in its definition of battery.[130] Instead, it deals with consent in a chapter entitled 'Defenses Applicable to All Tort Claims'.[131] This treatment arguably implies that the Reporters regarded consent as a defence. However, one cannot be certain that this is what they meant because it seems that the purpose of the chapter in question is to address generally applicable rules that prevent liability from arising[132] rather than defences specifically. Not all rules of general application that preclude liability in tort from accruing are defences. For instance, the doctrine of illegality is an answer to liability in all torts[133] but, in the United Kingdom, it is not a defence.[134]

Fleming's the Tort Law of Torts is more carefully expressed. In Fleming's words, 'Arguably, consent is not a privilege at all, because lack of it is the very gist of assault and battery, false imprisonment, and trespass to land or goods.'[135] This presents consent as a denial. Unfortunately, Fleming cited *Freeman* as authority for this proposition and, as has just been noted, *Freeman* indicates only how the onus of proof in relation to the issue of consent is assigned; it does not stipulate how the issue of consent is to be categorised. Fleming also quoted a passage from the reasons of Patteson J in *Christopherson v Bare*, who said that 'An assault must be an act done against the will of the party assaulted: and therefore it cannot be said that a party has been assaulted by his own permission.'[136] This passage is unhelpful, because it is unclear what Patteson J meant by 'assault'. Did he think that an 'assault' is committed as soon as the elements of the action in assault are satisfied? Or did he believe that there was an assault only if the elements of the action are present and there was no defence? If Patteson J thought that an assault is committed once the elements of the action are established then his remarks cast the plea of consent as a denial. Conversely, if Patteson J believed that an assault was perpetrated once the action in assault was constituted and the defendant had no defence then his opinion gives no instruction on how the issue of consent should be allocated between the tort and defence categories. Lord Denman CJ's opinion in the same case is more helpful. His Lordship said that the suggestion that liability in assault could be confessed and avoided by a plea of consent involved a 'manifest contradiction in terms'.[137] This presents the plea of consent as a denial.

---

[130] See § 18.
[131] See § 892A.
[132] See ch 45, Introductory Note.
[133] See ch 1, n 50.
[134] See 3.4.6.
[135] Sappideen and Vines (n 20) 90 [5.30]. The passage is unchanged from the 9th edition: JG Fleming, *The Law of Torts*, 9th edn (Sydney, Law Book Co, 1998) 86.
[136] (1848) 11 QB 473, 477; 116 ER 554, 556.
[137] *Ibid.*

Prosser and Keeton wrote in their textbook that 'Consent ordinarily bars recovery for intentional interferences with person or property. It is not, strictly speaking, a privilege, or even a defense, but goes to negative the existence of any tort in the first instance.'[138] In support of this claim, which reveals clearly that they believed the plea of consent to be a denial, Prosser and Keeton quoted a passage from one of Holmes's opinions that '[t]he absence of lawful consent is part of the definition of an assault',[139] and then asserted that 'The same is true of false imprisonment, conversion, and trespass.'[140] However, it is not clear what Holmes meant by 'assault'. His language suffers from the same ambiguity as that of Patteson J in *Christopherson v Bare*.

In summary, it is extremely difficult to discover whether the plea of consent is a denial or a defence in the context of the action in trespass to the person. There are many causes of this unhappy situation: the incautious use of the word 'defence', a tendency to conflate defences with rules that govern the allocation of the onus of proof, and a general failure of judges and writers to explain whether they believe that a defendant still commits a tort if he has a defence. However, when, exceptionally, language is used sufficiently cleanly, the consensus seems to be that to plead consent is to attack a definitional element of the action in trespass. It is tentatively concluded, therefore, that to plead consent in proceedings in trespass is to offer a denial rather than a defence.

It is not easy to ascertain how consent precludes liability from arising in trespass to land and to goods. The conclusions that have been reached in relation to trespass to the person do not necessarily carry over to trespass to land and to goods. Consent need not operate in the same fashion in relation to these actions as it does in the context of trespass to the person. However, the dominant position seems to be that consent is also a denial in trespass to land and to goods. According to Lord Hope of Craighead DPSC in *Bocardo SA v Star Energy UK Onshore Ltd*, 'a trespass [to land] occurs when there is an unjustified intrusion by one party upon land which is in the possession of another'.[141] Lord Hope treats consent as a justification[142] and, by incorporating the absence of justification within the definition of trespass to land, regards non-consent as an element of the tort. Barwick CJ in *Public Transport Commission (NSW) v Perry* appeared to be of the same view. His Honour asserted that 'It is trespass to be on the land of another without legal right, invitation or permission.'[143] In *Inland Revenue Commissioners v Rossminster Ltd*, Lord Diplock asserted that 'the act of handling a man's goods without his permission is prima facie tortious.'[144] Although it is far from clear, this statement seems to be sympathetic to construing consent as a denial to liability arising in trespass to goods.

---

[138] Keeton *et al* (n 10) 112 (footnotes omitted).
[139] *Ford v Ford* 143 Mass 577, 578; 10 NE 474, 475 (1887).
[140] Keeton *et al* (n 10) 112 (footnotes omitted).
[141] [2010] UKSC 35; [2011] 1 AC 380, 390 [6].
[142] On this point, see the text in ch 5 accompanying nn 69–70.
[143] (1977) 137 CLR 107, 126 (HCA).
[144] [1980] AC 952, 1011 (HL).

A different view of the role played by consent in relation to trespass to land and to goods appears to be promoted by the Restatement (Second) of Torts. In § 158, trespass to land is defined simply as an intentional entry upon land in possession of another person. No mention is made in this section of consent or justifying circumstances. Trespass to goods is likewise defined in § 217 without any reference being made to consent.[145] Presumably, therefore, the Reporters regard consent as a defence to these torts.

3.6.2. Prescription

The doctrine of prescription can prevent liability from arising in trespass to land[146] and in private nuisance.[147] Shorn of its details, which are unimportant for present purposes, the doctrine applies where the use of, or interference with, the claimant's land is sufficiently longstanding. According to Lord Hoffmann, its rationale is to 'prevent the disturbance of long-established de facto enjoyment'.[148] If a defendant relies on the doctrine, is he offering a denial or a defence? The position is uncertain. The fact that the doctrine is sometimes described as a 'defence' by judges[149] and scholars[150] is an unreliable guide because of the dizzying diversity of meanings that that word bears.[151]

At first glance, it might seem that the doctrine is a defence. This is because it comes into play only once the action in trespass or private nuisance is constituted. Unless there has been an actionable use of the claimant's land by the defendant, or an actionable interference by the defendant with the claimant's enjoyment of his land, time will not start to run for the purposes of the doctrine.[152] Nevertheless, the better view is that the doctrine is a denial. Note that it is an element of both the actions in trespass[153] and private nuisance[154] that the claimant enjoyed title to

---

[145] See also *Attorney-General v Leason* [2011] NZHC 1053 [32] ('The constituent elements of the tort of trespass to goods are: (a) the plaintiff must have had possession of goods; (b) There must have been a direct physical inference with the goods by the defendant; (c) If the goods have not been taken away or used, it may be necessary for damage to be caused; and (d) The trespass must have been committed intentionally' (footnotes omitted)).

[146] Eg, *London Tara Hotel Ltd v Kensington Close Hotel Ltd* [2010] EWHC 2749 (Ch).

[147] The doctrine of prescription does not apply in the context of public nuisance: *R v Cross* (1812) 3 Camp 224, 227; 170 ER 1362, 1363 ('It is immaterial how long the practice may have prevailed' (Lord Ellenborough)).

[148] *R v Oxfordshire County Council, ex p Sunningwell Parish Council* [2000] 1 AC 335, 349 (HL).

[149] Eg, *Sturges v Bridgman* (1878) 11 Ch D 852, 855 (CA); *Hulley v Silversprings Bleaching and Dyeing Co Ltd* [1922] 2 Ch D 268, 282 (Ch D); *Garfinkel v Kleinberg* [1955] OR 388; [1955] 2 DLR 844 (Ont CA); *Lawrence v Fen Tigers Ltd* [2011] EWHC 360 (QB); [2011] 4 All ER 1314, 1318 [224].

[150] Eg, J Murphy, *The Law of Nuisance* (Oxford, Oxford University Press, 2010) 105; AM Dugdale and MA Jones (eds), *Clerk & Lindsell on Torts*, 21th edn (London, Sweet & Maxwell, 2014) [20.85] esp nn 425, 432.

[151] Meanings attributed to the word 'defence' are discussed in 1.2.

[152] 'Before time can commence to run ... there must be an invasion of some legal right': *Liverpool Corporation v H Coghill & Son, Ltd* [1918] 1 Ch 307, 314 (Ch D).

[153] *Wellaway v Courtier* [1918] 1 KB 200 (Div Ct).

[154] *Hunter v Canary Wharf Ltd* [1997] AC 655 (HL).

sue. It is arguable that the doctrine attacks this element: where the doctrine applies, the claimant's rights in respect of his land will be insufficient to sustain an action in trespass or in private nuisance against the defendant. The apparent inconsistency in characterising the doctrine as a denial despite the fact that it can arise only after the relevant action has been constituted can be resolved on the basis of a legal fiction: the doctrine retrospectively unconstitutes the action by treating the defendant as having been expressly granted a prescriptive right at some point in the past. In John Fleming's words, the trespass or private nuisance 'is retrospectively legalised as if it has been authorised by a grant from the owner of the servient land'.[155]

3.6.3. Exclusion of Liability by Contract or Notice

There are several ways in which a contract or a notice can prevent liability in tort from arising.[156] Consider, first, a situation in which the defendant issues the claimant with a notice in which he disclaims responsibility for a particular act or representation. A defendant who relies on such a notice may be offering a denial. The decision in *Hedley Byrne & Co Ltd v Heller & Partners Ltd*[157] illustrates the point. The defendant in this case was found not to owe a duty of care to the claimant in respect of advice that it gave concerning a third party's creditworthiness because it included in the advice a notice in which it disclaimed responsibility for the consequences of relying on the advice. Because such a disclaimer negated a duty of care – an element of the action in negligence – pleading the disclaimer functioned as a denial. Take, secondly, a contractual clause in which the claimant states that he will not rely on the defendant's representations. A defendant who places weight on such a clause in proceedings in negligent misstatement is denying the reliance element of that action. Lastly, consider a clause in a contract or notice that purports to prevent liability generally from arising. It is difficult to determine whether, in pointing to such a clause, the defendant is offering a denial or a defence. Judges and textbook writers generally talk simply of exclusion clauses as 'protect[ing]'[158] defendants and 'binding'[159] claimants. Such language gives no guidance as to how exclusion clauses operate to prevent liability from arising. But intuition suggests that they are denials. It is true that it is not easy to point to a particular element of any tort that exclusion clauses target. A possible way of overcoming this hurdle to

---

[155] Fleming (n 135) 490. These words are preserved in the current edition of Fleming's work: Sappideen and Vines (n 20) 517 [21.230].

[156] There are many statutory restrictions on the circumstances in which a defendant can take advantage of a contract or a notice to avoid liability in tort: eg, Unfair Contract Terms Act 1977 (UK), s 2; Road Traffic Act 1988 (UK), s 149. It is unnecessary to consider such restrictions for present purposes. For discussion, see E Peel (ed), *Treitel on the Law of Contract*, 14th edn (London, Sweet & Maxwell, 2015) ch 7.

[157] [1964] AC 465 (HL).

[158] *Thornton v Shoe Land Parking Ltd* [1971] 2 QB 163, 167 (CA).

[159] Ibid, 169–71, 174.

viewing exclusion clauses as denials is by perceiving all torts as incorporating the absence of an exclusion clause as an implicit element.

3.6.4. Voluntary Assumption of Risk

It has already been explained that when the phrase 'voluntary assumption of risk' is used in the tort law context, the speaker frequently means to say 'no breach'[160] or 'no causation'.[161] But there is also evidence that this phrase can also mean 'no duty'. The wide range of ways in which the plea of voluntary assumption of risk can function as a denial was noted by Lord Walker of Gestingthorpe in *Stone & Rolls Ltd v Moore Stephens*.[162] Lord Walker perceptively observed that 'The volenti principle is far from precise and it may sometimes operate [as a denial of causation and] to negative any duty (or any breach).'[163] Several legal writers think that the plea of voluntary assumption of risk *always* operates as denial of a duty of care. For example, John Fleming wrote that 'Volenti is a waiver of duty . . .'.[164] Likewise, Fleming James asserted that the doctrine 'is simply a confusing way of stating certain no-duty rules . . .'.[165] Similarly, Francis Bohlen said that 'Voluntary assumption of risks negatives the idea of even *prima facie* liability . . . [If the doctrine of voluntary assumption of risk applies,] the defendant owes [the claimant] no duty . . .'.[166]

There is a wealth of judicial authority supporting the views of these writers. In *Car and General Insurance Corp Ltd v Seymour*, Kellock J claimed that 'A finding of *volenti* involves the consequence that no . . . duty [of care] existed . . .'.[167] Sopinka J in *Hall v Hebert* claimed that 'The *volenti* defence is another example of the application of policy to negate a duty of care which would otherwise arise.'[168] According to Asquith J in *Dann v Hamilton*, 'As a matter of strict pleading it seems that the plea volenti is a denial of any duty at all and, therefore, of any breach of duty, and an admission of negligence cannot strictly be combined with the plea.'[169]

---

[160] See 3.3.8.

[161] See 3.4.5.

[162] [2009] UKHL 39; [2009] AC 1391.

[163] *Ibid*, 1498 [178].

[164] Fleming (n 135) 327, n 2. This passage is preserved in the 10th edition: Sappideen and Vines (n 20) 335, n 134.

[165] F James, 'Assumption of Risk: Unhappy Reincarnation' (1968) 78 *Yale Law Journal* 185, 188.

[166] FH Bohlen, 'Contributory Negligence' (1908) 21 *Harvard Law Review* 233, 245.

[167] [1956] SCR 322, 331.

[168] [1993] 2 SCR 159, 192. See also *ibid*, 193.

[169] [1939] 1 KB 509, 512 (KBD).

3.6.5. Illegality[170]

It was explained above that, in England, the plea of illegality in proceedings in negligence is a denial of causation.[171] A different approach is taken in several other jurisdictions. For example, in Australia it was recently held in *Miller v Miller*[172] that, for the purposes of proceedings in negligence, a duty of care will not be owed to a claimant who was injured while acting illegally if to find that a duty existed would be inconsistent with the criminal law statute that the claimant violated. This principle was developed in a case in which the claimant was injured while engaged in a joint illegal enterprise with the defendant, but it does not seem to be restricted to joint illegal enterprise cases. It is unclear how the doctrine of illegality prevents liability arising in torts other than negligence. The position in Scotland is similar. Scots law withholds a duty of care as between parties to serious joint illegal enterprises.[173] A like rule also appears to apply in Ireland.[174]

3.6.6. Contributory Negligence

Since the apportionment legislation[175] was enacted, a claimant who is guilty of contributory negligence may have his damages reduced on account of that negligence. A defendant who relies on the apportionment legislation offers neither a denial nor a defence.[176] This is because the apportionment provision is part of the law of remedies and not the law of liability.[177] But this does not mean that the plea of contributory negligence never relates to liability. For example, that plea can constitute a denial in the context of the tort of negligent misstatement. This is because this tort has as one of its elements a requirement that the claimant's reliance on the defendant's misstatement be reasonable. A defendant who pleads contributory negligence in the setting of this action might intend to attack this element.[178]

---

[170] This is a highly condensed account of the way in which the plea of illegality can prevent a duty of care from arising. See further J Goudkamp, 'The Defence of Joint Illegal Enterprise' (2010) 34 *Melbourne University Law Review* 425.

[171] See 3.4.6.

[172] [2011] HCA 9; (2011) 242 CLR 446.

[173] *Lindsay v Poole* 1984 SLT 269 (OH); *Sloan v Triplett* 1985 SLT 294 (OH); *Wilson v Price* 1989 SLT 484 (OH); *Ashcroft's Curator Bonis v Stewart* 1988 SLT 163 (OH); *Andersen v Hameed* [2010] CSOH 99; 2010 Rep LR 132.

[174] *Anderson v Cooke* [2005] IEHC 221; [2005] 2 IR 607 (no duty owed by driver to passenger who photographed speedometer while driver accelerated the vehicle to its maximum speed).

[175] Law Reform (Contributory Negligence) Act 1945 (UK), s 1.

[176] See 1.2.2.

[177] See further J Goudkamp, 'Rethinking Contributory Negligence' in SGA Pitel, JW Neyers and E Chamberlain (eds), *Tort Law: Challenging Orthodoxy* (Oxford, Hart Publishing, 2013) 336–38.

[178] It has been held that damages awarded in proceedings for negligent misstatement can be reduced for contributory negligence: *Grand Restaurants of Canada Ltd v City of Toronto* (1981) 32 OR (2d) 757 (HCJ); *Gran Gelato Ltd v Richcliffe (Group) Ltd* [1992] Ch 560, 572–73 (Ch D); cf *JEB Fasteners Ltd v Marks, Bloom & Co* [1981] 3 All ER 289, 297 (QBD). It might be suggested that this is contradictory

3.6.7. Truth

It was contended earlier that the plea of truth in proceedings in defamation is a denial and not a defence.[179] The element that the plea attacks is that of damage. Loss caused by a true defamatory statement does not count as damage. This is not, however, the only way in which the plea of truth can be characterised as a denial. Statements can occasionally be found in the case law and academic commentary that falsity is an element of the action in defamation. For example, in *Hodgkinson v Economical Mutual Insurance Co*, Morden JA, with whom the other members of the court concurred, said that 'falsity of the defendant's statements is an element of the cause of action for defamation'.[180] If these statements are accurate, it is this element to which the plea of truth pertains.

Despite the decision in *Hodgkinson* and other sources that take a like view of the action of defamation, it is unclear whether falsity is an element of the action. Statements can also be found that expressly deny that falsity is an element of the tort. An illustration of such a statement is found in the reasons of the Constitutional Court of South Africa in *Khumalo v Holomisa*.[181] The Court said:[182]

> At common law, the elements of the delict of defamation are: (a) the wrongful and (b) intentional (c) publication of (d) a defamatory statement (e) concerning the plaintiff. It is not an element of the delict in common law that the statement be false.

Furthermore, there are authoritative cases in which courts have enumerated the elements of the action in defamation in which the issue of falsity does not feature.[183] The oft-repeated statement that it is presumed that defamatory statements are false[184] supplies no real guidance regarding the constitution of the tort of defama-

given that the absence of contributory negligence is a prerequisite to liability in the tort of negligent misstatement. However, in actuality, it is only the case that a claimant cannot be found guilty of contributory negligence in relation to his *reliance* on the defendant's misstatement of fact. It is conceivable that a claimant might be careless with respect to his interests in some other way and that such carelessness may be penalised by the apportionment provision. Suppose that C, a mortgagee, relied on a valuation report prepared by D that negligently overvalued the property in issue. If the elements of the tort of negligent misstatement are satisfied, C's damages cannot be reduced on the ground that his reliance was unreasonable. Such an outcome would be inconsistent with the fact that the elements of the tort of negligent misstatement are present. But he could have his damages reduced for carelessness that is unconnected with the reliance. For instance, a reduction in C's damages might be warranted if he failed to check the mortgagor's credit history.

[179] See 3.5.1.

[180] [2003] 68 OR (3d) 587, 597 [33]; (2004) 235 DLR (4th) 1, 11 (CA). See also P Milmo and WVH Rogers, *Gatley on Libel and Slander*, 11th edn (London, Sweet & Maxwell, 2008) 11 [1.6], in which it is asserted that 'Defamation is committed when the defendant publishes to a third person words or matter containing an *untrue* imputation against the reputation of the claimant' (emphasis added). This text does not appear in the twelfth edition of this work.

[181] [2002] (5) SA 401.

[182] *Ibid*, 413 [18].

[183] See, eg, the quote from the reasons of McLachlin CJ in *Grant v Torstar Corp* [2009] SCC 61; [2009] 3 SCR 640, 658 [28] set out at the text accompanying n 114 above.

[184] Eg, *Grant v Torstar Corp* [2009] SCC 61; [2009] 3 SCR 640, 658 [28]; *Jameel v Wall Street Journal Europe SPRL (No 3)* [2005] EWCA Civ 74; [2005] QB 904, 915 [4]; *Adelson v Anderson* [2011] EWHC

tion. The most that this statement can with certainty be said to establish is that the defendant bears the onus of proving that his impugned statement was true.

3.6.8. Common Enemy Rule

The common enemy rule is relevant in the context of private nuisance. It holds that a person will not incur liability in this tort if he modifies his land in order to protect it from surface water, which is a threat common to all occupiers, with the result being that his neighbour's land is flooded. The rule was carefully analysed by Laws LJ in *Arscott v The Coal Authority*.[185] His Lordship explained that the rule is subject to three qualifications. First, the defendant must not alter an established watercourse.[186] Secondly, the rule does not apply if the defendant causes water that is already on his land to flow to the claimant's land.[187] Thirdly, the measures taken by the defendant to protect his land must not be excessive.[188] A defendant who pleads the common enemy rule is contending that his use of his land was reasonable. As Laws LJ explained, 'Where works done to protect land from the common enemy are [within the common enemy rule], they may be considered a natural use of the land which is *prima facie* also a reasonable use.'[189] If the defendant is making reasonable use of his land, the claimant will not be able to show that the interference with his land is unreasonable. Without proof of such interference, the action in private nuisance will be incomplete. It follows that to rely on the common enemy rule is to offer a denial.

3.7. Conclusion

A great many pleas that defendants may be able to offer in an attempt to avoid incurring liability in tort are denials of one or more elements of the tort in which the claimant sues. These pleas must be expelled from the category of defences. If they are allowed to intrude into the category of defences they will threaten attempts to understand how defences operate. This chapter has identified a significant number of denials. The results of this analysis are captured in Table 1 below.

2497 (QB) [76].
[185] [2004] EWCA Civ 892.
[186] *Ibid* [35].
[187] *Ibid* [37]–[39].
[188] *Ibid* [40].
[189] *Ibid* [40].

Table 1: Denials

Denials of the act element	Denials of the fault element	Denials of causation	Denials of the damage element	Denials of other elements
Involuntariness	Involuntariness Infancy Insanity Intoxication Inevitable accident Act of God Mistake Voluntary assumption of risk	Inevitable accident Act of God Act of third party Claimant default Voluntary assumption of risk Illegality *Novus actus interveniens*	Truth	Consent Prescription Exclusion of liability by contract or notice Voluntary assumption of risk Illegality Contributory negligence Truth? Common enemy rule

Before leaving the subject of denials, two general observations need to be made about them. First, certain denials can attack more than one element. Take, for instance, the plea of inevitable accident. As has been demonstrated, this plea can entail a denial of fault[190] and a denial of causation.[191] It might be thought that presenting some pleas as going to more than one element is confusing. On the contrary, it is not the analysis in this chapter that it is confusing but the terminology used by judges and commentators. Indeed, one of the main strengths of the analysis that has been undertaken here is that it reveals this confusion. It shows that certain denials sometimes operate in more than one way. It is obviously undesirable for a single label to be used to describe attacks on different elements of the tort in which the claimant sues. Doing so creates a significant risk of confusion.

Secondly, some of the conclusions that have been reached in this chapter are tentative. This is because it is sometimes impossible to determine with certainty how certain pleas that defendants might make prevent liability from arising. For instance, it is not crystal clear that the plea of truth is a denial. It is arguably a defence. The same might be said of the plea of voluntary assumption of risk. The uncertainty in this regard is a product of the general failure of law-making bodies and commentators to attend to the fundamental distinction between torts and defences. The imprecise way in which the word 'defence' is usually used, coupled with doubt as to the elements of many torts, means that efforts to determine how some pleas operate are sometimes destined to fail.

---

[190] See 3.3.5.
[191] See 3.4.1.

4

A Taxonomy of Tort Law Defences

[A]n academical expounder of the laws should . . . consider his course as a general map of the law, marking out the shape of the country, its connexions and boundaries, it's [*sic*] greater divisions and principal cities: it is not his business to describe minutely the subordinate limits, or to fix the longitude and latitude of every inconsiderable hamlet.[1]

The business of the jurist is to make known the content of the law; that is, to work upon it from within, or logically, arranging and distributing it, in order, from its *stemmum genus* to its *infima species*, so far as practicable.[2]

4.1. Introduction

In contrast with the efforts that have been made to categorise torts,[3] no one has made a serious attempt to classify tort law defences. Indeed, some theorists have counselled against making an attempt. For example, John Fleming contended that it would be futile to seek to organise tort law defences. In his words, 'the countless situations in which harm is held uncompensable defy explanation by reference to any systematic index of "exceptions" or "defences".'[4] There is no doubt that the number and diversity of defences are formidable obstacles to the development of a satisfactory taxonomy. But Fleming was surely too pessimistic. It is far from clear that defences are substantially more plentiful or varied than torts, which most theorists, including Fleming,[5] regard as susceptible to categorisation. The goal of this chapter is, therefore, to suggest a system by which defences may be classified.[6]

[1] W Blackstone, *Commentaries on the Laws of England*, vol 1 (Oxford, Clarendon Press, 1765) 35.

[2] OW Holmes, *The Common Law* (Boston, Mass, Little, Brown, & Co, 1881) 219.

[3] See the text accompanying n 36 in ch 1.

[4] JG Fleming, *The Law of Torts*, 9th edn (Sydney, Law Book Co, 1998) 8. This passage is preserved in the 10th edition of Fleming's book: C Sappideen and P Vines (eds), *Fleming's The Law of Torts*, 10th edn (Sydney, Lawbook Co, 2011) 8.

[5] Fleming (n 4) 18–19.

[6] For useful discussions of how one should go about constructing legal taxonomies, see DN Husak, *Philosophy of Criminal Law* (Totowa, Rowman & Littlefield, 1987) ch 7; P Birks, 'Equity in the Modern Law: An Exercise in Taxonomy' (1996) 26 *University of Western Australia Law Review* 1; P Birks, 'Definition and Division: A Meditation on *Institutes* 3.13' in P Birks (ed), *The Classification of Obligations* (Oxford, Clarendon Press, 1997); V Tadros, *Criminal Responsibility* (Oxford, Oxford University Press, 2005) 119–21; R Stevens, *Torts and Rights* (Oxford, Oxford University Press, 2007) ch 13.

4.2. The Taxonomy

It is submitted that tort law defences should be arranged pursuant to a taxonomy the first level of which divides into:

(1) justification defences; and
(2) public policy defences.

For present purposes, justifications will be defined simply as defences that relieve the defendant of liability on the basis that he acted reasonably in committing a tort. This definition will be fleshed out as the analysis proceeds. Public policy defences are defences that are insensitive to the rational defensibility of the defendant's conduct. In other words, when advancing a public policy defence, the defendant does not attempt to explain why he committed a tort. Public policy defences exist in recognition of the fact that the goals of tort law (whatever they might be) must on occasion play second fiddle to other concerns. Liability must sometimes be withheld from a tortfeasor in order to promote an aim that is external to tort law.

The remainder of this chapter consists largely in attempts to fend off the many challenges that might be made to this proposed arrangement of tort law defences. The next chapter endeavours to show which defences belong to which category and how these categories should be subdivided.

4.3. Challenges to the Taxonomy

4.3.1. Justifications

4.3.1.1. Denials of wrongdoing or explanations for wrongdoing?

Justificatory defences have been defined as defences that enable the defendant to escape from liability because, in committing a tort, the defendant acted reasonably. In other words, justificatory defences have been conceptualised as defences that release the defendant from liability because he behaved reasonably in committing a wrong. This definition of a justificatory defence differs fundamentally from that accepted by many theorists. According to conventional learning, an actor who is justified commits no wrong. The following passages demonstrate the extent of the commitment to this traditional understanding. Peter Cane asserts that 'justifications deny wrongdoing'.[7] Arthur Ripstein contends that '[j]ustifications exculpate by showing that an apparently wrongful act was not wrongful'.[8] Jules Coleman

---

[7] P Cane, *Responsibility in Law and Morality* (Oxford, Hart Publishing, 2002) 90.
[8] A Ripstein, *Equality, Responsibility, and the Law* (Cambridge, Cambridge University Press, 1999) 138.

argues that 'when an actor *justifies* what she has done, she denies that the action is, all things considered, wrong'.[9] This understanding of what it means to be justified will be called the 'conventional view'.[10] The definition of a justification that has been adopted in this chapter will be referred to as the 'radical view'.

Because torts are wrongs, conventionalists are committed to the proposition that a justified defendant does not commit any tort. So, for conventionalists, a person does not commit a battery in making an arrest[11] or in using reasonable force to protect himself[12] or his property,[13] 'a landlord commits no trespass if he distrains for rent'[14] neither does a 'bailiff who enters private premises on civil process',[15] a person does not convert a chattel by recapturing it,[16] a gaoler who imprisons a person in circumstances where the State authorised the imprisonment does not commit false imprisonment[17] and so on. In the eyes of conventionalists, justifications are, consequently, exceptions to torts. This understanding was captured by Stevenson VC in *Alfred W Booth & Bro v Burgess* when he said that 'There is no justification for a tort. The so-called justification is an exceptional fact which shows that no tort was committed. Such exceptional fact makes the

[9] J Coleman, *Risks and Wrongs* (Oxford, Oxford University Press, 1992) 217 (emphasis in original); cf at 371: 'justifiable . . . conduct can constitute a wrong'.

[10] For further endorsement of the conventional view, see GP Fletcher, *Rethinking Criminal Law* (Boston, Mass, Little, Brown & Co, 1978) 759 ('[c]laims of justification . . . challenge whether the act is wrongful'); MS Moore, *Law and Psychiatry: Rethinking the Relationship* (Cambridge, Cambridge University Press, 1984) 84 ('justifying circumstances make the act not wrong as performed on this occasion'); DN Husak, 'Conflicts of Justifications' (1999) 18 *Law and Philosophy* 41, 52 ('a defendant has a justification for his presumptively wrongful conduct if and only if his conduct is not actually wrongful all things considered'); M Baron, 'Justifications and Excuses' (2005) 2 *Ohio State Journal of Criminal Law* 387, 389 ('to say that an action is justified is to say . . . that though the action is of a type that is usually wrong, in these circumstances it was not wrong'). This sentence does not feature in the fifth edition of their text.

[11] Eg, Nicholas McBride and Roderick Bagshaw claim that 'if A runs out of a store with some goods which he has stolen, B – one of the store's security guards – *will commit no battery* if she chases A and wrestles him to the ground in an attempt to apprehend him': NJ McBride and R Bagshaw, *Tort Law*, 4th edn (Harlow, Pearson Education, 2012) 55 (emphasis added). This sentence does not feature in the fifth edition of this text.

[12] Eg, 'It is not tautologous to define assault as an unlawful offer or application of force': *Blackburn v Bowering* [1994] 3 All ER 380, 384; [1994] 1 WLR 1324, 1328–29 (CA) (Sir Thomas Bingham MR).

[13] Eg, WP Keeton, DB Dobbs, RE Keeton and DG Owen (eds), *Prosser and Keeton on Torts*, 5th edn (St Paul, Minn, West Publishing Co, 1984) 131, where it is asserted that the defence of one's property 'is the privilege to resist a trespass, by force *which would otherwise amount to assault, battery or false imprisonment*' (emphasis added).

[14] WVH Rogers (ed), *Winfield & Jolowicz on Tort*, 18th edn (London, Sweet & Maxwell, 2010) 696–97 [13.11].

[15] *Ibid*, 697 [13.11].

[16] Eg, NJ McBride and R Bagshaw, *Tort Law*, 5th edn (Harlow, Pearson, 2015) 515, where the doctrine of recapture is identified as a 'lawful justification or excuse for doing something *that would normally amount to conversion of another's property*' (emphasis added).

[17] Eg, 'it is of the essence of the tort of false imprisonment that the imprisonment is without lawful justification': *R v Governor of Brockhill Prison, ex p Evans (No 2)* [2001] 2 AC 19, 32 (Lord Hope of Craighead) (HL); 'the ingredients of the tort [of false imprisonment] are clear. There must be a detention and the absence of lawful authority to justify it': *Lumba v Secretary of State for the Home Department* [2011] UKSC 12; [2012] AC 245, 276 [71] (Lord Dyson JSC); 'False imprisonment is established if there has been a detention and an absence of lawful authority justifying it': *Lumba v Secretary of State for the Home Department* [2011] UKSC 12; [2012] AC 245, 321 [239] (Lord Kerr).

case an exception to the definition of a tort.'[18] Similarly, Webster J in *Shearson Lehman Hutton Inc v Maclaine Watson & Co Ltd* said that 'there can be no justification for a civil wrong'.[19] It follows that, on the conventional view, the absence of justification is actually an element of all torts. Thus, it turns out that, if conventionalists are correct, all pleas of justification are in fact denials.

In contrast with conventionalists, radicals believe that a defendant who has a justification defence commits a tort but, because of the defence, is not liable in tort. Radicals think, therefore, that a person commits a battery if he uses reasonable force to resist an attack[20] or to make an arrest,[21] that one who enters another's land or who destroys chattels in circumstances of public necessity commits a justified trespass[22] and so on. Expressed differently, a defendant who asserts that he was justified in his acts is, on the radical view, not denying that he committed a wrong but is offering an explanation for *admitted wrongdoing*. Radicals do not, of course, mean to claim that a justified defendant is blameworthy. The radical position is simply that a defendant who has a justificatory defence has committed, but is not liable for, a tort.

The difference between the conventional view and the radical view has gone largely unnoticed by torts scholars. There seems to have been little or no recognition of the fact that when, for example, the tort of battery is in issue, some writers define a battery as 'unjustified contact with the body of another person' whereas others use the very different formulation of 'contact with the body of another person' and then assert that liability in battery can be avoided by way of a justification defence. However, the difference between the conventional view and the radical view is of critical importance for the purposes of the taxonomy of defences that has been advanced in this chapter. This is because the conventional view, which conceives of pleas of justification as denials, is a threat to the taxonomy's coherence. If the conventional view is correct, there is no such thing as a justification defence and, consequently, no category should be reserved for justifications within a taxonomy of tort law defences. Conversely, the inclusion of a category for justifications is coherent on the radical view.

Although the conventional view is firmly entrenched, there are at least two reasons for thinking that it is mistaken.[23] In the first place, the conventional view

---

[18] 72 NJ Eq 181, 188; 65 A 226, 229 (1906).

[19] [1989] 2 Lloyd's Rep 570, 633 (QBD).

[20] Eg, John Goldberg and Benjamin Zipursky write that 'a person who commits the tort of battery by intentionally shooting another can justify the battery, and thereby escape liability, by proving that the shooting was in *self-defense*': JCP Goldberg and BC Zipursky, *The Oxford Introductions to US Law: Torts* (Oxford, Oxford University Press, 2010) 110 (emphasis in original).

[21] Eg, Diplock LJ in *Dallison v Caffery* [1965] 1 QB 348, 370 (CA) said: 'Since arrest involves trespass to the person and any trespass to the person is prima facie tortious, the onus lies on the arrestor to *justify the trespass* by establishing reasonable and probable cause for the arrest' (emphasis added).

[22] 'In exceptional circumstances necessity may *justify trespass* to land or to goods': *Monsanto v Tilly* [2000] Env LR 313, 318 (CA) (emphasis added).

[23] John Gardner, drawing on M Nussbaum, *The Fragility of Goodness*, rev edn (Cambridge, Cambridge University Press, 2001) especially chs 2 and 11, doubts the conventional view in the context of the criminal law: J Gardner, *Offences and Defences: Selected Essays in Philosophy of Criminal Law* (Oxford, Oxford University Press, 2007) esp at 77–82, 96–97. The analysis here largely tracks Gardner's argument applied, *mutatis mutandis*, to tort law.

leads to the startling conclusion that wrongs (including torts) cannot be justified (since if one is justified, no wrong (and no tort) is committed). The conclusion that wrongs cannot be justified is a reason for looking askance at the conventional view, because if anything calls for justification, it is wrongs. In John Gardner's words, 'One might think that the fact that an action is wrong yields a powerful rational objection to its performance, and that wrongdoing therefore calls for justification if anything does.'[24]

Secondly, the conventional view cannot easily explain why adverse normative consequences often obtain in respect of justified acts. Suppose that D is murderously attacked by C, an upstanding citizen who has temporarily gone insane because an enemy of his injected him against his will with a powerful hallucinogenic drug. D can save himself only by hitting C with a hammer that he happens to be holding. D strikes C with the hammer, causing C to suffer serious injury. Although C is an 'innocent aggressor', D is surely justified in hitting him[25] (and would not be liable to him in tort). But there are several adverse normative consequences that D would nevertheless incur. For example, D would be morally obliged to apologise to C. D should also regret that he needed to injure C in order to save himself. Conventionalists would have a difficult time explaining these normative consequences. If D's act was not wrong, why should he bear them? This problem does not arise on the radical view.

What can be said in support of the conventional view? It might be argued that, despite the foregoing, the conventional view should be accepted because justified acts are commendable. This argument runs as follows:

(1) justified acts are commendable;
(2) therefore, the conventional view is correct since commendable acts cannot be wrong.

The suggestion that justified acts are commendable enjoys significant support. For instance, George Fletcher argues that a justified act is 'right and proper'.[26] Likewise, Paul Robinson claims that 'Justified behavior is correct behavior and

---

[24] Gardner (n 23) 77.

[25] There is a general consensus among scholars that it is justifiable to use reasonable defensive force against an innocent aggressor: see, eg, PH Robinson, 'Criminal Law Defenses: A Systematic Analysis' (1982) 82 *Columbia Law Review* 199, 275; JC Smith, *Justification and Excuse in the Criminal Law* (London, Stevens & Sons, 1989) 19–20; JJ Thomson, 'Self-Defense' (1991) 20 *Philosophy & Public Affairs* 283, 284–85; GP Fletcher, 'The Psychotic Aggressor – A Generation Later' (1993) 27 *Israel Law Review* 227; J Horder, 'Redrawing the Boundaries of Self-Defence' (1995) 58 *Modern Law Review* 431, 432.

[26] GP Fletcher, 'Should Intolerable Prison Conditions Generate a Justification or an Excuse for Escape?' (1979) 26 *University of California Los Angeles Law Review* 1355, 1357. Fletcher specifically rejects the view that justified conduct is merely permissible at 1359–60. See also EB Arnolds and NF Garland, 'The Defense of Necessity in Criminal Law: The Right to Choose the Lesser Evil' (1974) 65 *Journal of Criminal Law & Criminology* 289, 290; BS Byrd, 'Wrongdoing and Attribution: Implications beyond the Justification-Excuse Distinction' (1987) 33 *Wayne Law Review* 1289, 1293; CO Finkelstein, 'Self-Defense as a Rational Excuse' (1996) 57 *University of Pittsburgh Law Review* 621, 625; ER Milhizer, 'Justification and Excuse: What They Were, What They Are, and What They Ought to Be' (2004) 78 *St John's Law Review* 725, 856.

therefore is not only tolerated but encouraged.'[27] Other theorists argue, however, that justified acts are not necessarily commendable. For example, Joshua Dressler asserts that in order for an act to be justified, 'It is not necessary that the conduct be affirmatively desirable or morally good.'[28] Similarly, John Gardner says that 'an action is justified only if performed for an undefeated reason, which need not be a noble or admirable one'.[29] In the same vein, Douglas Husak contends that conduct that is justified 'should be understood as conduct that is permissible, although not necessarily commendable or praiseworthy'.[30] Which view is preferable? Although there is no doubt that justified conduct is sometimes commendable, it is better to say that conduct can be justified without being commendable. It is easy to think of scenarios involving acts that are justified but not praiseworthy. Suppose that C, a baby, waves a loaded gun in D's direction. D is in danger of being shot.[31] Accordingly, D shoots C with a gun that he is holding. D is plainly justified in defending himself,[32] but he hardly acted commendably. On the contrary, we would applaud D if he *did not* shoot C and preferred C's life to his own. The argument that the conventional view is correct since justified conduct is commendable should be rejected.

For the foregoing reasons, it is submitted that the radical view of what it means to be justified is preferable to the conventional view. Unlike the conventional view, the radical view is compatible with the inclusion of a category for justification defences within a taxonomy of tort law defences.

4.3.1.2. *Does tort law accept pleas of justification?*

John Gardner is the author of several ground-breaking pieces of scholarship concerning justificatory defences in the context of the criminal law.[33] It is crystal clear

---

[27] PH Robinson, 'A Theory of Justification: Societal Harm as a Prerequisite for Criminal Liability' (1975) 23 *University of California Los Angeles Law Review* 266, 274; cf PH Robinson, *Structure and Function in Criminal Law* (Oxford, Clarendon Press, 1997) 82 ('Justified conduct . . . is behaviour that is to be encouraged (or at least tolerated)').

[28] J Dressler, 'New Thoughts about the Concept of Justification in the Criminal Law: A Critique of Fletcher's Thinking and *Rethinking*' (1984) 32 *University of California Los Angeles Law Review* 61, 83.

[29] J Gardner, 'Justification under Authority' (2010) 23 *Canadian Journal of Law & Jurisprudence* 71, 81. Elsewhere Gardner writes that 'more is required for credit than is required for mere justification. An action may still be justified even though performed without any technical proficiency and for a most banal, trivial, and unimpressive reason': Gardner (n 23) 104.

[30] DN Husak, 'Justifications and the Criminal Liability of Accessories' (1989) 80 *Journal of Criminal Law & Criminology* 491, 500. See also Husak (n 10) 53–55; Coleman (n 9) 218; RF Schopp, *Justification Defenses and Just Convictions* (Cambridge, Cambridge University Press, 1998) 16–21; Baron (n 10) 395; V Bergelson, 'Rights, Wrongs, and Comparative Justifications' (2007) 28 *Cardozo Law Review* 2481, 2488–90.

[31] Let us make all additions to this scenario necessary to prevent it from becoming contaminated with distractions. For instance, assume that D bears no responsibility for C gaining possession of the gun, that he did not realise that C was holding a gun until C began waving it in his direction (and that the reasonable person would not have become aware of the fact that C had a gun beforehand), that D knows that C's gun is loaded and that D had no other means of preventing C from shooting him than firing his gun at C.

[32] See n 25 and accompanying text above.

[33] See, especially, Gardner (n 23) chs 4–5.

from his work that he thinks that such defences play a central role in the criminal law. But he appears to think that justificatory defences are much less important in tort law. Indeed, he even seems to go so far as to claim that tort law does not recognise justificatory defences. Gardner asserts: 'That a norm-violation was justified is . . . irrelevant to the law of torts. Torts are wrongs – breaches of obligation – and one owes damages for their commission even if one's wrong was justified . . .'.[34] He also claims that 'In general one owes reparative damages for torts as wrongs, never mind whether they are justified.'[35] Gardner does not deny that the fact that the defendant was justified in some relevant aspect of his life may be of significance for the purposes of tort law. He accepts, for instance, that some torts can be committed only if the defendant was unjustified, such as the action in negligence.[36] In the terminology that has been adopted in this book, Gardner recognises that to assert that one was justified in one's behaviour may constitute a denial of an element of the tort in which the claimant sues. But it certainly appears that Gardner believes that tort law does not recognise any justificatory defences. This is not because Gardner accepts the conventional view of the concept of justification discussed in the preceding section. Gardner in fact argues powerfully against that view.[37] Rather, Gardner claims that there are no justification defences because, as a matter of substantive law, tort law does not let justified defendants out of liability. Gardner's position in this regard is incompatible with the taxonomy of tort law defences that has been proposed. If Gardner is correct, there should not be a category for justifications.

Gardner cites the famous decision in *Vincent v Lake Erie Transportation Co*[38] (and only *Vincent*) as authority for the proposition that tort law does not recognise justificatory defences. It is worth recounting the facts of, and the holding in, *Vincent*.[39] The *SS Reynolds*, which was owned by the defendant, was moored at the claimant's dock. A severe storm spontaneously developed. The captain of the *Reynolds* signalled for a tugboat to assist her to leave the dock. But no tugboat operator was willing to help owing to the ferocity of the storm. Accordingly, the captain of the *Reynolds* decided that the ship would remain docked (had the captain cast off, the

---

[34] J Gardner, 'What is Tort Law For? Part 1. The Place of Corrective Justice' (2011) 30 *Law and Philosophy* 1, 42.

[35] *Ibid*, 43.

[36] '[T]here are some torts, such as the tort of negligence, that are not committed if one acted with certain justifications. That one acted with reasonable (ie justified) care means that one did not commit this tort': *ibid*, 42 (footnote omitted). See also the text accompanying nn 48–49 in ch 1.

[37] See n 23 above.

[38] 109 Minn 456; 124 NW 221 (1910).

[39] *Vincent* has been extensively analysed. For a small selection of the literature, see FH Bohlen, 'Incomplete Privilege to Inflict Intentional Invasions of Interests of Property and Personality' (1926) 39 *Harvard Law Review* 307; RE Keeton, 'Conditional Fault in the Law of Torts' (1959) 72 *Harvard Law Review* 401, 410–18; FB Sussmann, 'The Defence of Private Necessity and the Problem of Compensation' (1967) 2 *Ottawa Law Review* 184; D Friedmann, 'Restitution of Benefits Obtained through the Appropriation of Property or the Commission of a Wrong' (1980) 80 *Columbia Law Review* 504, 542–46; A Brudner, 'A Theory of Necessity' (1987) 7 *Oxford Journal of Legal Studies* 339, 365–68; Coleman (n 9) 291–302, 369–72; D Klimchuk, 'Necessity and Restitution' (2001) 7 *Legal Theory* 59. See also the special issue on *Vincent* in (2005) Issues in Legal Scholarship (downloadable at <http://www.bepress.com/ils/vincent/>).

Reynolds would almost certainly have been destroyed). The storm repeatedly threw the *Reynolds* against the dock with the result being that the dock was damaged. The claimant sued the defendant in negligence and trespass. The defendant pleaded what is usually known as the defence of private necessity. O'Brien J, with whom Jaggard J concurred, rejected the claim in negligence on the ground that the defendant acted reasonably, but upheld the action in trespass.

Strictly speaking, all that the decision in *Vincent* establishes, relevantly, is that private necessity is not a defence to liability in trespass.[40] It is extremely doubtful that it is authority for the far more general proposition that there are no justificatory defences whatsoever to liability in tort. That is simply not the ratio decidendi of the case. Gardner is mistaken in suggesting otherwise, and it is unsurprising that none of the numerous theorists who have analysed *Vincent* has made a similar claim. Indeed, it is tolerably clear that tort law recognises a wide array of justificatory defences to liability in trespass. Such defences include arrest, discipline, public necessity and self-defence. It is equally clear that there are justificatory defences to many other torts. It is the burden of the next chapter to demonstrate the variety of justificatory defences recognised by tort law.

While Gardner erred in claiming that there are no justificatory defences to liability arising in tort, his claims in this connection serve as a valuable reminder that not every reason that a defendant might be able to cite in an attempt to explain why he committed a tort forms the basis of a defence, irrespective of the strength of the reason in question outside of the law. Tort law is highly selective (for reasons that cannot be explored properly here) in choosing which reasons for committing a tort will furnish the defendant with a defence. As has been noted, *Vincent* shows that tort law places no weight whatsoever on the fact that a defendant who commits a trespass to land committed the trespass to preserve his own, more valuable, chattels. It is suspected that the law would also deny a defence to a defendant who argues that the reason why he committed a trespass was to save himself from suffering personal injury.[41]

4.3.2. Excuses

4.3.2.1. Introduction

It seems to be universally accepted that the criminal law recognises excuses.[42] In contrast, it appears to be generally thought that tort law does not. For example,

---

[40] English law is arguably at odds with *Vincent*: consider *Cope v Sharpe (No 2)* [1912] 1 KB 496 (CA).

[41] This was Blackstone J's view in his dissenting opinion in *Scott v Shepherd* (1773) 2 Wm Bl 892, 896; 96 ER 525, 527.

[42] Criminal law theorists have invested a vast amount of energy developing taxonomies of defences to criminal liability. Although many ways of arranging criminal law defences have been suggested, virtually all of these proposals reserve a category for excuses. Paul Robinson argues for a five-fold system comprising: (1) absent element defences; (2) offence modification defences; (3) justifications; (4) excuses; and (5) non-exculpatory public policy defences (Robinson (n 25)). Douglas Husak

John Gardner writes that tort law 'makes no room for excuses'.[43] Likewise Jules Coleman declares that 'tort liability is not generally defeasible by excuses'.[44] Joseph Raz apparently joined in this view when he said that 'Excuses excuse from punishment and more, but are not relevant to compensation.'[45] The main dissentient from this position is George Fletcher. In his famous article, 'Fairness and Utility in Tort Theory', Fletcher contends that 'nonreciprocal risk-creation may sometimes be excused'.[46] He identifies duress and unavoidable ignorance as excuses accepted by tort law. The possibility that tort law recognises excuses is a challenge to the proposed taxonomy of tort law defences. If excuses exist, a separate category must be reserved for them. The aim of this section is, therefore, to investigate whether there are any excusatory defences to liability in tort.

4.3.2.2. *Excuses are assertions of responsibility*

For reasons that will not become fully apparent until later, it is essential to weed out at the outset a fundamental mistake that is routinely committed when the concept of an excuse is discussed. According to a widely-accepted view (the 'traditional view'), an excuse is a defence the application of which depends on the defendant not being responsible for his deed. John Austin embraced this view when he claimed that to plead an excuse is to 'admit that [the impugned act] was bad but [not to] accept full, or even any, responsibility'.[47] Likewise, Peter Cane asserts that 'excuses deny responsibility'.[48] Paul Robinson also accepted the traditional view when he wrote that 'Excuses admit that the deed may be wrong, but excuse the actor because conditions suggest that the actor is not responsible for

---

defends a tripartite scheme consisting of: (1) denials of the elements of offences; (2) justifications; and (3) excuses (Husak (n 6) 187–90). Victor Tadros supports a threefold system constituted by: (1) justifications; (2) excuses; and (3) exemptions (Tadros (n 6) 121–29). Joshua Dressler proposes that defences should be separated into: (1) justifications; (2) excuses; (3) specialised defences; and (4) extrinsic defences (J Dressler, *Understanding Criminal Law* (New York, Matthew Bender, 1987) 176–78). Antony Duff argues for a system consisting of: (1) justifications; (2) warrants; (3) excuses; and (4) exemptions (RA Duff, *Answering for Crime: Responsibility and Liability in the Criminal Law* (Oxford, Hart Publishing, 2007) ch 11). Andrew Simester's taxonomy involves: (1) irresponsibility defences; (2) justifications; (3) excuses; and (4) mistake-based defences (A Simester, 'On Justification and Excuse' in L Zedner and JV Roberts (eds), *Principles and Values in Criminal Law and Criminal Justice: Essays in Honour of Andrew Ashworth* (Oxford, Oxford University Press, 2012) 96–98). The richest classificatory system is that proposed by Jeremy Horder. Horder's schema consists of seven categories: (1) justifications that negate wrongdoing; (2) justifications for wrongdoing; (3) full excuses; (4) excuses which take a predominantly normative form; (5) excuses which assume a predominantly ascriptive character; (6) the partial excuse of diminished capacity; and (7) denials of responsibility (J Horder, *Excusing Crime* (Oxford, Oxford University Press, 2004) ch 3).

[43] Gardner (n 29) 92.

[44] Coleman (n 9) 224. See also *ibid*, 259–61.

[45] J Raz, 'Responsibility and the Negligence Standard' (2010) 30 *Oxford Journal of Legal Studies* 1, 10. See also M Hale, *History of the Pleas of the Crown*, vol 1 (Philadelphia, Pa, Robert H Small, 1847) 13–15; DB Dobbs, *The Law of Torts* (St Paul, Minn, West Publishing Co, 2000) 157; P Kelly, 'Infancy, Insanity, and Infirmity in the Law of Torts' (2003) 48 *American Journal of Jurisprudence* 179, 218–19.

[46] GP Fletcher, 'Fairness and Utility in Tort Theory' (1972) 85 *Harvard Law Review* 537, 551.

[47] JL Austin, *Philosophical Papers* (Oxford, Clarendon Press, 1961) 124.

[48] Cane (n 7) 90.

his deed.'[49] Traditionalists generally regard pleas such as insanity, infancy, provocation and duress[50] as excuses.

It is important to grasp what the traditional view of excuses entails. What exactly is meant when it is said that a defendant who offers an excuse denies his responsibility? John Gardner distinguishes between two senses in which the word 'responsibility' is used in legal contexts.[51] First, a defendant can be 'consequentially responsible'. This form of responsibility refers to responsibility to bear the adverse moral or legal consequences of some wrong. Clearly, proponents of the traditional view cannot be using the word 'responsibility' in this sense. It is true that excuses, when applicable in a legal context, deny that the defendant is consequentially responsible for a legal sanction (or certain types of legal sanctions), but this is something that excuses have in common with all defences. If excuses are distinct from other defences on the basis that they deny the actor's responsibility, the word 'responsibility' must be being used to mean something else. This brings us to the idea of 'basic responsibility', which is the second sense identified by Gardner in which a person can be responsible. A person is responsible in this sense if he has the capacity to be guided by reasons.[52] One whose mind is so disordered that he is not a rational agent is not responsible within this meaning of the word. Although it is not entirely clear, it seems that basic responsibility is what advocates of the traditional view have in mind when they say that excuses deny a defendant's responsibility. It is significant, in this connection, that those who accept this view typically emphasise the importance of impairments of the defendant's cognitive functioning.[53]

A significant problem with the traditional view of excuses is that several pleas that are widely accepted as excuses do not deny the defendant's responsibility in

[49] Robinson (n 25) 221. See also Coleman (n 9) 218 ('[i]n offering an excuse, an actor typically seeks to deny responsibility or blame for action she may be otherwise prepared to acknowledge is wrong').

[50] Significant argument has broken out as to the proper classification of the plea of duress. Most theorists think that it is an excuse: eg, Fletcher (n 10) 829–33; Robinson (1997) (n 27) 85–87; K Huigens, 'Duress is not a Justification' (2004) 2 *Ohio State Journal of Criminal Law* 303; Gardner (n 23) 137–38. However, some commentators argue that duress is a justification: eg, P Westen and J Mangiafico, 'The Criminal Defense of Duress: A Justification, Not an Excuse – And Why it Matters' (2003) 6 *Buffalo Criminal Law Review* 833. Others contend that duress can operate as a justification or an excuse depending on the relevant factual matrix: eg, K Greenawalt, 'The Perplexing Borders of Justification and Excuse' (1984) 84 *Columbia Law Review* 1897, 1912; Tadros (n 6) 117–18; Duff (n 42) 287–88; A Ashworth, *Principles of Criminal Law*, 6th edn (Oxford, Oxford University Press, 2009) 205–12.

[51] Gardner (n 23) ch 9. See also J Gardner, 'Hart and Feinberg on Responsibility' in MH Kramer, C Grant, B Colburn and A Hatzistavrou (eds), *The Legacy of HLA Hart: Legal, Political, and Moral Philosophy* (Oxford, Oxford University Press, 2008).

[52] The concept of basic responsibility is discussed in more detail in 8.2.

[53] For instance, Kent Greenawalt writes that 'a worker who is experiencing extreme distress at home and who, in a fit of uncontrollable rage, strikes a blameless fellow employee is not justified in doing so, but his emotional state might constitute a total or partial excuse': Greenawalt (n 50) 1899–1900. Similarly, Paul Robinson says that excuses are concerned with whether the defendant suffered from a 'dysfunction' in his 'cognitive processes': PH Robinson, 'Four Distinctions that Glanville Williams did not Make: The Practical Benefits of Examining the Interrelation Among Criminal Law Doctrines' in D Baker and J Horder (eds), *The Sanctity of Law and the Criminal Law: The Legacy of Glanville Williams* (Cambridge, Cambridge University Press, 2013) 110.

the basic sense.[54] A good example is the plea of provocation. A defendant who kills in response to provocation may have suffered a loss of self-control, but this does not mean that such a defendant will be unable to explain himself rationally. On the contrary, he will be able to point to the fact that he was justified in becoming angry in response to the provocation to which he was exposed. As Jeremy Horder puts it, the plea of provocation is, to an extent, 'justificatory in character because it requires defendants to explain their conduct, in part, by reference to the "moral warrant" that they believed the gravity of the provocation gave them for retaliating so violently in anger.'[55] Accordingly, the better view is that a defendant who claims an excuse actually endeavours to demonstrate that he was operating within the realm of reason. It follows that pleas that really do entail a denial of basic responsibility, such as insanity and infancy, need to be ignored in considering whether tort law admits of excuses.

4.3.2.3. *Justifications and excuses*

Criminal lawyers have gone to great lengths to distinguish between justifications and excuses in their field.[56] It is widely accepted that the difference between these types of defences is one of the most important features of the architecture of the criminal law.[57] In contrast, tort law theorists tend to treat the concepts of justification and excuses as synonymous.[58] This is a serious mistake, and one that has the potential, if it is not corrected, to distract from the task of considering whether tort law provides for excuses. This is not the place to explore comprehensively all of the possible ways in which justifications come apart from excuses. To undertake that task would require much more space than is available. It will suffice for

---

[54] Attacks on the traditional view are made in Gardner (n 23) 82–87, 131–35, 178–82; Horder (n 42) 103–08; Duff (n 42) 284–91.

[55] J Horder, *Provocation and Responsibility* (Oxford, Clarendon Press, 1992) 112.

[56] Joshua Dressler writes that 'Enough justification-excuse literature now exists to merit the publication of a bibliography': J Dressler, 'Justifications and Excuses: A Brief Review of the Concepts and the Literature' (1987) 33 *Wayne Law Review* 1155, 1159, n 16. Mitchell Berman remarks that 'In the field of Anglo-American criminal law theory perhaps no subject has been more in vogue in the past twenty-odd years than the distinction between justification and excuse': MN Berman, 'Justification and Excuse, Law and Morality' (2003) 53 *Duke Law Journal* 1, 3. Douglas Husak observes that 'Perhaps the most significant and controversial research program among contemporary criminal theorists is the investigation of the advantages and limitations of applications of the distinction between justification and excuse': Husak (n 30) 491 (footnote omitted).

[57] Criminal law theorists generally agree that the distinction between justification and excuse is of considerable explanatory power. For instance, Kent Greenawalt argued that 'the basic distinction between justification and excuse is very important for moral and legal thought . . .': Greenawalt (n 50) 1927. HLA Hart asserted that 'the distinction between [justification and excuse] is . . . of great moral importance': HLA Hart, *Punishment and Responsibility: Essays in the Philosophy of Law*, 2nd edn (Oxford, Oxford University Press, 2008) 13. George Fletcher wrote that '[t]he distinction between justification and excuse is of fundamental theoretical and practical value': GP Fletcher, 'The Right and the Reasonable' (1985) 98 *Harvard Law Review* 949, 955. Joshua Dressler claimed that '[t]he nature of justification, and its attendant relationship to the concept of excuse, are subjects of great moral, and potentially practical, significance . . .': Dressler (n 28) 61 (footnote omitted).

[58] For a good example of this tendency, see ch 45 of the Restatement (Second) of Torts. That chapter is entitled 'Justification and Excuse', but the Reporters make no effort to disentangle these terms.

present purposes to note that while justifications and excuses are both concerned with the rational defensibility of the defendant's impugned behaviour, to offer an excuse is to give a qualitatively inferior answer to a justification. A defendant who claims that he was justified asserts that he acted reasonably; in contrast, a defendant who pleads an excuse accepts that he did not achieve the same success in terms of leading a rational life as a defendant who enjoyed a justificatory defence. Accordingly, justifications reflect more favourably on defendants than excuses. This is because an excused defendant, while still offering a rational explanation for his conduct, does not assert that his conduct was reasonable. Although there were one or more reasons for an excused defendant to do that which he did, those reasons were insufficiently strong to result in the defendant being justified in his acts.

4.3.2.4. Fletcher's analysis

George Fletcher's ground-breaking article 'Fairness and Utility in Tort Theory' was mentioned at the start of the discussion of excuses. It is now time to address his contribution head-on. In order to appreciate why Fletcher's article is relevant to excuses, it is necessary to say a few words about his wider thesis. Fletcher maintains that tort law can be conceptualised in terms of two competing paradigms: the paradigm of reasonableness and the paradigm of reciprocity. According to the paradigm of reasonableness, liability is imposed when imposing liability will maximise utility. In contrast, under the paradigm of reciprocity, liability is visited upon D in respect of injury that results from a non-reciprocal risk that D imposed on C unless D is excused. Unlike the paradigm of reasonableness, the paradigm of reciprocity has its field of vision restricted to the relationship between C and D. The interests of others are given no weight.

In attempting to marshal evidence in support of his contention that the paradigm of reciprocity has influenced tort law's liability rules, Fletcher points to several cases in which, in his view, excuses are implicitly recognised. For instance, Fletcher cites *Cordas v Peerless Transportation Co*[59] as an example of a case in which the defendant succeeded on the basis of an excuse of duress. In *Cordas*, the defendant cab driver leapt from his moving vehicle when a bandit jumped on to the sideboard and threatened him with a gun. The cab collided with, and injured, the three claimant pedestrians. The court held that in light of the emergency with which he was presented, the driver had not acted negligently. However, Fletcher argues that, in truth, the driver succeeded because he was excused. Fletcher writes:[60]

> In view of the crowd of pedestrians nearby, the driver clearly took a risk that generated a net danger to human life. It was thus an unreasonable, excessive, and unjustified risk. Yet the overwhelmingly coercive circumstances meant that he, personally, was excused from fleeing the cab.

[59] 27 NYS 2d 198 (City Ct 1941).
[60] Fletcher (n 46) 552.

In addition to the excuse of duress, Fletcher contends that tort law contains an excuse of unavoidable ignorance:[61]

> An example of unavoidable ignorance excusing risk-creation is *Smith v Lampe*,[62] in which the defendant honked his horn in an effort to warn a tug that seemed to be heading toward shore in a dense fog. As it happened, the honking coincided with a signal that the tug captain expected would assist him in making port. Accordingly the captain steered his tug toward the honking rather than away from it. That the defendant did not know of the prearranged signal excused his contributing to the tug's going aground. Under the facts of the case, the honking surely created an unreasonable risk of harm. If instantaneous injunctions were possible, one would no doubt wish to enjoin the honking as an excessive, illegal risk. Yet the defendant's ignorance of that risk was also excusable.

Fletcher also refers at some length to the famous decision of the King's Bench in *Weaver v Ward*,[63] which is discussed below.[64] Fletcher claims that various examples given by the court in this case of when liability would not arise in trespass despite the fact that the defendant had directly injured the claimant, are excuses. Referring to *Weaver*, Fletcher writes: 'One kind of excuse would be the defendant being physically compelled to act, as if someone took his hand and struck a third person.'[65] He also says that 'Another kind [of excuse] would be the defendant's accidentally causing harm, as when the plaintiff suddenly appeared in the path of his musket fire.'[66]

Several points should be noted about Fletcher's analysis. First, it subscribes to the fallacy of the excluded middle. Fletcher thinks that demonstrating that the defendants in *Cordas* and *Smith* were unjustified supports the conclusion that they were excused. However, even if it is accepted that the defendants in these cases were unjustified, it does not follow that they were excused. To prove that an unjustified defendant who is let out of liability enjoyed an excuse, Fletcher needs to show that there is no defence of a third kind. Secondly, Fletcher does not come clean on what he means by the concept of 'excuse'. He simply stipulates that certain pleas are excuses. At no point is even a general definition of an excuse offered. Thirdly, Fletcher takes it for granted that a defendant will not be justified unless his conduct is supported by the balance of reasons. He does not regard that a defendant who reasonably believes that justifying facts exist might be justified. Fletcher's view in this connection is controversial. Whether or not a reasonable belief in the existence of justifying facts is sufficient to provide the defendant with a justification is considered later.[67] Lastly, even if Fletcher is correct in so far as he asserts that tort law recognises pleas that take the form of an excuse, his analysis does not show (and is perhaps not intended to show) that such pleas seek to

---

[61] *Ibid*, 552–53.

[62] 64 F 2d 201 (6th Cir 1933). Fletcher could have also cited the famous decision of the English Court of Appeal in *Roe v Ministry of Health* [1954] 2 QB 66 (CA).

[63] (1616) Hob 134; 80 ER 284.

[64] See 4.3.3.1.

[65] Fletcher (n 46) 551 (footnote omitted).

[66] *Ibid* (footnote omitted).

[67] See 4.3.2.6.

enliven defences rather than to make good a denial. Just as pleas of justification can sometimes strike at the element of a tort as opposed to triggering a defence,[68] perhaps the same is true of excusatory pleas. Indeed, it is tolerably clear that several of the pleas that Fletcher identifies as excuses are denials. For instance, in his discussion of *Weaver*, Fletcher says that a defendant whose body is used by another person as a weapon against a claimant has an excuse; yet, as has already been shown, such a defendant will be able to refer to the fact of physical compulsion to deny the act element of the action in battery.[69] Similar remarks can be made in relation to Fletcher's treatment of the plea of inevitable accident, which he identifies as an excuse. It was explained earlier why this plea is a denial of fault[70] or of causation.[71] Fletcher actually states towards the end of his discussion of excuses that the elements of some torts, such as the proximate cause element of the tort of negligence, are used to accommodate certain excusatory pleas.[72]

In conclusion, Fletcher's article does not show that tort law admits of excusatory defences. While Fletcher gathers evidence that pleas that sound in the theory of excuse feature in the law of torts, it is far from clear that such pleas are not merely denials.

4.3.2.5. *Provocation, duress and excessive self-defence*

The purpose of this section is to ask whether three pleas that are often regarded as excusatory in nature, provocation, duress and excessive self-defence, are defences to liability in tort. Provocation can be dealt with quickly. It is firmly established in all of the major common-law jurisdictions that the fact that the defendant was provoked merely diminishes the claimant's entitlement to damages. (It is settled that provocation can reduce punitive damages,[73] but the effect of provocation on compensatory damages is unclear.[74]) Provocation does not go to liability.[75] Provocation is not, therefore, a defence.

There are only two reported decisions in the common-law world, both very old, in which the availability of duress as a defence in tort has been directly considered. The first is *Gilbert v Stone*.[76] In this unusual case, 12 bandits threatened to

---

[68] See the text accompanying nn 48–49 in ch 1.

[69] See 3.3.1.

[70] See 3.3.5.

[71] See 3.4.1.

[72] Fletcher (n 46) 554–55.

[73] *Fontin v Katapodis* (1962) 108 CLR 177 (HCA), appd in *Lane v Holloway* [1968] 1 QB 379 (CA); *Hoebergen v Koppens* [1974] 2 NZLR 597 (SC); *Hurley v Moore* (1993) 112 Nfld & PEIR 40, 50; (1994) 107 DLR (4th) 664, 682 (CA).

[74] Consider the apparently inconsistent positions that Lord Denning took on this issue in *Lane v Holloway* [1968] 1 QB 379, 387 (CA) and *Murphy v Culhane* [1977] 1 QB 94, 98 (CA). The position in Canada has been described as 'muddled': *Hurley v Moore* (1993) 112 Nfld & PEIR 40, 56; (1994) 107 DLR (4th) 664, 675 (CA). The situation in the United States is comprehensively described in AG Nadel, 'Provocation as Basis for Mitigation of Compensatory Damages in Action for Assault and Battery' (1985) 35 ALR 4th 947.

[75] Cf a line of authority in Queensland: *White v Connolly* [1927] St R Qd 75 (SC); *Grehan v Kann* [1948] QWN 40 (SC); *Love v Egan* (1971) 65 QJPR 102 (Dist Ct).

[76] (1647) Style 72; 82 ER 539 (see also the report in (1647) Aleyn 35; 82 ER 902).

kill the defendant if he did not help them to steal the claimant's horse. The defendant yielded to this threat and was sued by the claimant in trespass. It was held that the fact that the defendant's acts were coerced was no defence. The other decision is *Waller v Parker*.[77] The claimant in this matter bailed cotton to the defendant. While in possession of the cotton, the defendant was confronted by a party of marauding soldiers who declared that if he did not destroy it, they would incinerate the building in which it was stored. The defendant caved into the soldiers' threat and the claimant sued him in conversion. The court ruled that the defendant had a defence. In view of the scarcity of relevant authority,[78] it seems unlikely that duress is a defence to liability in tort.[79] This conclusion is reinforced by the fact that most tort law textbooks make no mention of duress and those that do declare that it is not a defence.[80]

In relation to the defence of self-defence, the official position taken by the courts is that the defence only covers acts of defensive force that are in proportion to the exigency.[81] A defendant who uses excessive force to defend himself has no defence at all.[82] However, matters may be more complicated than they initially seem. Jeremy Horder contends that the test of reasonableness for the purposes of the defence of self-defence in the criminal law is applied very leniently. Indeed, it is applied so leniently, according to Horder, that defendants who fall just short of acting reasonably in defending themselves are sometimes found to be within the defence. Such defendants, Horder asserts, are excused. In Horder's words:[83]

> English law governing the . . . limits of self-defence harbours a concealed, very limited, complete 'excuse' of excessive defence. If D has to use force to defend himself . . . in law

---

[77] 45 Tenn 476 (1868).

[78] The courts have had relatively little to say about *Gilbert* or *Waller*. However, it is worth noting that Holmes J singled *Gilbert* out for mention on several occasions. Overall, he remained agnostic on whether it was correctly decided: *Miller v Horton* 152 Mass 540, 547; 26 NE 100, 102 (1891); *Spade v Lynn & BRR* 172 Mass 488, 489; 52 NE 747, 747 (1899); *The Eliza Lines* 199 US 119, 130–31 (1905). Blackstone J, in his dissenting opinion in *Scott v Shepherd* (1773) 2 Black W 892, 896; 96 ER 525, 527, cited *Gilbert* with approval and asserted that 'Not even menaces from others are sufficient to justify a trespass against a third person'.

[79] A person who commits a tort under duress may have a claim in tort against the person who compelled him to act. It is doubtful that such a claim would be defeated by the defence of illegality, at least where the claimant would be able to resist the imposition of criminal liability via the criminal law defence of duress. It seems that the defence of illegality is not engaged where the claimant commits an offence but possesses a criminal law defence: *Miller v Miller* [2009] WACA 199; (2009) 54 MVR 367, 384 [78] (the issue was not dealt with on appeal to the High Court: [2011] HCA 9; (2011) 242 CLR 446). See further J Goudkamp, 'The Defence of Joint Illegal Enterprise' (2010) 34 *Melbourne University Law Review* 425, 432–33.

[80] 'In general, one cannot excuse a tort by showing that he committed it under duress': TM Cooley, *A Treatise on the Law of Torts, or, The Wrongs which arise Independent of Contract* (Chicago, Ill, Callaghan and Co, 1880) 115; 'duress [is] not recognised as an excuse': Fleming (n 4) 107; 'Duress, or threatened injury to a person unless he commits a tort, was held many years ago to be no defence if he does commit it': Rogers (n 14) 1173 [25.37].

[81] See the text accompanying n 10 in ch 2.

[82] The law on this point has been modified by statute in New South Wales: Civil Liability Act 2002 (NSW), s 53(1). For discussion of this provision, see J Goudkamp, 'Self-Defence and Illegality Under the *Civil Liability Act* 2002 (NSW)' (2010) 18 *Torts Law Journal* 61, 20–21.

[83] Horder (n 42) 56.

that force must . . . have been reasonable if it is to be truly justified. English law takes a generous view, however, of how the jury should go about its task of judging the element of reasonableness in D's use of force. It is within this generous view that a complete excuse for a slightly excessive defensive reaction lies concealed.

In support of his argument Horder cites cases in which it has been stressed that allowances should be made where a defendant had to act on the spur of the moment in assessing whether the defensive force that he applied was in proportion to the threat or perceived threat.[84] As judges have made equivalent remarks in tort cases,[85] it is worth asking whether tort law recognises a hidden defence of excessive self-defence. The difficulty with the suggestion that tort law provides for such a defence, and with Horder's analysis generally, is that it overlooks the fact that a court's determination that a defendant acted reasonably is conclusive for legal purposes. One might, like Horder, disagree with a court's conclusion in this connection. But in doing so, one is adopting a private perspective from which to assess whether a defendant is justified.

4.3.2.6. Mistaken belief in the existence of justifying circumstances

Suppose that D sees C walking towards him and concludes, reasonably, that C is a mugger who is about to attack him. D disables C on account of his belief that C is a mugger. It transpires that D was mistaken and that C is an innocent pedestrian. Is D justified in committing a battery against C? Or is he merely excused? These questions bear upon the satisfactoriness of the taxonomy of tort law defences which has been advanced in this chapter. Because tort law sometimes extends defences that ordinarily apply only where it was reasonable to commit a tort to defendants who mistakenly but reasonably believed that committing a tort was justified,[86] it is crucial to determine whether such defendants are justified or excused. If they are merely excused, the taxonomy of defences that has been promoted would need to be revised.

---

[84] The classic remark to this effect is Holmes J's statement that '[d]etached reflection cannot be demanded in the presence of an uplifted knife': *Brown v United States* 256 US 335, 343 (1921). See also *Palmer v R* [1971] AC 814, 832 (PC) (Lord Morris of Borth-y-Gest):'If there has been attack so that defence is reasonably necessary it will be recognised that a person defending himself cannot weigh to a nicety the exact measure of his necessary defensive action.' These observations have recently been put on a statutory footing: Criminal Justice and Immigration Act 2008 (UK), s 76(7).

[85] In *Reed v Wastie* [1972] Crim LR 221 (QBD), Geoffrey Lane J said 'one does not use jewellers' scales to measure reasonable force'. Similarly, in *Cross v Kirkby* The Times, 5 April 2000 (CA), Judge LJ remarked that the law does not require D 'to measure the violence to be deployed with mathematical precision'.

[86] Examples of such defences include self-defence (*Ashley v Chief Constable of Sussex Police* [2008] UKHL 25; [2008] 1 AC 962 (HL); *Attorney-General v Leason* [2011] NZHC 1053 [67]), defence of others (*Gambriell v Caparelli* (1974) 7 OR (2d) 205; (1974) 54 DLR (3d) 661 (CC)) and arrest (Police and Criminal Evidence Act 1984 (UK), s 24). It seems that the defence of justification to the action for inducing a breach of contract departs from this trend: *Read v The Friendly Society of Operative Stonemasons of England, Ireland and Wales* [1902] 2 KB 88, 96 (Div Ct). The same may be the case in relation to public necessity: *Scott v Wakem* (1862) 3 F & F 328, 334; 176 ER 147, 150.

The case of the defendant who reasonably but mistakenly believes that his impugned act was justified has been debated at great length in criminal law circles. It is possible to draw on this literature, given that criminal law scholars have not attached their own special meaning to the concept of justification.[87] That concept is obviously one known outside the law to which both the criminal law and tort law have helped themselves. The two most conspicuous contributors to the criminal law scholarship concerning defendants who committed an offence due to a reasonable mistake are Paul Robinson[88] and George Fletcher.[89] They first locked horns on the issue in the mid-1970s and have argued over it ever since. Robinson champions the 'deeds theory' of justification. This theory holds that a defendant is justified in Φing so long as the reasons in favour of Φing outweigh the countervailing reasons. It is irrelevant on this account whether the defendant was aware of the reasons in favour of Φing. Fletcher defends the 'dual theory' of justification. On this theory, a defendant is not justified in Φing unless there was an undefeated reason for Φing *and* the defendant was aware of that reason. A third theory of justification is the 'reasons theory'. Pursuant to the reasons theory, a defendant is not justified in Φing unless he reasonably believed that there was an undefeated reason for Φing. It is immaterial on this view whether there was such a reason.

The three theories often lead to the same conclusion. For example, a defendant who Φs believing there to be an undefeated reason to Φ, is justified on all three theories if such a reason exists. However, there are two situations in which the theories yield different outcomes. The first is the case of the defendant who labours under a mistaken belief that his acts are supported by an undefeated reason. Such a defendant is not justified according to the deeds theory or the dual theory. Most proponents of the deeds or dual theory think, however, that such a defendant is excused, provided that his mistake was reasonable. The second and much less common situation in which the theories yield different results involves so-called 'unknowingly justified defendants'. Unknowingly justified defendants

[87] Kent Greenawalt writes that '"[j]ustified" is most definitely not a special legal term': Greenawalt (n 50) 1903 (footnote omitted)). Similarly, John Gardner states that [t]he legal point of view ... is widely noted for putting its own specialized glosses on everyday words. But English criminal law, at any rate, has not yet paid that particular compliment to the word "justification"': Gardner (n 23) 94.

[88] Robinson (1975) (n 27); Robinson (n 25) 239–40; PH Robinson, *Criminal Law Defenses*, vol 2 (St Paul, Minn, West Publishing Co, 1984) 7–29; PH Robinson, 'Rules of Conduct and Principles of Adjudication' (1990) 57 *University of Chicago Law Review* 729, 749–52; PH Robinson, 'The Bomb Thief and the Theory of Justification Defenses' (1997) 8 *Criminal Law Forum* 387; Robinson (1997) (n 27) 100–24; PH Robinson, 'Justification Defenses in Situations of Unavoidable Uncertainty: A Reply to Professor Ferzan' (2005) 24 *Law & Philosophy* 775; PH Robinson, 'Objective versus Subjective Justification: A Case Study in Function and Form in Constructing a System of Criminal Law Theory' in PH Robinson, SP Garvey and KK Ferzan (eds), *Criminal Law Conversations* (Oxford, Oxford University Press, 2009); PH Robinson and JM Darley, 'Testing Competing Theories of Justification' (1998) 76 *North Carolina Law Review* 1095.

[89] GP Fletcher, 'The Right Deed for the Wrong Reason: A Reply to Mr Robinson' (1975) 23 *University of California Los Angeles Law Review* 293; Fletcher (n 10) 762–69; Fletcher (n 25) 239–45; Fletcher (n 26); Fletcher (n 57); GP Fletcher, 'Domination in the Theory of Justification and Excuse' (1996) 57 *University of Pittsburgh Law Review* 553, 563–67; GP Fletcher, *Basic Concepts of Criminal Law* (Oxford, Oxford University Press, 1998) 101–06.

are defendants who commit a justifiable act without realising that it is justifiable. Imagine that D wants to murder C. D locates C in a crowded shopping mall and shoots him dead. Unbeknownst to D, C was a terrorist and was about to detonate a bomb that was strapped to his body. By shooting C, D saved the lives of many people. D is justified in shooting C on the deeds theory. The fact that he did not know that C was a terrorist is irrelevant. But he is not justified on either the reasons theory or the dual theory as he was unaware of C's nefarious plot. Indeed, because D did not operate under a reasonable mistake, both the reasons theory and the dual theory hold that D is not even excused. These outcomes are summarised in Table 2 below. The crucial column for present purposes is the third column. It reveals that if either the deeds theory or the dual theory is correct, tort law provides for excuses.

Table 2: Outcomes of the Three Theories of Justification

	Defendant knows that facts justify	Defendant knows that facts do not justify	Defendant reasonably but mistakenly believes that facts justify	Defendant unreasonably believes that facts justify	Defendant unaware that facts justify (unknowing justification)
Deeds theory	Justified	Unjustified and unexcused	Excused	Unjustified and unexcused	Justified
Reasons theory	Justified	Unjustified and unexcused	Justified	Unjustified and unexcused	Unjustified and unexcused
Dual theory	Justified	Unjustified and unexcused	Excused	Unjustified and unexcused	Unjustified and unexcused

The deeds theory enjoys little support, primarily because it holds that unknowingly justified defendants are justified, an outcome that strikes many people as self-evidently wrong. It has been described as 'impossible to accept',[90] 'absurd'[91] and 'offen[sive to] one's intuitive moral sense'.[92] Paul Robinson, who has argued tirelessly in favour of it, is virtually its only proponent.[93] Many of Robinson's arguments quickly descend into confusion. Consider, for instance, Robinson's attempt to support the deeds theory by reference to the distinction between justifications and excuses.[94] Robinson claims that whereas excuses deal with the actor, justifications focus on the act.[95] He then asserts that the fact that justifications are

---

[90] M Corrado, 'Notes on the Structure of a Theory of Excuses' (1991) 82 *Journal of Criminal Law & Criminology* 465, 489.

[91] B Hogan, 'The *Dadson* Principle' [1989] *Criminal Law Review* 679, 680.

[92] K Greenawalt, 'Distinguishing Justifications from Excuses' (1986) 49 *Law and Contemporary Problems* 89, 102.

[93] Although see Byrd (n 26) 1315–21; Schopp (n 30) 35–40.

[94] Robinson (1975) (n 27) 274–75, 280, 283–84.

[95] 'In determining whether given conduct is justified, the focus is upon the *act*, not the *actor* . . . Excuse, on the other hand, focuses on the actor, rather than the act': *ibid*, 274–75 (emphasis in original).

concerned with acts supports the deeds theory.[96] This argument fails since it assumes to be true that which it sets out prove, namely, that justifications are concerned exclusively with acts. Furthermore, the distinction between justifications and excuses does not correspond to that between acts and actors.[97] The suggestion that justification defences are concerned with acts ignores, among other things, the fact that certain justification defences depend on the role played by the actor. Take, for example, the defence of discipline.[98] A person is eligible for this defence in respect of force used to chastise a child only if he is the child's parent.[99] A person who does not occupy a parental role with respect to a child whom he disciplines cannot take advantage of this defence. It is irrelevant that the child's parent would also have punished the child and would have done so in precisely the same way. Similarly, take the provisions in the Police and Criminal Evidence Act 1984 (UK)[100] that authorise constables to stop and search persons for stolen or prohibited articles. These provisions furnish constables with a justificatory defence to any liability in tort that they would otherwise incur by detaining and searching persons. However, this defence is not available to an ordinary citizen who stops and searches another citizen for contraband. This is so even if the first citizen acts in way that would attract the defence were he a constable.

Another of Robinson's arguments depends on supposed inter-party effects of justifications.[101] This argument can be illustrated with an example. Imagine that D uses force to disable C on account of his reasonable but mistaken belief that C is an aggressor. If the reasons theory is right, D is justified and, Robinson tells us, C must submit to D's attack since a person should not resist justified acts. Robinson says that this result is counter-intuitive. He concludes that the deeds theory is, therefore, preferable, since it holds that D is unjustified and that C can, therefore, resist him. Two problems loom large for this argument. First, it does nothing to show that the deeds theory is superior to the dual theory. The dual theory, like the deeds theory, holds that D's attack is unjustified. Secondly, this argument takes for granted that which it seeks to prove. It is only impermissible to resist a justified actor if the deeds or dual theory is right. However, if the reasons theory is correct, it may be justifiable to resist a justified actor.

A key defect in the deeds theory is that it does not recognise fully the importance of the role that reasons play in relation to the concept of justification. Because of the connection between reasons and the idea of justification, justifications reflect on one's success as a rational being. To claim that one is justified is to make a claim

---

[96] '[T]he principle of justification should not contain actor-orientated considerations, such as ... belief': *ibid*, 280.

[97] The analysis here draws on Greenawalt (n 50) 1915–18. See also M Thorburn, 'Justifications, Powers, and Authority' (2008) 117 *Yale Law Journal* 1070, 1072.

[98] See 5.2.2.5.

[99] Teachers may no longer inflict corporal punishment: Education Act 1996 (UK), s 548. This is so even if the teacher is 'authorised' by the child's parent to administer such punishment: *R v Secretary of State for Education and Employment, ex p Williamson* [2005] UKHL 15; [2005] 2 AC 246, 256 [12]–[14].

[100] Police and Criminal Evidence Act 1984 (UK), pt 1.

[101] Robinson (1997) (n 27) 106–08.

about the quality of one's life. Consequently, the deeds theory cannot possibly be correct, since one cannot claim that the fact that one's act was supported by the balance of reasons reflects favourably on one as a rational agent unless, among other things, one was aware of the relevant reasons. The deeds theory should be rejected.

Whereas the deeds theory has been rejected by most theorists, the dual theory has many supporters.[102] The dual theory, it will be recalled, holds that a defendant is not justified unless he both had an undefeated reason for committing his impugned act *and* was aware of that reason. Fletcher is one of the main advocates for the dual theory.[103] Fletcher argues that the supposed effects that justification defences have on the permissibility of assistance and resistance support the dual theory.[104] He invites us to imagine the following scenario. A group of robbers break into a shop. The shopkeeper fires at them in an attempt to drive them away. A plain-clothes police officer arrives on the scene. The shopkeeper thinks, reasonably, that the police officer is one of the robbers and shoots at him. The police officer, who realises that the shopkeeper has made a mistake, must fire back or risk being killed or seriously injured. Fletcher argues that if the shopkeeper is justified in shooting at the police officer, it is impermissible for the officer to fire back. Because this result is counter-intuitive, Fletcher says that the dual theory of justification should be adopted since, on this theory, the shopkeeper is merely excused and it is therefore permissible for the police officer to resist him. This argument is not up to the task that Fletcher sets for it. In the first place, it equally supports the deeds theory.[105] On the deeds theory, the shopkeeper's act is also unjustified since there was no reason to shoot the police officer. Another problem with this argument is that it assumes that it is impermissible to resist justified conduct. This is true only if the dual theory (or the deeds theory) is correct. This argument therefore takes as its premise something that it is trying to prove.

Fletcher also appeals to supposed differences in our emotional responses to harming an aggressor as opposed to a person who is mistakenly perceived to be an aggressor to support the dual theory. He writes:[106]

> Consider the difference in personal sentiments that follow upon justified self-defense as compared with putatively justified self-defense. If I have disabled an aggressor who was trying to injure me or a member of my family, I should feel that I have done the right thing. I would not be inclined to feel regret or remorse about the injury that I necessarily inflicted in repelling the attack. I would feel no need to apologize to the injured aggressor. Nor would it be appropriate to think about making amends. But if I have killed an innocent person who seemed, perhaps reasonably, to be attacking me, should I not feel differently about the harm done? The appropriate response would be at least

---

[102] Eg, Horder (n 42) 49; KK Ferzan, 'Justifying Self-Defense' (2005) 24 *Law and Philosophy* 711; F Leverick, *Killing in Self-Defence* (Oxford, Oxford University Press, 2006) 23–37; Bergelson (n 30) 2486; Duff (n 42) 280–81; Gardner (n 23) 95–103.

[103] See n 89 above.

[104] Fletcher (n 10) 763–68.

[105] Robinson makes precisely the same argument in defence of the deeds theory: see the text accompanying n 101 above.

[106] Fletcher (n 26) 1363.

to be concerned that I have saved my life at the expense of an innocent and unoffending person. If I had done the right thing in acting on my reasonable beliefs, I should hardly feel it appropriate to make amends. But my remorse is appropriate for it is wrong, a great wrong, to kill an innocent person. The reasonableness of my mistake hardly alleviates the wrong in killing. My mistake might excuse my wrongdoing; it might check efforts to hold me criminally or tortiously liable. But my mistake hardly converts a wrongful act into one that is right and proper.

This argument proceeds on the footing that adverse normative consequences do not obtain in respect of justified acts. This is simply untrue.[107] People often have to bear adverse normative consequences in respect of justified acts. This has already been demonstrated.[108] There are always reasons not to kill or injure persons, even aggressors. These reasons render it appropriate, among other things, to regret the fact that the exigencies of a situation required one to injure or kill to save oneself.

There are at least two reasons for looking askance at the dual theory. First, it leads to the counter-intuitive conclusion that a person may find himself in a situation, through no fault of his own, where he is unjustified no matter how he acts.[109] Suppose that D appears to pose a threat to T, C's baby, but in fact poses no threat. C has a choice: he can either disable D or do nothing. C is unjustified on the dual theory no matter what he decides to do. He is unjustified if he disables D, since D in fact posed no threat to C. He is unjustified in doing nothing, since he was unaware of the fact that makes this choice justifiable, namely, that D was not an aggressor. It is difficult to accept that scenarios exist in which no course of action is justified. If, as seems to be the case, the hypothetical reasonable person is always justified, a theory that admits of the possibility that situations exist where there is no justified available course of action should not be accepted.

A second reason for doubting the dual theory is that, if it is right, it follows that it is impossible to tell for certain whether a given act is justified.[110] It is impossible to ascertain whether a particular act is justified on the dual theory because it is always possible that future facts will reveal that an act that appeared to be unjustified when it was performed was actually justified and vice versa. The fact that, on the dual theory, it cannot be known whether a given act is justified weds dual theorists to the unattractive proposition that whenever it is said that a person is justified (or unjustified), what is really being said is that the person concerned is provisionally justified (or unjustified).

The analysis so far has identified reasons for doubting the deeds theory and the dual theory of justification. Attention will now be turned to the reasons theory of

---

[107] Tellingly, Fletcher retreats from this argument in later work. For instance, in GP Fletcher, 'The Right to Life' (1979) 13 *Georgia Law Review* 1371, 1385–86 he concedes that there are instances where we may regret harming an aggressor.

[108] See 4.3.1.1.

[109] This argument is based on the analysis in H Stewart, 'The Role of Reasonableness in Self-Defence' (2003) 16 *Canadian Journal of Law & Jurisprudence* 317, 321–23.

[110] The argument here has been heavily influenced by Tadros (n 6) 288–89.

justification, which, like the dual theory, enjoys considerable support.[111] One complaint that has frequently been made about the reasons theory is that it leads to the conclusion that justified acts can conflict.[112] It is certainly true that justifications can conflict on the reasons theory. Two people who reasonably but mistakenly think that the other is an aggressor and use defensive force against each other are both justified on the reasons theory. But why should this incident of the reasons theory stand in the way of accepting it? Given that justification defences are permissions not duties,[113] it is hard to see why the proposition that justified acts can conflict is unpalatable.

A second criticism that is often levelled against the reasons theory is that, by labelling as justified persons who act under a mistaken belief that their act is justified, the reasons theory regards persons who might regret or feel the need to apologise for their behaviour as justified.[114] It is true that persons who (for example) mistakenly believe on reasonable grounds that they are about to be attacked and disable the perceived aggressor may regret their act and want to apologise. But, as has already been explained,[115] this is true also of persons who commit a justifiable act knowing that it is justified.

It has been show that some criticisms of the reasons theory are misguided, but what can be said in support of this theory? One point in its favour is that it is the only theory of justification that does not draw morally meaningless distinctions between actors. Suppose that D1 and D2 each kill a person. They both believed on reasonable grounds that killing was justified (they both thought, say, that the person they killed was an aggressor who was about to launch a lethal attack on them). However, only the person whom D1 killed was in fact an aggressor. Why should D1 and D2 have different labels applied to them, given that there is nothing to separate them in terms of their thought processes, the way in which they acted or the outcomes of their acts? Do they not stand in a morally identical, or substantially identical, situation?

The analysis in this section has been long. It has asked whether persons who mistakenly but reasonably commit a justifiable act are justified or excused. This issue is of great importance for the purposes of constructing a taxonomy of tort law defences since tort law often gives such persons a defence. Three theories of justification were considered in this regard: the deeds theory, the dual theory and the reasons theory. If either the deeds theory or the dual theory is correct, defend-

---

[111] Proponents of the reasons theory of justification include C Fried, *Right and Wrong* (Cambridge, Mass, Harvard University Press, 1978) 48; Greenawalt (n 50) especially at 1908–09; Greenawalt (n 92) 101–04; RL Christopher, 'Mistake of Fact in the Objective Theory of Justification: Do Two Rights Make Two Wrongs Make Two Rights . . .?' (1994) 85 *Journal of Criminal Law & Criminology* 295; L Crocker, 'Improving the Codes' (1999) 10 *Criminal Law Forum* 151, 154–57; Stewart (n 109); Baron (n 10) 393, 398–406; Tadros (n 6) 280–90; A Botterell, 'Why We Ought to be (Reasonable) Subjectivists about Justification' (2007) 26 *Criminal Justice Ethics* 36.

[112] Eg, Fletcher writes that 'incompatible actions cannot both be justified': Fletcher (n 57) 975.

[113] See 2.3.6.

[114] See, for example, the passage in the paragraph accompanying n 106 above.

[115] See the text accompanying n 25 above.

ants who act on the basis of a reasonable mistake about the existence of justifying facts are excused and not justified. It would follow that the taxonomy of defences that has been promoted in this chapter would need to be revised and a category would need to be reserved for excuses. Conversely, if the reasons theory is correct, a defendant who acts due to a reasonable but mistaken belief that justifying facts exist is justified. It was argued that the reasons theory is correct. If this is right, the case of the defendant who mistakenly believes that committing a tort is justified does not show that tort law provides for excuses.

4.3.2.7. *Defective motive*

Consider the following scenario. D is out walking and sees C murderously attacking T. D despises C and decides to hurt him. D attacks C. D realises that doing so will save T but he does not care one iota about T; he attacks C solely because he wants to injure him. It is clear that it was justifiable for D to disable C: disabling C would save T. D was aware of the reason that made his conduct justifiable, but he did not act for that reason. This raises the question whether mere knowledge of, or a reasonable belief in the existence of, an undefeated reason to commit an act is sufficient to establish that a defendant is justified in performing the act concerned. If it is necessary to act for the right reason in order to be justified, any defence that tort law would extend to D might be an excuse.[116]

The threat to the two-fold taxonomy of tort law defences posed by the case of the defendant who commits a justifiable act for the wrong reason needs to be considered by way of asking two questions. First, are such defendants justified? If this question is answered in the affirmative, the present challenge to the bipartite taxonomy of defences falls away. But if this question is answered in the negative, it is necessary to ask a second question: Are defences that are reserved for defendants who commit a justifiable act insensitive to the motivation with which the justifiable act is performed? If an affirmative answer is given to this question then the two-fold taxonomy would be inadequate.

Can a defectively motivated defendant be justified? George Fletcher was the first legal theorist to consider the connection between justification and motivation in any real detail, but he could not make up his mind as to whether motivation matters. In one part of *Rethinking Criminal Law* he wrote that 'actors may avail themselves of justifications only if they act with a justificatory intent'.[117] This suggests that the fact that a given act is justifiable must have been the main or exclusive reason why the defendant committed the act concerned. A few pages later, Fletcher appeared to change tack and claimed that to be justified 'the actor must at least be cognizant of the justificatory circumstances'.[118] In *The Grammar of Criminal Law*, however, Fletcher no longer equivocated. He came down decisively in support of

---

[116] Tadros thinks that a defendant who committed a justifiable act for the wrong reason might be excused: Tadros (n 6) 280.

[117] Fletcher (n 10) 557.

[118] *Ibid*, 559. See also at 563.

the view that only those defendants who are properly motivated in performing justifiable acts are justified.[119]

What have other theorists said on the subject? Those who embrace the reasons or dual theory of justification generally believe that a defendant's motive bears upon the issue of justification.[120] In contrast, deeds theorists naturally reject the suggestion that justification depends on motivation.[121] They deny the existence of a distinction between justifiable and justified acts. In their view, a defendant is justified so long as there was an undefeated reason in support of his action. It is unnecessary for him to be conscious of, let alone act for, that reason.[122]

It is doubtful that the label of justification should be applied to defectively motivated defendants.[123] To claim that one is justified is to claim some credit for the way in which one led one's life in some relevant respect. It is surely the case, however, that one should not speak more highly of a person as a rational being than would otherwise be the case simply because he is conscious of the existence of an undefeated reason for action. Why should it be thought that a person who knows of an undefeated reason for action but who does not act for that reason is in a morally different position from a person who commits a justifiable act without realising that it is justifiable? Because no credit can be earned from pointing to the fact that one knew of a reason for which one did not act, defectively motivated defendants are not justified.

The conclusion that defectively motivated defendants who commit a justifiable act are unjustified leads to the second question, which is whether defences that are reserved for defendants who commit justifiable acts are available regardless of the motivation with which the justifiable act is performed. It is necessary to turn here to the substantive law. It seems that the defences in issue are sensitive to the defendant's motivation. Several examples will be given. Take, first, the defence of qualified privilege. This defence, which is restricted to defendants who act justifiably in publishing a defamatory statement about the claimant,[124] requires the defendant to be properly motivated. It is well established that a defendant who acts maliciously in publishing a defamatory statement on an occasion that attracts qualified privilege will not enjoy the defence.[125]

---

[119] GP Fletcher, *The Grammar of Criminal Law: American, Comparative, and International*, vol 1 (Oxford, Oxford University Press, 2007) 14.

[120] Eg, AM Dillof, 'Unraveling Unknowing Justification' (2002) 77 *Notre Dame Law Review* 1547, 1595–99; Tadros (n 6) 273–80; MN Berman, 'Lesser Evils and Justification: A Less Close Look' (2005) 24 *Law and Philosophy* 681, 705–08; Duff (n 42) 280–81; Gardner (n 23) 94–103.

[121] Eg, Robinson (1975) (n 27) 287; Byrd (n 26) 1304.

[122] Some theorists who do not seem to be dyed-in-the-wool deeds theorists have also argued that being justified does not depend on one's motivation: eg, L Alexander, 'Unknowingly Justified Actors and the Attempt/Success Distinction' (2004) 39 *Tulsa Law Review* 851, 852–53; L Alexander, 'Lesser Evils: A Closer Look at the Paradigmatic Justification' (2005) 24 *Law and Philosophy* 611, 619–20; L Crocker, 'Justification and Bad Motives' (2008) 6 *Ohio State Journal of Criminal Law* 277. Peter Cane expresses some sympathy for the proposition that a bad motive does not bar the defendant from being justified, in P Cane, *The Anatomy of Tort Law* (Oxford, Hart Publishing, 1997) 35.

[123] The argument in this paragraph is essentially that made by Gardner (n 23) 94–103.

[124] See further 5.2.1.7.

[125] The role that malice plays in relation to the defence of qualified privilege is discussed in 2.2.2.

A second example is the defence of discipline. This defence is confined to defendants who act justifiably in committing a tort.[126] It too depends on the defendant's motive. In *R v Hopley*, Cockburn CJ remarked:[127]

> [A] parent . . . may for the purpose of correcting what is evil in the child inflict moderate and reasonable corporal punishment . . . *If it be administered for the gratification of passion or of rage* . . . the punishment is excessive, the violence is unlawful.

A third illustration is the defence of responsible journalism. This defence is evidently confined to situations where it is justifiable to publish defamatory statements.[128] It seems, although authority on this point is admittedly scanty, that the defence is conditional upon the defendant's motive. In *Flood v Times Newspapers Ltd*,[129] Lord Phillips of Worth Matravers PSC[130] and Lord Mance JSC[131] appeared to think that a defendant's reasons for publishing a defamatory statement might bear upon the defence's availability.[132]

A fourth example concerns the defence of recapture of land. It appears that this defence, which is justifactory in nature,[133] will be unavailable unless the reason that the defendant used force against the claimant occupier was to eject him. This is the view expressed in the Restatement (Second) of Torts. Section 93 provides:

> Force used against another in taking possession of land is not privileged unless the force is used for the purpose of regaining possession of the land or of effecting an entry upon it.

It is unclear whether the defence of self-defence, which is restricted to defendants whose tort is justifiable,[134] adheres to this pattern. *Presidential Security Services of Australia Pty Ltd v Brilley*[135] suggests that it does not. In this case, an armed security guard in the employ of the defendant was patrolling the defendant's sports club. He spotted the claimant preparing to break in and lay in wait for him. When the claimant gained entry to the club, the guard opened fire. The guard continued firing at the claimant after the claimant began to retreat. One of the bullets struck the claimant. The defendant, resisting an action for damages, argued that its guard was acting in self-defence. The claimant contended that the defence was inapplicable as the guard had been motivated primarily by a desire to cause injury rather than to defend himself. The judge at first instance accepted this argument and rejected the defence of self-defence. An appeal to the New South Wales Court of Appeal succeeded. Ipp JA, speaking for the Court on this point, said that the trial judge's 'finding of callous intention to cause injury says nothing

---

[126] See further 5.2.2.5.
[127] (1860) 2 F & F 202, 206; 175 ER 1024, 1026 (emphasis added).
[128] See further 5.2.2.6.
[129] [2012] UKSC 11; [2012] 2 AC 273.
[130] *Ibid*, 297–98 [69].
[131] *Ibid*, 330 [179].
[132] Cf *ibid*, 335–36 [200]–[202] (Lord Dyson JSC).
[133] See further 5.2.1.4.
[134] See further 5.2.1.1.
[135] [2008] NSWCA 204; (2008) 73 NSWLR 241. For further analysis of this decision, see Goudkamp (n 82) 79–80.

about whether, in causing that injury, the [guard] acted in self-defence'.[136] A criminal law case that is on all fours with *Brilley* in this respect is *Golden v State*. In this matter the Court said:[137]

> Whenever the circumstances of the killing would not amount to murder, the proof even of express malice will not make it so. One may harbor the most intense hatred toward another; he may court an opportunity to take his life; may rejoice while he is imbruing his hands in his heart's blood; and yet, if, to save his own life, the facts showed that he was fully justified in slaying his adversary, his malice shall not be taken into account. This principle is too plain to need amplification.

Laws v State,[138] another criminal case, points in the opposite direction. This was an appeal against a murder conviction on the basis that the trial judge had instructed the jury that the defendant could not escape liability on the ground that he was defending his property if he was badly motivated in doing so. The Court said that 'If the killing was upon malice, and not to prevent a theft, or the consequences of a theft, it would not be justified . . . although a theft . . . was actually being committed . . . at the time he was killed.'[139]

The defence of justification to an action for inducing a breach of contract may be another deviation from this trend. In several American cases it was held that the motive of a defendant who has a good reason for interfering with a contract is irrelevant. According to these authorities, the defendant's motives 'are not to be inquired into',[140] and it is thus irrelevant that the defendant might have been motivated by bitterness and hostility towards the claimant.[141] A contrary view was apparently taken by Collins MR in *Read v The Friendly Society of Operative Stonemasons of England, Ireland and Wales*. The Master of the Rolls said that 'the justification to be of any avail must cover [the defendants'] whole conduct, the means they used as well as the end they had in view'.[142]

The balance of authority appears to favour the view that defences that depend upon the justifiability of the defendant's conduct are not generally available where the defendant acted for the wrong reason. If this is correct, it follows that the case of the defectively motivated defendant who commits a tort in circumstances where doing so is justifiable does not pose a threat to the two-fold taxonomy of tort law defences developed in this chapter.

---

[136] [2008] NSWCA 204; (2008) 73 NSWLR 241, 263 [132]. The defendant succeeded in the retrial: *Brilley v Presidential Security Services of Australia Pty Ltd* [2009] NSWDC 14.

[137] 25 Ga 527, 532 (1858).

[138] 26 Tex App 643; 10 SW 220 (Ct App 1888).

[139] *Ibid*, Tex App 655; SW 221. See also *People v Williams* 32 Cal 280, 285–86 (1867); *Wortham v State* 70 Ga 336 (1883); *Lyons v People* 137 Ill 602, 618–19; 27 NE 677, 682 (1891); *Surges v State* 88 Tex Crim 288, 292; 225 SW 1103, 1105 (1920); *Garcia v State* 237 SW 279, 281 (Tex Crim App 1922).

[140] *O'Brien v Western Union Telegraph Co* 114 P 441, 442; 62 Wash 598, 603 (1911).

[141] *Bentley v Teton* 153 NE 2d 495, 498; 19 Ill App 2d 284, 289 (App Ct 1958). See also *Stevens v Siegel* 18 AD 2d 1109; 239 NYS 2d 827 (Sup Ct App Div 1963).

[142] [1902] 2 KB 732, 737 (CA).

4.3.2.8. Conclusion

This section asked whether tort law provides for excuses. It considered numerous possible ways in which excuses might creep into tort law. The analysis failed to undercover clear evidence of the existence of excuses in tort law. Accordingly, it is submitted that a taxonomy of tort law defences does not need to include a category for excuses.

4.3.3. Denials of Responsibility

The concept of a denial of basic responsibility was discussed earlier in this chapter.[143] A denial of basic responsibility is a plea by the defendant that he was incapable of understanding reasons. The criminal law recognises several defences that constitute denials of basic responsibility, the most important of which are insanity,[144] infancy[145] and unfitness to plead.[146] The purpose of this section is to consider whether tort law also provides for these or any other types of denial of basic responsibility defences. If tort law recognises any such defences, a separate category must to be reserved for them (they should not be lumped together with excuses for the reasons that have already been given[147]).

4.3.3.1. Insanity[148]

The fact that the defendant was insane at the time of committing a tort is not, and has never been, a defence. The early case of *Weaver v Ward*[149] is widely regarded as the *fons et origo* of this rule.[150] The parties to this dispute were soldiers who were skirmishing in a military exercise. The defendant 'by chance and misadventure' fired his gun and wounded the claimant. The King's Bench found the defendant liable. However, in reaching this conclusion the court took the opportunity to provide some illustrations of instances in which a person would not incur liability

---

[143] See 4.3.2.2. See also 8.2.

[144] Criminal Procedure (Insanity) Act 1964 (UK), s 1.

[145] Children and Young Persons Act 1933 (UK), s 50.

[146] Criminal Procedure (Insanity) Act 1964 (UK), s 4.

[147] See 4.3.2.2.

[148] Tort law's treatment of insane defendants has been much discussed. Some of the more important contributions include WGH Cook, 'Mental Deficiency in Relation to Tort' (1921) 21 *Columbia Law Review* 333; FH Bohlen, 'Liability in Tort of Infants and Insane Persons' (1924) 23 *Michigan Law Review* 9; GJ Alexander and TS Szasz, 'Mental Illness as an Excuse for Civil Wrongs' (1967) 43 *Notre Dame Law Review* 24; JW Ellis, 'Tort Responsibility of Mentally Disabled Persons' [1981] *American Bar Foundation Research Journal* 1079; SI Splane, 'Tort Liability of the Mentally Ill in Negligence Actions' (1983) 93 *Yale Law Journal* 153; Law Reform Commission of Ireland, *Report on the Liability in Tort of Mentally Disabled Persons* Report 18 (Dublin, Law Reform Commission of Ireland, 1985); P Kelley, 'Infancy, Insanity, and Infirmity in the Law of Torts' (2003) 48 *American Journal of Jurisprudence* 179.

[149] (1616) Hob 134; 80 ER 284 (KB), analysed in GT Schwartz, 'Weaver v Ward' (1996) 74 *Texas Law Review* 1271.

[150] Although see the earlier case of *Cross v Andrews* (1598) Cro Eliz 622; 78 ER 863.

despite making direct non-consensual contact with the body of another. The report reads:[151]

> [F]or though it were agreed, that if men tilt or turney in the presence of the King, or if two masters of defence playing their prizes kill one another, that this shall be no felony; or if a lunatick kill a man, or the like, because felony must be done animo felonico: yet in trespass, which tends only to give damages according to hurt or loss, it is not so; and therefore if a lunatick hurt a man, he shall be answerable in trespass: and therefore no man shall be excused of a trespass (for this is in the nature of an excuse, and not of a justification, prout ei bene licuit) except it may be judged utterly without his fault.

Two points in particular are worth noting about this passage. First, it is obiter since none of the facts mentioned obtained. Secondly, it seems to harbour a contradiction. On the one hand, it states that a 'lunatick' will be held liable for any trespass that he commits. On the other hand, it provides that liability in trespass will not be imposed on those who are 'utterly without fault'. If the reference to 'fault' means 'blame', this passage is confusing, since a 'lunatic' who commits a trespass will not usually be culpable. Despite the foregoing, this passage has been widely embraced as authority for the proposition that insanity is not a defence to liability in tort generally. Consequently, insane defendants have been held liable in battery,[152] false imprisonment,[153] trespass to land[154] and goods,[155] negligence[156] and even the now extinct torts of criminal conversation and alienation of affections.[157] Admittedly, there is a handful of cases that go the other way and admit insanity as a defence.[158] However, these decisions run counter to the clear preponderance of authority.[159] It can be concluded, therefore, with a reasonable degree of

---

[151] (1616) Hobart 134, 134; 80 ER 284, 284.

[152] Eg, *Taggard v Innes* (1862) 12 UCCP 77; *Mordaunt v Mordaunt* (1870) LR 2 P & D 109; *Ward v Conatser* 63 Tenn 64 (1874); *Donaghey v Brennan* (1900) 19 NZLR 289 (CA); *McGuire v Almy* 297 Mass 323; 8 NE 2d 760 (1937); *Van Vooren v Cook* 273 AD 88 (NY Sup Ct App Div 1947); *Tindale v Tindale* [1950] 4 DLR 363 (BCSC); *Morriss v Marsden* [1952] 1 All ER 925 (QBD); *Donohue v Coyle* [1953–1954] Ir Jur Rep 30 (Circuit Ct); *Phillips v Soloway* (1956) 64 Man R 280; (1956) 6 DLR (2d) 570 (QB); *Shapiro v Tchernowitz* 155 NYS 2d 1011 (Sup Ct 1956); *Beals v Hayward* [1960] NZLR 131 (SC); *Squittieri v de Santis* (1976) 15 OR (2d) 416; (1976) 75 DLR (3d) 629 (SC); *Williams v Kearbey* 13 Kan App 2d 564; 775 P 2d 670 (1989); *Delahanty v Hinckley* 799 F Supp 184 (DDC 1992).

[153] Eg, *Krom v Schoonmaker* 3 Barb 647 (NY 1848).

[154] Eg, *Cross v Kent* 32 Md 581 (Ct App 1870); *In Re Guardianship of Meyer* 218 Wis 381; 261 NW 211 (1935).

[155] Eg, *Morse v Crawford* 17 Vt 499 (1845). Consider also *Williams v Cameron's Estate* 26 Barb 172 (NY Sup Ct 1857).

[156] Eg, *Williams v Hays* 143 NY 422; 38 NE 449 (1894); *Sforza v Green Bus Lines, Inc* 268 NYS 446 (Mun Ct 1934); *Adamson v Motor Vehicle Insurance Trust* (1957) 58 WALR 56 (SC); *Creasy v Rusk* 730 NE 2d 659 (Ind 2000); *Carrier v Bonham* [2001] QCA 234; [2002] 1 Qd R 474.

[157] Eg, *Shedrick v Lathrop* 106 Vt 311; 172 A 630 (1934); *Sweeney v Carter* 24 Tenn App 6; 137 SW 2d 892 (1939).

[158] Eg, *Buckley v Smith Transport Ltd* [1946] OR 798; [1946] 4 DLR 721 (CA) (negligence); *Hutchings v Nevin* (1992) 9 OR (3d) 776 (OCJ) (same); *White v Pile* (1950) 68 WN (NSW) 176 (Div Ct) (battery). There are also some obiter dicta to this effect: see *Emmens v Pottle* (1885) 16 QBD 354, 356 (CA); *Hanbury v Hanbury* (1892) 8 TLR 559, 560 (CA).

[159] That insanity is not a tort defence is confirmed by the Restatement (Second) of Torts. Section 895J provides: 'One who has deficient mental capacity is not immune from tort liability solely

confidence, that those who commit a tort while insane, while they may be able to point to their insanity to deny an element of the tort in which the claimant sues,[160] are not afforded a defence.[161]

4.3.3.2. *Infancy*[162]

It is firmly established throughout the common-law world that the fact that the defendant was an infant at the time of committing a tort is not a defence.[163] As Lord Keynon CJ said in *Jennings v Rundall*, 'if an infant commit an assault, or utter slander, God forbid that he should not be answerable for it in a Court of Justice'.[164] Of course, the fact that the defendant is an infant may open the door to a successful denial.[165] But if all of the elements of the tort in question are in place, the defendant's youth is of no consequence in so far as liability is concerned.[166]

4.3.3.3. *Unfitness to plead*

It is trite law that unfitness to plead is not a tort defence. The defendant will not be able to escape from liability merely because, at the time of the trial, he was, for instance, severely brain-damaged, an infant, deceased[167] or suffering from a mental illness that prevented him from understanding the proceedings.

---

for that reason.' The Reporters supplied the following light-hearted example to illustrate this rule: 'A, who is insane, believes that he is Napoleon Bonaparte, and that B, his nurse, who confines him in his room, is an agent of the Duke of Wellington, who is endeavouring to prevent his arrival on the field of Waterloo in time to win the battle. Seeking to escape, he breaks off the leg of a chair, attacks B with it and fractures her skull. A is subject to liability to B for battery.'

[160] See 3.3.3.

[161] It is argued below that the law in this respect is deficient: see ch 8.

[162] Bohlen (n 148); Law Reform Commission of Ireland, *Liability in Tort of Minors and the Liability of Parents for Damage Caused by Minors*, Report 17 (Dublin, Law Reform Commission of Ireland, 1985); R Bagshaw, 'Children through Tort' in J Fionda (ed), *Legal Concepts of Childhood* (Oxford, Hart Publishing, 2001).

[163] *Ellis v D'Angelo* 116 Cal App 2d 310; 253 P 2d 675 (Ct App 1953) (4-year-old capable of being held liable for battery); *Seaburg v Williams* 16 Ill App 2d 295; 161 NE 2d 576 (1958) (child nearly aged 6 years capable of incurring liability for setting a building on fire); *Baldinger v Banks* 201 NYS 2d 629 (1960) (6-year-old liable for battery). Consider also the remarks in *Hackshaw v Shaw* (1984) 155 CLR 614, 664 (HCA). The Restatement (Second) of Torts, § 895I provides: 'One who is an infant is not immune from tort liability solely for that reason . . .'. An exception to this rule may exist where the conduct also constitutes a breach of contract, at least where the minor is not liable, on account of his age, for the breach of contract. According to *Treitel: The Law of Contract*, 'If a minor engages in [conduct amounting to a breach of contract and a tort, the minor] can sometimes set up the invalidity of the contract as a defence to the tort claim': E Peel (ed), *Treitel: The Law of Contract*, 14th edn (London, Sweet & Maxwell, 2015) 651 [12.034].

[164] (1799) 8 TR 335, 337; 101 ER 1419, 1420–21.

[165] See 3.3.2.

[166] It is argued in ch 8 that this rule should be revised.

[167] Except in relation to actions in defamation: see 5.3.2.10.

4.3.4. Public Policy Defences

One might claim that public policy defences are not really distinct from other types of defences since all defences have (or should have) a foundation in public policy. If all defences are public policy defences then the taxonomy of tort law defences promoted in this chapter is incoherent. It is certainly true that all defences need to be justified: their advantages should outweigh their disadvantages. If a defence, of any type, has more cons than pros, it should be banished from tort law or trimmed down to the extent to which it is supported. But this does not mean that all tort defences are public policy defences. The fact remains that justification defences pose an entirely different type of enquiry from public policy defences. Justifications are concerned with the rational defensibility of the defendant's conduct in question. Public policy defences are not.

4.4. Conclusion

It has been argued that tort defences should be divided into:

(1) justification defences; and
(2) public policy defences.

The categories that constitute this system draw morally significant lines around the different types of arguments that defendants can advance in an attempt to avoid incurring liability in tort. By offering a justification, the defendant admits that he committed a tort but asserts that he acted reasonably in doing so. A defendant who relies on a public policy defence makes no claim whatsoever about the justifiability of his acts.

5

Applying the Taxonomy

5.1. Introduction

It was argued in the previous chapter that all tort law defences can be separated into:

(1) justifications; and
(2) public policy defences.

Justifications, simply stated, relieve the defendant of liability on the ground that he acted reasonably in committing a tort. Public policy defences release the defendant from liability for committing a tort regardless of the justifiability of the defendant's conduct. The aim of this chapter is to identify the category to which individual defences belong. Because tort law provides for so many defences, it is not possible to discuss within the available space how they should all be allocated. Some defences will be skated over, others ignored. However, the analysis that follows demonstrates, it is hoped, that most defences can be neatly slotted into the taxonomy. It is stressed that the goal here is not to elucidate the circumstances in which the defences discussed apply and do not apply. Neither is it to demonstrate when the defences under consideration should or should not apply.

5.2. Justification Defences

This section canvasses a selection of justification defences. It is convenient to sub-divide justifications into private justifications and public justifications.[1] Private

---

[1] Other ways of categorising justifications have been suggested. The Restatement (Second) of Torts, § 10(2) separates justifications into: (1) consent-based justifications; (2) justifications that enable an important interest to be protected; and (3) justifications that enable one to perform an essential function. Robinson organises criminal law justifications into: (1) the 'lesser evils' justification; (2) defensive force justifications; and (3) public authority justifications: PH Robinson, 'Criminal Law Defenses: A Systematic Analysis' (1982) 82 *Columbia Law Review* 199, 213–16. Thornburn arranges justifications to criminal liability by reference to the relationship between the defendant and the person whose rights are affected by the defendant's act in issue. This yields a classification based on justifications available to: (1) fiduciaries; (2) public officials; and (3) ordinary citizens with public powers: M Thorburn, 'Justifications, Powers, and Authority' (2008) 117 *Yale Law Journal* 1070, 1098. Bergelson divides criminal law justifications into: (1) public duty justifications; (2) justifications based on special relationships; (3) justifications that have their foundation in preserving autonomy; and (4) justifications

justifications are defences that relieve the defendant of liability when he acted reasonably in committing a tort in the furtherance of his own interests. In contrast, public justifications are defences that are available when the defendant acted reasonably in committing a tort in order to promote the interests of a section of society or the public generally.

5.2.1. Private Justifications

5.2.1.1. Self-defence

The plea of self-defence falls to be considered in the context of trespass to the person and, under that umbrella concept, generally in relation to the tort of battery, although it is also available in relation to assault and false imprisonment.[2] It is convenient for present purposes to focus on the tort of battery.

Before turning attention to the classification of the defence of self-defence, it is worth pausing to enquire briefly as to whether to plead self-defence is to offer a defence or a denial. Unfortunately, due to the fact that the tort of battery has not been defined consistently, it is not a straightforward task to determine how the plea of self-defence operates. There are many formulations on offer, which often differ wildly from each other, a fact that seems to have passed unnoticed. In *Letang v Cooper*, Lord Denning MR defined a battery as the 'intentional ... [application of] force directly to another'[3] person. In contrast, according to Robert Goff LJ in *Collins v Wilcock*, 'a battery is the actual infliction of unlawful force on another person'.[4] These descriptions differ quite fundamentally in several respects. But most importantly for current purposes, they put a different spin on the doctrine of self-defence. By using the word 'unlawful', Robert Goff LJ incorporates the absence of self-defence within the definition of a battery. Lord Denning MR's definition does not. If Robert Goff LJ is correct, it is doubtful that to plead self-defence is to offer a defence. Rather, an assertion by the defendant that he acted in self-defence appears to be a denial. In contrast, self-defence seems to be a defence on Lord Denning MR's definition of a battery.

Despite the occasional judicial remark that suggests that the absence of justification as an element of the tort of battery,[5] it is doubtful whether these statements

---

that promote efficiency: V Bergelson, 'Rights, Wrongs, and Comparative Justifications' (2007) 28 *Cardozo Law Review* 2481, 2484.

[2] Restatement (Second) of Torts, § 67.

[3] [1965] 1 QB 232, 239 (CA).

[4] [1984] 3 All ER 374, 377; [1984] 1 WLR 1172, 1177 (QBD).

[5] In addition to the passage quoted from Robert Goff LJ's reasons in *Collins v Wilcock*, see *Reibl v Hughes* [1980] 2 SCR 880, 890 (Laskin CJC) ('[the tort of battery] is an intentional one, consisting of an unprivileged and unconsented to invasion of one's bodily security') and *Fagan v Commissioner of Metropolitan Police* [1969] 1 QB 439, 444 (QBD) (James J) ('[the term "battery" means] "the actual intended use of unlawful force to another person without his consent"').

reflect the law. It seems likely that the remarks in question are instances of loose language. The dominant view is that self-defence is a rule that is external to the definition of battery and hence a defence.[6] Where, exceptionally, the effort has been made to enumerate the elements of battery, self-defence is not mentioned.[7] Hence, the analysis will proceed on the assumption that the doctrine of self-defence is a defence.

Within the category of defences, self-defence is evidently a justification. Indeed, it is commonly regarded as the paradigmatic private justification. It is available when the damage about which the claimant complains was inflicted through the application of reasonable defensive force. A defendant who uses unreasonable force is not within the defence,[8] at least to the extent that the force was excessive. The limits of reasonable defensive measures are marked by the rule that protective force must come neither too soon nor too late in order to attract the defence.[9] This principle reflects the fact that it is unreasonable to launch strikes to eliminate a threat that is not imminent, since if one has sufficient notice of an impending attack, one can secure assistance from the authorities. The requirement that defensive force must not come too late[10] excludes acts of revenge and retaliation from the defence.[11] Such acts are unreasonable primarily because the defendant lacks the authority to mete out punishment.[12]

---

[6] Eg, '[a battery is] committed by intentionally bringing about a harmful or offensive contact with another person's body': C Sappideen and P Vines, *Fleming's The Law of Torts*, 10th edn (Sydney, Lawbook Co, 2011) 31 [2.60]; 'A harmful or offensive contact with a person, resulting from an act intended to cause the plaintiff or a third person to suffer such a contact, or apprehension that such a contact is imminent, is a battery': WP Keeton, DB Dobbs, RE Keeton and DG Owen (eds), *Prosser and Keeton on Torts*, 5th edn (St Paul, Minn, West Publishing Co, 1984) 39 (footnote omitted); 'Battery is the intentional and direct application of force to another person': WVH Rogers, *Winfield & Jolowicz on Tort*, 18th edn (London, Sweet & Maxwell, 2010) 104 [4.5]; 'a consideration of self-defence follows only after the elements of the offence have been satisfied, including the proof of an intention to injure': *Presidential Security Services of Australia Pty Ltd v Brilley* [2008] NSWCA 204; (2008) 73 NSWLR 241, 264 [135] (Ipp JA).

[7] Eg, § 18 of the Restatement (Second) of Torts offers a list of the elements of battery that does not contain a reference to self-defence.

[8] See 2.2.2, 4.3.2.5.

[9] *Cockcroft v Smith* (1705) 11 Mod 43; 88 ER 872.

[10] 'Self-defense justifies the use of force only while the apparent danger continues. The right to use force in self-defense ends when the apparent danger ends': *Gortarez v Smitty's Super Valu, Inc* 104 Ariz 97, 105; 680 P 2d 807, 815 (1984).

[11] Although a defendant who acts too late for his conduct to qualify as self-defence may nevertheless be able to benefit from the doctrine of provocation to diminish the damages that he is liable to pay: see 4.3.2.5.

[12] Regarding the distinction between self-defence and punishment, see GP Fletcher, 'Punishment and Self-Defense' (1989) 8 *Law and Philosophy* 201, esp 207–08.

5.2.1.2. Defence of one's property[13]

The plea of defence of one's property is a variation on the same theme as that of self-defence[14] and is, therefore, also a private justification.[15] Like self-defence, it can defeat liability from arising in all of the varieties of trespass to the person, and it is available only when it was reasonable to use force and the force used was proportionate.[16] However, the defence of property defence differs from self-defence in several ways. Most importantly, the maximum amount of force that it permits a defendant to use without incurring liability is lower. Because the law regards interests in property as less valuable than interests in bodily security, all things being equal,[17] a defendant is not permitted to use as much force merely to defend his land or chattels as he may to defend his person. Consequently, whereas it is permissible to kill in self-defence where one is threatened with harm that is sufficiently serious,[18] a person cannot apply lethal force merely to protect his property.[19] Indeed, it is probably the case that the defence of one's property does not even authorise one to subject a trespasser to a significant risk of serious physical injury.[20]

5.2.1.3. Abatement

The doctrine of abatement is often referred to as a remedy.[21] It is better described as a defence[22] since it relieves of liability a person who commits the tort of trespass to land in order to ameliorate or terminate a nuisance. Its resemblance to the plea of defence of one's property is obvious and, like that defence, it is also a private justification. It is a justification because it extends only to reasonable steps taken

[13] See generally FH Bohlen and JJ Burns, 'The Privilege to Protect Property by Dangerous Barriers and Mechanical Devices' (1926) 35 *Yale Law Journal* 525; RA Posner, 'Killing or Wounding to Protect a Property Interest' (1971) 14 *Journal of Law & Economics* 201.

[14] 'The privilege to defend the possession of property rests upon the same considerations of policy as that of self-defense. . . . The limitations upon the privilege are much the same as in the case of self-defense': Keeton *et al* (n 6) 131 (footnote omitted).

[15] There are several other defences that are closely related to, or are specific applications of, that of defence of property, such as the defence afforded to those who destroy dogs that worry their livestock: Animals Act 1971 (UK), s 9. For discussion of this provision, see R Bagshaw, 'The Animals Act 1971' in TT Arvind and J Steele (eds), *Tort Law and the Legislature: Common Law, Statute and the Dynamics of Legal Change* (Oxford, Hart Publishing, 2012) 223–24.

[16] *Attorney-General's Reference (No 2 of 1983)* [1984] QB 456 (CA).

[17] 'The safety of human lives belongs to a different scale of values from the safety of property. The two are beyond comparison': *Southport Corporation v Esso Petroleum Co Ltd* [1953] 2 All ER 1204, 1209; [1953] 3 WLR 773, 779 (QBD) (Devlin J).

[18] Eg, *Brown v Wilson* (1975) 66 DLR (3d) 295 (BCSC).

[19] Restatement (Second) of Torts, § 77; Civil Liability Act 2002 (NSW), s 52(3); cf *Hackshaw v Shaw* (1984) 155 CLR 614 (HCA).

[20] *Kline v The Central Pacific Railroad Company of California* 37 Cal 400 (1869); *Jordan House Ltd v Menow* [1974] SCR 239.

[21] Eg, *Lagan Navigation Co v Lambeg Bleaching, Dyeing and Finishing Co Ltd* [1927] AC 226, 244 (HL); *Melaleuca Estate Pty Ltd v Port Stephens Council* [2006] NSWCA 31; (2006) 143 LGERA 319, 330 [38]; K Barker, M Lunney, P Cane and F Trindade, *The Law of Torts in Australia*, 5th edn (Oxford, Oxford University Press, 2012) 224.

[22] For further discussion, see the text accompanying n 21 in ch 1.

to reduce a nuisance or to bring one to an end. It will be forfeited if, for instance, one uses disproportionate force to eliminate the nuisance,[23] if the more prudent course of action would have been to request the occupier of the land on which the nuisance was situated to bring it to an end[24] or if one delayed to such an extent before taking steps to address the nuisance that one could have waited for relief through 'the slow progress of the ordinary forms of justice'.[25]

5.2.1.4. Recapture of land[26]

A person who enters land in respect of which he has a right to immediate possession and who uses no more force than is reasonably necessary to evict a trespasser will have a defence in any action brought by the trespasser for battery and interference with his chattels.[27] It is unnecessary for such an individual to resort to proceedings for possession,[28] although the practicality of obtaining judicial relief may cast light on the reasonableness of forcibly re-entering land. This defence is closely related to that of defence of one's property. It too is justificatory in nature,[29] although the courts are slow to find that it is satisfied owing to the fact that forcibly re-entering land poses an obvious risk of disorder.

5.2.1.5. Recapture of chattels[30]

One who has a right to the immediate possession of a chattel can commit a battery or a trespass to land to reclaim the chattel from one who wrongfully has control of it without incurring liability, provided that doing so is reasonable and no more force than is reasonable is used.[31] The defence will be unavailable if the defendant could have recovered his chattel by peaceful means,[32] or if the force used to reclaim it was excessive. This defence is a variant of that of recapture of land, and the principles that govern its availability are, *mutatis mutandis*, more or less the

---

[23] Such as demolishing a house simply because it was used as a brothel: *Ely v Supervisors of Niagara County* 36 NY 297 (1867).

[24] *Lagan Navigation Co v Lambeg Bleaching, Dyeing and Finishing Co Ltd* [1927] AC 226 (HL).

[25] W Blackstone, *Commentaries on the Laws of England*, vol 3 (Oxford, Clarendon Press, 1768) 6.

[26] This defence is also known as the defence of forcible entry.

[27] *Hemmings v The Stoke Poges Golf Club Ltd* [1920] 1 KB 720 (CA); *Manchester Airport plc v Dutton* [2000] QB 133 (CA); Restatement (Second) of Torts, §§ 88, 94.

[28] 'The owner is not obliged to go to the courts to obtain possession. He is entitled, if he so desires, to take the remedy into his own hands. He can go in himself and turn [trespassers] out without the aid of the courts of law': *McPhail v Persons, Names Unknown* [1973] Ch 447, 456 (CA) (Lord Denning MR).

[29] The defence has been abrogated where the occupier is a tenant who has held over: Protection from Eviction Act 1977 (UK), s 2.

[30] See generally CA Branston, 'The Forcible Recaption of Chattels' (1912) 28 *Law Quarterly Review* 262; C Hawes, 'Recaption of Chattels: The Use of Force against the Person' (2006) 12 *Canterbury Law Review* 253.

[31] *Blades v Higgs* (1861) 10 CB (NS) 713; 142 ER 634; Restatement (Second) of Torts, §§ 100, 106. According to *Toyota Finance Australia Ltd v Dennis* [2002] NSWCA 369; (2002) 58 NSWLR 101, the defence is restricted to cases in which the chattel was wrongfully appropriated.

[32] *Stear v Scott* [1992] RTR 226n (QBD); *Lloyd v Director of Public Prosecutions* [1992] 1 All ER 982, 992 (QBD); *R v Mitchell* [2003] EWCA Crim 2188; [2004] RTR 224, 230 [19].

same. However, this justification is, it seems, somewhat more generous than that of recapture of land owing to the fact that chattels can be destroyed, concealed and removed from the jurisdiction (hence sometimes requiring urgent action on the part of the defendant), although again, for self-evident reasons, it too is kept on a tight rein.

5.2.1.6. Distress

Where a chattel belonging to the claimant is on the defendant's land without the defendant's consent and causes actual damage to the land, the defendant may be entitled to seize it and impound it as security for a claim for compensation without incurring liability. This rule is usually described as a 'remedy'.[33] But it is better referred to as a defence since it operates to defeat liability despite the fact that all of the elements of the action in conversion will be satisfied once the defendant seizes the chattel in question. The defence is a private justification since it is available if and only if taking the chattel is reasonable, the defendant acquired it in a reasonable way and the defendant took reasonable care of it.[34] Thus, the defence will not lie if, for example, the value of the chattel taken far exceeds the value of the claim that he might have for compensation.[35] The defence of distress will often be enlivened in tandem with that of defence of one's property, but unlike the latter defence, the defence of distress has the advantage of permitting the defendant to acquire security for any claim to compensation that he decides to bring. However, it is clear that the defence is to a large degree a relic of a bygone era and that it will rarely be enlivened in the modern world.

5.2.1.7. Qualified privilege

The fact that an impugned statement was published on an occasion that attracts a qualified privilege insulates against liability that may arise in the torts of defamation and injurious falsehood. Because the absence of privilege is not an element of

---

[33] Eg, *Arthur v Anker* [1997] QB 564, 573 (CA).

[34] This is a highly compact statement of the scope of this complex defence. It is hedged with numerous qualifications. It is neither possible nor necessary to explore these here. Distraining chattels for arrears of rent is no longer within the defence: Tribunals, Courts and Enforcement Act 2007 (UK), s 71. Where the chattel distrained is a trespassing animal the defence was known as 'distress damage feasant'. For exhaustive discussion, see GL Williams, *Liability for Animals: An Account of the Development and Present Law of Tortious Liability for Animals, Distress Damage Feasant and the Duty to Fence in Great Britain, Northern Ireland and the Common-Law Dominions* (Cambridge, Cambridge University Press, 1939) chs 1–7. Distress damage feasant was abolished by the Animals Act 1971 (UK), s 7 and replaced with a substantially equivalent defence of detention of livestock. This defence is also a private justification.

[35] As Blackstone (n 25) 12 said (emphasis in original) (footnote omitted): 'Distresses must be proportioned to the thing distrained for. . . . [I]f the landlord distrains two oxen for twelvepence rent; the taking of *both* is an unreasonable distress; but, if there were no other distress nearer the value to be found, he might reasonably have distrained *one* of them.' This rule did not, apparently, apply to distress damage feasant. Glanville Williams, speaking of this species of distress, wrote that there is no 'rule that the distress must be . . . proportionate to the amount claimed': Williams (n 34) 83.

these actions,[36] qualified privilege is a defence to both of them.[37] Conventionally, an occasion will be covered by qualified privilege if the defendant publisher had a moral or legal duty to publish a statement about the claimant or his goods to the recipient, and the recipient had a reciprocal interest in receiving it.[38] This test has been held to be satisfied where an employer provided a defamatory character reference regarding the claimant to a prospective employer,[39] where an invigilator told a group of examinees that one of their number had cheated,[40] where a businessperson dictated a defamatory letter to his secretary[41] and where a company director showed a note that was defamatory of one of his company's employees to the company's chairman.[42]

Qualified privilege is a justification. Its justificatory nature is revealed clearly by the duty/interest test. The fact that the defendant who is sued in defamation or injurious falsehood was under a duty to publish the impugned statement makes it reasonable to commit these torts. That qualified privilege is a justification is also apparent from the many rules that orbit the duty/interest test and guide its application. Consider, for example, the fact that in determining whether a defendant was under a duty to publish particular information, regard is had to how the reasonable person in his position would have acted.[43] Also noteworthy is the principle that the privilege will be forfeited if the defendant publishes the statement in question more extensively than the reasonable needs of the occasion require,[44] such as by circulating it via the mass media when the audience with an interest in receiving it is limited.

The duty/interest test is not the only test that determines when the defence of qualified privilege will be available. Thus, an occasion will also be privileged if the defendant was responding, in a proportionate way, to an attack on his reputation

---

[36] See the judicial attempts to enumerate the elements of defamation mentioned in 3.5.1 and 3.6.7. The essentials of the tort of injurious falsehood are stated in *Kaye v Robertson* [1991] FSR 62, 67 (CA) and in *Palmer Bruyn & Parker Pty Ltd v Parsons* [2001] HCA 69; (2001) 208 CLR 388, 404 [52], 425 [114].

[37] Lord Mansfield in *Weatherston v Hawkins* (1786) 1 TR 110; 99 ER 1001, a defamation suit, seemed to think otherwise. His Lordship suggested that where the occasion on which the statement was made was privileged, there is no publication. Speaking of qualified privilege (TR 111, ER 1002), he wrote that 'to every libel there may be a necessary and implied justification from the occasion. So that what, taken abstractedly, would be a publication, *may from the occasion prove to be none*, as if it were read in a judicial proceeding' (emphasis added). Put differently, in Lord Mansfield's view, to plead privilege is to deny the publication element of the action in defamation. There is little in the authorities, both in Lord Mansfield's time and subsequently, to support his view.

[38] Defamation Act 2005 (NSW), s 30; *Adam v Ward* [1917] AC 309, 334 (HL).

[39] *Weatherston v Hawkins* (1786) 1 TR 110; 99 ER 1001; *Spring v Guardian Assurance plc* [1995] 2 AC 296 (HL).

[40] *Bridgman v Stockdale* [1953] 1 All ER 1166; [1953] 1 WLR 704 (QBD).

[41] *Bryanston Finance Ltd v de Vries* [1975] QB 703, 719–20 (CA).

[42] *Watt v Longsdon* [1930] 1 KB 130 (CA) (although showing the letter to the employee's wife was not a privileged occasion).

[43] *Howe v Lees* (1910) 11 CLR 361, 369 (HCA).

[44] *Oddy v Lord George Paulet* (1865) 4 F & F 1008; 176 ER 886; *Williamson v Freer* (1874) LR 9 CP 393; *Clift v Slough Borough Council* [2010] EWCA Civ 1484; [2011] 3 All ER 118; [2011] 1 WLR 1774.

launched by the claimant.[45] In this manifestation, the justificatory character of the defence of qualified privilege is particularly obvious as it is governed by rules that are analogous to those that control the defence of self-defence,[46] a paradigmatic justification. For instance, just as the defence of self-defence is inapplicable where the defendant uses excessive force to defend himself,[47] the defence of qualified privilege will be forfeited if the defendant's defamatory statement goes beyond refutation and constitutes retaliation.[48]

The defence of qualified privilege is probably best categorised as a private justification rather than a public justification. It is true that it has been said that the defence serves 'the common convenience and welfare of society'[49] and that 'Considerations of public good and public policy run through all the common law cases on this topic.'[50] It is also the case that a defendant may be discharging a public duty in publishing the statement in question. However, this defence, unlike certain other defences to liability in defamation and injurious falsehood, does not require that the statement be on a subject that is of public interest.[51] More significantly, a defendant who acts in a self-interested manner may be entitled to the defence of qualified privilege.

5.2.1.8. Innocent dissemination

It was noted earlier that it is unnecessary for the claimant in an action in defamation to show that the defendant knew that his impugned statement was defamatory.[52] Accordingly, all persons who are complicit in the distribution of a statement that is defamatory of the claimant are prima facie liable. However, distributors other than authors, editors and publishers are afforded a defence so long as they took reasonable care in relation to the publication of the statement.[53] This defence protects, for instance, a newsagent who commits the tort of defamation by selling a newspaper that contains a defamatory imputation about the claimant, so long as he reasonably believed that the newspaper did not make any such imputation. By virtue of its reasonableness requirement, this defence is a justification.

---

[45] For comprehensive discussion, see RP Reynolds, 'Self-Defense in Defamation or "Re-Tort not Reply"' (1969) 34 *Albany Law Review* 95. Where the claimant has defamed the defendant, the claimant may be deemed to have consented to the publication of a defamatory reply by the defendant. Consent as a defence to liability arising in defamation is discussed in 5.2.1.9. The relationship between the defences of qualified privilege and consent is the subject of illuminating analysis by Dixon J in *Loveday v Sun Newspapers Ltd* (1938) 59 CLR 503, 523–25 (HCA).

[46] 'There is . . . an analogy between the . . . law of self defence and a man's right to defend himself against written or verbal attacks': *Turner v Metro-Goldwyn-Mayer Pictures Ltd* [1950] 1 All ER 449, 470 (HL) (Lord Oaksey).

[47] See the text accompanying n 10 in ch 2 and 4.3.2.5.

[48] *French v The Herald and Weekly Times Pty Ltd (No 2)* [2010] VSC 155; (2010) 27 VR 171, 189 [70].

[49] *Toogood v Spyring* (1834) 1 Cr M & R 181, 193; 149 ER 1044, 1049 (Parke B).

[50] *Telegraph Newspaper Co Ltd v Bedford* (1934) 50 CLR 632, 655 (HCA) (Evatt J).

[51] Although see s 15(3) of the Defamation Act 1996 (UK).

[52] See 3.3.7.

[53] Defamation Act 1996 (UK), s 1; Defamation Act 2005 (NSW), s 32.

5.2.1.9. Consent

The claimant's consent to the defendant's impugned act can, as has been explained, prevent the tort of trespass from being constituted.[54] Thus, in the language used in this book, the plea of consent is sometimes a denial. But it can also function as a justificatory defence to several torts that do not treat the lack of consent as a definitional matter. These torts include defamation, private nuisance and the action in *Rylands v Fletcher*. The absence of consent on the part of the claimant is not an ingredient of these wrongs.[55] But the claimant's consent to conduct that satisfies their definitions can relieve the defendant of liability in them.

It is relatively rare for the defence of consent to be raised in an action in defamation. However, it has been held the claimant will be taken to have consented to a defamatory statement being published if he entraps the defendant into publishing a defamatory statement in order to maintain an action against the defendant,[56] if the statement was published by the defendant pursuant to terms and conditions to which the claimant agreed when he entered into a relationship with the defendant[57] and if the statement was published on the claimant's website in circumstances where the claimant had the power to remove the statement but omitted to do so.[58] A claimant does not consent to the publication of statements that are defamatory of him merely because he invites a discussion of his own conduct[59] or buys a copy of a book in which the statement is contained in order to prove the fact of publication.[60]

It is well established that consent is a defence to liability arising in private nuisance.[61] For example, a claimant who occupies part of a building owned by the defendant takes the building as it stands and cannot maintain an action in private nuisance in respect of any defect in the way in which it was constructed.[62] Likewise, a claimant who contracts with the defendant for grazing rights, the enjoyment of which he knows will be disturbed as a result of the defendant working on a quarry on adjoining land, cannot complain about the disturbance.[63] Neither can a landlord who lets a portion of his building to university students obtain relief when

---

[54] See 3.6.1.

[55] In so far as defamation is concerned, see the text accompanying n 114 and n 182 in ch 3. Attempts to describe the elements of private nuisance are made in *Copart Industries, Inc v Consolidated Edison Co of New York, Inc* 41 NY 2d 564, 570; 362 NE 2d 968, 972 (1977); *Lippiatt v South Gloucestershire Council* [2000] QB 51, 56 (CA). The absence of consent is not mentioned in any of these definitions. The ingredients of the action in *Rylands v Fletcher* are identified in *Transco plc v Stockport Metropolitan Borough Council* [2003] UKHL 61; [2004] 2 AC 1, 23 [54]. Again, no mention is made of a lack of consent.

[56] *Weatherston v Hawkins* (1786) 1 TR 110; 99 ER 1001; *King v Waring* (1803) 5 Esp 13; 170 ER 721.

[57] *Chapman v Lord Ellesmere* [1932] 2 KB 431, 463–65 (CA); *Russell v Duke of Norfolk* [1949] 1 All ER 109, 120 (CA); *Friend v Civil Aviation Authority* [1998] IRLR 253 (CA); *Spencer v Sillitoe* [2003] EWHC 1651 (QB).

[58] *Carrie v Tolkien* [2009] EWHC 29 (QB).

[59] *Loveday v Sun Newspapers Ltd* (1938) 59 CLR 503, 513–14 (HCA).

[60] *Brunswick v Harmer* (1849) 14 QB 185; 117 ER 75.

[61] For discussion, see J Murphy, *The Law of Nuisance* (Oxford, Oxford University Press, 2010) 107–08.

[62] *Kiddle v City Business Properties Ltd* [1942] 1 KB 269 (KBD).

[63] *Thomas v Lewis* [1937] 1 All ER 137 (Ch D). See also *Lyttelton Times Co Ltd v Warners Ltd* [1907] AC 476 (PC); *Pwllbach Colliery Co Ltd v Woodman* [1915] AC 634 (HL).

the students create noise which the landlord would have reasonably expected them to have generated.[64]

The defence of consent crops up periodically in actions in the rule in *Rylands v Fletcher*. For example, it has been held that a claimant will consent to the risk that a dangerous object kept on the defendant's land will escape and cause him damage if the object was stored on the defendant's property for the parties' joint benefit.[65] A claimant will also consent to the risk that a dangerous object will escape and cause harm if he takes occupation of premises in a building that is shared with the defendant, knowing that the defendant keeps a dangerous object in his part of the building.[66] However, negligence on the part of the defendant vitiates any consent given by the claimant. For instance, a claimant will not consent to the presence of water in proximity to his land in circumstances where it is stored in a dangerous way.[67] Neither will a claimant consent to the storage of petroleum products where the defendant negligently failed to institute proper safety procedures.[68]

Consent is a unique form of justification. The fact that C consented to a particular act is not a reason to do anything. For example, the bare fact that C consents to being punched, kissed or having his book burned does not give anyone a reason to do any of these things. It follows that the fact of consent cannot be an undefeated reason to commit a tort. However, the defence of consent is nevertheless a justification, because D must act in reliance on the fact that C consented in order to benefit from the defence of consent.[69] It is doubtful whether a defendant who, for example, defames another person not realising that the latter was consenting to the publication of the statement could succeed on the defence of consent.[70]

5.2.2. Public Justifications

5.2.2.1. Public necessity

The archetypal public justification is the defence of public necessity.[71] This defence, which is in principle an answer to liability arising in all torts other than those that require proof of negligence,[72] allows defendants to commit torts against

---

[64] *Clarey v Principal and Council of the Women's College* (1953) 90 CLR 170 (HCA).

[65] *Carstairs v Taylor* (1871) LR 6 Exch 217, esp at 222; *Blake v Woolf* [1898] 2 QB 426 (Div Ct).

[66] *Ross v Fedden* (1872) LR 7 QB 661 (QBD); *Peters v Prince of Wales Theatre (Birmingham) Ltd* [1943] KB 73 (CA).

[67] *A Prosser & Son Ltd v Levy* [1955] 3 All ER 577; [1955] 1 WLR 1224 (CA).

[68] *Colour Quest Ltd v Total Downstream UK plc* [2009] EWHC 540 (Comm). The issue of consent fell away on appeal: *Shell UK Ltd v Total UK Ltd* [2010] EWCA Civ 180; [2011] QB 86.

[69] The analysis here follows J Gardner, 'Justification under Authority' (2010) 23 *Canadian Journal of Law and Jurisprudence* 71, 78–82.

[70] See the text accompanying nn 90–92 in ch 4.

[71] Private necessity is not a tort defence. For discussion, see the text accompanying n 40 in ch 4.

[72] *Rigby v Chief Constable of Northamptonshire* [1985] 2 All ER 985; [1985] 1 WLR 1242 (QBD). Public necessity, like all justification defences, is unavailable to negligence-based torts since the absence of justification is a definition element of such torts: see the text accompanying nn 48–49 in ch 1.

innocent people free from the obligation to pay compensation where it is reasonably necessary to do so to protect an important public interest from an imminent peril. Thus, to give some classic illustrations, this defence would apply were the defendant to tear down a house to stop a conflagration from spreading,[73] to jettison cargo from a ship to prevent it from sinking and those aboard from drowning,[74] or to incinerate clothing that is contaminated with a virulent disease.[75] A rescuer who acts to save a person in circumstances where the latter had no opportunity to consent (such as by dragging a pedestrian out of the path of a speeding car that the latter failed to notice bearing down on him) may also be within the defence,[76] as may a doctor who performs life-saving and urgently-needed surgery on an unconscious patient.[77] More recently, and controversially, the defence was held to be available to police officers to defeat claims in trespass to the person where the officers concerned had detained suspected offenders in a police van while searching their abode for illegal firearms[78] and kept several hundred people in cramped conditions in Oxford Circus in London until safe crowd dispersal could be arranged.[79] The defence was denied to environmental activists who destroyed genetically-modified crops[80] and to anti-war campaigners who damaged a military installation.[81]

The defence of public necessity is sometimes elided with that of self-defence,[82] but the two defences are fundamentally different and consequently need to be kept apart from each other. Public necessity permits force to be used against an innocent person or his property, whereas self-defence applies principally where force is applied against aggressors, although this line is admittedly blurred by the fact that a person can act in self-defence against one who he mistakenly but reasonably thinks is an aggressor.[83] Because public necessity is concerned with conflicts between innocents, the maximum amount of force that it regards as proportionate is less than is permitted in the case of self-defence. Thus, whereas the defence of self-defence may authorise the use of greater force than that with which one is threatened (eg, a person threatened with grievous bodily harm or rape may

---

[73] '[F]or the commonwealth, a man shall suffer damage; as, for saving a city or town, a house shall be plucked down if the next be on fire . . . and a thing for the commonwealth every man may do without being liable to an action': *Saltpetre Case* (1606) 12 Co Rep 12, 13; 77 ER 1294, 1295. Cf *Burmah Oil Co (Burma Trading) Ltd v Lord Advocate* [1965] AC 75, 164 (HL). See generally HC Hall and JH Wigmore, 'Compensation for Property Destroyed to Stop the Spread of a Conflagration' (1907) 1 *Illinois Law Review* 501.

[74] *Mouse's Case* (1608) 12 Co Rep 63; 77 ER 1341.

[75] *Seavey v Preble* 64 Me 120 (1874).

[76] *In re F (Mental Patient: Sterilisation)* [1990] 2 AC 1, 74 (HL).

[77] *Wilson v Pringle* [1987] QB 237, 252 (CA). But see the statutory defences made available to doctors: 5.2.2.7.

[78] *Connor v Chief Constable of Merseyside Police* [2006] EWCA Civ 1549; The Times, 4 December 2006.

[79] *Austin v Commissioner of Police of the Metropolis* [2009] UKHL 5; [2009] 1 AC 564.

[80] *Monsanto Plc v Tilly* [2000] Env LR 313 (CA).

[81] *Attorney-General v Leason* [2011] NZHC 1053.

[82] Eg, NJ McBride and R Bagshaw, *Tort Law*, 5th edn (Harlow, Pearson, 2015) 50 (discussing the defences under a single heading).

[83] *Ashley v Chief Constable of Sussex Police* [2008] UKHL 25; [2008] 1 AC 962.

be entitled to kill[84]), it is doubtful whether the defence of public necessity allows the defendant to cause a net harm. It is not for nothing that the defence of public necessity is sometimes known as that of 'lesser evils'.

The defence of public necessity is in a state of flux owing to the recent developments in the case law to which reference has been made. Consequently, its limits are difficult to state with precision. Nevertheless, it is clear that public necessity is a justificatory defence as it is available only to those defendants who act reasonably in committing a tort. It is a public justification on account of the fact that it applies only where the defendant acts to preserve the common good.

5.2.2.2. *Defence of another person*

Under the early common law, the defence of defence of another person was restricted to certain relationships. It was, at one time, limited to masters who used reasonable force to defend their servants from aggressors[85] and vice versa,[86] and to husbands who protected their wives.[87] Today, however, the defence is no longer confined in this way. It is of general application. For example, one who intervenes to protect a stranger may be eligible for it.[88] The principles that govern this defence track closely those that control that of self-defence.[89] Most importantly, like the defence of self-defence, the defence of another defence is available if and only if it was reasonable to use force and the force used was proportionate to the threat. Like self-defence, the defence of another defence is a justification.

5.2.2.3. *Defence of another's property*

It has already been noted that tort law provides for a defence where the defendant uses reasonable force to protect his own property from a trespasser.[90] Although relevant cases are few and far between, it seems that a defence will also be granted where proportionate force is used to prevent a trespass from being committed against a third party's property. Lord Parker CJ recognised the existence of such a defence in *Workman v Cowper*,[91] a criminal law case. The Lord Chief Justice said that the test for the defences of defence of one's own property and defence of another's property 'must be the same'.[92] It follows that the latter defence, like the former, is a justification.

---

[84] 'Only an archaic system of justice would suggest that a woman cannot use deadly force to defend herself against common-law rape': *People v Heflin* 434 Mich 482, 511; 456 NW 2d 10, 22 (1990).

[85] *Seaman v Cuppledick* (1614) Owen 150; 74 ER 966.

[86] *Barfoot v Reynolds* (1733) 2 Strange 953; 93 ER 963.

[87] W Blackstone, *Commentaries on the Laws of England*, vol 4 (Oxford, Clarendon Press, 1769) 186.

[88] *Goss v Nicholas* [1960] Tas SR 133 (SC); *Gortarez v Smitty's Super Valu, Inc* 104 Ariz 97, 106; 680 P 2d 807, 816 (1984).

[89] '[T]he criteria are essentially the same for both defences': *Glover v Fell* [1999] BCJ No 1333 [37] (SC).

[90] See 5.2.1.2.

[91] [1961] 2 QB 143 (Div Ct).

[92] *Ibid*, 150. See also Restatement (Second) of Torts, § 86.

5.2.2.4. Arrest

The doctrine of arrest[93] exists for the protection of the public and to enable offenders to be brought to justice. It is closely related to the defences of self-defence[94] and defence of another person. It permits the use of reasonable force[95] to apprehend and temporarily detain a person who is about to commit, is in the process of committing or has committed an offence. The ambit of the doctrine of arrest is determined by intricate statutory provisions.[96] Different rules apply depending on whether the person effecting the arrest is a constable or a private citizen. It is unnecessary for present purposes to delve into these details,[97] since it is reasonably clear that the doctrine of arrest is a defence. It is a defence because it permits liability to be evaded even though all of the elements of the tort of trespass to the person are present. As Diplock LJ stated in *Dallison v Caffrey*, 'arrest involves trespass to the person'.[98] This brings out clearly the fact that the action in trespass will be constituted when an arrest is made. So the plea of arrest cannot be denial. Within the category of defences, the doctrine of arrest is a public justification. It is justificatory in nature because it insists that the force applied be reasonable.

5.2.2.5. Discipline

The doctrine of discipline,[99] when enlivened, prevents liability from arising in trespass to the person (typically in the tort of battery). The main context in which it applies is that of parental control over children.[100] A parent who uses force to discipline his child satisfies all of the elements of the action in battery. However, if it was reasonable to use force and if the degree of force applied was proportionate

[93] There are numerous associated statutory 'law-and-order' defences, including the defence of stop and search of persons and vehicles, the defence of entry and search of premises, the defence of entry and arrest (Police and Criminal Evidence Act 1984 (UK), pts 1–2; Criminal Justice and Police Act 2001 (UK), pt 2), and the defence of prevention of crime (Criminal Law Act 1967 (UK), s 3). It is not practical to discuss these defences here. For analysis, see AM Dugdale and MA Jones (eds), *Clerk & Lindsell on Torts*, 21st edn (London, Sweet & Maxwell, 2014) chs 15, 19.

[94] The connection between arrest and self-defence is explored in J Gardner, 'Justification under Authority' (2010) 23 *Canadian Journal of Law & Jurisprudence* 71, 89–90.

[95] The principles in this regard parallel those that apply to self-defence. 'The degree of permissible force should be the same in both cases': *R v Clegg* [1995] 1 AC 482, 496 (HL) (Lord Lloyd of Berwick).

[96] The most important provisions are contained in the Police and Criminal Evidence Act 1984 (UK), pt 3.

[97] For discussion, see Dugdale and Jones (n 93) [15.65]–[15.92].

[98] [1965] 1 QB 348, 370 (CA). Cf the sources mentioned in n 17 in ch 4 which cast the plea of arrest as a denial.

[99] See SH Bitensky, 'Spare the Rod, Embrace our Humanity: Toward a New Legal Regime Prohibiting Corporal Punishment of Children' (1998) 31 *University of Michigan Journal of Law Reform* 353; H Keating, 'Protecting or Punishing Children: Physical Punishment, Human Rights and English Law Reform' (2006) 26 *Legal Studies* 394; JA Scutt, 'Sparing Parents Pain or Spoiling the Child by the Rod: Human Rights Arguments against Corporal Punishment' (2009) 28 *University of Tasmania Law Review* 1.

[100] The doctrine is no longer available in Britain to teachers who administer corporal punishment: Education Act 1996 (UK), s 548. See further 9.3.5.1.

in the circumstances,[101] the doctrine will apply. Hence, the doctrine is a defence. It is a justification because of the twin reasonableness requirements, and public in nature because it exists in order to enable a child to be controlled for his own benefit and for the benefit of those with whom the child interacts. The doctrine has a presence in a very limited range of other settings. For example, it also authorises the captains and crew of aircraft and ships[102] to use reasonable force against passengers in order to maintain order.[103]

5.2.2.6. Responsible journalism

As explained earlier,[104] the defence of qualified privilege conventionally applied if and only if the publisher of a defamatory statement had a duty to publish the statement and the recipient had an interest in receiving it. This defence was unlikely to encompass, therefore, statements made via the mass media. As Lord Carswell observed in *Seaga v Harper*:[105]

> The law has been slow to accept that a communication to the world at large, such as in a newspaper, is protected by qualified privilege. It has traditionally been held either that there is no duty on the part of the maker to publish it so widely or that the breadth of the class of recipients is too wide for them all to have an interest in receiving it.

Hence, untrue defamatory statements of fact published by the media stood a fair chance of generating liability even if the publisher acted reasonably in disseminating the statement in question. As a result of concerns about the compatibility of this situation with the right to freedom of expression guaranteed by article 10 of the European Convention on Human Rights, the House of Lords created a defence of 'responsible journalism' in *Reynolds v Times Newspapers Ltd*.[106] This defence[107] is available to defendants who act reasonably in publishing defamatory

---

[101] 'Proportionate force' is narrowly defined for the purposes of the doctrine. Factors to be considered in this respect are discussed in *R v H (Assault of Child: Reasonable Chastisement)* [2001] EWCA Crim 1024; [2001] 2 FLR 431, 438–39 [31]. In England, the infliction of actual bodily harm is, by legislative fiat, unreasonable: Children Act 2004 (UK), s 58(3). See further 9.3.5.1.

[102] *King v Franklin* (1858) 1 F & F 360; 175 ER 764; *Hook v Cunard Steamship Co Ltd* [1953] 1 All ER 1021; [1953] 1 WLR 682 (Winchester Assizes).

[103] The common law in this connection has been supplemented with numerous statutory provisions: eg, Civil Aviation Act 1982 (UK), s 94; Merchant Shipping Act 1995 (UK), s 105.

[104] See 5.2.1.7.

[105] [2008] UKPC 9; [2009] AC 1, 7 [6]. Consider also Lord Nicholls of Birkenhead's remark in *Reynolds v Times Newspapers Ltd* [2001] 2 AC 127, 195 (HL), that 'Frequently a privileged occasion encompasses publication to one person only or to a limited group of people. Publication more widely, to persons who lack the requisite interest in receiving the information, is not privileged'.

[106] [2001] 2 AC 127 (HL). See further 9.3.5.1. The Defamation Act 2013 (UK), s 4, abolishes this defence and installs a roughly similar defence in its place.

[107] According to one view, the defence of responsible journalism is an outgrowth of the traditional defence of qualified privilege (which is discussed in 5.2.1.7). A different view, and the one preferred here, is that the responsible journalism defence is *sui generis*. The House of Lords split 3:2 in *Jameel v Wall Street Journal Europe Sprl* [2006] UKHL 44; [2007] 1 AC 359 on this issue, with three law lords favouring the first-mentioned view: see at 376–77 [30], 381 [46], 395 [107], 402 [130], 404 [135], 405 [137], 408 [146].

statements on subjects of public interest.[108] Due to its reasonableness requirement, it is a justification.

5.2.2.7. Medical treatment

The common law, via the defence of public necessity, enabled people to provide
medical treatment to persons who were incapable of consenting to treatment. The
role of the defence of public necessity in this regard has already been discussed.[109]
The judge-made law in this regard has been supplemented by intricate statutory
schemes that facilitate the provision of medical treatment to those who require
treatment but who are unable to consent. The most important statutes are the
Mental Health Act 1983 (UK) and the Mental Capacity Act 2005 (UK). It is
unnecessary to delve into these Acts here.[110] It suffices to say that they enable
treatment to be administered or an assessment to be undertaken non-consensually,
in limited circumstances, without liability in tort being incurred. The relevant
provisions are defences since they relieve the person providing treatment or
undertaking the assessment from liability even though, in providing treatment, all
of the elements of the tort of trespass to the person are satisfied. The provisions
are justificatory on account of the fact that they authorise the administration of
treatment or admission to hospital for assessment on the condition that it is necessary and reasonable to provide treatment or to conduct an assessment.[111] They
are public justifications because persons entitled to them are not acting to advance
their own interests.

5.2.2.8. Justification

Lord Hoffmann's ground-breaking speech in *OBG Ltd v Allan* reveals that the tort
of inducing a breach of contract has at least four elements.[112] These elements are:

(1) a breach of contract;
(2) the breach must have been induced by the defendant;
(3) the defendant knew that he was inducing a breach; and
(4) the claimant suffered damage due to the breach.

Liability will not arise in this tort if the defendant was justified in inducing the
breach of contract. Thus, to give some examples, inducing a breach was held to be
justified where the defendant encouraged a group of chorus girls who were so

---

[108] Due to the defence's title – responsible *journalism* – it was initially thought in some circles that it
was restricted to media defendants. However, it has been held that it is not so confined: *Jameel v Wall
Street Journal Europe Sprl* [2006] UKHL 44; [2007] 1 AC 359, 383 [54], 398 [118], 408 [146]; *Seaga v
Harper* [2008] UKPC 9; [2009] AC 1, 9 [11].

[109] See 5.2.2.1.

[110] They are dealt with comprehensively in J Herring, *Medical Law and Ethics*, 3rd edn (Oxford,
Oxford University Press, 2013) ch 3.

[111] See, eg, s 64G of the Mental Health Act 1983 (UK) (emergency treatment for patients lacking
capacity or competence).

[112] *OBG Ltd v Allan* [2007] UKHL 21; [2008] 1 AC 1, 29–31 [39]–[44] (HL) (Lord Hoffmann).

underpaid by the claimant employer that they had to resort to prostitution to leave the claimant's employment,[113] where the defendant counselled his son, a minor, to break his promise to marry an immoral woman[114] and where the defendant lender pressured a property developer to dismiss architects in order to protect its right to be repaid a loan that it had made to the developer.[115]

Is justification a defence, or is the absence of justification an element of the tort of inducing a breach of contract? The position is misty.[116] No guidance can be extracted from Lord Hoffmann's speech in *OBG*. In *Greig v Insole*,[117] Slade J said that

> even if *all the other ingredients* of the tort [of inducing a breach of contract] are present in a given case, the defendant may still escape liability, if he can in the particular circumstances show sufficient 'justification' in law for what he did.[118]

This implies that the absence of justification is an element of the tort. But this is hardly conclusive. Perhaps Slade J was not as careful with his language as he should have been and failed, as so many do, to pay attention to the distinction between torts and defences. Dyson Heydon, writing extra-judicially, appears to regard justification as a defence. Referring to the doctrine of justification, he said that 'once certain facts are proved, certain legal consequences follow unless certain other facts are proved'.[119] By 'other facts', Heydon means to refer to defences, and he seems to count as one of the 'other facts' the fact that the defendant was justified in inducing a breach of contract. But Heydon's convoluted expression renders it impossible to be certain what stance he takes on the issue in question. More useful is Jenkin LJ's statement in *Thomson v Deakin* that the action for inducing a breach of contract involves 'direct persuasion or procurement or inducement applied by the third party to the contract breaker, with knowledge of the contract and the intention of bringing about its breach'.[120] It is significant that Jenkins LJ did not mention the doctrine of justification in this definition of the tort. He presumably considers it to be a defence.

Although precious little guidance can be derived from the authorities and literature as to how the doctrine of justification should be classified, the stronger analysis seems to be that it is a defence. The tort of inducing a breach of contract works in partnership with the action in defamation in so far as the two torts are

---

[113] *Brimelow v Casson* [1924] 1 Ch 302 (Ch D).

[114] *Findlay v Blaylock* 1937 SC 21 (Ct of Sess). See also *G v B* (1926) 22 Alta LR 126; [1926] 1 DLR 855 (SC App Div).

[115] *Edwin Hill & Partners (a firm) v First National Finance Corp Plc* [1988] 3 All ER 801; [1989] 1 WLR 225 (CA).

[116] '[A]t times the tort and its justification are mixed together to provide an unsatisfactory analysis': H Carty, *An Analysis of the Economic Torts* (Oxford, Oxford University Press, 2001) 73.

[117] [1978] 3 All ER 449, 491; [1978] 1 WLR 302, 340 (Ch D) (emphasis added).

[118] See, additionally, at All ER 484–85; WLR 332, where the absence of justification is described as one of five 'conditions' that must be satisfied in order for the tort of inducing to be constituted.

[119] JD Heydon, 'The Defence of Justification in Cases of Intentionally Caused Economic Loss' (1970) 20 *University of Toronto Law Journal* 139, 139.

[120] *Thomson v Deakin* [1952] Ch 646, 694 (CA).

concerned with protecting relationships. The fact that the various privileges that exist in the context of defamation are defences[121] might offer some reason for thinking that the doctrine of justification, which is often referred to as a privilege,[122] is a defence to liability for inducing a breach of contract. It should also be noted that the defendant bears the onus of proof in relation to the issue of justification,[123] although this is admittedly a highly unreliable guide as to whether a particular issue is a defence.[124]

If, as has been contended, the doctrine of justification is a defence, it is plainly a justificatory defence since it relieves the defendant of liability if and only if the defendant acted reasonably in inducing the breach of contract. The defence will not be enlivened unless the defendant had a good reason for interfering with the contract.[125] It is more difficult to determine how to classify this defence within the category of justifications. As the examples given earlier of when the defence applies indicate, it cannot be slotted neatly into either the private justification or public justification category. It straddles this divide, since it may apply both where the defendant is acting to protect his own rights or to promote a public interest. The defence is treated in this part of the chapter simply because most of the cases in which it has succeeded have tended to be cases where the defendant was advancing the interests of the public or a section of it.

5.2.2.9. *Statutory authority*

The doctrine of statutory authority[126] typically features in the context of public and private nuisance, and it is convenient to discuss it in relation to these torts.[127] This doctrine is sometimes spoken of in words that portray it as a denial. For instance, Blackburn J said that[128]

> if the Legislature authorizes the doing of an act (which if unauthorized would be a wrong and a cause of action) no action can be maintained for that act, on the plain ground that no Court can treat that as a wrong which the Legislature has authorized.

The remark that an activity that is within the doctrine of statutory authority is not 'a wrong' is consistent with understanding the plea of statutory authority as a denial. But this interpretation of the effect of statutory authorisation cannot be

---

[121] See 5.2.1.7 (qualified privilege), 5.2.2.6 (responsible journalism), 5.3.1.2 (report of court proceedings) and 5.3.1.3 (Parliamentary and executive privilege).

[122] Eg, Sappideen and Vines (n 6) 779 [30.100].

[123] *Edwin Hill & Partners v First National Finance Corporation plc* [1988] 3 All ER 801, 804; [1989] 1 WLR 225, 228 (CA). Cf *Greig v Insole* [1978] 3 All ER 449, 485; [1978] 1 WLR 302, 332 (Ch D), where it is suggested that the claimant bears the burden of proof in relation to the issue of justification.

[124] See the text accompanying nn 6–8 in ch 3.

[125] The authorities are discussed in R O'Dair, 'Justifying an Interference with Contractual Rights' (1991) 11 *Oxford Journal of Legal Studies* 227, 243–45.

[126] The leading discussion of statutory authority is AM Linden, 'Strict Liability, Nuisance and Legislative Authorization' (1966) 4 *Osgoode Hall Law Journal* 196.

[127] Statutory authority can also prevent liability from arising under the rule in *Rylands v Fletcher*. *JP Porter Co v Bell* [1955] 1 DLR 62, 69 (NS Full Ct).

[128] *Hammersmith and City Railway Co v Brand* (1869) LR 4 HL 171, 196 (HL).

upheld. This is because the absence of statutory authorisation is not an element of the actions in public or private nuisance.[129] This being the case, statutory author-ity must be a defence. Is it a justification or a public policy defence? Statutory authority is often referred to as an 'immunity',[130] which lends weight to under-standing it as a public policy defence. However, the better view is that the defence is a justification. This is because when the legislature authorises a particular activ-ity, the defendant is shielded from liability only if he acts with reasonable care. Thus, as Lord Wilberforce observed in *Allen v Gulf Oil Refining Ltd*:[131]

> It is now well settled that [statutory authorisation eliminates liability subject to] the qualification, or condition, that the statutory powers are exercised without 'negligence' – that word here being used in a special sense so as to require the undertaker, as a condition of obtaining immunity from action, to carry out the work and conduct the operation with all reasonable regard and care for the interests of other persons . . .

5.3. Public Policy Defences

Tort law and the procedural regime by which it is administered provide for a large number of public policy defences. These defences are rather eclectic. Nevertheless, they can be separated, in a rough and ready way, into two groups: those that arise at the time the tort was committed, and those that arise subsequently.

5.3.1. Public Policy Defences That Arise at the Time of the Tort

5.3.1.1. *Judicial process immunities*

Immunities against liability are held by certain participants in the judicial process, most notably judges,[132] jurors,[133] witnesses[134] and prosecutors.[135] Persons who play

---

[129] See n 55 above.

[130] See, eg, *Allen v Gulf Oil Refining Ltd* [1981] AC 1001, 1011 (HL); *Transco plc v Stockport Metropolitan Borough Council* [2003] UKHL 61; [2004] 2 AC 1, 32 [88]. Regarding the meaning of the term 'immunity', see n 10 in ch 6.

[131] *Allen v Gulf Oil Refining Ltd* [1981] AC 1001, 1011 (HL).

[132] *Anderson v Gorrie* [1895] 1 QB 668 (CA); *Nakhla v McCarthy* [1978] 1 NZLR 291 (CA); *Morier v Rivard* [1985] 2 SCR 716; *Rajski v Powell* (1987) 11 NSWLR 522 (CA). See further AA Olowofoyeku, *Suing Judges: A Study of Judicial Immunity* (Oxford, Clarendon Press, 1993) ch 2; J Murphy, 'Rethinking Tortious Immunity for Judicial Acts (2013) 33 *Legal Studies* 455. Justices of the Peace are immune to liability for acts committed within jurisdiction and for acts committed in good faith outside jurisdiction: Courts Act 2003 (UK), ss 31–32. Arbitrators also enjoy immunity: Arbitration Act 1996 (UK), s 29(1).

[133] *Sutton v Johnstone* (1786) 1 TR 493, 503; 99 ER 1215, 1221; *Cabassi v Vila* (1940) 64 CLR 130, 140 (HCA).

[134] In the United Kingdom, only lay witnesses are immune: *Jones v Kaney* [2011] UKSC 13; [2011] 2 AC 398. In Australia, the immunity extends to all witnesses: *Commonwealth of Australia v Griffiths* [2007] NSWCA 370; (2007) 70 NSWLR 268 (special leave to appeal refused: [2008] HCATrans 227). For critical analysis of the conferral of immunity on expert witnesses, see A Edis, 'Privilege and Immunity: Problems of Expert Evidence' (2007) 26 *Civil Justice Quarterly* 40.

[135] *Elguzouli-Daf v Commissioner of Police of the Metropolis* [1995] QB 335 (CA); cf *Nelles v Ontario* [1989] 2 SCR 170.

one of these roles are not liable for anything that they say or do in connection with court proceedings. In particular, they cannot be held responsible in negligence or defamation.[136] These immunities exist not for the personal benefit of the persons entitled to them, but in order to safeguard the administration of justice. They ensure that the aforementioned participants in the judicial process are not hindered in the discharge of their duties to the court by litigation, or the threat thereof, by disappointed litigants. They also prevent decided issues from being re-agitated outside of appellate routes.

The judicial process immunities are excellent examples of public policy defences. They are defences since they are rules that prevent liability from arising that are external to the definitions of the torts to which they pertain. To plead an immunity cannot amount to offering a denial since the absence of an immunity is not an ingredient of any tort. The immunities (like all immunities) are public policy defences because their application is not dependent upon the reasonableness of the defendant's impugned behaviour. It is irrelevant, in so far as the immunities are concerned, that the defendant's behaviour was utterly without justification.

5.3.1.2. *Report of court proceedings*

Standing shoulder to shoulder with the judicial process immunities is the absolute privilege that obtains in respect of reports of court proceedings.[137] This privilege, which is a public policy defence since its availability does not depend on the justifiability of the defendant publisher's conduct, aims to keep the administration of justice under the public's gaze by allaying fears that reporting on it may result in liability.

5.3.1.3. *Parliamentary and executive privilege*

Absolute privilege is also conferred upon statements made by Members of Parliament in the course of Parliamentary proceedings[138] and on certain documents published by the order of, or under the authority of, Parliament.[139] The main rationale for this head of privilege is that it increases the range of issues that may be debated in Parliament and raises public awareness of the business of Parliament. Likewise, high-level executive communications (for example, inter-ministerial communications) are absolutely privileged.[140] Executive communications privilege is defensible on the ground that it facilitates the efficient discharge of governmental business.

---

[136] '[N]o action of libel or slander lies, whether against judges, counsel, witnesses, or parties, for words written or spoken in the course of any proceeding before any Court recognised by law, and this though the words written or spoken were written or spoken maliciously, without any justification or excuse, and from personal ill-will and anger against the person defamed': *Royal Aquarium and Summer and Winter Garden Society Ltd v Parkinson* [1892] 1 QB 431, 451 (CA) (Lopes LJ).

[137] Defamation Act 1996 (UK), s 14.

[138] Bill of Rights 1688, Art 9.

[139] Parliamentary Papers Act 1840 (UK), s 1.

[140] *Chatterton v Secretary of State for India in Council* [1895] 2 QB 189 (CA).

5.3.1.4. Diplomatic, consular and related immunities

Foreign Heads of State and their diplomatic agents are immune to liability under the law of the receiving State.[141] So too are consular officials[142] and certain international organisations and their agents.[143] The purpose of these immunities is to ensure that those who enjoy them are not hindered in the discharge of their responsibilities by liability or the threat thereof. They have also been supported on the grounds of sovereign independence and dignity. Because these immunities are not conditional upon the reasons that the immune persons had for committing a tort, they are public policy defences.

5.3.1.5 Foreign State immunity

Section 1(1) of the State Immunity Act 1978 (UK) provides:

> A State is immune from the jurisdiction of the courts of the United Kingdom . . .

This rule, which is subject to a range of exceptions, is obviously allied with the diplomatic, consular and associated immunities discussed in the previous section.[144] It is justified on the ground that it promotes 'good relations between States through the respect of another State's sovereignty'.[145] It is a public policy defence since it does not turn on the justifiability of the tortious act of the foreign State in question.

5.3.1.6. Act of State

The common law recognises a defence of act of State. The House of Lords in *Regina v Bow Street Metropolitan Stipendiary Magistrate, ex p Pinochet Ugarte* insisted that this defence is distinct from the immunity of foreign States discussed in the preceding paragraph,[146] but failed rather spectacularly to explain the difference between the defences, even in general terms. Several members of the House of Lords quoted with apparent approval the celebrated passage by Fuller CJ in *Underhill v Hernandez*, who identified the act of State defence as the principle that 'the courts of one country will not sit in judgment on the acts of the government of another, done within its own territory'.[147] This description does nothing to separate the act of State defence from the immunity of foreign States since it is a valid description of foreign State immunity too. Despite the uncertain ambit of the act of State defence and the hazy nature of its relationship with the foreign State immunity, it is clear that the act of State defence is a public policy defence since it is unconcerned with the reasons why a tort was committed.

---

[141] Diplomatic Privileges Act 1964 (UK), s 2; State Immunity Act 1978 (UK), s 20.

[142] Consular Relations Act 1968 (UK), s 1.

[143] International Organisations Act 1968 (UK), s 5.

[144] The connections between these rules are explored in *Regina v Bow Street Metropolitan Stipendiary Magistrate, ex p Pinochet Ugarte* [2000] 1 AC 61, 74–75 (HL).

[145] *Al-Adsani v United Kingdom* (2002) 34 EHRR 273, 289 [54] (ECtHR).

[146] [2000] 1 AC 61, 85 ('The two doctrines are separate'), 90 ('in legal theory they are separate'), 105 ('it is necessary to distinguish [the] principles') (HL).

[147] 168 US 250, 252 (1897).

5.3.1.7. *Trade union immunity*[148]

From around the middle of the nineteenth century until the start of the twentieth century, the courts generally aggressively developed the economic torts.[149] The result of the expansion of these torts was that most forms of industrial action became tortious. Parliament responded by enacting the Trade Disputes Act 1906 (UK). That Act insulated those striking from liability in the economic torts.[150] The scope of the immunity was adjusted many times over the twentieth century, with the last significant changes to it being made by the Thatcher Government.[151] Like all immunities, the trade union immunity is a public policy defence.

5.3.1.8. *Crown immunity*[152]

Historically, no tort action lay against the Crown: an extensive immunity sheltered it from liability. The basis of this immunity was the fiction that the King could do no wrong.[153] The impact of this rule was mollified in various ways, principally by permitting suits against servants of the Crown that the Crown would satisfy despite not being legally obliged to do so.[154] Eventually, the immunity was severely restricted by the Crown Proceedings Act 1947 (UK).[155] This Act placed the Crown essentially on the same footing as a private litigant.[156] However, vestiges of the immunity remain. For example, the Crown continues to enjoy immunity in respect of liability for wrongs committed by judicial officers.[157] This remnant of the immunity (which is a close cousin of the judicial process immunities[158]) exists primarily to prevent collateral attacks on judicial findings.

---

[148] See generally J Bowers, M Duggan and D Reade, *The Law of Industrial Action and Trade Union Recognition*, 2nd edn (Oxford, Oxford University Press, 2011) ch 4.

[149] See, eg, *Lumley v Gye* (1853) 2 E & B 216; 118 ER 749; *Quinn v Leathem* [1901] AC 495 (HL); *South Wales Miners' Federation v Glamorgan Coal Co Ltd* [1905] AC 239 (HL); *Taff Vale Railway Co v The Amalgamated Society of Railway Servants* [1901] AC 426 (HL). The context is discussed in L Hoffmann, 'The Rise and Fall of the Economic Torts' in S Degeling, J Edelman and J Goudkamp (eds), *Torts in Commercial Law* (Sydney, Thomson Reuters Australia, 2011).

[150] The immunity is currently housed in the Trade Union and Labour Relations (Consolidation) Act 1992 (UK), s 219.

[151] The Thatcher Government enacted numerous relevant Acts. The process began with the Employment Act 1980 (UK).

[152] See generally GL Williams, *Crown Proceedings: An Account of Civil Proceedings By and Against the Crown as affected by the Crown Proceedings Act, 1947* (London, Stevens & Sons Ltd, 1948).

[153] In Blackstone's words, the 'law supposes an incapacity of doing wrong from the excellence and perfection of [the monarch's] person': Blackstone (n 87) 32–33. Elsewhere in his *Commentaries* Blackstone wrote that 'The king, moreover, is not only incapable of *doing* wrong, but even of *thinking* wrong: he can never mean to do an improper thing: in him is no folly or weakness': W Blackstone, *Commentaries on the Laws of England*, vol 1 (Oxford, Clarendon Press, 1765) 239 (emphasis in original).

[154] This and other palliatives are discussed in *Matthews v Ministry of Defence* [2003] UKHL 4; [2003] 1 AC 1163, 1169 [4].

[155] Amendments to this Act further whittled down the immunity: see, eg, Crown Proceedings (Armed Forces) Act 1987 (UK).

[156] Crown Proceedings Act 1947 (UK), s 2(1).

[157] *Ibid*, s 2(5).

[158] See 5.3.1.1.

Crown immunity also survives to prevent the monarch from being held personally liable.[159] This facet of the immunity is explicable on several grounds. It is
arguably needed to prevent the dignity of the monarch from being diminished. A
second possibility is that lawsuits against the monarch are disallowed since they
might impede him in the discharge of his official functions. Less convincingly, it
might be argued that since judges represent the monarch,[160] the immunity exists
in this setting in recognition of the fact that it would be impossible for the monarch to be called to account owing to the fundamental principle of law, enshrined
in article 6(1) of the European Convention on Human Rights, that justice must be
dispensed by a tribunal that is independent of the litigants.

Crown immunity, to the extent that it survives, is obviously a defence. Because
the immunity is not contingent upon the justifiability of the tortious conduct in
question, it is a public policy defence.

5.3.1.9. *Honest comment*[161]

The defence of honest comment protects the expression of defamatory opinions
based on true or privileged facts on matters of public interest. Remarks can be
found in several older cases to the effect that the defence of honest comment is
restricted to opinions that the reasonable person could have expressed.[162] But it is
clear that, today, the defence is not subject to any such limitation. In *Reynolds v
Times Newspapers Ltd*, Lord Nicholls of Birkenhead said that 'The true test [con-
trolling the defence] is whether the opinion, however exaggerated, obstinate or
prejudiced, was honestly held by the person expressing it.'[163] In order words, the
reasonableness of the opinion is of no consequence. It follows that honest comment is a public policy defence. It exists primarily in recognition of the fact that
the ability to express one's opinions is essential to human flourishing.

5.3.1.10. *Illegality at common law*

It was noted earlier that the plea of illegality sometimes functions as a denial of a
duty of care for the purposes of the tort of negligence.[164] However, it can also deny a
claimant redress even though all of the elements of the tort in which he sues are
present. A good example is *Cross v Kirkby*.[165] In this case, the claimant hunting pro-
tester trespassed upon the land of a farmer across which a hunt was riding and

---

[159] Crown Proceedings Act 1947 (UK), s 40(1).

[160] Blackstone wrote that as 'the sole executive power of the laws is vested in the person of the king,
it will follow that all courts of justice, which are the medium by which he administers the laws, are
derived from the power of the crown': Blackstone (n 25) 23–24.

[161] Formerly known as the defence of fair comment. It was rebranded in *Joseph v Spiller* [2010]
UKSC 53; [2011] 1 AC 852, 888 [117]. The Defamation Act 2013 (UK) provides in s 3 for a defence of
'honest opinion'.

[162] Even as late as the landmark decision in *London Artists Ltd v Littler Grade Organisation Ltd*
[1969] 2 QB 375, 392–93 (CA), Lord Denning MR repeatedly suggested that the defence protected
only opinions that the 'fair minded man' might have held.

[163] [2001] 2 AC 127, 193 (HL).

[164] See 3.6.5.

[165] The Times, 5 April 2000 (CA).

assaulted the farmer. The farmer retaliated and caused the claimant to suffer serious injuries. An action in trespass by the claimant failed on account of the claimant's criminal conduct.[166] Because all of the elements of the action in trespass to the person were satisfied, it follows that the doctrine of illegality must have functioned in this case as a defence. When the doctrine operates as a defence, it is a public policy defence. This is because it is not concerned with the reasonableness of the defendant's tortious conduct but with the claimant's infraction of the criminal law.

5.3.1.11. *Statutory illegality defences*

The legislatures in some jurisdictions, evidently dissatisfied with the scope of the common law illegality defence, created statutory counterparts to it. It is convenient to focus on the English provision,[167] which is contained in section 329 of the Criminal Justice Act 2003 (UK).[168] This section has sometimes been overlooked by torts scholars, no doubt because it is concealed within an Act that is concerned mainly with the criminal law.[169] It operates in tandem with its common law sibling.[170] Broadly speaking, it provides that liability will not arise when:

(1) the defendant committed a trespass against the claimant;
(2) the claimant was convicted of an imprisonable offence in respect of conduct committed at the time of the defendant's trespass;
(3) the force used by the defendant was not 'grossly disproportionate'; and
(4) the defendant committed the trespass because he believed[171] that it was necessary to prevent the claimant from committing an offence, to protect life or property, or to apprehend the claimant.

Section 329 creates a defence since it is enlivened only where the defendant commits a trespass to the claimant's person. It is a public policy defence since it may apply even if the defendant acted unreasonably, such as by using disproportionate force against the claimant,[172] or by proceeding on the basis of an incorrect and unreasonable belief that it was necessary to use force.

[166] The Court of Appeal also held that the defence of self-defence applied.

[167] Potent statutory illegality defences also exist in Australia: Civil Liability Act 2002 (NSW), ss 54–54A; Civil Liability Act 2003 (Qld), s 45; Civil Liability Act 1936 (SA), s 43; Civil Law (Wrongs) Act 2002 (ACT), s 94; Personal Injuries (Liabilities and Damages) Act 2003 (NT), s 10. These defences are discussed in J Goudkamp, 'A Revival of the Doctrine of Attainder? The Statutory Illegality Defences to Liability in Tort' (2007) 29 *Sydney Law Review* 445; J Goudkamp, 'Self-Defence and Illegality Under the *Civil Liability Act* 2002 (NSW)' (2010) 18 *Torts Law Journal* 61.

[168] For discussion of s 329, see *Andorian v Commissioner of Police of the Metropolis* [2009] EWCA Civ 18; [2009] 1 WLR 1859; JR Spencer, 'Legislate in Haste, Repent at Leisure' (2010) 69 *Cambridge Law Journal* 19. The primary motivation for the creation of this defence was the Tony Martin saga. For discussion of the Tony Martin case, see J Goudkamp, 'Statutes and Tort Defences' in J Steele and TT Arvind (eds), *Tort Law and the Legislature: Common Law, Statute and the Dynamics of Legal Change* (Oxford, Hart Publishing, 2013) 40.

[169] Regarding the tendency of the legislature to 'hide' tort defences, see 9.1.4.

[170] Criminal Justice Act 2003 (UK), s 329(6).

[171] The belief does not need to be reasonable: s 329(8)(b).

[172] It is true that the defence in s 329 is not completely insensitive to the rational defensibility of the defendant's act, since it does not apply where the force used is 'grossly disproportionate'. To this extent, it is admitted that the description of s 329 as creating a public policy defence is not entirely accurate.

5.3.1.12. Defunct defences

A suite of extinct defences would have fallen within the first subcategory of public policy defences had they survived to the present day. Six such defences will be mentioned briefly. The first is interspousal immunity.[173] Subject to certain exceptions, this immunity prevented litigation from being maintained between spouses. It existed for various reasons. It was thought that to permit spouses to bring litigation *inter se* would undermine the institution of marriage and disturb domestic tranquillity.[174] It was also propped up by the legal fictions that upon marrying, a wife's legal identity merged with her husband's[175] and that marriage entails irrevocable consent to any act committed by one's spouse. Additionally, the immunity was supported on the ground that it protected insurers from collusion between spouses.[176] The immunity was gradually removed throughout the common law world.[177]

A second deceased defence that would have belonged to the first subcategory of public policy defences had it survived is the immunity of highway authorities.[178] This immunity protected highway authorities from liability in negligence and public nuisance in respect of damage caused by a failure to maintain a highway. The primary justification for this immunity was that it saved highway authorities from the risk of being crippled financially by lawsuits. In England, this immunity met its end with the fall of the legislative axe.[179]

A third defence that has been extinguished that would have fallen into the first subcategory of public policy defences is the defence of common employment. This defence was previously a formidable weapon in the arsenal available to employers to resist suits brought by their employees.[180] It provided employers

---

[173] See generally Law Reform Committee, *Liability in Tort between Husband and Wife* (London, HMSO, 1961); Note, 'Litigation between Husband and Wife' (1966) 79 *Harvard Law Review* 1650; WF Foster, 'Modern Status of Interspousal Immunity in Personal Injury and Wrongful Death Actions' (1979) 92 ALR 3d 901; C Tobias, 'Interspousal Tort Immunity in America' (1989) 23 *Georgia Law Review* 359.

[174] 'The flames which litigation would kindle on the domestic hearth would consume in an instant the conjugal bond': *Ritter v Ritter* 31 Pa 396, 398 (1858).

[175] *Holman v Holman* 73 Ga App 205; 35 SE 2d 923 (1945); *Taylor v Vezzani* 109 Ga App 167; 135 SE 2d 522 (1964); *Bencomo v Bencomo* 200 So 2d 171 (Fla 1967); *Boone v Boone* 345 SC 8; 546 SE 2d 191 (2001).

[176] *Varholla v Varholla* 56 Ohio St 2d 269; 383 NE 2d 888 (1978); *Raisen v Raisen* 379 So 2d 352 (Fla 1979).

[177] Family Law Act 1975 (Cth), s 119; Law Reform (Husband and Wife) Act 1962 (UK), s 1(1).

[178] See G Sawer, 'Non-Feasance Revisited' (1955) 18 *Modern Law Review* 541; B McDonald, 'Immunities under Attack: The Tort Liability of Highway Authorities and their Immunity from Liability for Non-Feasance' (2000) 22 *Sydney Law Review* 411.

[179] Highways (Miscellaneous Provisions) Act 1961 (UK), s 1(1). The immunity was killed off in Australia by *Brodie v Singleton Shire Council* [2001] HCA 29; (2001) 206 CLR 512. However, it was reborn, in modified form, in most jurisdictions: Civil Law (Wrongs) Act 2002 (ACT), s 113; Civil Liability Act 2002 (NSW), s 45; Civil Liability Act 2003 (Qld), s 37; Civil Liability Act 1936 (SA), s 42; Civil Liability Act 2002 (Tas), s 42; Road Management Act 2004 (Vic), s 102; Civil Liability Act 2002 (WA), s 52.

[180] It was invented in *Priestley v Fowler* (1837) 3 M & W 1; 150 ER 1030.

with an answer to liability in respect of torts that their employees committed against each other. One reason why this defence was recognised was that it was considered that, without it, the process of industrialisation would have been retarded. This defence was gradually restricted by both legislation[181] and judicial decision.[182] Unable to bear the strain of the intense and sustained criticism directed at it, it was eventually abolished by Parliament.[183]

A fourth defence formerly recognised by the common law that would have belonged to the first category of public policy defences but for its abolition is the immunity of charities. This immunity[184] existed due to a belief that liability would hamper charities in the discharge of their altruistic work and discourage donations. It was only short-lived in England.[185] It flourished in the United States,[186] but there too it has been removed (or substantially eradicated).[187]

Fifthly, it is necessary to mention the doctrine of contributory negligence. Prior to the enactment of the apportionment provision,[188] negligence on the part of the claimant that contributed to his damage was an answer to liability. However, it is unclear by what route the doctrine prevented liability from arising. There are two and only two possibilities: the doctrine is either a denial or a defence.[189] Bowen LJ in *Thomas v Quartermaine* regarded the doctrine, when applicable, as a denial of the causation element of the action in negligence. His Lordship wrote that the doctrine[190]

> rests upon the view that though the defendant has in fact been negligent, yet the plaintiff has by his own carelessness severed the causal connection between the defendant's negligence and the accident which has occurred; and that the defendant's negligence accordingly is not the true proximate cause of the injury.

The other view is that the doctrine introduces an issue into the proceedings not raised by the claimant's statement of case and is hence a defence. Fleming James preferred this analysis. He wrote that 'Contributory negligence is *never* properly invoked when plaintiff's negligence alone causes the damage but only when the negligence of both the plaintiff and defendant are contributing proximate causes of it.'[191] This is not the place to explore the merits of these competing interpretations

---

[181] Employers' Liability Act 1880 (UK).

[182] Several significant cases are discussed in PH Winfield, 'The Abolition of the Doctrine of Common Employment' (1949) 10 *Cambridge Law Journal* 191, 192–93.

[183] Law Reform (Personal Injuries) Act 1948 (UK), s 1(1).

[184] Apparently invented in *The Feoffees of Heriot's Hospital v Ross* (1846) 12 Cl & Fin 507; 8 ER 1508.

[185] Abolished in *The Mersey Docks and Harbour Board Trustees v Gibbs* (1866) 11 HLC 686; 11 ER 1500.

[186] See DB Dobbs, *The Law of Torts* (St Paul, Minn, West Publishing Co, 2000) 760–65.

[187] 'One engaged in a charitable, educational, religious or benevolent enterprise or activity is not for that reason immune from tort liability': Restatement (Second) of Torts, § 895E.

[188] Law Reform (Contributory Negligence) Act 1945 (UK), s 1(1).

[189] 'The plea of contributory negligence is either an argumentative traverse of the necessary averment that the defendant's negligence was the sole cause of the injury, or a plea in confession and avoidance': *Logan v O'Donnell* [1925] 2 IR 211, 227 (SC).

[190] (1887) 18 QBD 685, 697 (CA).

[191] F James, 'Contributory Negligence' (1953) 62 *Yale Law Journal* 691, 697 (footnote omitted).

of the doctrine of contributory negligence.[192] To do so comprehensively would be a very significant undertaking. It suffices for present purposes to note that if the doctrine was a defence it would, had it survived, have pertained to the first subcategory of public policy defences.

The sixth defence is the immunity of advocates. Formerly, advocates were afforded immunity against liability in negligence in respect of 'in court work' and work done outside of the courtroom that was intimately connected to 'in court work'.[193] This immunity, which has been removed in most jurisdictions,[194] was previously thought to be essential to ensure the efficient administration of justice.[195] For example, it was believed that it was necessary to prevent advocates from neglecting their paramount duty to the court by a fear of being sued by their disgruntled clients. It was also thought that, but for the immunity, advocates might refuse to abide by the cab-rank rule and that unpopular or maligned individuals would, consequently, be unable to secure legal representation.[196]

5.3.2. Public Policy Defences That Arise After the Tort

5.3.2.1. Limitation bars

The common law never developed a system of limitation bars.[197] Actions, once they accrued, could in principle be brought at any time. This position was altered by statute. The default rule is that actions in tort are lost if proceedings are not commenced within six years of the date on which they arose.[198] (There are, unfortunately, many haphazard exceptions to this rule, the most important of which concerns personal injury actions, the limitation period for which is three years.[199])

Limitation bars are an indispensable feature of a good legal system. They promote the smooth functioning of the judicial system in several ways, but mainly by rendering it less likely that disputes will be determined on the basis of seriously incomplete evidence. With the passage of time, certain types of evidence tend to

---

[192] For criticism of the view that the plea of contributory negligence was a denial of the causation element of the action in negligence, see FH Bohlen, 'Contributory Negligence' (1908) 21 *Harvard Law Review* 233, 234–42; James (n 191) 697–98.

[193] Decisions that established the immunity include *Rondel v Worsley* [1969] 1 AC 191 (HL); *Saif Ali v Sydney Mitchell & Co* [1980] AC 198 (HL); *Giannarelli v Wraith* (1988) 165 CLR 543 (HCA).

[194] *Demarco v Ungaro* (1979) 21 OR (2d) 673 (HCJ); *Arthur J S Hall & Co v Simons* [2002] 1 AC 615 (HL); *Lai v Chamberlains* [2006] NZSC 70; [2007] 2 NZLR 7. It lingers on in Australia: *D'Orta-Ekenaike v Victoria Legal Aid* [2005] HCA 12; (2005) 223 CLR 1.

[195] For discussion of its suggested rationales, see M Newman, 'The Case against Advocates' Immunity: A Comparative Study' (1995) 9 *Georgetown Journal of Legal Ethics* 267; R English, 'Forensic Immunity Post-*Osman*' (2001) 64 *Modern Law Review* 300; J Goudkamp, 'Is there a Future for Advocates' Immunity?' (2002) 10 *Tort Law Review* 188.

[196] While advocates can now be sued in negligence, they are, presumably, immune to liability in certain other torts, such as defamation (see *Munster v Lamb* (1883) 11 QBD 588 (CA)), on account of the absolute privilege discussed in 5.3.1.1.

[197] The position in equity is different, where the doctrine of laches was developed.

[198] Limitation Act 1980 (UK), s 2.

[199] *Ibid*, s 11(4).

deteriorate. Memories fade. Witnesses may die or leave the jurisdiction. Physical evidence may be lost or destroyed. All other things being equal, resolving disputes when important evidence is missing or is of low quality tends to be more time-consuming and diminishes the accuracy of decisions. Limitation bars also have a range of other desirable effects. For example, a system of limitation bars reduces any anxiety that one might experience at the prospect of being pursued in respect of one's transgressions. Limitation bars also assist the victims of torts to forgive and forget wrongs committed against them by foreclosing legal redress after a sufficient period of time has elapsed.

It scarcely needs to be said that limitation bars are defences. It is axiomatic that the absence of a limitation bar is not part of any action in tort. Within the category of defences, it is equally clear that limitation bars are public policy defences. This is because limitation bars are enlivened by the mere passage of time. They are completely insensitive to the rational defensibility of the defendant's impugned conduct.

5.3.2.2. Res judicata

The doctrine of *res judicata* prevents matters that have already been decided from being re-litigated. It contributes to the efficient administration of justice by preventing court resources from being squandered on re-litigation and by stopping courts of co-ordinate jurisdiction from reaching inconsistent holdings (public confidence in the judicial system would not be fostered if the courts spoke with a forked tongue). The doctrine also gives litigants and other interested persons an assurance that judicial findings will not be disturbed. This enables them to plan their affairs more effectively than would be the case if findings could be challenged repeatedly or indefinitely. Lastly, it insulates defendants from being harassed in relation to a matter that has already been decided, and prevents claimants from recovering compensation more than once in respect of a single injury.

It could not be seriously disputed that the doctrine of *res judicata* is a defence. The doctrine is a public policy defence since it is uninterested in the quality of the defendant's impugned conduct.

5.3.2.3. Abuse of process

The doctrine of abuse of process advances the administration of justice by preventing the court's process from being corrupted. It applies when a litigant uses a process for a purpose that is significantly different from that for which it was intended. For example, the doctrine has been invoked to stay proceedings that are an attempt to circumvent the special procedure that governs claims for judicial review[200] or which constitute a collateral attack on the verdict of a criminal

---

[200] *O'Reilly v Mackman* [1983] 2 AC 237 (HL); *Clark v University of Lincolnshire and Humberside* [2000] 1 WLR 1988 (CA).

court.[201] It has also been used to stay actions in defamation where the value of the damage suffered by the claimant as a result of the publication of the defendant's defamatory statement is insignificant relative to the cost of the proceedings.[202] Clearly, the doctrine of abuse of process is a defence. It is not an element of any tort that the proceedings commenced by the claimant are not an abuse of process. The doctrine is a public policy defence since it is unconcerned with the reasons that the defendant had for acting tortiously.

5.3.2.4. Contract of settlement

An accord and satisfaction is a contract between the parties in which the claimant agrees to surrender the right to pursue his cause of action in return for valuable consideration (the 'accord' is the contract and the 'satisfaction' is the passing of consideration).[203] Once such a contract (which, in the interests of using more helpful terminology, will be called a 'contract of settlement') has been executed, the claimant will be estopped from pursuing his tort claim. If he wishes to proceed against the defendant, it is to the contract to which he must turn. He must either attack the contract or sue for breach of it.

Contracts of settlement are a means by which the parties can agree to resolve their dispute. By providing this avenue by which claims can be settled, the law reduces backlogs in judicial lists and enables parties to resolve disputes in a way that may be more economical and psychologically satisfying to them than a court-imposed solution. A contract of settlement is obviously a defence. No tort includes among its elements the absence of a contractual settlement. Within the field of defences, a contract of settlement falls within the public policy defence category, as this defence does not enquire as to the justifiability of the defendant's conduct.

5.3.2.5. Release

A release is an undertaking by the claimant contained in a deed to relinquish his action. Once a deed containing a release has been executed, the claimant will be precluded from bringing proceedings against the claimant in respect of the tort that was the subject of the release. A release also provides the defendant with an answer to the claimant's action. Everything that was said in preceding section in relation to contracts of settlement applies *mutatis mutandis* to releases.

---

[201] *Hunter v Chief Constable of the West Midlands Police* [1982] AC 529 (HL).

[202] *Jameel v Dow Jones & Co Inc* [2005] EWCA Civ 75; [2005] QB 946; *Carrie v Tolkien* [2009] EWHC 29 (QB) [19]; *Kaschke v Osler* [2010] EWHC 1075 (QB); *Kaschke v Gray* [2010] EWHC 1907 (QB); *Khader v Aziz* [2010] EWCA Civ 716; [2010] 1 WLR 2673. It is suspected that this defence will become less significant once the Defamation Act 2013 (UK) comes into force. Section 1 of this Act provides that statements are not defamatory unless they cause 'serious harm' to the claimant's reputation.

[203] See generally, S Williston, 'Accord and Satisfaction' (1904) 17 *Harvard Law Review* 459; JF Kelly, 'Accord and Satisfaction – Availability as a Defense' (1932) 6 *St John's Law Review* 342.

5.3.2.6. *Offer to make amends*[204]

An 'offer to make amends' is made when the defendant, having published a statement that is defamatory of the claimant, offers to publish a suitable correction, to make a sufficient apology and to pay compensation plus costs. Liability will not arise if the claimant accepts the offer. In this respect, this defence is similar to those of contract of settlement and release. It provides a means of achieving an expeditious and economical resolution of disputes. If the offer is rejected the defendant will also enjoy a defence unless he knew, at the time of publishing the statement, that it was defamatory of the claimant and false. The defence is extended in this situation in order to prevent claimants from maintaining defamation actions for purely vindictive reasons. In this respect, this answer to liability bears a resemblance to that of abuse of process. Offer to make amends is a public policy defence, since the fact that the defendant may have acted reasonably in publishing the defamatory statement is insufficient to enliven it.

5.3.2.7. *Prior criminal proceedings*

Suppose that C brings a private prosecution against D for assault and battery. Irrespective of the outcome of the prosecution, the fact that the prosecution was brought will, in England, provide D with a defence to any civil liability that he might have otherwise incurred in respect of the act on which the prosecution was based.[205] The apparent rationale for this defence is that it would be wasteful and unjust to permit the claimant to pursue the defendant in the civil sphere in light of the prior prosecution. Because this defence presents no issue as to the reasonableness of the defendant's conduct, it is a public policy defence.[206]

5.3.2.8. *Bankruptcy*

Generally speaking, liabilities incurred before becoming a discharged bankrupt are extinguished upon being discharged.[207] Bankruptcy of the defendant is, therefore, a defence. It is a public policy defence, since it is insensitive to the reasonableness of the defendant's tortious conduct. Bankruptcy of the claimant can also constitute a defence. Broadly speaking, if the claimant becomes a discharged bankrupt, any right that he had to sue the defendant will be lost to him (it will pass to his trustee in bankruptcy). This has the effect of giving the defendant a defence as against the

[204] See the Defamation Act 1996 (UK), ss 2–4. This defence and its rationales are discussed in *Milne v Express Newspapers Ltd* [2004] EWCA Civ 664; [2005] 1 All ER 1021, 1026–30 [17]–[26]; *Warren v The Random House Group Ltd* [2008] EWCA Civ 834; [2009] QB 600, 630–31 [13]–[15]. It has rendered the defence of apology (see Libel Act 1843 (UK), s 2) redundant.
[205] Offences Against the Person Act 1861 (UK), ss 44–45.
[206] The Law Commission recommended that this defence be abolished: Law Commission, *Legislating the Criminal Code: Offences against the Person and General Principles*, Report 218 (London, HMSO, 1993) 138 [12.2]. In *Wong v Parkside Health NHS Trust* [2001] EWCA Civ 1721; [2003] 3 All ER 932, 938 [16] Hale LJ described it as 'anomalous'.
[207] However, if a bankrupt defendant is insured, the claimant may be able to proceed against the defendant's insurer under s 1 of the Third Parties (Rights against Insurers) Act 2010 (UK).

claimant (but not against his trustee in bankruptcy) in respect of any action brought against him in relation to a tort committed prior to the claimant's discharge. Bankruptcy is also a public policy defence in this manifestation.

5.3.2.9. Reportage

Reportage is a defence to liability in defamation.[208] It applies when the defendant reports the fact that one person made defamatory allegations against another person when doing so is in the public interest. As Ward LJ explained in *Roberts v Gable*:[209]

> To qualify as reportage the report, judging the thrust of it as a whole, must have the effect of reporting, not the truth of the statements, but the fact that they were made. . . . If upon a proper construction of the thrust of the article the defamatory material is attributed to another and is not being put forward as true, then a responsible journalist would not need to take steps to verify its accuracy. He is absolved from that responsibility because he is simply reporting in a neutral fashion the fact that it has been said without adopting the truth.

This defence is widely regarded as a species of the defence of responsible journalism.[210] However, it is a different juristic creature[211] since, unlike responsible journalism,[212] it is unconcerned with the reasonableness of the defendant's acts. It is irrelevant, for instance, whether the defendant had grounds for believing that the allegations he was reporting were true. Because the reportage defence is not contingent upon the justifiability of the defendant's conduct, it is a public policy defence.

5.3.2.10. Death

At common law, the death of either party subsequent to the commission of a tort extinguished liability: *actio personalis moritur cum persona*.[213] This principle was eventually reversed for all but a few torts,[214] the only surviving one of which is that of defamation.[215] The common law rule was adopted by the legislature in so far as the death of the claimant is concerned when it provided for the statutory action for bereavement.[216] Because the defence of death applies regardless of the reasonableness of the defendant's impugned conduct, it is a public policy defence.

---

[208] The term 'reportage' entered the case law in *Roberts v Gable* [2006] EWHC 1025; [2006] EMLR 692, 696 [6].

[209] [2007] EWCA Civ 721; [2008] QB 502, 527 [61].

[210] See, eg *Roberts v Gable* [2007] EWCA Civ 721; [2008] QB 502, 526 [60]; *Charman v Orion Publishing Group Ltd* [2007] EWCA Civ 972; [2008] 1 All ER 750, 765 [48]; *Flood v Times Newspapers Ltd* [2012] UKSC 11; [2012] 2 AC 273, 287 [35], 299 [77].

[211] See J Bosland, 'Republication of Defamation under the Doctrine of Reportage – The Evolution of Common Law Qualified Privilege in England and Wales' (2011) 31 *Oxford Journal of Legal Studies* 89.

[212] Responsible journalism is discussed above in 5.2.2.6.

[213] See generally P Winfield, 'Death as Affecting Liability in Tort' (1929) 29 *Columbia Law Review* 239.

[214] Law Reform (Miscellaneous Provisions) Act 1934 (UK), s 1(1).

[215] It was also retained for the actions in seduction, alienation of affections and criminal conversation, but these actions have been abolished: Law Reform (Miscellaneous Provisions) Act 1970 (UK), ss 4–5; Matrimonial Causes Act 1857 (UK), s 59.

[216] Law Reform (Miscellaneous Provisions) Act 1934 (UK), s 1(1A).

5.4. Conclusion

The widespread failure on the part of the courts and commentators to make it clear which issues relevant to liability constitute elements of torts and which issues are defences has generated significant confusion. This chapter has sought to reduce this confusion by identifying doctrines that are defences, and by separating them into justifications and public policy defences. It was not possible to consider all of the defences for which tort law provides. However, a large number of defences were dealt with. The results of the analysis are summarised in Table 3 below.

Table 3: Application of the Taxonomy

Justification Defences	*Public Policy Defences*
Private justifications	*Public policy defences that arise at the time of the tort*
Self-defence	Judicial process immunities
Defence of one's property	Absolute privilege
Abatement	Diplomatic, consular and related immunities
Recapture of land	Foreign State immunity
Recapture of chattels	Act of State
Distress	Trade union immunity
Qualified privilege	Crown immunity
Innocent dissemination	Honest comment
Consent	Illegality at common law
	Statutory illegality defences
Public justifications	*Public policy defences that arise after the tort*
Public necessity	Limitation bars
Defence of another person	*Res judicata*
Defence of another's property	Abuse of process
Arrest	Contract of settlement
Discipline	Release
Responsible journalism	Offer to make amends
Medical treatment	Prior criminal prosecution
Justification	Bankruptcy
Statutory authority	Reportage
	Death

6

Implications

6.1. Introduction

Classification can aid in the description of the law. This is reason enough to organise tort law defences systematically (and to separate them from denials), especially considering that no detailed system for classifying defences has previously been developed. But the way in which a body of law is organised can also have practical implications. The purpose of this chapter is, therefore, to delineate several ways in which the classificatory exercise that has been undertaken in preceding chapters of this book has real-world significance. It will be argued that a great deal turns in practice on whether a given response offered by a defendant is a denial or a defence and, in the case of those responses that are defences, whether the defence in question is a justification or a public policy defence.[1]

6.2. Unwanted Side-effects

The way in which a plea is classified arguably gives some indication of the likely extent of its adverse social impact (if any) when it is accepted, and in turn the reception that it is likely to receive from the courts.[2] Any harmful side-effects resulting from a successful denial are attributable to the way in which the tort in question has been designed rather than the fact that the defendant can avoid liability by way of denying an element of the tort in which he is sued as opposed to via a defence. Certain justifications have some undesirable by-products. Many justificatory defences are instances of self-help,[3] such as abatement[4] and recapture

---

[1] In thinking about the practical implications of the way in which responses available to defendants can be classified, I have found much of value in GP Fletcher, *Rethinking Criminal Law* (Boston, Mass, Little, Brown & Co, 1978) ch 7, especially at 552–55; PH Robinson, 'Criminal Law Defenses: A Systematic Analysis' (1982) 82 *Columbia Law Review* 199, 243–91.

[2] A similar claim is made by Robinson in the criminal law context: Robinson (n 1) 243–50.

[3] For exhaustive analysis of the circumstances in which tort law permits self-help, see DI Brandon, ML Cooper, JH Greshin, AL Harris, JM Head, KR Jacques and L Wiggins, 'Self-Help: Extrajudicial Rights, Privileges and Remedies in Contemporary American Society' (1984) 37 *Vanderbilt Law Review* 845, 852–72.

[4] See 5.2.1.3.

of land[5] and chattels.[6] It is well known that the law takes a dim view of self-help.[7] As Edmund Davies LJ remarked in *Southwark London Borough Council v Williams*,[8] 'the law regards with the deepest suspicion any remedies of self-help, and permits those remedies to be resorted to only in very special circumstances'.[9] The main reason for this attitude is that it is feared that self-help will result in violence or the escalation thereof. Public policy defences tend to have the most objectionable consequences. They operate indiscriminately, that is to say, without regard to the extent to which their application is prone to thwart the realisation of the goals of tort law (whatever those may be). By definition, they are insensitive to the justifiability of the defendant's behaviour and gravity of his wrongdoing. Some types of public policy defences, such as immunities,[10] are particularly odious since they are liable to create the impression that the law is guilty of favouritism.[11] (This is part of the reason why immunities are overrepresented among extinct defences.[12]) Consequently, a defendant who asks the courts to forge a new

---

[5] See 5.2.1.4.

[6] See 5.2.1.5.

[7] Holdsworth claimed that the suppression of self-help was 'the first business of the law, and more especially of the law of crime and tort': WS Holdsworth, *History of English Law*, vol 3, 3rd edn (London, Methuen & Co Ltd, 1922) 278. Blackstone wrote that 'if individuals were once allowed to use private force as a remedy for private injuries, all social justice must cease, the strong would give law to the weak, and every man would revert to a state of nature': W Blackstone, *Commentaries on the Laws of England*, vol 3 (Oxford, Clarendon Press, 1769) 4.

[8] [1971] Ch 734, 745 (CA).

[9] See also *Sedleigh-Denfield v O'Callaghan* [1940] AC 880, 899–900 (HL); *R v Jones* [2006] UKHL 16; [2007] 1 AC 136, 174–76 [76]–[83]; *R v Burns* [2010] EWCA Crim 1023; [2010] 2 Cr App R 117, 120–21 [11]–[14].

[10] The term 'immunity' is widely used in the context of tort law. There seems to be a general understanding of what it means. However, attempts to define it are few and far between. It was defined, in circular terms, in *Brodie v Singleton Shire Council* [2001] HCA 29; (2001) 206 CLR 512, 555 [94] by Gaudron, McHugh and Gummow JJ when they said that 'The term "immunity" is used in various areas of the law to indicate an immunity to action in respect of rights and duties which otherwise exist in the law.' In *Lai v Chamberlains* [2005] NZCA 37; [2005] 3 NZLR 291, 323 [169], Hammond J said that an immunity was 'a state of freedom from the operation of otherwise applicable legal rules'. According to Hohfeld, the term 'immunity' correlates with 'disability' and is the opposite of 'liability': WN Hohfeld, 'Some Fundamental Legal Conceptions as Applied Judicial Reasoning' (1913) 23 *Yale Law Journal* 16, 30. The nearest synonym is said to be 'exemption': at 57.

[11] This problem is particularly acute when lawyers are afforded immunity since this presents a risk that the public will conclude that the law is guilty not only of favouritism but also of feathering the nests of its own disciples. This was one of the reasons why the immunity of advocates (see 5.3.1.12) has been abolished in most jurisdictions. In *Rondel v Worsley* [1967] 1 QB 443, 468 (QBD), Lawton J noted that this immunity was liable to convey the impression that advocates had 'with the connivance of judges, built for themselves an ivory tower and have lived in it . . . at the expense of their clients'. See also the comments in *Arthur J S Hall & Co v Simons* [2002] 1 AC 615, 688–89 (HL); *D'Orta-Ekenaike v Victoria Legal Aid* [2005] HCA 12; (2005) 223 CLR 1, 100 [319].

[12] The decline of immunities is discussed in 1.3 and 5.3.1.12. Prosser and Keeton remarked that 'The description of immunities today is largely the description of abandonment of and limitation on the immunities erected in an earlier day': WP Keeton, DB Dobbs, RE Keeton and DG Owen (eds), *Prosser and Keeton on Torts*, 5th edn (St Paul, Minn, West Publishing Co, 1984) 1032 (footnote omitted). The Reporters of the Restatement (Second) of Torts wrote that 'the modern tendency has been to view immunities with a considerable degree of disapproval and to insist upon good reasons for their continued existence. They have been restricted within increasingly narrow limits, either by statute or by decision': ch 45A, Introductory Note.

public policy defence or extend the reach of an existing one will generally be fighting an uphill battle.[13]

6.3. Burden of Pleading

The rules of pleading are sensitive to the type of plea offered by a defendant who wishes to contest liability.[14] Since the claimant should describe in his statement of case a set of facts that constitute a tort, the facts that he alleges in it ought to be inconsistent with any denials. The claimant should not, however, anticipate any justifications or public policy defences on which the defendant may rely. This is because attempting to do so will detract from one of the main goals of pleadings, which is to isolate the issues in respect of which the parties are in dispute. The defendant, in his statement of defence, can offer a denial, a justification or a public policy defence. The distinctions between these pleas are unimportant, therefore, in so far as the contents of statements of defence are concerned. But the type of plea made by a defendant is important at the reply stage, since replies should be limited to denying justifications and public policy defences. Replies should not touch upon any denials presented by the defendant. This is because, as has been noted, the claimant should have already pleaded facts in his statement of case that are inconsistent with denials of elements of the tort in which the claimant sues.

6.4. Burden of Proof

The general rule concerning the allocation of the onus of proof in the tort context is clear and uncontroversial: the claimant bears the onus of proof (both the evidential onus and the persuasive onus) in relation to the elements of the tort in which he sues, whereas the defendant carries the onus of proof with regard to defences.[15] It follows that the type of plea offered by a defendant to resist the imposition of liability has implications for the assignment of the burden of proof in respect of it. Denials are attacks on elements of the tort in which the claimant

---

[13] This is especially true of immunities: see the remarks in *Lincoln v Daniels* [1962] 1 QB 237, 263 (CA); *Puntoriero v Water Administration Ministerial Corporation* [1999] HCA 45; (1999) 199 CLR 575, 594–95 [59]; *Darker v Chief Constable of the West Midlands Police* [2001] 1 AC 435, 453 (HL); *D'Orta-Ekenaike v Victoria Legal Aid* [2005] HCA 12; (2005) 223 CLR 1, 73–74 [225], 98–99 [314], 99 [317], 101–02 [324], 105 [334], 108 [345]; *Commonwealth of Australia v Griffiths* [2007] NSWCA 370; (2007) 70 NSWLR 268, 289 [98], 293 [118]; *Westcott v Westcott* [2008] EWCA Civ 818; [2009] QB 407, 422 [32]; *Jones v Kaney* [2011] UKSC 13; [2011] 2 AC 398, 419 [51], 432–33 [108]–[115].

[14] This is touched on above in 2.2.2.

[15] See the text accompanying n 66 in ch 1.

sues. Therefore, they are for the claimant to disprove.[16] In contrast, justifications and public policy defences are defences. Consequently, the defendant carries the onus of establishing them.

6.5. Permissible Vagueness

Torts are wrongs, and liability in tort is a sanction. Accordingly, the rule of law demands that fair notice be given of conduct that constitutes a tort.[17] Vagueness in relation to pleas that count as denials is therefore objectionable, since it creates doubt as to when conduct falls within the definition of a tort. Such uncertainty should be reduced as far as is reasonably practical.[18] The situation is arguably different in relation to justifications and public policy defences.[19] Whereas the fact that Φing is a tort is a reason not to Φ, the fact that the law provides for a justificatory defence is no reason to act in any particular way.[20] For example, the fact that the law admits of the defence of self-defence does not give persons confronted by aggressors any reason to defend themselves that they would not already have. Because justifications are not supposed to guide people in their behaviour in the same way as the duties created by the causes of action in tort, it might be less objectionable, for the purposes of the rule of law, if their ambits are uncertain.[21] The same is true *a fortiori* of public policy defences.[22]

---

[16] This is sometimes overlooked by the courts and commentators. Consider the doctrine of illegality. This doctrine can function as a denial of the existence of a duty of care for the purposes of the tort of negligence (see 3.6.5). When it functions in this way, it should be up to the claimant to show that it does not apply. Illogically, however, the courts have held that the defendant carries the onus of establishing it: ch 3, n 7. The same problem arises in relation to the plea of truth. This plea is probably a denial of the damage element of the action in defamation: see 3.5.1. Thus, it should fall to the claimant to show that the defendant's statement is untrue, at least where that issue is put into contention by the defendant. Wrongly, the courts have held that the onus rests with the defendant to establish that his statement is true: *Lawrence v Chester Chronicle & Associated Newspapers Ltd* The Times, 1 January 1986.

[17] For further discussion, see 2.3.6 and 8.6.1.

[18] The qualification 'as far as is reasonably practical' is needed, as there would seem to be a point at which reducing vagueness is no longer worth the candle or is positively counter-productive. There is insufficient space in which to explore this interesting possibility in any detail (some relevant discussion can be found in TAO Endicott, *Vagueness in Law* (Oxford, Oxford University Press, 2000) ch 9). Briefly, however, it is at least arguable that vagueness should be countenanced if efforts to reduce it would result in the law becoming so detailed and voluminous that it would be unacceptably difficult to discover and comprehend.

[19] The argument here has been influenced by Fletcher (n 1) 570–73; Robinson (n 1) 264–73.

[20] See 2.3.6.

[21] Of course, vagueness in the definitions of justifications (and public policy defences) may be objectionable for reasons that are unconnected with the rule of law. For instance, the more uncertain the scope of a justification defence, the more likely it is that it will provoke litigation.

[22] Robinson goes further (and perhaps too far). He asserts that vagueness in relation to public policy defences to criminal liability is *beneficial*. In his words, 'vagueness and ambiguity in these defenses may serve the useful purpose of deterring undesirable conduct by persons who in fact qualify for the defense': Robinson (n 1) 272.

6.6. Defendant's Knowledge of the Material Facts

Is it necessary that the defendant know of the facts that furnish him with an escape route from liability in order to benefit from that escape route? This question should be answered in the negative in so far as denials are concerned. If the defendant is ignorant of the fact that one or more of the elements of a tort are present, liability will nevertheless not arise. Suppose, for example, that the defendant firebombs his own car believing that it belongs to his enemy. The defendant is not liable to his enemy since the tort of trespass to goods is not constituted (no property of the defendant's enemy was damaged). It is irrelevant for the purposes of tort law that the defendant did not realise that the car which he destroyed was his own.[23] To give another illustration, imagine that the defendant, intending to steal the claimant's coat, mistakes his own coat for that of the claimant and goes home with it. Liability will not arise in conversion because the action is incomplete (the defendant did not interfere with the claimant's property). It matters not one jot for tort law's purposes that the defendant was unaware of the fact that he was not handling the claimant's coat. As a third illustration, take a case in which the defendant has sexual intercourse with the claimant, mistakenly believing that the claimant was withholding consent. The defendant commits no battery since the element of non-consent is not present. Consistently with the fact that the plea of consent in the context of proceedings in trespass to the person is a denial,[24] it is irrelevant in so far as tort law is concerned that the defendant mistakenly believed that he was raping the claimant. As a final example, consider a situation where the defendant publishes defamatory statements about the claimant, not realising that they are true. In line with the fact that the plea of truth is a denial in an action in defamation,[25] the plea's success is not conditional upon the defendant knowing of the truth of the defamatory facts which he published.[26]

Analogous remarks can, on the whole, be made about public policy defences. Take the doctrine of illegality, which sometimes functions as a public policy defence.[27] This defence will be triggered only if, among other requirements, the claimant was committing an offence at or around the same time he was injured by the defendant's tort. However, it is irrelevant to this defence whether the defendant knew that the claimant's acts in question were illegal when he injured the claimant. Consider, secondly, the immunity of witnesses.[28] If a defendant makes defamatory statements about the claimant in an affidavit, he will benefit from the

---

[23] Although the claimant might be guilty of an impossible attempt under the criminal law.

[24] See 3.6.1.

[25] See 3.5.1.

[26] *Maisel v Financial Times Ltd* [1915] 3 KB 336, 340, 342 (CA); *Pamplin v Express Newspapers Ltd* [1988] 1 WLR 116n, 121 (CA); *Lowe v Associated Newspapers Ltd* [2006] EWHC 320; [2007] QB 580, 600–01 [62]; *Spiller v Joseph* [2010] UKSC 53; [2011] 1 AC 852, 883 [89].

[27] See 5.3.1.10–5.3.1.11. The doctrine of illegality can also provide the defendant with a denial (see 3.4.6, 3.6.5) and diminish the damages to which a successful claimant is entitled (see 1.2.1.3).

[28] See 5.3.1.1.

immunity[29] even though he does not realise, when he swears the affidavit, that he is performing a testimonial act. As a final illustration, take limitation bars.[30] A defendant will benefit from a limitation defence even if he has no inkling that the applicable limitation period has expired. One public policy defence that does not conform to this pattern is that of honest comment.[31] This defence lies when the defendant's impugned statement about the claimant is an opinion based on true or privileged facts that are of public interest. Significantly for present purposes, the courts have held that the defendant can only rely on facts of which he was aware at the time of making the comment in order to succeed on this defence.[32]

In contrast with the position that generally obtains in relation to denials and public policy defences, a defendant must be aware of the facts that render his acts justifiable in order to be eligible for a justification defence.[33] Suppose that the defendant shoots the claimant in a crowded shopping mall. Unbeknownst to the defendant, the claimant was a terrorist who was about to detonate a bomb. Had the defendant known what the claimant was planning to do, he would have been able to avoid liability on the ground that he was defending others. But the defendant's ignorance of the claimant's nefarious plot renders him ineligible for this defence.[34] The point is also nicely illustrated by the defence of responsible journalism. Consistently with the fact that this defence is a justification,[35] it was held in *Loutchansky v Times Newspapers Ltd* that in deciding whether the defence applied, only those facts of which the defendant was aware at the time of publication should be considered.[36]

6.7. The Relevance of the Defendant's Motive

For the most part, the definitional elements of torts are unconcerned with the defendant's motive.[37] Therefore, the defendant's motive for committing his impugned act is generally irrelevant to the issue of whether a defendant would be able to mount a successful denial. The fact that the defendant was maliciously motivated will not prevent a defendant from showing that an element of the

---

[29] *KJM Superbikes Ltd v Hinton* [2008] EWCA Civ 1280, [2009] 3 All ER 76, 81–82 [11]; [2009] 1 WLR 2406, 2410–11.

[30] See 5.3.2.1.

[31] See 5.3.1.9.

[32] *Cohen v Daily Telegraph Ltd* [1968] 1 WLR 916, 920; cf 919–20 (CA); *Lowe v Associated Newspapers Ltd* [2006] EWHC 320; [2007] QB 580, 604 [75]; *Spiller v Joseph* [2010] UKSC 53; [2011] 1 AC 852, 884 [95], 886–87 [108]–[111]. It seems, although it is not entirely clear, that this limitation on the defence has been removed by the Defamation Act 2013 (UK), s 3.

[33] It was argued in 4.3.2.6 that in order for a defendant to be justified he must, among other things, know of the justifying circumstances.

[34] Restatement (Second) of Torts, §63, cmt f.

[35] See 5.2.2.6.

[36] [2001] EWCA Civ 536; [2002] QB 321, 345 [80]–[82] (Brooke LJ). See also the concurring remarks of Sir Martin Nourse at 345 [85].

[37] 'Although the rule may be otherwise with regard to crimes, the law of England does not, according to my apprehension, take into account motive as constituting an element of civil wrong': *Allen v Flood* [1898] AC 1, 92 (HL) (Lord Watson).

relevant tort is absent. A classic example of the insensitivity of the elements of torts to the defendant's motive is that of defamation. It was shown earlier that the plea of truth is a denial of the damage element of this tort.[38] Consistently with the fact that the plea of truth is a denial, it is irrelevant to this plea that the defendant published the defamatory statement in question with the sole objective of humiliating the claimant. As Lord Nicholls of Birkenhead observed in *Reynolds v Times Newspapers Ltd*, the plea of truth 'avails a defendant even if he was acting spitefully'.[39] There are some relatively minor exceptions to the principle that the defendant's motive is irrelevant for the purposes of determining if the elements of a tort are satisfied. One tort that pays attention to the defendant's motive is private nuisance.[40] The fact that a given interference with the claimant's enjoyment of land was created maliciously may render it actionable.[41]

The defendant's motive is obviously irrelevant to public policy defences. Public policy defences are, by definition, unconcerned with the justifiability of the defendant's impugned act. The defendant's conduct need not be supported by an undefeated reason or, indeed, any reason. Naturally, therefore, public policy defences are not in the slightest bit interested in the defendant's reasons for acting. Thus, a judge who decided a case against the claimant litigant because the other party bribed him will nevertheless be immunised against liability,[42] a sadist who tortures a claimant in order to fulfil his twisted desires can enjoy a limitation defence and a defendant who defames a person who subsequently dies in circumstances where the defendant had only base reasons for publishing the defamatory statement is entitled to the defence of death.

Justifications are different from both denials and public policy defences in relation to the significance of the defendant's motive. It has already been explained in an earlier chapter[43] that the availability of justification defences is generally conditional upon the defendant acting for the reasons that rendered it justifiable to commit a tort. Thus, if the defendant commits a tort when doing so is justifiable for reasons other than those that made the commission of the tort justifiable, justification defences are typically unavailable. For example, a parent who uses force against his misbehaving child in circumstances where it was reasonable to discipline the child and the force used was reasonable is entitled to the defence of discipline only if he acted in order to discipline the child.[44] If he acted for sadistic reasons, for example, the defence is unavailable.

---

[38] See 3.5.1.

[39] [2001] 2 AC 127, 192 (HL). See also *KJO v XIM* [2011] EWHC 1768 (QB) [12] and n 111 in ch 3. In England, the sole (and minor) exception to the rule that the defendant's motive is irrelevant if his statement is true is created by the Rehabilitation of Offenders Act 1974 (UK), s 8.

[40] See GHL Fridman, 'Motive in the English Law of Nuisance' (1954) 40 *Virginia Law Review* 583.

[41] *Christie v Davey* [1893] 1 Ch 316 (Ch D); *Hollywood Silver Fox Farm Ltd v Emmett* [1936] 2 KB 468 (KBD).

[42] '[I]f the judge has accepted bribes or been in the least degree corrupt, or has perverted the course of justice, he can be punished in the criminal courts. That apart, however, a judge is not liable to an action for damages': *Sirros v Moore* [1975] QB 118, 132 (CA).

[43] See 4.3.2.7.

[44] See the text accompanying nn 126–127 in ch 4.

6.8. Benefiting from a Defence Enjoyed by a Confederate

The type of route by which a defendant is able to escape from liability may affect whether that escape route can be shared by another defendant who acts together with the first defendant. Suppose that D1 successfully denies an objective element of the tort that he is alleged to have committed. D2, who acted together with D1, should benefit from that denial too. This is because no tort will have been committed by either D1 or D2. Suppose, for instance, that D2 hands D1 a megaphone so that D1 can make defamatory remarks about C from his rooftop. If these remarks do not cause damage to C, D1 will be able to make good on a denial. D2 should benefit from this denial as well.

The position is different where D1 is able to avoid liability by denying only a subjective element of the tort in question. Suppose that D1, a bank employee, attempts to close the door to the bank's vault. The door is heavy and D1 struggles to move it. D2 comes to D1's assistance and, through their combined effort, they manage to lock the vault. C, another employee, is trapped inside it. D2 but not D1 knew that C was inside the vault when they closed the door. D1 is not liable in false imprisonment because the fault element of this tort is not satisfied. Plainly, however, D2 should not be able to enjoy the denial available to D1.

If the reasons theory of justifications that was defended earlier is correct,[45] justification defences are personal to the actor entitled to the defence in question and cannot be shared. On this theory, to be entitled to a justification defence, the defendant must reasonably believe that committing a tort was supported by an undefeated reason. It is insufficient that committing a tort was justifiable. Suppose that D1 uses reasonable defensive force against C, an aggressor, knowing that C is an aggressor. D1 is justified. D2 comes to D1's aid. Simply because D1 enjoys a justification defence does not mean that D2 will too. Whether or not D2 is justified depends on whether he realised that D1 was justified in defending himself.

It is doubtful whether public policy defences should be shared.[46] Suppose that D1, a diplomat, attacks C. D2 assists D1. Plainly, D2 should not benefit from the immunity that D1 enjoys by virtue of his status as a diplomat. The mere fact that D1 is immune provides no reason for exempting D2 from liability. Of course, D2 may be entitled to a public policy defence of his own. The point that is being made here is simply that D2 cannot resist the imposition of liability on the back of D1's defence.

To summarise, only denials of objective elements of the tort in which the claimant sues can be shared by confederates. Denials of subjective elements of the relevant tort, justifications and public policy defences cannot be shared.

---

[45] See 4.3.2.6.

[46] The Restatement (Second) of Torts, § 880 provides: 'If two persons would otherwise be liable for a harm, one of them is not relieved from liability by the fact that the other has an absolute privilege to act or an immunity from liability to the person harmed.'

6.9. Invocation by the Court

In an earlier chapter, it was noted that, as a general rule, it is up to the defendant (or, rather, his insurer) to raise defences.[47] But it was also observed that the court can sometimes interpose a defence. Arguably, the way in which a defence is classified affects whether the court can consider it on its own motion.[48] There is something to be said for permitting the court to raise public policy defences, or at least certain types of public policy defences, if the defendant fails to do so. If the court is unable to raise some or particular types of public policy defences, the administration of justice or the realisation of some other important social goal may be imperilled. Suppose that a defendant, because he is represented by incompetent lawyers, fails to invoke the defence of abuse of process in circumstances when it is clearly available. If the court is not permitted to consider the defence, the claimant would be free to misuse the court's process. This would obviously be unacceptable, and it is unsurprising that the courts have held that they can consider the defence of abuse of process on their own accord.[49] The defences of *res judicata*[50] and illegality[51] can also be raised by the court. Limitation bars[52] seem to be treated differently. It appears that defendants are free to waive limitation bars.[53]

In contrast with the situation that obtains in relation to most public policy defences, it is doubtful whether the court can or should invoke denials or justification defences. Were the court permitted to raise denials or justifications, little or nothing would remain of the principle that the courts should decide only those issues that are in dispute between the parties, which is a lodestar of civil procedure.[54]

---

[47] See 1.8.

[48] Cf F Bennion, *Bennion on Statutory Interpretation: A Code*, 5th edn (London, LexisNexis, 2008) 58, who writes that 'In general it is taken that when Parliament provides for . . . a defence it intends the party entitled to the defence to be able to waive it (whether by conduct or by an express agreement not to rely on the defence).'

[49] CPR 3.4(2)(b).

[50] 'Because "res judicata belongs to courts as well as to litigants," a court may invoke res judicata *sua sponte*': *Nwachukwu v Karl* 222 FRD 208, 212 (DCC, 2004) (citation omitted).

[51] See ch 1, n 105.

[52] See 5.3.2.1.

[53] *Wright v John Bagnall & Sons Ltd* [1900] 2 QB 240 (CA); *Lubovsky v Snelling* [1944] KB 44 (CA).

[54] This principle is discussed in 1.8.2 and 8.5.1.2. The conclusions reached in this section lead to the odd conclusion that the court can raise the doctrine of illegality in so far as it operates as a public policy defence, but not when it works as a denial. This anomaly should be removed by changing the doctrine of illegality so that it functions only as a public policy defence. This step has been taken in Canada: *Hall v Hebert* [1993] 2 SCR 159. For argument in support of the Canadian approach, see J Goudkamp, 'The Defence of Joint Illegal Enterprise' (2010) 34 *Melbourne University Law Review* 425, esp at 435–36.

6.10. Bad Character Evidence

The fact that a defendant has been able to avoid liability in tort will not necessarily insulate him from other adverse legal consequences of his behaviour. For example, the impugned conduct of a defendant who has been released from liability may be adduced as evidence of bad character in subsequent proceedings.[55] However, it is much less likely that a defendant's underlying behaviour will amount to evidence of bad character if the defendant was able to avoid liability on the basis of a denial or a justification as opposed to a public policy defence. Consider the following scenarios:

(1) C1 sues D1 in deceit. D1 can make out a denial as the evidence establishes that D1 did not intend to defraud C1.
(2) C2 sues D2 in false imprisonment. D2 has a justification defence as he was lawfully arresting C2.
(3) C3 sues D3 in battery. The allegation that underlies the action is that D3 raped C3. C3 cannot hold D3 liable because D3 has a public policy defence; a limitation bar has descended.

On these bare facts, D1 and D2 have not engaged in any behaviour that discloses evidence of bad character on their part. This is not so in the case of D3: the fact that a limitation bar prevents D3 from being held liable does not alter the moral nature of his behaviour. Accordingly, evidence that D3 raped C3 may be admissible to establish D3's bad character in subsequent proceedings. Of course, it does not follow automatically from the fact that a defendant could not be held liable because he enjoyed a public policy defence that his underlying conduct will qualify as bad character evidence. This is partly because a defendant who has a public policy defence may also be able to succeed on a denial or a justification.

6.11. Non-implications

It might be thought that the classificatory exercises that have been conducted so far in this book yield further practical implications. Additional ramifications arguably exist. But the goal of this section is to identify some limits on the implications of this taxonomic project.

---

[55] Regarding the admissibility of bad character evidence, see generally C Tapper, *Cross & Tapper on Evidence*, 12th edn (Oxford, Oxford University Press, 2010) chs 7–8.

6.11.1. Liability for Resisting the Conduct of an Aggressor

Imagine that C is an aggressor who is not liable in tort. Can D resist C's conduct, say, by disabling him? The answer to this question might be thought to depend on why C is not liable. If C is not liable despite being an aggressor because an element of a relevant tort is missing, D is probably entitled to use reasonable force to resist C. Suppose that C involuntarily strikes D. The voluntary act requirement of the action in battery is unsatisfied, so C commits no battery against D. However, it would seem that D would be entitled to resist C nevertheless. It seems implausible to say that D would incur liability to C in tort if he did not submit to C's attack.

It has often been said that it is impermissible to resist justified actors.[56] But whether or not one should agree with this view depends on which theory of justification one accepts.[57] If the reasons theory of justification should be accepted (it was supported earlier[58]), this principle must be rejected. On this theory of justification, it is impossible to lay down a rule for all situations, as everything depends on whether the defendant reasonably believed that he was justified. Suppose that C is not liable because he was lawfully arresting D. If D realises that the arrest is lawful, D would indeed be liable in tort if he resisted C; D would be required to submit to C. But things are different where D reasonably but mistakenly thinks that justifying circumstances exist. Imagine that D resists being arrested by C because he reasonably but mistakenly thinks that C is a mugger. Both C and D are justified on the reasons theory of justification. Neither is liable to the other.

Lastly, it seems that, as a general rule, liability in tort will not arise for merely resisting the acts of an aggressor who is able to avoid liability only because he has a public policy defence. Acts that do not attract liability solely because of the application of a public policy defence are typically thoroughly objectionable. For example, a person who is attacked by another individual who cannot be held liable in battery because he enjoys diplomatic immunity should not have to submit to the attack.

In conclusion, contrary to what some theorists might believe, the issue of whether or not it is permissible to resist an aggressor who is not liable in tort law cannot be resolved by reference to the avenue by which the aggressor is able to avoid liability. Although it is permissible to resist aggressors who can avoid liability only by way of a denial or a public policy defence, if the reasons theory of justification is correct, no general rule can be laid down as to whether or not it is permissible to resist a justified aggressor. It follows, therefore, that the differences

---

[56] See, eg, Fletcher (n 1) 759–62; PH Robinson, *Criminal Law Defenses*, vol 1 (St Paul, Minn, West Publishing Co, 1984) 164–78; A Brudner, 'A Theory of Necessity' (1987) 7 *Oxford Journal of Legal Studies* 339, 363; JG Fleming, *Law of Torts*, 9th edn (Sydney, Lawbook Co, 1998) 83 (see at 87 [5.10] in the 10th edition: C Sappideen and P Vines, *Fleming's The Law of Torts*, 10th edn (Sydney, Lawbook Co, 2011)); A Ashworth, *Principles of Criminal Law*, 6th edn (Oxford, Oxford University Press, 2009) 114.

[57] For illuminating discussion on this point, see DN Husak, 'Conflicts of Justifications' (1999) 18 *Law and Philosophy* 41.

[58] See 4.3.2.6.

between denials, justification and public policy defences do not convey any useful information for present purposes.

6.11.2. Vicarious Liability

It might be thought that the route by which a tortfeasor can avoid liability is relevant to whether another defendant can be held vicariously liable for the tort. Imagine the following scenario: D1 is employed by D2. C commences proceedings against D1 and D2, claiming that he was injured by D1's tortious conduct committed in the scope of his employment. If D1 can avoid liability, might the legal basis on which D1 is able to escape from liability affect whether C is able to hold D2 vicariously liable? It is arguable that D2's liability should turn on whether D1 has a denial, a justification or a public policy defence. However, the law on this point is clear: because masters are vicariously liable only if their servant is liable,[59] *any* rule that enables the servant to evade liability will prevent the master from being held vicariously liable.[60] The taxonomic exercise that has been conducted in this book has, therefore, no bearing on vicarious liability.

6.11.3 Costs

If a defendant is able to avoid being held liable, does it matter for the purposes of costs orders whether the defendant had a denial, a justification or a public policy defence? It is clear that it does not. Generally speaking, in Commonwealth jurisdictions the successful party is entitled to have his costs paid by his opponent (the 'costs rule').[61] As 'success' is defined simply as obtaining a verdict in one's favour, the legal route by which a defendant is able to avoid liability does not, in the ordinary course of things, impact upon his entitlement to have his costs paid by the claimant.

Should the legal avenue by which a defendant is let out of liability impact upon the orders that the court should make as to costs? This question should also be answered in the negative. The route by which a defendant who succeeds in litigation escaped from liability does not change the fact that he had to go to the

---

[59] This is because the servant's theory of vicarious liability has found favour with the courts: *New South Wales v Lepore* [2003] HCA 4; (2003) 212 CLR 511, 611 [299]; *Majrowski v Guy's and St Thomas's NHS Trust* [2006] UKHL 34; [2007] 1 AC 224, 230 [15]. On this theory the only tort is the servant's; his liability is merely duplicated on the master. Hence, if the servant is not liable, the master cannot be vicariously liable. See further G Williams, 'Vicarious Liability: Tort of the Master or of the Servant?' (1956) 72 *Law Quarterly Review* 522; JG Fleming, 'Vicarious Liability for Breach of Statutory Duty' (1957) 20 *Modern Law Review* 655; PS Atiyah, *Vicarious Liability in the Law of Torts* (London, Butterworths, 1967) 6–7; R Stevens, *Torts and Rights* (Oxford, Oxford University Press, 2007) 259–67.

[60] *Darling Island Stevedoring and Lighterage Co Ltd v Long* (1957) 97 CLR 36, 57–58 (HCA); *Parker v Commonwealth* (1965) 112 CLR 295, 300–03 (HCA); *Commonwealth of Australia v Griffiths* [2007] NSWCA 370; (2007) 70 NSWLR 268, 289–93 [100]–[116] (special leave to appeal refused: [2008] HCATrans 227); cf *Imperial Chemical Industries Ltd v Shatwell* [1965] AC 656, 686 (HL).

[61] CPR 44.3(2)(a).

expense of resisting a claim to a remedy to which the claimant was not entitled. Furthermore, if the application of the costs rule depended upon the basis on which the defendant was able to escape liability (suppose that it did not apply where the defendant won on a justification or a public policy defence), it would be necessary whenever a defendant has a justification or public policy defence to determine whether he did not also have a denial. This enquiry would be a waste of resources.

6.11.4. The tribunal

Might the type of plea offered by a defendant who hopes to resist liability affect whether responsibility for determining if it applies rests with the judge or jury (where, exceptionally, a jury is used in tort litigation)? Apparently it does not.[62] It does not seem possible to generalise in this respect. Some denials are for the judge to consider (eg, a denial of the existence of a relevant duty of care[63]) while others are for the jury (eg, a denial of an allegation of negligence[64]). Similar remarks can be made about justifications. Consider, for example, the defence of qualified privilege, which requires the judge and jury to work together to determine its applicability. Whether a given occasion is privileged is a question of law for the judge. However, if the judge decides this issue in favour of the defendant, it is for the jury to decide whether the statement in question was published on the occasion concerned and whether the defendant abused the privilege.[65] Likewise, public policy defences are not the exclusive province of either the judge or the jury. Some public policy defences contain elements that are matters for the jury, such as honest comment (it is for the jury to determine whether the defendant's impugned statement is a comment[66]) and illegality (whether the claimant committed an offence is a jury question). Others are, in whole or in the main, for the judge, such as the defences of abuse of process and *res judicata*.

6.11.5. Defendant Causing the Conditions of his Own Defence

Criminal law theorists have spent a great deal of time discussing the problem of the defendant who brings about the conditions of his own defence.[67] Classic

---

[62] Robinson reached the same conclusion in relation to the criminal law: see PH Robinson, *Criminal Law Defenses*, vol 1 (St Paul, Minn, West Publishing Co, 1984) 53–54.

[63] *Wicks v State Rail Authority (NSW)* [2010] HCA 22; (2010) 241 CLR 60, 73 [33].

[64] *Qualcast (Wolverhampton) Ltd v Haynes* [1959] AC 743, 757 (HL); Restatement (Third) of Torts, § 8.

[65] *Adam v Ward* [1917] AC 309, 318 (HL).

[66] *London Artists Ltd v Littler Grade Organisation Ltd* [1969] 2 QB 375, 385–86 (CA).

[67] Eg, M Gur-Arye, *Actio Libera in Causa in Criminal Law* (Jerusalem, Harry Sacher Institute, 1984); PH Robinson, 'Causing the Conditions of One's Own Defense: A Study in the Limits of Theory in Criminal Law Doctrine' (1985) 71 *Virginia Law Review* 1; C Finkelstein and L Katz, 'Contrived Defenses and Deterrent Threats: Two Facets of One Problem' (2008) 5 *Ohio State Journal of Criminal Law* 479.

illustrations of this problem are the defendant who starts a fight and then kills the victim in self-defence, and the defendant who voluntarily puts himself in a position where he may be subjected to duress. It does not seem that this issue has received any serious attention from torts scholars. The relevant question for present purposes is whether tort law handles the problem differently depending on whether justifications or public policy defences are in issue. It is doubtful that a public policy defence would be lost because the defendant conspired to take advantage of it, with the possible exception of limitation bars, which will not apply where the defendant concealed from the claimant a fact relevant to his action.[68] The way in which tort law would respond to a defendant bringing about his own justification defence is unclear. Virtually the only justification in respect of which guidance exists in this regard is that of public necessity. In *Southport Corporation v Esso Petroleum Co Ltd*,[69] Devlin J opined (dictum) that a defendant who was at fault for causing a situation of peril could not rely on the defence of public necessity to destroy property to avoid the peril.[70] Given the lack of authority in relation to the effect of a defendant's causing conditions necessary to enliven a justification, it is impossible to say whether tort law treats justifications differently from public policy defences in this connection.

6.11.6. Context Sensitivity

Can it plausibly be argued that the type of plea offered by a defendant casts light on whether the plea concerned is confined to specific contexts or is available throughout tort law generally? Clearly, it cannot be so argued. The truth of the matter is that the type of plea advanced by a defendant does not determine whether it is context-specific. Some denials are limited to certain contexts, such as the plea of truth. Other denials prevent liability from arising in all torts, such as involuntariness. Much the same is true of justifications. For example, the defences of consent and public necessary are general defences, whereas the defences of abatement or qualified privilege are confined to particular torts. There are also both general and specific public policy defences. Certain public policy defences are available to all torts, such as illegality[71] and limitation bars. Others have specific spheres of application, such as the defence of honest comment.

---

[68] Limitation Act 1980 (UK), s 32(1)(b).
[69] [1953] 2 All ER 1204, 1210; [1953] 3 WLR 773, 779 (QBD). The issue was not considered on appeal to the House of Lords: *Esso Petroleum Co Ltd v Southport Corporation* [1956] AC 218 (HL).
[70] See also *Rigby v Chief Constable of Northamptonshire* [1985] 2 All ER 985, 994; [1985] 1 WLR 1242, 1253 (QBD).
[71] See ch 1, n 50.

Implications

6.12. Summary

In this short chapter it has been argued that much turns on whether the defendant has a denial or a defence and, if the defendant has a defence, on whether the defence is a justification or a public policy defence. The type of plea available to a defendant may affect:

(1) the reception that it is likely to receive from the courts;
(2) the allocation of the onus of pleading in respect of it;
(3) the assignment of the burden of proof in relation to it;
(4) the maximum degree of vagueness from which the underlying rule can suffer for the purposes of the rule of law;
(5) whether the underlying rule requires that the defendant know of the facts that are necessary to enliven it;
(6) whether the underlying rule will be forfeited if the defendant was improperly motivated;
(7) whether the underlying rule can be shared with the defendant's confederate;
(8) whether the court can raise the underlying rule on its own motion; and
(9) whether the defendant's act in issue constitutes evidence of bad character on his part.

7

Rival Taxonomies

Flawed classification is a source and symptom of intellectual disorder.[1]

7.1. Introduction

The bipartite taxonomy of tort defences that has been developed in this book is not the only way in which tort defences can be organised. There are numerous other possible arrangements. This chapter considers briefly 10 other classifications that have been adopted, expressly or implicitly, elsewhere. It is rather difficult to assess these rival taxonomies since they are all in a skeletal state. As was noted earlier,[2] no comprehensive taxonomic analysis of tort defences has been offered. No more than a sentence or two has been written in support of most of the taxonomies that will be considered here. Indeed, some of them are endorsed only by implication in the chapter structure of tort law textbooks. However, despite the limited materials available in this regard, it is clear that there is little hope that, even once fleshed out, any of these rival taxonomies would be particularly illuminating. As mechanisms for understanding how defences operate as a system, they all compare unfavourably with the bipartite taxonomy that has been defended.

7.2. A Derived System of Classification

One could derive a taxonomy of defences from whatever schema one uses to organise torts. Suppose, for instance, that one agrees with Holmes that torts should be categorised according to the basis on which they impose liability.[3] Separating torts from each other in this way yields the following categories: torts that require subjective fault; negligence-based torts; and torts that impose strict liability. Defences could then be ordered as follows: defences to intentional torts; defences to negligence-based torts; and defences to strict liability torts. It should

[1] P Birks, *Unjust Enrichment*, 2nd edn (Oxford, Oxford University Press, 2005) 20.
[2] See 1.3, 4.1.
[3] This schema was proposed in an anonymous article: 'The Theory of Torts' (1873) 7 *American Law Review* 652. Holmes is generally credited as the author.

be noted that, technically, what is being discussed here is not so much a system for classifying defences as a method by which a system of defences can be generated. Applying this method will yield different schemas of defences depending on the system of torts with which one starts.

Tort law textbooks frequently use the derivative method to produce a system of defences.[4] It may seem appropriate for defences to be organised in this way. Defences are, after all, dependent upon torts for their existence. While it is theoretically possible to construct a system of tort law that lacks defences,[5] it is impossible to have defences without torts. On closer reflection, however, it emerges that a derived system of defences is unlikely to be illuminating. This is because there is no reason for thinking that such a schema will tell us anything interesting about defences. A given taxonomy of torts might be useful when it comes to understanding the wrongs that qualify as torts, but it is by no means guaranteed that a system for categorising tort defences that is derived from that taxonomy will cast any light on defences. For example, what practical implications of a classificatory system of defences can be derived from Holmes's taxonomy of torts? None is immediately apparent. Conversely, a substantial number of potential ramifications of the taxonomy supported in this book have been identified.[6]

7.3. General Defences and Special Defences

Most tort law textbooks that do not employ the derivative method of classification divide defences into those that apply to all torts (general defences) and those that apply to only some torts (special defences).[7] General defences include limitation bars, illegality[8] and most immunities. Examples of defences that are typically regarded as special defences include self-defence, abatement, recapture of land and chattels, and honest comment. It may be convenient to embrace this system of defences for the purposes of writing a tort law textbook. It makes it possible for a (usually brief) discussion of special defences to be tacked onto the ends of chapters that deal with particular torts, while analysis of general defences can be placed in a

---

[4] See, eg, WP Keeton, DB Dobbs, RE Keeton and DG Owen (eds), *Prosser and Keeton on Torts*, 5th edn (St Paul, Minn, West Publishing Co, 1984); C Sappideen and P Vines (eds), *Fleming's The Law of Torts*, 10th edn (Sydney, Lawbook Co, 1998); DB Dobbs, *The Law of Torts* (St Paul, Minn, West Publishing Co, 2000); K Barker, P Cane, M Lunney and F Trindade, *The Law of Torts in Australia*, 5th edn (Oxford, Oxford University Press, 2012); C Witting (ed), *Street on Torts*, 14th edn (Oxford, Oxford University Press, 2015).

[5] See 2.3.

[6] See ch 6.

[7] See, eg, MA Jones, *Textbook on Torts*, 8th edn (Oxford, Oxford University Press, 2002); A Dugdale and MA Jones (eds), *Clerk & Lindsell on Torts*, 21st edn (London, Sweet & Maxwell, 2014); K Oliphant (ed), *The Law of Tort*, 3rd edn (London, LexisNexis, 2013); S Deakin, A Johnston and B Markesinis, *Markesinis and Deakin's Tort Law*, 7th edn (Oxford, Oxford University Press, 2012); NJ McBride and R Bagshaw, *Tort Law*, 5th edn (Harlow, Pearson Longman, 2015).

[8] See ch 1, n 50.

separate chapter (usually relegated to the end of the book). This might enable words to be saved. It might also mean that textbooks can cover the law of torts in manner that is convenient given the constraints of a university term. Splitting defences into general and special defences may also appeal to practitioners.[9] Practitioners want to be able to discover, with the minimum amount of effort, which defences are available to which torts. The general defence/special defence classification might enable this information to be conveyed more simply than some other models.

While arranging defences into general defences and special defences might be useful for certain purposes, it is not particularly helpful if one is interested in obtaining a sound theoretical understanding of how the law of defences operates as a system. One problem with it is that there is no crisp distinction between the two categories. For instance, is a defence that is available to three torts (such as qualified privilege, which is an answer to liability arising in injurious falsehood, slander and libel) a special defence or a general defence? It is doubtful whether a sensible answer can be given to this question. Another weakness in this schema, which is not shared by the system of defences that has been promoted in this book, is that it is not clear that it uncovers anything of philosophical or practical significance.

7.4. Cane's System

Peter Cane suggests that tort defences can be separated into those that are 'claimant relative' and those that are 'defendant relative'.[10] He contends that the defendant-relative category has three subcategories: justifications, excuses and immunities. Cane identifies self-defence, consent and statutory authority as justifications. Excuses are said to include necessity.[11] Cane offers the judicial process immunities as illustrations of defences that fall within the last subcategory of defendant-relative defences. Defences in the claimant-relative category comprise consent, contributory negligence and voluntary assumption of risk.

This taxonomy has at least three significant downsides. First, Cane does not explain why certain defences, such as that of consent, feature in both the claimant-relative and defendant-relative categories. It is contradictory to say that a given defence is both claimant relative and defendant relative.

Secondly, Cane's system fails to capture many defences. Numerous defences are more or less equally interested in the claimant's and the defendant's behaviour or, more to the point, are concerned with the nature of the parties' *interaction*,

[9] It may not be a coincidence that the two leading books about tort law for practitioners in England organise defences into general defences and special defences: Dugdale and Jones (n 7); Oliphant (n 7).

[10] P Cane, *Responsibility in Law and Morality* (Oxford, Hart Publishing, 2002) 90. Cane says that he is offering a schema of 'answers' and that he 'deliberately avoided the narrower term "defences"'. Unfortunately, Cane does not explain what he means by 'answer' and 'defence'.

[11] Cf 5.2.2.1, where it is argued that necessity is a justification.

and so do not fall neatly within either category. An example of a defence that straddles these categories is that of self-defence. Cane identifies self-defence as a defendant-relative defence. In doing so, he misses an important part of the truth. This defence does not scrutinise the reasonableness of the defendant's acts in isolation from the claimant's. It is also concerned, for instance, with the force that the claimant applied or threatened to apply. Similar remarks can be made about the defence of arrest. Cane claims that this defence is defendant relative. It is true that it is interested in the defendant's behaviour. For example, the defence will be unavailable if the defendant uses more force than is reasonably necessary to make an arrest.[12] But it does not follow, as Cane seems to believe, that the claimant's conduct is unimportant. For instance, the defence's scope depends on whether the claimant committed or is about to commit an offence.

Cane's system is also incapable of organising those defences that are not connected in any significant way to either party. An example of a defence that has no claim to belong to either category is that of *res judicata*. This defence is concerned with whether the issue in respect of which the parties are in dispute has already been decided, a matter that is not linked to either party. Another example of a defence that defies classification within Cane's scheme is that of prior private prosecution. It is difficult to see how this defence, the application of which depends solely on whether a private prosecution was brought against the defendant, is associated in any significant way with either party.

Thirdly, Cane does not detail ways in which his taxonomy might illuminate interesting features of defences. What implications might it entail? The category to which a given defence is assigned might be thought to have a bearing on the onuses of pleading and proof, with claimant-relative defences being for claimants to establish and the burden falling to defendants to make out defendant-relative defences. But, on inspection, it emerges that it does not have this consequence. For example, illegality, a claimant-relative defence, is for the defendant to plead and prove.[13] The same is true in relation to voluntary assumption of risk,[14] which is also a claimant-relative defence. In short, Cane's taxonomy does not really advance learning regarding defences.

Before leaving Cane's system of defences, it worth noting that his adoption of it is animated by his thinking about tort law generally. A theme that permeates his writing about tort law is that[15]

---

[12] *R v Clegg* [1995] 1 AC 482 (HL).

[13] *Gala v Preston* (1991) 172 CLR 243, 254 (HCA); *Brown v Harding* [2008] NSWCA 51 [40]; *Wills v Bell* [2002] QCA 419; [2004] 1 Qd R 296, 304 [12].

[14] *Smith v Baker & Sons* [1891] AC 325, 336, 338 (HL); *Osborne v The London and North Western Railway Co* (1888) 21 QBD 220, 224–25 (Div Ct); *Roggenkamp v Bennett* (1950) 80 CLR 292, 300 (HCA); *Car and General Insurance Corp Ltd v Seymour* [1956] SCR 322, 331; *Multinational Gas and Petrochemical Co v Multinational Gas and Petrochemical Services Ltd* [1983] Ch 258, 282 (CA); *Joslyn v Berry* [2003] HCA 34; (2003) 214 CLR 552, 561–62 [24].

[15] Cane (n 10) 49–50 (footnote omitted). See also P Cane, *The Anatomy of Tort Law* (Oxford, Hart Publishing, 1997) 1, 11–15; P Cane, 'Retribution, Proportionality, and Moral Luck in Tort Law' in P Cane and J Stapleton (eds), *The Law of Obligations: Essays in Celebration of John Fleming* (Oxford, Clarendon Press, 1998) 141.

[r]esponsibility in [it] is two-sided, concerned not only with agent-conduct, but equally with the impact of that conduct on others. Victims play a central role in the civil justice process. Responsibility in civil law is always *to* someone as well as *for* something.

The critique of Cane's taxonomy of defences offered here should not be regarded as casting doubt on the accuracy of the proposition that tort law is a two-part affair. Cane is clearly correct to say that this is an important feature of tort law. The overarching point that has been made in this section is simply that it is not useful to arrange defences into defences that are claimant-relative and those that are defendant-relative.

7.5. Wigmore's System

John Wigmore, in an article that has not enjoyed nearly as much attention as it deserves, considered the classification of tort law defences. Despite being over 100 years old, Wigmore's analysis is the most serious effort made by far to organise tort defences. Although it describes a tort system that is rather different in significant respects from the modern law of torts, it is worth giving it close consideration.

Wigmore contended that defences ought to be grouped according to 'the essential policy of the excuse, – that which gives it character, and explains its varying application by the courts'.[16] He thought that this yielded three categories. The first category comprises defences that are interested 'solely in the condition, conduct, or other circumstances of the plaintiff'.[17] This category consists in three subcategories. The first subcategory is reserved for the defence of consent. The second subcategory is the province of defences that, according to Wigmore, amount to an assumption of the risk of harm. Wigmore placed in this subcategory the doctrine of 'avoidable damage' (or, mitigation, as it tends to be known outside of the United States), illegality and contributory negligence (which was a defence in all jurisdictions in the United States in Wigmore's time[18]). The third subcategory contained a defence that applies where the claimant is in a situation 'calling for humane assistance'.[19]

The second category of defences is constituted by 'excuses starting from the interest of others than the plaintiff'.[20] Wigmore subdivided this group into 'excuses resting on the needs of public justice, and the excuses resting on the

---

[16] JH Wigmore, 'A General Analysis of Tort-Relations' (1895) 8 *Harvard Law Review* 377, 390. In this article, Wigmore builds on JH Wigmore, 'The Tripartite Division of Torts' (1894) 8 *Harvard Law Review* 200.

[17] Wigmore (1895) (n 16) 390.

[18] The decline of the defence of contributory negligence in the United States is masterfully described in JG Fleming, 'Comparative Negligence at Last – By Judicial Choice' (1976) 64 *California Law Review* 239.

[19] Wigmore (1895) (n 16) 391.

[20] *Ibid*, 390.

interests of the community in general or of the defendant in particular'.[21] Defences based on the needs of the administration of justice included arrest, execution of judicial order and the various absolute privileges to utter defamatory statements in connection with judicial proceedings. Defences that exist in view of the community's or the defendant's interests include public necessity, nuisance resulting from reasonable use of land, qualified privilege and honest comment.

The last category of defences is described as an intermediate group in the sense that elements of both of the preceding categories enter into it. Wigmore splits this category into 'the various forms of Self-redress and Self-defence',[22] and 'limitations allowable in favor of parents, teachers, masters, ship-captains, and the like'.[23] The 'Self-redress and Self-defence' subcategory includes the defences of self-defence, defences of others, defence of property, recapture, re-entry and abatement. The other subcategory includes discipline, arrest and State-sanctioned imprisonment. Because Wigmore's system of defences is extremely complex, it is worth describing it diagrammatically. See Table 4 below.

To a degree, Wigmore's system of defences is similar to Cane's. The first two categories in Wigmore's taxonomy correspond roughly to the groupings of defences that Cane proposed. But, unlike Cane's taxonomy, Wigmore's schema

Table 4: Wigmore's system of defences

Defences concerned solely with the claimant	Defences concerned with interests of society or of the defendant	Defences in which elements of both categories enter
Consent	*Defences based on the needs of the administration of justice*	*Self-redress and self-defence*
Consent		Self-defence
Assumption of the risk of harm		Defences of others
	Arrest	Defence of property
	Execution of judicial order	Recapture
Doctrine of avoidable damage	Absolute privileges to defame in connection with judicial proceedings	Re-entry
		Abatement
Illegality		
Contributory negligence	*Defences based on other community interests or the defendant's interests*	*Limitations allowable in favour of parents, teachers, masters, ship-captains, etc*
Claimant needing assistance		
Humane assistance of claimant	Public necessity	Discipline
	Nuisance caused by reasonable user	Arrest
	Qualified privilege	State-sanctioned imprisonment
	Honest comment	

[21] *Ibid.*
[22] *Ibid*, 391.
[23] *Ibid*, 392.

recognises a category to accommodate defences that are interested in the conduct of both the claimant and the defendant. In this regard, Wigmore's system is superior to Cane's. But it suffers from numerous limitations nonetheless. As an initial point, note that, contrary to what Wigmore thought, the doctrines of avoidable damage, illegality and contributory negligence are not based on an assumption of risk (and, bafflingly, Wigmore did not discuss the voluntary assumption of risk principle at all).[24] These rules were independent of each other in Wigmore's time,[25] as they are today. Secondly, Wigmore did not explain why the defence of arrest features in both his second and third category. This is something that he appeared not to notice. Thirdly, in contrast to what Wigmore believed, many of the defences that he placed in his second category manifest concern for the claimant. For example, the defence of qualified privilege, at least in certain contexts, such as when the defendant is responding to an attack made by the claimant, openly shows regard for the interests of the claimant, as has already been explained.[26] Fourthly, it is unclear whether Wigmore applied his professed criterion of classification to create his taxonomy. As noted earlier, he declared that defences should be organised according to their 'policy', by which he presumably meant to refer to the reason why the law recognises them. But the three categories seem to be drawn not on the basis of particular policies that underpin defences but on the basis of the concern that defences show for different stakeholders. Fifthly, Wigmore conflates in his second category defences that advance society's interests and defences that promote the defendant's interests. Sixthly, Wigmore did not set out any practical ramifications of his taxonomy (and none is immediately apparent).

7.6. The Division Adopted by the Restatement (Second) of Torts

The Restatement (Second) of Torts addresses defences under the following chapter titles: 'Justification and Excuse'; 'Immunities'; and 'Discharge'.[27] Justifications and excuses are said to include the defences of consent, abatement, arrest and self-defence. The chapter on immunities canvasses absolute privilege and governmental immunity. The chapter on discharge treats the doctrine of *res judicata*, limitation bars, death, contract of settlement, release and bankruptcy. This system

---

[24] These doctrines are disentangled in J Goudkamp, 'Rethinking Contributory Negligence' in SGA Pitel, JW Neyers and E Chamberlain (eds), *Tort Law: Challenging Orthodoxy* (Oxford, Hart Publishing, 2013) 328–34; J Goudkamp, 'The Defence of Joint Illegal Enterprise' (2010) 34 *Melbourne University Law Review* 425, 428–29.

[25] Voluntary assumption of risk and contributory negligence are distinguished in FH Bolhen, 'Contributory Negligence' (1908) 21 *Harvard Law Review* 233, 243–51.

[26] See 5.2.1.7.

[27] Restatement (Second) of Torts, chs 45, 45A and 46.

is highly unsatisfactory. Things go awry at the very beginning as the Reporters do not mark clearly the borders of the categories that they identify. Consider the Reporters' attempt to delimit the justification and excuse category. They write that 'a justification or excuse avoids liability for tortious conduct under particular circumstances because those circumstances make it just and reasonable that the liability not be imposed'.[28] This definition is hopelessly inadequate because it does not separate justifications and excuses from immunities or discharges. So defined, the category for justifications and excuses engulfs the other two categories set out by the Reporters. Immunities, we are told, differ from 'justifications and excuses ... but the difference would appear to be largely differences of degree'.[29] This is manifestly incorrect. There is a fundamental difference between these types of answers to liability. The former are sensitive to the reasonableness of the defendant's conduct,[30] whereas the latter are not. Immunities are concerned not with the justifiability of what the defendant did but with whether he occupied a particular role or enjoyed a certain status.[31] The Reporters do not say explicitly what a 'discharge' is. However, they seem to have thought that discharges are defences that are enlivened by events that take place subsequent to the commission of a tort. It is unclear, however, whether this is a theoretically interesting basis for identifying discharges as a separate category.

7.7. Defences That Apply Immediately and Delayed-onset Defences

Several tort law textbooks adopt a chapter structure that distinguishes between defences that apply at the time of the defendant's tort and defences that accrue at a later point in time[32] (typically, the second category of defences is termed rules that 'extinguish liability'). Defences that are generally regarded as arising immediately include pleas such as arrest, self-defence, abatement, public necessity and qualified privilege. Delayed-onset defences are normally thought to consist in rules such as limitation bars, contract of settlement and release. It might be that the best way of arranging certain types of defences is to divide them into those that accrue at the time of the tort and those that are enlivened subsequently. Indeed, this is how public policy defences are broken down in this book.[33] It is arguable that this is the cleanest way of arranging these defences. But this system

---

[28] *Ibid*, ch 45A, Introductory Note.

[29] *Ibid*.

[30] See 4.3.2.2–4.3.2.3.

[31] Some further remarks on what the word 'immunity' means are offered in n 47 below and in ch 6, n 10.

[32] Eg, WVH Rogers (ed), *Winfield & Jolowicz on Tort*, 18th edn (London, Sweet & Maxwell, 2010) chs 25–26.

[33] See 5.3.

of classifying the whole of the law of tort defences is not particularly revealing. Nothing much would seem to turn on whether a defence is engaged at the time of the tort or later. For this reason, to organise all defences in this manner would seem to be ill-advised. It is an inferior system of classification to the bipartite structure promoted in this book.

7.8. Dobbs's System

Dan Dobbs in *The Law of Torts*[34] makes some brief remarks about the classification of defences. He organises defences into:

(1) justifications (he says that justifications include self-defence, defence of property and discipline);
(2) defences based on policy (he gives a limitation bar as an example of such a defence);
(3) defences that are founded on the claimant's own misconduct (he identifies contributory negligence as an example of such a defence); and
(4) defences that are rooted in the defendant's status (he gives the example of governmental immunity).

The central difficulty with Dobbs's system is that many defences defy classification within it. For example, is the defence of illegality a policy defence or a defence that is based on the claimant's own misconduct? How should the defence of self-defence be classified in a case where the defendant uses reasonable defensive force to repel an attack by someone who is criminally liable? Is it a justification, as Dobbs claims? Why should it not be placed instead in the category for defences that spring from the claimant's misconduct? What about the defence of discipline in the context of an action brought by a child who had been chastised? That defence is contingent upon the defendant using no more than reasonable force.[35] This is presumably why Dobbs regards it as a justification. But note that this defence is available only to a child's parent or a person in *loco parentis*. It is denied to all other defendants.[36] Why, therefore, should discipline not be regarded as a defence that is based on the defendant's status? Dobbs seems to have overlooked the fact that many defences that are justificatory in nature depend upon the status or role of the defendant.[37] The same point can be made in relation to the legislative provisions that furnish constables with a defence to any liability in tort that they would otherwise incur by detaining and searching persons for stolen or

---

[34] DB Dobbs, *The Law of Torts* (St Paul, Minn, West Publishing Co, 2000) 155.
[35] See 5.2.2.5.
[36] See the text accompanying nn 98–99 in ch 4.
[37] For discussion, see K Greenawalt, 'The Perplexing Borders of Justification and Excuse' (1984) 84 *Columbia Law Review* 1897, 1915; M Thorburn, 'Justifications, Powers, and Authority' (2008) 117 *Yale Law Journal* 1070, 1072.

prohibited articles.[38] It seems tolerably clear from Dobbs's textbook that he would regard this defence as a justification.[39] However, this defence is not available to an ordinary citizen who stops and searches another citizen for contraband. This is so even if the citizen acts in a way that would attract the defence were he a constable.[40] Hence, this defence has a claim to being placed in the category for defences that depend upon the defendant's status.

7.9. Bipolar and Non-bipolar Defences

Ernest Weinrib argues that the rules that constitute tort law look to the parties' relationship. In his words, tort law 'single[s] out . . . two parties and bring[s] them together . . . [It] looks neither to the litigants individually nor to the interests of the community as a whole, but to a bipolar relationship of liability'.[41] It is this feature of tort law, Weinrib claims, that gives it a coherent structure and enables it to be understood from an internal perspective. Although Weinrib did not make a serious attempt to show that defences conform to his understanding of tort law,[42] some defences seem to be consistent with it. Examples of such defences include those of self-defence, abatement, and recapture of land and chattels. These defences certainly appear to be concerned with the interaction between the parties. But many defences are animated not by the relationship between the claimant and the defendant but by considerations that pertain to just one of the parties. Take, for instance, the immunity enjoyed by diplomats.[43] This immunity, like all immunities, does not spring from the connection between the parties. Rather, it is concerned exclusively with the defendant. Its existence can be explained, therefore, only by reference to considerations that have nothing to do with the parties' relationship (specifically, the fact that it purchases reciprocal protection for diplomats abroad). A prominent defence that is not bipolar is that of illegality. This defence is interested in the fact that the claimant committed an offence at the time at which he was injured. Because it looks at the claimant in isolation from the defendant, it cannot be explained by reference to the parties' relationship, a point that Weinrib concedes.[44]

The fact that Weinrib's theory of tort law can explain only some defences reveals that some defences are bipolar whereas others are not. This affords a basis for organising defences. McLachlin J had this classificatory criterion in mind when she said in *Hall v Hebert* that 'The law of tort recognizes many types of

---

[38] Police and Criminal Evidence Act 1984 (UK), pt 1.
[39] Dobbs (n 34) 194–204.
[40] See the text accompanying n 100 in ch 4.
[41] EJ Weinrib, *The Idea of Private Law* (Cambridge, Mass, Harvard University Press, 1995) 2.
[42] See ch 1, n 38.
[43] Diplomatic immunity is discussed in 5.3.1.4.
[44] Weinrib (n 41) 169, n 53.

defence. Some go to the relationship between the parties . . . But others go to matters unrelated to that relationship.'[45] Before the merits of this system are discussed, it should be observed that the separation between bipolar and non-bipolar defences does not map precisely onto the distinction between justifications and public policy defences promoted in this book. While it is true that public policy defences are non-bipolar defences, not all justifications are bipolar defences. A good illustration of a justification that is not bipolar is that of public necessity.[46] This justification defence fails to connect the claimant with the defendant. This is because its availability hinges on considerations that are external to their relationship, specifically, whether the defendant's tort advances the greater public good.

A classificatory system that took bipolarity as its criterion of organisation has certain merits. It would capture all tort defences. Its categories would not overlap. However, it is unclear whether such an arrangement would answer any questions regarding defences. What turns on the fact that a given defence is bipolar or non-bipolar? Of course, this is not to deny that it may be useful for certain purposes to ask whether a given defence is bipolar or not. Posing this question directs attention to the extent to which tort law as a whole is correlatively structured. But when it comes to understanding defences specifically, it is unclear whether much stands to be gained from determining whether a given defence is bipolar or non-bipolar.

7.10. Goldberg and Zipursky's System (I)

Goldberg and Zipursky sketch a system of tort defences in their *The Oxford Introductions to US Law: Torts*. They write:[47]

> Some tort affirmative defenses, such as *statute of limitations* defenses that bar claims simply for being brought too late, are procedural. Others amount to justifications for conduct that would otherwise be tortious. To use an example involving a tort other than negligence, a person who commits the tort of battery by intentionally shooting another can justify the battery, and thereby escape liability, by proving that the shooting was in *self-defense* and was a proportionate response to the threat from the victim. Still others take the form of status-based *immunities*. For example, the law renders certain governmental entities immune from tort liability simply by virtue of their being government entities.

Goldberg and Zipursky do not explain exactly what they mean by a 'procedural defence'. Perhaps they think that a procedural defence is a defence that facilitates the efficient administration of justice. If this is the meaning that they intend, their

---

[45] [1993] 2 SCR 159, 183.
[46] Public necessity is discussed in 5.2.2.1.
[47] JCP Goldberg and BC Zipursky, *The Oxford Introductions to US Law: Torts* (Oxford, Oxford University Press, 2010) 110 (emphasis in original).

system is problematic since several immunities[48] exist in order to promote the smooth functioning of the judicial system (such as the immunities afforded to judges, jurors, witnesses and prosecutors[49]). In other words, the procedural defence category and immunities category overlap. Another difficulty with Goldberg and Zipursky's model is that it is not exhaustive. Consider the defence of illegality. This defence does not fall within any of the categories on offer.[50]

7.11. Goldberg and Zipursky's System (II)

The system described in the previous section is not the only taxonomy of tort defences proposed by Goldberg and Zipursky. Elsewhere in their *The Oxford Introductions to US Law: Torts* they say 'Recognized defenses rest on various grounds: that the defendant's conduct was justified (or excused), that the plaintiff is ineligible to complain about it, or because of a concern to ensure that the legal system functions fairly.'[51] Goldberg and Zipursky identify self-defence an example of a defence falling within the first category, the doctrine of consent in the context of the action in false imprisonment as a defence that renders the claimant ineligible to complain about the defendant's conduct, and limitation bars as a defence that is designed to preserve the integrity of the legal process.

Goldberg and Zipursky's second system obviously differs significantly from their first arrangement (they do not explain why they embrace two schemas and do not compare them). In the second model, unlike the first, they seem to recognise the existence of excuses, although they do not make it clear whether they think that justifications differ from excuses and, if they do believe that they are distinct types of defences, what they take the nature of the difference to be. In their second taxonomy, no category is reserved for immunities but provision is made for rules that render the claimant ineligible to complain about the defendant's conduct.

Goldberg and Zipursky's second system, like their first, suffers from the fundamental problem of overlapping categories. The major difficulty in this connection flows from their category of defences that render 'the plaintiff . . . ineligible to complain' about the defendant's conduct. This definition is so wide that it results in their second category swallowing up both of their other categories, since all defences disentitle the claimant to a remedy.

---

[48] Goldberg and Zipursky define an immunity as 'a defense that blocks the imposition of liability on an actor because of the actor's status or identity': *ibid*, 178.

[49] These immunities are discussed in 5.3.1.1.

[50] It is worth noting that Goldberg and Zipursky's insistence that the doctrine of voluntary assumption of risk is a defence (see the text accompanying n 75 in ch 3) is inconsistent with their taxonomy of defences that is under consideration here. None of the categories that Goldberg and Zipursky articulate captures this doctrine.

[51] Goldberg and Zipursky (n 47) 183.

7.12. Conclusion

This short chapter delineated 10 other ways in which tort law defences might be classified. While some of these systems might be useful if one is writing a book the aim of which is to impart the bare details of tort law to university students or to acquaint busy practitioners with the state of the law, in terms of providing a sound theoretical understanding of how defences operate as a coherent system, they are all inferior to the bipartite taxonomy promoted in this book. The rival taxonomies are all inferior in this regard because they suffer from at least one of three basic drawbacks. The first is that many of them are not exhaustive. This is an intolerable defect, for it means that some defences are left out in the classificatory cold. The second problem is that of overlapping categories. The third problem is the failure of a classificatory enterprise to reveal any insights as to the way in which the law of tort defences operates.

8

Denials of Responsibility

8.1. Introduction

In an earlier chapter,[1] reference was made to a distinction that John Gardner draws between consequential responsibility and basic responsibility.[2] Consequential responsibility, recall, refers to one's responsibility for something that has gone awry. One is consequentially responsible if one is required to bear the adverse moral or legal consequences of some wrong. Basic responsibility, on the other hand, looks to whether one can account for oneself as a rational agent. A person is responsible in the basic sense if he has the capacity to be guided by reasons. In both tort law and the criminal law, when a defendant denies an element of a tort or crime or invokes a defence, he asserts that he is not consequentially responsible for the sanctions that these bodies of law mete out to those who are held liable.[3] Reliance on certain criminal law defences also involves a claim by the defendant that he was not responsible in the basic sense at some point in time. The most important of these defences are insanity,[4] infancy[5] and the doctrine of unfitness to plead.[6] The defences of insanity and infancy are engaged when the defendant lacked basic responsibility due, respectively, to a mental illness or immaturity at the time that he committed the offence. The defence of unfitness to plead is triggered if the defendant is not responsible in the basic sense at the time of the trial. The existence of these defences means that consequential responsibility to bear criminal liability requires basic responsibility. Tort law stands in stark contrast with the criminal law in this respect. As has been explained earlier, insanity, infancy

---

[1] See 4.3.2.2.

[2] J Gardner, *Offences and Defences: Selected Essays in the Philosophy of Criminal Law* (Oxford, Oxford University Press, 2007) ch 9.

[3] The criminal law, unlike tort law, provides for partial defences, such as diminished responsibility and provocation. Partial defences reduce rather than eliminate one's consequential responsibility for legal sanctions. The absence of partial defences to liability in tort is discussed in 1.7.

[4] Criminal Procedure (Insanity) Act 1964 (UK), s 1.

[5] Children and Young Persons Act 1933 (UK), s 50.

[6] Criminal Procedure (Insanity) Act 1964 (UK), s 4. Counting unfitness to plead as a defence is contentious. For example, Kenneth Campbell (K Campbell, 'Offence and Defence' in IH Dennis (ed), *Criminal Law and Justice: Essays from the W.G. Hart Workshop, 1986* (London, Sweet & Maxwell, 1987) 76–77), John Gardner (Gardner (n 2) 182–83) and Paul Robinson (PH Robinson, 'Criminal Law Defenses: A Systematic Analysis' (1982) 82 *Columbia Law Review* 199, 231) regard unfitness to plead as a defence, while Antony Duff does not (RA Duff, *Answering for Crime: Responsibility and Liability in the Criminal Law* (Oxford, Hart Publishing, 2007) 179–81).

and unfitness to plead are not tort defences[7] (although, exceptionally, insanity and infancy may undercut the definitional elements of certain causes of action[8]). It follows that tort liability may descend upon a person who does not enjoy basic responsibility.

The goal of this chapter is to determine whether tort law should follow the criminal law and grant defendants who lack basic responsibility a defence. Should tort law provide for defences of insanity, infancy and unfitness to plead? This question is clearly not of a great deal of practical relevance. The insane, infants and persons who are unfit to plead are not usually worth suing unless they are insured and their insurance policy covers the tort that they commit. But it is of great importance for the purposes of this book, because if these defences are welcomed into tort law, the bipartite structure of defences would need to be expanded.[9] A new category would be needed to accommodate them. They obviously could not be put together with justifications, since possession of basic responsibility is a prerequisite to being justified.[10] And they cannot be placed in the public policy defence category either. Whereas public policy defences are unconcerned with the rational defensibility of the defendant's impugned conduct, defences that are triggered by a lack of basic responsibility require proof that the defendant positively lacked the capacity for rational action. If a new category is required, it should not be labelled 'excuses'. Although the pleas of insanity and infancy are routinely described as excuses, this language should be avoided. That is because, for the reasons given earlier,[11] excuses, like justifications, are explanations that can be offered only by persons who can cite reasons in support of their impugned behaviour. Excuses, as is the case with justifications, are assertions of responsibility in the basic sense. It is suggested that any new category that might be needed should be called 'denials of responsibility'.

8.2. Unpacking the Concept of Basic Responsibility

Because this chapter is about basic responsibility – the ability to understand and respond to reasons – it is worth expanding upon this concept slightly before

---

[7] See 4.3.3.

[8] See 3.3.2–3.3.3.

[9] The issue of whether tort law should admit of defences that are enlivened by a lack of basic responsibility is also important for various other theoretical purposes. Consider, for example, the sustained attempts that have been made in recent years to demonstrate that tort law is an exercise in corrective justice (see, especially, EJ Weinrib, *The Idea of Private Law* (Cambridge, Mass, Harvard University Press, 1995). If tort law refused to release those who are not responsible in the basic sense from liability, it cannot be exhaustively explained by any theory of corrective justice. This is because a correctible injustice can occur only through the actions of a rational agent. For discussion, see Weinrib, 183, n 22; J Coleman, *Risks and Wrongs* (Oxford, Oxford University Press, 1992) 333–35.

[10] Only the deeds theory of justification admits of the possibility that a person who lacks basic responsibility might be justified. This theory should be rejected for the reasons given earlier: see 4.3.2.6.

[11] See 4.3.2.2.

considering whether insanity, infancy and unfitness to plead should be tort defences. The first point to note is that a loss of basic responsibility need not be permanent. A temporary loss of basic responsibility will occur, for instance, if a person experiences a transient insane delusion. Similarly, a baby will lack basic responsibility until such time as he develops the cognitive powers necessary to endow him with rational agency.

Secondly, it is entirely possible for a person to be responsible in the basic sense in some aspects of his life but not in others.[12] Suppose that D believes that he is an agent of God and that C is Satan. D drives to C's house in order to kill him. D will lack basic responsibility in so far as his interactions with C are concerned owing to his irrational beliefs regarding C. However, D may be responsible in this sense in so far as his conduct as a driver is concerned. He may, notwithstanding his delusions concerning C, be fully capable of understanding and responding to reasons that bear on the way in which one who is in charge of a motor vehicle should act.

Thirdly, it is important not to confuse having a merely causal explanation for one's behaviour with the ability to cite reasons in support of one's behaviour. Possessing an explanation for one's conduct in the sense of being able to identify the forces that precipitated it does not mean that one was basically responsible at the time of the conduct concerned. One must be able to point to facts that supplied reasons for engaging in the conduct. The point can be illustrated by the facts in *Breunig v American Family Insurance Co.*[13] The defendant motorist in this case steered her vehicle on to the wrong side of the road and accelerated. She drove in this manner because she believed that God was controlling her car and that she could 'fly because Batman does it'. She was surprised when she did not become airborne and, instead, collided with the claimant's oncoming vehicle. The defendant had a causal explanation for her acts. She could point to the fact that she suffered from insane delusions to account for her driving. But obviously, this fact did not generate any reasons for the defendant to steer into the path of the claimant's vehicle. There is no justificatory capital that can be extracted from this fact. This being the case, the defendant was not responsible in the basic sense at the time of the accident.

8.3. Should Insanity Be a Tort Defence?

For much of the history of the common law, the prevailing view among theorists has been that insanity should not be a tort defence. Sir Francis Bacon, writing in relation to tort law, said that if 'a madman . . . put out a man's eye, or do him like corporal hurt, he shall be punished in trespass'.[14] Sir Matthew Hale concurred. He

---

[12] This point is discussed in Gardner (n 2) 182–83.
[13] 45 Wis 2d 536; 173 NW 2d 619 (1970).
[14] J Spedding, RL Ellis and DD Heath (eds), *The Works of Francis Bacon*, vol 7 (London, Longman, 1861–1879) 348.

argued that the mentally ill should be held liable for their torts, 'because such a recompense is not by way of penalty, but a satisfaction for damage done'.[15] At around the beginning of the twentieth century, the wisdom of this position was questioned. Particularly influential in this respect was a contribution by Francis Bohlen.[16] Bohlen, who was at the time the Reporter of the American Law Institute's Restatement (First) of Torts,[17] declared that the refusal of the courts to absolve the mentally disordered of liability was supported only by '*dicta* contained in English cases decided at a time [before the rise of] the modern concept that liability must be founded on fault'.[18] Today, theorists are more or less evenly divided on the issue. Some contend that the absence of a defence of insanity is an anachronism founded on prejudice towards those who suffer from mental illnesses.[19] Others argue that a defence of insanity should be withheld.[20] This debate is the subject of this section. It is convenient to begin the analysis by considering the case for maintaining the status quo.

8.3.1. The Case Against Recognition

8.3.1.1. *The causation argument*

Suppose that D, who is insane, causes C loss. (For insulation from possible distractions, assume that C had no responsibility for D and that neither party caused D's insanity or had any warning that D might become insane.) Both parties in this scenario are blameless. How should tort law allocate the loss between them? It has

---

[15] M Hale, *The History of the Pleas of the Crown*, vol 1 (Philadelphia, Pa, Robert H Small, 1847) 15. See also WS Holdsworth, *A History of English Law*, vol 3, 3rd edn (London, Methuen & Co Ltd, 1923) 375–77.

[16] FH Bohlen, 'Liability in Tort of Infants and Insane Persons' (1924) 23 *Michigan Law Review* 9. Other theorists writing near the beginning of the 20th century who argued for the recognition of a defence of insanity include T Brown, 'The Liability of Persons of Unsound Mind and Infants for Torts in Civil Actions' (1875–1876) 1 *Southern Law Review (New Series)* 346; OW Holmes, *The Common Law* (Boston, Mass, Little, Brown, & Co, 1881) 109; WB Hornblower, 'Insanity and the Law of Negligence' (1905) 5 *Columbia Law Review* 278; HD Bamford, 'Unsoundness of Mind in Relation to Torts' (1906) 4 *Commonwealth Law Review* 3; JB Ames, 'Law and Morals' (1908) 22 *Harvard Law Review* 97, 99–100.

[17] Bohlen's influence on the position taken by the Restatement (First) of Torts with respect to insanity is discussed in PJ Kelley, 'The First Restatement of Torts: Reform by Descriptive Theory' (2007) 32 *Southern Illinois University Law Journal* 93, 100–06.

[18] Bohlen (n 16) 32.

[19] See, eg, P Picher, 'The Tortious Liability of the Insane in Canada . . . With a Comparative Look at the United States and Civil Law Jurisdictions and a Suggestion for an Alternative' (1975) 13 *Osgoode Hall Law Journal* 193; Law Reform Commission of Ireland, *Report on the Liability in Tort of Mentally Disabled Persons* (Law Com No 18, 1985); HJF Korrell, 'The Liability of Mentally Disabled Tort Defendants' (1995) 19 *Law & Psychology Review* 1.

[20] See, eg, GJ Alexander and TS Szasz, 'Mental Illness as an Excuse for Civil Wrongs' (1967) 43 *Notre Dame Law Review* 24; RA Epstein, 'Defenses and Subsequent Pleas in a System of Strict Liability' (1974) 3 *Journal of Legal Studies* 165, 169–70; SI Splane, 'Tort Liability of the Mentally Ill in Negligence Actions' (1983) 93 *Yale Law Journal* 153; WM Landes and RA Posner, *The Economic Structure of Tort Law* (Cambridge, Mass, Harvard University Press, 1987) 127–30, 182–83; P Kelley, 'Infancy, Insanity, and Infirmity in the Law of Torts' (2003) 48 *American Journal of Jurisprudence* 179.

often been contended that, since D caused the loss, it should be imposed on him. As one court put it, 'as between an insane person who injures another and an innocent person, it is more just for the insane person to bear the loss he caused than to visit the loss on the injured person'.[21] This line of reasoning, which will be called the 'causation argument', is, in essence, a plea for insane persons to be held strictly liable for harm that would not have occurred but for the fact that they were insane.[22] Before it can be accepted, it is necessary to identify a convincing reason for holding insane persons strictly liable.

Landes and Posner claim to have identified such a reason. They maintain that the insane are highly dangerous and that the same arguments that weigh in favour of imposing strict liability on those who participate in ultrahazardous activities therefore also support holding the insane strictly liable. They write:[23]

> [P]eople whose insanity is severe enough to affect their ability to avoid physical injury to themselves and others are generally kept under restraint. They are highly dangerous – one might say ultrahazardous – and the same considerations that argue for strict liability for ultrahazardous activities argue for strict liability for the torts of the insane.

This argument is unpersuasive. It ignores the fact that the main reason why strict liability is imposed for harm resulting from abnormally dangerous activities is that, typically, those who cause harm while engaged in such activities will be at fault. The imposition of strict liability saves the effort and expense of inquiring as to fault when fault will normally be present. Clearly, though, a person who causes damage while insane will rarely be to blame.[24]

Can the imposition of strict liability on insane persons be supported by analogy to any other situation in which defendants are held strictly liable? Those who belong to a class of persons who tend to be in a good position to bear or distribute losses are sometimes held strictly liable. The classic illustration of such a class is employers, who are vicariously (strictly) liable for the torts of their employees acting in the course of their employment. For the sake of argument, assume that it is

---

[21] *Williams v Kearbey* 13 Kan App 2d 564, 567; 775 P 2d 670, 672 (1989). See also *Beals v See* 10 Pa 56, 61 (1848); *Williams v Hays* 143 NY 442, 447; 38 NE 449, 450 (1894); *Seals v Snow* 123 Kan 88; 254 P 348, 349 (1927); *Kuhn v Zabotsky* 9 Ohio St 2d 129, 134; 224 NE 2d 137, 141 (1967); *Vosnos v Perry* 43 Ill App 3d 834, 836; 357 NE 2d 614, 615 (Ct App 1976); Epstein (n 20) 169–70; K Barker, P Cane, M Lunney and FA Trindade, *The Law of Torts in Australia*, 5th edn (Oxford, Oxford University Press, 2006) 65.

[22] This argument has been criticised on the ground that tort law has largely rejected strict liability: see, eg, RM Ague, 'The Liability of Insane Persons in Tort Actions' (1956) 60 *Dickinson Law Review* 211, 221–22; OC Dark, 'Tort Liability and the "Unquiet Mind": A Proposal to Incorporate Mental Disabilities into the Standard of Care' (2004) 30 *Thurgood Marshall Law Review* 169, 183. This criticism is unconvincing. There are still large swathes of strict liability in tort law. Moreover, the fact that tort law generally requires proof of fault before imposing liability does not mean that holding insane persons strictly liable is unwarranted.

[23] Landes and Posner (n 20) 128.

[24] One might also question the premise that the insane are highly dangerous: see M Moran, *Rethinking the Reasonable Person: An Egalitarian Reconstruction of the Reasonable Person* (Oxford, Oxford University Press, 2003) 43.

justifiable to impose strict liability on those who are good loss bearers or distributors. Is levying strict liability on insane persons thereby warranted? Obviously it is not. The insane are unlikely to have deep pockets (particularly if they are institutionalised).

Is there any other theory by which holding the insane strictly liable can be justified? An important general defence of strict liability was offered by Tony Honoré in his famous essay 'Responsibility and Luck'.[25] Honoré argues that since we take the benefit of good luck when we do not deserve it, it is fair for us to be burdened with responsibility for the bad consequences of our acts even if we were not at fault in bringing them about. It is just, he says, because, in the long run, people tend to come out in front in the sense that they will have more credits from good outcomes than debits from bad ones. Does this logic, assuming that it is sound, support holding the insane strictly liable? It does not. This is because it is unlikely that the insane will be winners overall. This was noted by Honoré. He said that it is only fair to impose liability on persons who are not at fault if they 'possess a minimum capacity for reasoned choice and action'.[26]

It would be possible to continue exploring the grounds on which the imposition of strict liability generally has been defended. But it should be apparent from what has already been said that doing so is unlikely to uncover an argument that will support holding the insane strictly liable. Accordingly, it will be concluded that, unless a compelling reason is identified for imposing strict liability on insane persons, the causation argument is unconvincing. As it stands, it is merely a question-begging statement.

8.3.1.2. The fraud argument

It has been argued that insanity should not be a defence since, were it an answer to liability, sane defendants might invoke it.[27] Built into this argument is an assumption that it would be hard to identify sane defendants who succumb to this temptation. This logic (the 'fraud argument') has been criticised on the ground that sane defendants would be unlikely to concoct a defence of insanity, since being found insane carries an indelible stigma, the possibility of civil commitment and the risk of suffering various civil disabilities, such as the loss of the right to practise one's profession. Critics of this argument have also observed that, since most

---

[25] T Honoré, *Responsibility and Fault* (Oxford, Hart Publishing, 1999) ch 2. For searching discussion of this essay, see J Gardner, 'Obligations and Outcomes in the Law of Torts' in P Cane and J Gardner (eds), *Relating to Responsibility: Essays for Tony Honoré on his Eightieth Birthday* (Oxford, Hart Publishing, 2001).

[26] Honoré (n 25) 26.

[27] *McIntyre v Sholty* 121 Ill 660, 665; 13 NE 239, 241 (1887); *Williams v Hays* 143 NY 442, 447; 38 NE 449, 450 (1894); *Seals v Snow* 123 Kan 88; 254 P 348, 349 (1927); *Sforza v Green Bus Lines, Inc* 150 Misc 180, 181–82; 268 NYS 446, 448 (Mun Ct 1934); *In re Meyer's Guardianship* 218 Wis 381; 261 NW 211, 215 (1935); *Kuhn v Zabotsky* 9 Ohio St 2d 129, 134; 224 NE 2d 137, 141 (1967); *Vosnos v Perry* 43 Ill App 3d 834, 836; 357 NE 2d 614, 615 (Ct App 1976); *Jankee v Clark County* 235 Wis 2d 700, 744; 612 NW 2d 297, 316 (2000); Restatement (Second) of Torts, § 895J, cmt a.

defendants are insured, there would be little incentive for them to plead insanity. One theorist sums up this line of reasoning as follows:[28]

> A label of mental illness . . . carries with it a substantial stigma in our society. While some criminal defendants may be willing to assume the stigmatizing effect of such a label in order to escape . . . lengthy imprisonment, it does not necessarily follow that tort defendants would be equally willing when money damages are the only penalty at issue. The fact that many tort defendants are substantially insured to cover the cost of an adverse judgment further mitigates the concern about false claims of mental disability.

Proponents of the fraud argument and critics of it have both overlooked a breathtakingly obvious point. As noted in an earlier chapter,[29] due to the ubiquity of insurance, it is not defendants but their insurers who normally invoke defences. Insured defendants typically have no say as to the defences that will or will not be raised on their behalf. Insurers do not even usually notify or consult with defendants as to how they will proceed in this respect. Consequently, were insanity a defence, sane defendants would not often have the opportunity to plead it fraudulently. The fraud argument is therefore meritless. It also follows that the critics' observation that there would be many disincentives for sane defendants to contest their sanity were insanity a defence (although surely accurate[30]) is neither here nor there.

Advocates of the fraud argument could reformulate it to accommodate the fact that it is insurers who decide whether to raise a defence. So restructured, this rationale for holding the mentally disordered liable is that insanity should not be a defence since, were it an escape route from liability, *insurers* might dishonestly rely on it. Insurers, unlike defendants, have nothing to lose and everything to gain from succeeding on a defence of insanity, and so have an incentive to rely on it fraudulently. But the fraud argument surely cannot be rescued in this way. It is simply improbable that, were insanity a defence, many insurers would fraudulently enter a plea of insanity. This is partly because they could not entertain any realistic hope of succeeding in any such subterfuge without colluding with the defendant and, for the reasons that have just been mentioned, few defendants would want to contest their sanity.

---

[28] JW Ellis, 'Tort Responsibility of Mentally Disabled Persons' (1981) 6 *American Bar Foundation Research Journal* 1079, 1087. See also Law Reform Commission of Ireland (n 19) 48–49; WR Casto, 'The Tort Liability of Insane Persons for Negligence: A Critique' (1972) 39 *Tennessee Law Review* 705, 715; Picher (n 19) 229; Dark (n 22) 184; S Light, 'Rejecting the Logic of Confinement: Care Relationships and the Mentally Disabled under Tort Law' (1999) 109 *Yale Law Journal* 381, 387–88.

[29] See 1.8.1.

[30] Even in the criminal context, defendants rarely plead insanity. As Glanville Williams pointed out, '[u]sually, the defendant fears a verdict of insanity only slightly less than he fears a conviction, if indeed he does not fear it more' (GL Williams, 'Murder—Drunkenness—Insane and Non-Insane Automatism' (1962) 20 *Cambridge Law Journal* 3, 4). The accuracy of this observation has been confirmed by empirical studies: H McGinley and RA Pasewark, 'National Survey of the Frequency and Success of the Insanity Plea and Alternative Pleas' (1989) 17 *Journal of Psychiatry & Law* 205; LA Callahan, HJ Steadman, MA McGreevy and PC Robbins, 'The Volume and Characteristics of Insanity Defense Pleas: An Eight-State Study' (1991) 19 *Bulletin of the American Academy of Psychiatry and the Law* 331; RD Mackay, BJ Mitchell and L Howe, 'Yet More Facts about the Insanity Defence' [2006] *Criminal Law Review* 399.

There are further shortcomings in the fraud argument. These problems include the following:

(1) It is incompatible with the assumption that the courts are generally thought to be capable of identifying mendacity. The courts are trusted to verify the veracity of denials by the defendant (or, rather, the defendant's insurer) that he acted (for example) voluntarily or with an intention to bring about a particular result. Why should the courts not also be trusted to ascertain the truthfulness of pleas by the defendant that he was insane at the time of his conduct in question?[31]

(2) It is unsustainable in light of empirical studies establishing that insanity is not easily faked.[32]

(3) It cannot account for the fact that insanity is a defence to criminal liability.[33] Why should defendants in the civil side of things be denied a defence of insanity on the ground that it may be invoked fraudulently, but not those in the criminal context?

(4) It cannot explain why evidence that the defendant was insane may be taken into account in relation to the assessment of damages. Such evidence may be admitted to show that grounds for awarding punitive damages do not exist.[34] Neither can it account for the fact that evidence of a mental illness suffered by the claimant may be considered for the purposes of determining whether he is guilty of contributory negligence[35] or if his acts constitute a *novus actus interveniens*.[36]

(5) The risk that a defence of insanity would be fraudulently invoked were it recognised as an answer to liability does not establish that the insane should be held liable. Rather, it merely demonstrates that mechanisms are needed to weed out false insanity defences.[37]

---

[31] 'Courts must depend upon the efficacy of the judicial processes to ferret out the meritorious from the fraudulent in particular cases' (*Emery v Emery* 45 Cal 2d 421, 431; 289 P 2d 218, 225 (1955)). See also *Hambrook v Stokes Brothers* [1925] 1 KB 141, 158 (CA) (Atkin LJ) (quoting from *Dulieu v White & Sons* [1901] 2 KB 669, 681 (Div Ct) (Kennedy J) with approval).

[32] D Schretlen and H Arkowitz, 'A Psychological Test Battery to Detect Prison Inmates who Fake Insanity or Mental Retardation' (1990) 8 *Behavioral Science & the Law* 75; D Schretlen, SS Wilkins, WG Van Gorp and JH Bobholz, 'Cross-Validation of a Psychological Test Battery to Detect Faked Insanity' (1992) 4 *Psychological Assessment* 77; JS Hayes, DB Hale and WD Gouvier, 'Malingering Detection in a Mentally Retarded Forensic Population' (1998) 5 *Applied Neuropsychology* 33.

[33] Fears of false insanity defences being advanced in the criminal setting have often been ventilated. For argument that these fears are unfounded, see A Ashworth, 'Four Threats to the Presumption of Innocence' (2006) 10 *International Journal of Evidence & Proof* 241, 263–65.

[34] *McIntyre v Sholty* 121 Ill 660, 665; 13 NE 239, 241 (1887); *Moore v Horne* 153 NC 413; 69 SE 409, 410 (1910); *Parke v Dennard* 218 Ala 209; 118 So 396, 399 (1928).

[35] *Noel v McCaig* 174 Kan 677, 685–86; 258 P 2d 234, 241 (1953); *Lynch v Rosenthal* 396 SW 2d 272, 278 (Mo Ct App 1965); *Mochen v State* 352 NYS 2d 290, 295; 43 AD 2d 484, 488–89 (Sup Ct App Div 1974); *Baltimore & Potomac Railroad Co v Cumberland* 176 US 232, 238 (1990); cf *Galindo v TMT Transport, Inc* 152 Ariz 434, 435–37; 733 P 2d 631, 632–34 (Ct App 1986); GL Williams, *Joint Torts and Contributory Negligence* (London, Stevens & Sons, 1951) 357. For further discussion, see Restatement (Third) of Torts, § 11, cmt e.

[36] *Corr v IBC Vehicles Ltd* [2008] UKHL 13; [2008] 1 AC 884.

[37] Special measures have been put in place in the criminal context to ensure that only those defendants who were insane at the time of the offence succeed on an insanity defence. For instance, s 1 of the

(6) It does not give any weight to the unfairness inflicted upon insane defendants by denying them a defence. It myopically focuses on the need to prevent a defence of insanity from being fraudulently invoked.

(7) It cannot easily explain why actions in respect of psychiatric injuries are permitted. Until relatively late in the day, psychiatric injuries were not compensable unless intentionally inflicted[38] or consequential upon physical harm. There was a variety of reasons for this blanket rule, one of which was a concern that granting redress would invite counterfeit claims.[39] This concern was eventually cast aside.[40] Its dismissal would seem to be difficult to reconcile with accepting the fraud argument.

For these reasons, the argument that a defence of insanity should not be recognised on the ground that it would foment fraudulent reliance on it is unconvincing.

8.3.1.3. *The imported difficulties argument*

William Prosser argued against the recognition of an insanity defence on the basis that it spared 'the law of torts the confusion and unsatisfactory tests attending proof of insanity in criminal cases'.[41] This argument (the 'imported difficulties argument') still resonates in some quarters. For instance, the Reporters of the Restatement (Third) of Torts cited it with approval and opined that 'The awkwardness experienced by the criminal-justice system in attempting to litigate the insanity defense is at least instructive.'[42] Criminal lawyers are the first to admit that the *M'Naghten* test,[43] which controls the defence of insanity in their field, is plagued by formidable problems.[44] One theorist writes that 'It is widely accepted

Criminal Procedure (Insanity and Unfitness to Plead) Act 1991 (UK) requires evidence of two medical practitioners, at least one of whom is an experienced psychiatrist, before a defendant may be acquitted on the ground of insanity. The fear of false insanity defences also probably underpins to some extent the fact that, in derogation of the presumption of innocence, the defendant bears the onus of proving insanity.

[38] *Wilkinson v Downton* [1897] 2 QB 57 (QBD).

[39] For statements to this effect, see *Victorian Railway Commissioners v Coultas* (1888) 13 App Cas 222, 225 (PC); *Waube v Warrington* 216 Wis 603; 258 NW 497, 501 (1935); WP Keeton, DB Dobbs, RE Keeton and DG Owen (eds), *Prosser and Keeton on Torts*, 5th edn (St Paul, Minn, West Publishing Co, 1984) 361.

[40] *Dillon v Legg* 68 Cal 2d 728; 441 P 2d 912 (1968); *McLoughlin v O'Brian* [1983] 1 AC 410, 421 (HL); *White v Chief Constable of South Yorkshire Police* [1999] 2 AC 455, 493 (HL).

[41] Keeton *et al* (n 39) 1073 (footnote omitted).

[42] Restatement (Third) of Torts, § 11, cmt e. See also *McGuire v Almy* 297 Mass 323, 326–27; 8 NE 2d 760, 762 (1937); *Jolley v Powell* 299 So 2d 647, 649 (Fla Dist Ct App 1974).

[43] The test was enunciated by the House of Lords in *M'Naghten's Case* (1843) 10 Cl & Fin 200; 8 ER 718 (HL). It asks whether the 'accused was labouring under such a defect of reason, from disease of the mind, as not to know the nature and quality of the act he was doing, or, if he did know it, that he did not know he was doing what was wrong': Cl & Fin 210; ER 722.

[44] The *M'Naghten* test governs the defence of insanity in the United Kingdom and in some other parts of the Commonwealth. Several other tests are on offer. The *Durham* test, developed by the Federal Court of the District of Columbia in *Durham v United States* 214 F 2d 862 (DC Cir 1954), is well known. It was developed with the intention of reflecting developments in psychiatry and to mollify the perceived harshness of the *M'Naghten* test. It grants a defence if the defendant's 'unlawful act was the product of mental disease or mental defect' (at 875). Another test is that in the American Law

that the law in this area is inadequate . . .'.[45] Others describe the *M'Naghten* test as 'intractabl[y] . . . controvers[ial]',[46] 'impossible to administer . . . rationally and equitably'[47] and 'narrow, outmoded and deeply stigmatic'.[48] Senior judges have remarked that the test is 'at best obsolete and probably never scientifically sustainable',[49] 'the subject of persistent and powerful criticism'[50] and a 'quagmire'.[51] However, the fact that the *M'Naghten* test is problematic does not sustain the imported difficulties argument. If insane defendants should be exempted from liability, it is hardly fair to deny defendants who were insane at the relevant time a defence due to feared difficulties in administering it. It is unacceptable to say that such defendants must be held liable because a rule releasing them from responsibility cannot be tailored to the satisfaction of lawyers.[52] If a particular result is just, it behooves lawmaking bodies to develop rules that realise it.[53]

It is also worth noting that the imported difficulties argument assumes that, were insanity a tort defence, it would be governed by the *M'Naghten* test.[54] This assumption is unwarranted.[55] The criminal law is not the only field that is concerned with whether a person lacks basic responsibility. Many other bodies of law are too. For example, the absence of basic responsibility in some aspect of a person's life may be relevant to whether the person concerned possessed testamentary capacity,[56] can be

---

Institute's *Model Penal Code*, § 4.01. The rule states: 'A person is not responsible for criminal conduct if at the time of such conduct as a result of mental disease or defect he lacks substantial capacity either to appreciate the criminality (wrongfulness) of his conduct or to conform his conduct to the requirements of law.' It strikes a compromise between the *M'Naghten* test and the *Durham* test. It has been adopted in many American jurisdictions, including the District of Columbia in 1972: *United States v Brawner* 471 F 2d 969 (DC Cir 1972). As with the *M'Naghten* test, the satisfactoriness of these rival formulae has been robustly debated.

[45] AW Norrie, *Crime, Reason and History: A Critical Introduction to Criminal Law*, 2nd edn (Cambridge, Cambridge University Press, 2001) 174.

[46] DN Husak, *Philosophy of Criminal Law* (Totowa, Rowman & Littlefield, 1987) 196.

[47] SH Kadish, 'The Decline of Innocence' (1968) 26 *Cambridge Law Journal* 273, 277.

[48] RD Mackay, 'Diminished Responsibility and Mentally Disordered Killers' in A Ashworth and B Mitchell (eds), *Rethinking English Homicide Law* (Oxford, Oxford University Press, 2000) 83.

[49] *Corr v IBC Vehicles Ltd* [2008] UKHL 13; [2008] 1 AC 884, 912 [42] (Lord Walker).

[50] *Williams v Williams* [1964] AC 698, 720 (HL) (Lord Reid).

[51] *R v Quick* [1973] QB 910, 922 (CA) (Lawton LJ).

[52] Bohlen (n 16) wrote (37, n 38): '[I]t seems unworthy of the law, whose purpose should be to do justice and to perfect its machinery so that justice may be done, to deny immunity to persons so insane as to be incapable of culpability because of the difficulty of evolving a test satisfactory alike to lawyer and alienist by which the precise degree of mental deficiency which precludes culpability may be determined.'

[53] The prospect of administrative difficulties was often cited in the past in support of the historical refusal of the law to entertain actions in respect of negligently inflicted psychiatric injury. This argument was exposed as fallacious in this context too. The following remark in *Emden v Vitz* 88 Cal App 2d 313, 319; 198 P 2d 696, 700 (Ct App 1948) is instructive: '[The] contention that the rule permitting the maintenance of [negligence actions for psychiatric injury] would be impractical to administer . . . is but an argument that the courts are incapable of performing their appointed tasks, a premise which has frequently been rejected.'

[54] This assumption has often been stated expressly: see, eg, *White v Pile* (1950) 68 WN (NSW) 176, 178–80 (Div Ct).

[55] Some judges have rightly held that, were insanity a tort defence, it would not necessarily be controlled by the *M'Naghten* test: see, eg, *Morriss v Marsden* [1952] 1 All ER 925, 927 (QBD).

[56] The test for testamentary capacity was stated in *Banks v Goodfellow* (1870) LR 5 QB 549 (QBD).

civilly committed[57] or be the subject of a guardianship order,[58] can execute or revoke a power of attorney,[59] can commence and defend civil proceedings,[60] can have a limitation bar extended,[61] can make and escape from a contractual obligation[62] and can be called as a witness[63] or serve as a juror.[64] But only the criminal law uses the *M'Naghten* test to resolve the issue of capacity. Thus, were it decided that tort law should recognise a defence of insanity, tort law would not blindly have to embrace the *M'Naghten* test. Tort law is a *tabula rasa* in this respect. The test for insanity that is thought to fit its agenda best could be embraced.[65]

8.3.1.4. *The unsatisfactory evidence argument*

The absence of a defence of insanity has been defended on the basis of the 'unsatisfactory character of the evidence of mental deficiency in many cases'.[66] This logic, although deployed in many different contexts,[67] is utterly without merit.[68] It cannot explain why evidence of insanity is relevant to various other issues inside tort law[69] and in numerous other legal settings.[70] Even if evidence of insanity is typically 'unsatisfactory', no problem would arise were insanity a defence since the defence would fail when the evidence of insanity is sufficiently poor (because the defendant would not discharge his burden of proving that the defence applies).

8.3.1.5. *The deterrence argument*

It has been argued that withholding a defence of insanity encourages insane actors to implement measures to diminish the risk that they will injure others as a result of their insanity. In the words of one commentator, 'Just as holding average persons liable for their torts may make them behave more conscientiously, holding the mentally ill liable may have a similar effect.'[71] A fatal difficulty with this

---

[57] Mental Health Act 1983 (UK), ss 2–5, 135–136.
[58] *Ibid*, s 7.
[59] Mental Capacity Act 2005 (UK), ss 2, 9, 13.
[60] CPR 21. See further 8.5.
[61] Limitation Act 1980 (UK), s 28(1).
[62] *Hart v O'Connor* [1985] AC 1000 (PC).
[63] Youth Justice and Criminal Evidence Act 1999 (UK), s 53(3).
[64] Juries Act 1974 (UK), s 1, sch 1.
[65] It is unnecessary to speculate here as to the test for insanity that tort law should embrace in the event that it is decided that insanity should be admitted as a defence. The present concern is with the general issue of whether insanity ought to be a defence. The precise form that any insanity defence that is recognised should take is a subsidiary matter.
[66] Restatement (Second) of Torts, § 283B, cmt b(2).
[67] It was a major reason for the past refusal of the courts to countenance actions for negligently inflicted psychiatric injuries: see, eg, *Victorian Railway Commissioners v Coultas* (1888) 13 App Cas 222, 225 (PC).
[68] For a rare occasion on which this has been realised, see *Magill v Magill* [2006] HCA 51; (2006) 226 CLR 551, 617 [211] (Heydon J). Consider also *McLoughlin v O'Brian* [1983] 1 AC 410, 421 (HL) (Lord Wilberforce).
[69] See the text accompanying nn 34–36 above.
[70] See 8.3.1.2–8.3.1.3.
[71] Splane (n 20) 166 (footnote omitted). To like effect, see Landes and Posner (n 20) 183.

suggestion is that it is unlikely that the insane can be deterred by the threat of tort liability. Insane persons will often lack the cognitive or affective skills necessary for effective deterrence. Moreover, the insane will typically either be insured or judgment proof and will, consequently, have relatively little to lose by being held liable.

The fact that the insane are unlikely to be deterred by the threat of liability has led many philosophers and jurists interested in criminal justice to conclude that no argument from deterrence existed for holding them liable, including Bentham,[72] Austin[73] and Holmes.[74] But this conclusion is wrong. This was famously pointed out by Hart, who described it as a 'spectacular *non sequitur*'.[75] Visiting the insane with liability might incentivise *others* to behave in a way that reduces the rate at which wrongs are committed. Put differently, while imposing liability on the insane cannot be supported on the ground of specific deterrence, it may be defensible on the basis of general deterrence. Interestingly, tort lawyers were quicker than their criminal law colleagues to realise that this might be the case. It has often been contended that holding the insane accountable for their torts induces their guardians, carers and family members (these individuals will be referred to collectively as 'guardians' for convenience) to take proper care of them, since they may have an interest in their estate and would not wish to see it depleted through damages awards. One court expressed this idea as follows:[76]

> If an insane person is not held liable for his torts, those interested in his estate, as relatives, or otherwise, might not have a sufficient motive to so take care of him as to deprive him of opportunities for inflicting injuries upon others. There is more injustice in denying to the injured party the recovery of damages for the wrong suffered by him, than there is in calling upon the relatives or friends of the lunatic to pay the expense of his confinement, if he has an estate ample enough for that purpose. The liability of lunatics for their torts tends to secure a more efficient custody and guardianship of their persons.

---

[72] J Bentham, *An Introduction to the Principles of Morals and Legislation* (Oxford, Clarendon Press, 1876) ch XIII, § IX.

[73] J Austin, *Lectures on Jurisprudence*, vol 1 (London, John Murray, 1879) 506.

[74] Holmes (n 16) 109.

[75] HLA Hart, *Punishment and Responsibility: Essays in the Philosophy of Law*, 2nd edn (Oxford, Oxford University Press, 2008) 19. Hart directed his attack at Bentham. He wrote (emphasis in original): '[Bentham] sets out to prove that to *punish* the mad . . . must be inefficacious; but all that he proves (at the most) is the quite different proposition that the *threat* of punishment will be ineffective so far as the class of persons who suffer from [madness] is concerned. Plainly it is possible that though (as Bentham says) the *threat* of punishment could not have operated on them, the actual *infliction* of punishment on those persons, may secure a higher measure of conformity to law on the part of normal persons than is secured by the admission of [a defence of insanity].'

[76] *McIntyre v Sholty* 121 Ill 660, 664–65; 13 NE 239, 241 (1887). See also *Williams v Hays* 143 NY 442, 447; 38 NE 449, 450 (1894); *Seals v Snow* 123 Kan 88; 254 P 348, 349 (1927); *McGuire v Almy* 297 Mass 323, 326–27; 8 NE 2d 760, 762 (1937); *Van Vooren v Cook* 75 NYS 2d 362, 366; 273 AD 88, 92 (Sup Ct App Div 1947); *Schumann v Crofoot* 43 Or App 53, 57–58; 602 P 2d 298, 301 (Ct App 1979); Restatement (Second) of Torts, § 895J, cmt a; TM Cooley, *A Treatise on the Law of Torts: or the Wrongs which Arise Independent of Contract* (Chicago, Ill, Callaghan and Co, 1880) 100–01.

It is possible that holding the insane liable might prompt their guardians to act in such a way as will reduce the probability of the insane injuring others. But this seems extremely unlikely. In the first place, guardians already have a raft of powerful incentives to use reasonable care in discharging their responsibilities. Guardians may incur liability personally for injuries that their ward causes to a third party.[77] Concern for their own and for their ward's physical well-being provides additional reasons to take proper care, since an insane person is just as likely to injure his guardian or himself as a third party. These inducements for guardians to take care are much more powerful than that supplied by the risk that a potential legacy may be lost or diminished through liability. If they do not influence the behaviour of guardians, holding insane persons liable for their torts will hardly do so. Secondly, this argument assumes that guardians have a very considerable amount of control over their wards, a greater degree of control than they may in fact enjoy.[78] Thirdly, it is surely the case that many guardians do not stand to receive any substantial inheritance from their wards. Insane persons, as was noted earlier, are unlikely to have deep pockets. Fourthly, guardians may mistakenly assume that since insanity is a defence to criminal liability (a matter of common knowledge), it is also a tort defence.[79]

It is possible to point to various individuals other than guardians who might take notice of the fact that insanity is not a defence and alter their behaviour in a way that is desirable as a result.[80] These include those who are on the verge of insanity and those who might be tempted to feign insanity. However, the suggestion that such individuals might be deterred by holding the insane liable for their wrongs is just as implausible as the contention that holding the insane liable for their torts will incentivise their guardians to take reasonable care in the performance of their obligations. The fact of the matter is that the further removed the target of deterrence is from the individual held liable, the less likely it is that imposing liability will have the desired deterrent effect.

8.3.1.6. *The avoidance and deinstitutionalisation arguments*

There are two closely related but subtly different arguments to the effect that insanity ought not to be a tort defence since, were it an answer to liability, it would have deleterious consequences for insane persons. These arguments will be called the 'avoidance argument' and the 'deinstitutionalisation argument'. The gist of

---

[77] *Holgate v Lancashire Mental Hospitals Board* [1937] 4 All ER 19 (Liverpool Assizes); *Tarasoff v Regents of the University of California* 17 Cal 3d 425; 551 P 2d 334 (1976); AA Stone, 'The *Tarasoff* Decisions: Suing Psychotherapists to Safeguard Society' (1976) 90 *Harvard Law Review* 358.

[78] Section 1(6) of the Mental Capacity Act 2005 (UK), which determines when and how decisions may be made on behalf of persons lacking mental capacity, provides that '[b]efore [any act done or decision is made under this Act for or on behalf of a person who lacks capacity], regard must be had to whether the purpose for which it is needed can be as effectively achieved in a way that is *less restrictive of the person's rights and freedom of action*' (emphasis added).

[79] This point is persuasively made in Ague (n 22) 222.

[80] The argument here borrows from the analysis in GP Fletcher, *Rethinking Criminal Law* (Boston, Mass, Little, Brown & Co, 1978) 813–17.

the avoidance argument is that tort law should not recognise a plea of insanity since admitting insanity as a defence would discourage interaction with insane persons. George Alexander and Thomas Szasz put this contention as follows:[81]

> [A] person dealing with another who might raise the defense of insanity is bound to be affected by the decision made concerning liability for injury. Adults justifiably avoid dealing legally with children because of a recognition of their immunity to suit. Likewise, mentally healthy persons may be expected to avoid dealing with mentally sick ones . . . if the mentally sick are held harmless when they injure. . . . [A] policy [not to hold the insane liable] would thus create a class of irresponsible persons . . . However, persons in this hypothetical class might well be shut off from society and desocialized to an extent surpassing anything with which we are familiar today.

This argument is unpersuasive. Its central defect is that the analogy between contract and tort is a false one. People can, generally speaking, select carefully those with whom they contract. Consequently, they may, as Alexander and Szasz point out, avoid contracting with individuals who might have a defence to liability for breach of contract. However, it is not very possible to limit the people with whom one interacts to those from whom one might be able to recover damages in tort law in the event that one is injured by them. This is because, very often, the victims of torts and tortfeasors are strangers.

The thrust of the deinstitutionalisation argument is that insanity should not be a defence since exempting the insane from liability might increase opposition to the policy of deinstitutionalisation.[82] This logic is embraced in the Restatement (Third) of Torts. The Reporters claim that deinstitutionalisation 'becomes more socially acceptable if innocent victims are at least assured of opportunity for compensation when they suffer injury' at the hands of those who would escape from liability were insanity a defence.[83] Similarly, Stephanie Splane argues:[84]

> Allowing a defense of mental illness to tort liability may increase public resistance to having the mentally ill in the community. The public's attitudes toward the mentally ill vacillate capriciously and it takes only a few well-publicized cases absolving the mentally ill from tort liability to start a public outcry. If the law gives the mentally ill special immunities from liability for causing harm, then society might well restrict their opportunities to create injury. Opportunities for the mentally ill to obtain licenses, employment, or housing might be substantially circumscribed. Finally, such immunity would probably exacerbate the problems of social segregation and stigmatization of the mentally ill, since such immunity effectively labels them as a special class of irresponsible, incompetent persons that the general community would wish to avoid.

---

[81] Alexander and Szasz (n 20) 36.

[82] For discussion of this policy, see P Bartlett and R Sandland, *Mental Health Law: Policy and Practice*, 3rd edn (Oxford, Oxford University Press, 2007) ch 3.

[83] Restatement (Third) of Torts, § 11, cmt e.

[84] Splane (n 20) 165–66 (footnote omitted). See also *Creasy v Rusk* 730 NE 2d 659, 664–67 (Ind 2000); *Carrier v Bonham* [2001] QCA 234; [2002] 1 Qd R 474, 487–88 [36].

It is readily accepted that the public would be easily inflamed by reports of insane individuals escaping from tort liability by reason of their insanity. Some well-reported instances of defendants being absolved of responsibility in tort for injuries that they cause on the basis of insanity may well strengthen public opposition to the policy of deinstitutionalisation. But this is not a convincing reason for holding the insane liable for their torts. The inflammatory effect of exonerating insane defendants from tort liability would surely generally pale in comparison to the public hostility to the policy of deinstitutionalisation that is aroused by letting such defendants out of criminal liability.[85] Furthermore, tort law is unlikely to be a particularly efficacious tool for bolstering the policy of deinstitutionalisation. It would be much more sensible to advance it through educational and other modalities.[86]

In conclusion, the avoidance and deinstitutionalisation arguments are both unpersuasive. There are two further criticisms that can be made against them jointly. First, neither of them demonstrates that the suggested deleterious consequences of recognising a defence of insanity for the insane are worth tolerating. They look only to the downsides for the insane of providing them with a defence. Potential benefits are not considered. Secondly, several civil law jurisdictions admit insanity as a defence to delictual liability[87] but the feared consequences of releasing the insane from liability predicted by these arguments do not seem to have materialised.

---

[85] The public is clearly ardently opposed to the insanity defence in the criminal sphere. It is widely perceived to be a loophole that is frequently exploited. For empirical research concerning these views, see VP Hans, 'An Analysis of Public Attitudes Toward the Insanity Defense' (1986) 24 *Criminology* 393; E Silver, C Cirincione and HJ Steadman, 'Demythologizing Inaccurate Perceptions of the Insanity Defense' (1994) 18 *Law & Human Behavior* 63. Public opposition to the defence reached fever pitch following the acquittal of John Hinckley in respect of the attempted assassination of President Reagan on the basis of his insanity. The legislative response in the United States to Mr Hinckley's acquittal was swift: see L Callahan, C Mayer and HJ Steadman, 'Insanity Defense Reform in the United States – Post-Hinckley' (1987) 11 *Mental & Physical Disability Law Reporter* 54.

[86] Law Reform Commission of Ireland (n 19) 56.

[87] The Japanese Civil Code, art 713, relevantly provides: 'A person who has inflicted damages on others while he/she lacks the capacity to appreciate his/her own act due to mental disability shall not be liable to compensate for the same . . .'. Article 1457 of the Civil Code of Québec, SQ, 1991, c 64, materially states: 'Where [any person] is endowed with reason and fails in [a duty owed under this Code], he is responsible for any injury he causes to another person by such fault and is liable to reparation for the injury . . .'. By implication, persons who lack the capacity for rational thought are not liable for their acts. Article 425(1) of the Polish Civil Code reads: 'A person who for whatever reason is in a state excluding a conscious and free decision and expression of will, shall not be liable for an injury inflicted by him when in such a state.' France adopts the common law rule. Article 489–2 of the French Civil Code states: 'A person who has caused damage to another when he was under the influence of a mental disorder is nonetheless liable to compensation.' The position is the same in Switzerland (Swiss Civil Code, art 19(3); Bundesgesetzvom 30 März 1911 betreffend die Ergänzung des Schweizerischen Zivilgesetzbuches, FünfterTeil: Obligationenrecht, SR 220, art 54) and in the Netherlands (Dutch Civil Code, art 6:165(1)). In Germany, mentally disordered persons are exempt from civil liability if the victim can obtain compensation from a third party who had a duty of supervision over the insane person concerned (Civil Code, §§ 827, 829). For discussion of the Dutch, French and German provisions, see CC van Dam, *European Tort Law* (Oxford, Oxford University Press, 2006) 225–31.

8.3.1.7. The goal of tort law argument

Thomas Cooley, in an early and influential analysis, argued in favour of disregarding insanity in determining liability based on what he perceived to be the purpose of tort law. Cooley began by remarking that since the principal object of the criminal law is punishment, it rightly exempts the insane from liability. In his words, 'to punish, as for a wrong, a party incapable of indulging an evil intent is a mere barbarity; not useful as a discipline to the individual punished, and of evil example instead of warning to others.'[88] Cooley then contended that tort law properly parts company with the criminal law in refusing to recognise insanity as a defence, as the purpose of tort law is not punishment but compensation. He wrote:[89]

> A wrong is an invasion of right, to the damage of the party who suffers it. It consists in the injury done, and not commonly in the purpose, or mental or physical capacity of the person or agent doing it. It may or may not have been done with bad motive; the question of motive is usually a question of aggravation only. Therefore the law, in giving redress, has in view the case of the party injured, and the extent of his injury, and makes what he suffers the measure of compensation. . . . There is consequently no anomaly in compelling one who is not chargeable with wrong intent to make compensation for an injury committed by him; for, as is said in an early case, 'the reason is, because he that is damaged ought to be recompensed.'

This argument does not hold water for two reasons. In the first place, compensation per se is not the goal of tort law.[90] Those who think otherwise cannot explain why tort law does not award damages irrespective of the defendant's fault. Even the weaker claim that compensation is *a* goal of tort law is implausible. This is because the aim of compensating those who suffer loss is limited by the pursuit of whatever other goals tort law might be supposed to have, such as punishment and deterrence. Efforts to advance these goals will necessarily hinder the realisation of the goal of compensation.[91]

Secondly, Cooley's contrast between crime and tort is far too simple. It is of course true that the criminal law places more emphasis on punishment than tort law. But punishment is not alien to tort law. This is not just because tort law recognises punitive damages. It is primarily because tort liability, like criminal

---

[88] Cooley (n 76) 98.

[89] *Ibid*, 98–99. Essentially the same argument is made in RFV Heuston and RA Buckley (eds), *Salmond and Heuston on the Law of Torts*, 21st edn (London, Sweet & Maxwell, 1996) 415–16.

[90] To develop this point in full would require much more space than is available. Fortunately, to do so is unnecessary, since numerous other writers have defended it at length. See, eg, Coleman (n 9) 209 ('Compensation simpliciter is not a goal of tort law'); R Stevens, *Torts and Rights* (Oxford, Oxford University Press, 2007) 320–21 (concluding that he can put 'compensation [as a goal of tort law] to one side' (at 323)); Weinrib (n 9) 40 (asking rhetorically, 'If compensation is a worthwhile goal, why not compensate regardless of how the injury is produced?').

[91] For an illuminating discussion of the mutually limiting nature of these goals, see Weinrib (n 9) 40–41.

liability, is a sanction.[92] The imposition of tort liability is not equivalent to, say, burdening a person with an obligation to pay a tax. Like criminal liability, tort liability is designed to mark society's disapproval of a wrong committed by the defendant. Therefore, Cooley's observation that it is barbarous to hold an insane personal criminally liable also applies to visiting such persons with tort liability.

In the passage extracted, a supplementary argument in support of denying the insane a defence to liability in tort can be detected. Cooley asserts that because tort law typically disregards the defendant's motive and sometimes his intention, there is no anomaly in ignoring a lack of agency on the part of the defendant. Agency, however, is a fundamentally different concept from those of motive and intention. Thus, it does not follow from tort law's general insensitivity to the defendant's motive and whether he acted with the intention of bringing about a particular result that tort law should not attach importance to a lack of agency.

8.3.1.8. The self-support argument

Another argument in favour of liability is the 'self-support argument'. One court expressed it as meaning[93] 'that as an insane person must pay for his support, if he is financially able, so he ought also to pay for the damage which he does'. This argument is unsustainable. It is not a corollary of an ability to pay for one's necessaries that one should also pay for any damage that one causes. There is no rule that persons who are of sound mind and who have sufficient financial resources to pay for their sustenance are held liable for all of the losses that they occasion in the course of their lives. Why should the position be different for the insane? Additionally, this argument provides no support for imposing liability on insane persons who cannot pay for their upkeep and are dependent on the charity of others or the welfare system.

8.3.1.9. The distributive justice argument

Suppose that D owns an apartment in Park Lane. While strolling through Hyde Park, he suffers a fit of insanity during which he tackles a homeless person. The homeless person is badly injured. If D can escape from liability because he was

---

[92] Such significant support for this proposition exists in the theoretical literature that it is unnecessary to offer a detailed defence of it here. For a comprehensive argument in favour of this claim, see T Honoré, 'The Morality of Tort Law – Questions and Answers' in DG Owen (ed), *Philosophical Foundations of Tort Law* (Oxford, Clarendon Press, 1995) 73; P Cane, *The Anatomy of Tort Law* (Oxford, Hart Publishing, 1997); P Cane, 'Retribution, Proportionality, and Moral Luck in Tort Law' in P Cane and J Stapleton (eds), *The Law of Obligations: Essays in Celebration of John Fleming* (Oxford, Clarendon Press, 1998). It is worth briefly noting that the proposition that tort liability is a sanction cannot be refuted on the ground that one can insure against liability to pay tort damages. This is partly because contracts of insurance in respect of liability to pay punitive damages are not contrary to public policy: see *Lamb v Cotogno* (1987) 164 CLR 1 (HCA); *Lancashire County Council v Municipal Mutual Insurance Ltd* [1997] QB 897 (CA) (holding that it is at least permissible to insure against the risk of being held vicariously liable to pay punitive damages); *Gray v Motor Accidents Commission* [1998] HCA 70; (1998) 196 CLR 1, 12–13; cf 25–27.

[93] *McGuire v Almy* 297 Mass 323, 326–27; 8 NE 2d 760, 762 (1937).

insane at the time he executed the tackle, the homeless person will remain destitute. D, meanwhile, can continue to luxuriate in his apartment. The prospect of such distributive injustices in material wealth has prompted some courts to withhold a defence of insanity. In the words of one court, were insanity a defence, 'there would be no redress for injuries [caused by insane persons], and we might have the anomaly of an insane person having abundant wealth depriving another of his rights without compensation'.[94]

This argument is afflicted by serious confusion. The main problem with it is that it assumes that tort law is concerned to ameliorate distributive injustices in financial resources between litigants. This is plainly not the case. On the contrary, it may aggravate distributive injustices. Grindingly poor defendants who commit torts against the obscenely wealthy are liable to compensate the latter for their losses. Furthermore, the spectre that this argument raises is all but non-existent. There is virtually no prospect of extreme distributive injustices in economic resources resulting by virtue of the creation of an insanity defence since, as has been stressed several times, the insane will usually not be possessed of substantial means.

8.3.1.10. The justified expectations argument

According to Patrick Kelley, a defendant's insane state should not provide him with a defence in so far as letting him out of liability would frustrate the claimant's reasonable expectations that the defendant would comply with 'safety conventions'.[95] Kelley writes:[96]

> When the plaintiff coordinates her conduct with that of the defendant reasonably expecting him to follow the applicable safety conventions, a mentally ill or mentally deficient defendant should be held liable if he failed to follow that convention and caused injury to her. In that case, the defendant objectively wronged the plaintiff. When [the] plaintiff knew of [the] defendant's mental condition and appreciated the danger to herself threatened by that condition, and after acquiring that knowledge failed to act with ordinary care or voluntarily remained subject to that danger, she should not be able to recover even though [the] defendant breached a safety convention.

There are several oddities lurking in this argument. Kelley states that a claimant who is injured by a mentally-ill defendant should be denied compensation if he knew that the defendant was mentally ill but failed to take reasonable care for his own safety. But why should this be the case? Ordinarily, a failure by the claimant to take reasonable care for his interests results in apportionment rather than a verdict for the defendant. More seriously, this argument focuses on the claimant but leaves this focus unexplained. Why should the attention be on the claimant's reasonable expectations to the exclusion of the fairness of holding insane defendants liable? Kelley ignores the bilateral structure of tort law.

---

[94] *Seals v Snow* 123 Kan 88; 254 P 348, 349 (1927).

[95] Kelley (n 20). Kelley develops in this respect a line of thought suggested in DE Seidelson, 'Reasonable Expectations and Subjective Standards in Negligence Law: The Minor, the Mentally Impaired, and the Mentally Incompetent' (1981) 50 *George Washington Law Review* 17.

[96] Kelley (n 20) 236.

8.3.1.11. The price for membership of society argument

One of the more specious arguments in support of liability is that insane persons should pay for the damage that they cause in return for being permitted to live among the general population. The Reporters of the Restatement (Second) of Torts put this argument as follows:[97]

> [I]f mental defectives are to live in the world they should pay for the damage they do . . . [I]t is better that their wealth, if any, should be used to compensate innocent victims than that it should remain in their hands.

This contention, which is couched in rather backward language, is not so much an argument as it is a bald assertion. It does not explain *why* it is preferable for insane actors to pay for the damage that they cause than for them to apply it for their purposes. Neither does this argument explain why insane persons who are institutionalised should have to pay for damage that they inflict upon their carers and others with whom they have contact.

8.3.1.12. The consistency argument

Richard Epstein argues that withholding insanity as a defence is consistent with the refusal of certain other defences,[98] most notably private necessity[99] and duress.[100] He contends that this is because the plea of insanity, like the pleas of private necessity and duress, is an assertion by the defendant that he should be allowed to solve his own problems at the claimant's expense. This is true. But while insanity is similar to private necessity and duress in this respect, it is different from these defences in a deeper way. Private necessity is in the nature of a justification, while duress is an excuse. Because justifications and excuses can be offered by those who possess responsibility only in the basic sense,[101] private necessity and duress are fundamentally different from the plea of insanity. Epstein's argument founders due to this deep-seated distinction between the plea of insanity and the pleas of private necessity and duress.

8.3.1.13. The resistance and asset recovery argument

Imagine the following scenarios:

(1) C1 is walking to work. D1, who is insane, lunges for C1's briefcase.
(2) D2, who is insane, breaks into C2's house and absconds with C2's computer.

---

[97] Restatement (Second) of Torts, § 895J, cmt a. To like effect, see *Jolley v Powell* 299 So 2d 647, 648 (Fla Dist Ct App 1974); *Schumann v Crofoot* 43 Or App 53, 57–58; 602 P 2d 298, 300–01 (Ct App 1979).

[98] Epstein (n 20) 169–70.

[99] Private necessity is discussed in 4.3.1.2.

[100] Duress is discussed in 4.3.2.5.

[101] It is explained in 4.3.2.2 why to rely on an excuse is to assert one's responsibility in the basic sense.

If insanity were a defence, would it be permissible for C1 to resist D1? Similarly, would C2 be prevented from recovering his computer from D2? If recognising a defence of insanity would have these implications, this would be a reason not to let insane persons out of liability since, clearly, C1 should be able to resist D1 and C2 should be able to reacquire his computer from D2. Plainly, however, admitting insanity as a defence would not prevent the resistance of D1 or the recovery of the computer from D2. Insane persons who engage in criminal conduct may be resisted.[102] Why should tort law take a different position if insanity were a tort defence? Similarly, it is difficult to identify any reason why, if tort law recognised insanity as a defence, insane persons who convert another's property should be entitled to keep it.[103]

8.3.2. The Case for Recognition

In the previous section of this chapter, arguments upholding the rule that insanity is not a tort defence were considered. They were all found wanting. Indeed, most are so breathtakingly weak that it is surprising that they continue to enjoy support. In this section, the case in favour of recognising a defence of insanity will be sketched.

8.3.2.1. *The free will paradigm argument*

Like the criminal law, tort law is premised on the concept of free will; the idea that human beings are self-determining agents.[104] This notion finds expression in many of tort law's most basic principles. It will suffice to mention two (these examples could easily be multiplied). Take, first, the rule that involuntary conduct does not attract liability.[105] A person who strikes another individual due to an uncontrolled muscular reflex, or because a swarm of bees descended upon him,[106] or because he suffered from a coughing fit,[107] or while unconscious[108] and so on is not responsible in tort. Secondly, generally speaking, tort law treats the acts of human beings as intervening causes.[109] A deterministic view of the world is to this

---

[102] See the text accompanying n 25 in ch 4.

[103] See the remarks in *Morriss v Marsden* [1952] 1 All ER 925, 927 (QBD). The following passage in LL Fuller, *The Morality of Law*, rev edn (New Haven, Conn, Yale University Press, 1969) 73 is also pertinent: 'A lunatic, let us suppose, steals my purse. His mental condition may be such that it is impossible for him to understand or to obey the laws of private property. This circumstance furnishes a good reason for not sending him to jail, but it offers no reason at all for letting him keep my purse. I am entitled under the law to get my purse back, and he is, in this sense, under a legal liability to return it, even though in taking it he acted without fault and without any intention of doing wrong.'

[104] Expressly stated in *Perre v Apand Pty Ltd* [1999] HCA 36; (1999) 198 CLR 180, 223–24 [114] (McHugh J); *Gregg v Scott* [2005] UKHL 2; [2005] 2 AC 176, 196–97 [82] (Lord Hoffmann).

[105] For discussion, see 3.3.1.

[106] *Scholz v Standish* [1961] SASR 123, 127–28 (SC).

[107] *Robinson v Glover* [1952] NZLR 669, 672 (SC).

[108] *Slattery v Haley* (1922) 52 OLR 95 (Sup Ct App Div).

[109] HLA Hart and T Honoré, *Causation in the Law*, 2nd edn (Oxford, Clarendon Press, 1985) 136.

extent thereby rejected. Since insanity destroys or at least severely diminishes a person's capacity for self-determination, tort law, in failing to grant a defence of insanity, does not adhere faithfully to the paradigm of free will. In order to be consistent, it must, like the criminal law, release insane persons from liability.

8.3.2.2. The sanction argument

Another reason for exempting insane persons from liability was gestured towards earlier when 'the goal of tort law argument' was considered.[110] This argument, recall, draws a sharp contrast between tort law and the criminal law, identifying the former with compensation and the latter with punishment, and holds that, by reason of their different purposes, these bodies of law properly diverge in their treatment of insane defendants. It was contended that this view of the tort/crime divide is much too simple. This is mainly because it fails to acknowledge that tort liability, like criminal liability, is a sanction. Tort liability is not, as some theorists naively suggest, merely a mechanism for ensuring that accidents and other loss-causing events occur at an efficient rate. Once it is accepted that tort liability is a sanction, the conclusion that it is unfair to hold insane defendants liable in tort becomes irresistible. Just as it would be a travesty to impose criminal liability on mentally-disordered persons, it is unjust to visit them with tort liability.[111]

8.3.3. Conclusion

A large number of arguments have been offered in support of the rule that insanity is not a tort defence. Some rest on logical falsehoods. Others would only work in a world that is very different from the one in which we live. None of them is convincing. The stronger position is that insanity should be a tort defence.

8.4. Should Infancy Be a Tort Defence?

8.4.1. The Case Against Recognition

Do any of the arguments that have been mustered in support of tort law's refusal to recognise a defence of insanity, taken *mutatis mutandis,* justify the absence of a defence of infancy? It is obvious that many of these arguments are equally unconvincing when applied in explanation of the lack of an infancy defence. For example, the deterrence argument[112] is plainly not up to the job of rationalising tort

---

[110] See 8.3.1.7.

[111] This is why insane defendants are not liable for punitive damages: see the text accompanying n 34 above.

[112] See 8.3.1.5.

law's handling of the liability of infants. Threatening the very young with tort liability will not have any deterrent effect on them (they cannot be deterred by the threat of legal sanctions). Neither is threatening infants with liability necessary to encourage their carers to take cost-efficient precautions against the risk that they will tortiously injure others, since carers of infants already have very obvious and very considerable inducements to take reasonable care in the discharge of their responsibilities. Similarly, the 'resistance and asset recovery argument'[113] does not cut it when deployed in support of tort law's refusal to exempt infants from liability. Were infants granted a defence, tort law would not thereby enjoin resistance of their wrongful conduct. Neither would recognising a defence of infancy mean that tort law would be powerless to compel infants to return property that they wrongfully appropriate. Consider, lastly, the 'fraud argument'.[114] This line of reasoning cannot possibly justify tort law's treatment of the liability of infant defendants. This is primarily because there is no risk of infancy being successfully simulated.

Are there any other arguments that can be made against an infancy defence? It might be suggested that holding infants liable for their torts is warranted on the ground that it helps them to become responsible in the basic sense. Imposing liability on infants, one might say, assists them to become fully-fledged agents. This is an interesting possibility. But this argument should probably not be accepted. First, assuming *arguendo* that the imposition of sanctions (and the threat thereof) helps infants to mature, is it not sufficient that infants are exposed to moral sanctions? Why is it necessary to subject them to the risk of suffering legal sanctions? Secondly, this argument does not justify visiting very young infants with liability, since threatening such infants with liability will not shorten the biological timetable that determines when an infant will become responsible in the basic sense. At most this argument establishes that infants who are on the verge of acquiring basic responsibility, or who are responsible in the basic sense only in some facets of their life, may benefit from being exposed to the risk of incurring legal sanctions. Consequently, this argument goes to the debate about the age when a defence of infancy should be available, not to the issue of whether the law should recognise a defence of infancy.

8.4.2. The Case for Recognition

The arguments in favour of recognising a defence of insanity also appear to call for a defence of infancy. Two reasons were outlined earlier in support of the recognition of an insanity defence. The first was the 'free will paradigm argument'.[115] According to this argument, tort law, if it is to be consistent in embracing the paradigm of free will, must provide insane persons with a defence. It also calls for

---

[113] See 8.3.1.13.
[114] See 8.3.1.2.
[115] See 8.3.2.1.

the creation of an infancy defence, since the very young, like the insane, are not self-determining agents. The second reason that was offered for admitting insanity to the ranks of tort defences was the 'sanction argument'.[116] This argument holds that liability in tort is a sanction and that it is, therefore, unfair to impose it on insane persons. It clamours just as loudly for granting infants a defence.

One might respond to the foregoing along the following lines: 'Even if what was said about insane defendants is correct, the analysis cannot be extended to infants since there are significant differences between insanity and infancy.' Obviously, there are several not insignificant distinctions between insanity and infancy.[117] For instance, whereas insanity may be a permanent state, infancy is not. Infancy will invariably be outgrown. Another difference is that infancy is a socially acceptable condition while the same is not true of insanity. These and several other differences are incontestable. But they are eclipsed by a respect in which insane persons and sufficiently immature individuals stand in an equivalent position: they both lack responsibility in the basic sense. By virtue of this fundamental similarity, it is submitted that insane defendants and infant defendants should be treated equally. As the New York Court of Appeals put it in *Williams v Hays*, 'There can be no distinction as to the liability of infants and lunatics.'[118]

8.4.3. Conclusion

In conclusion, like the criminal law, tort law should exempt infants from liability. The argument on this score has been relatively brief. This has been possible since much of the legwork was done in considering whether insane defendants – who do not differ relevantly from infant defendants – should be released from liability in tort.

8.5. Should Unfitness to Plead Be a Tort Defence?

It is a fundamental principle of criminal justice that a defendant who does not enjoy basic responsibility cannot be tried:[119] he will be eligible for the defence of unfitness to plead.[120] As has been noted, tort law strikes off in a different direction from the criminal law in this respect. Unfitness to plead is not a tort defence. The fact that the defendant lacks responsibility in the basic sense is no impediment to

---

[116] See 8.3.2.2.

[117] See Alexander and Szasz (n 20) 34–35.

[118] 143 NY 442, 451; 38 NE 449, 451 (Ct App 1894).

[119] This principle is enshrined in art 6 of the ECHR (see especially art 6(3)(b)). See further *V and T v United Kingdom* (2000) 30 EHRR 121, 153–56 [98]–[107].

[120] The test for unfitness to plead is found in *R v Pritchard* (1836) 7 Car & P 303; 173 ER 135. The defence will apply if the defendant cannot comprehend the nature of the proceedings, cannot understand the evidence, does not understand his right to challenge jurors or cannot instruct counsel.

holding a civil trial. A civil trial can proceed despite the fact that the defendant is, for example, in a vegetative state, suffering from delusions that deprive him of the ability to understand the nature of the proceedings, is five years old, or is dead.[121] This is subject only to the proviso that defendants (and claimants) who are 'children'[122] or 'protected parties'[123] may participate in proceedings only through a 'litigation friend'.[124] The aim here is to consider the case for and against granting a defence triggered by a lack of basic responsibility on the part of the defendant at the time of the trial. Should tort law fall into line with the criminal law in this respect?[125]

8.5.1. The Case Against Recognition

At least two arguments militate against the recognition of a defence of unfitness to plead.

8.5.1.1. *The repugnant consequences argument*

Suppose that it was the law that tort trials cannot be held when the defendant is not responsible in the basic sense. What else would this entail? Would it not follow that a trial should also not be conducted if the *claimant* lacks basic responsibility? Such a state of affairs would clearly be objectionable. It would give defendants an incentive to injure claimants more severely, since the greater the injury inflicted the more likely it is that the claimant, as a consequence of his injuries, will be deprived of basic responsibility. It would also mean that tort law would not do much to discourage the commission of acts that injure those who do not enjoy basic responsibility in the first place, such as infants and the mentally disordered. This would be extremely odd. These consequences of recognising a defence of unfitness to plead suggest that it should not be welcomed into tort law.

---

[121] Death is, however, a defence to proceedings in defamation and to actions for damages for bereavement: see 5.3.2.10.

[122] A 'child' is defined in CPR 21.1(1) as a person under 18.

[123] Under CPR 21.1(1), a 'protected party' means 'a party, or an intended party, who lacks capacity to conduct the proceedings'. The words 'lacks capacity' have the meaning given to them in s 2 of the Mental Capacity Act 2005 (UK). This section provides that 'a person lacks capacity in relation to a matter if at the material time he is unable to make a decision for himself in relation to the matter because of an impairment of, or a disturbance in the functioning of, the mind or brain'. See further *Masterman-Lister v Brutton & Co (Nos 1 and 2)* [2002] EWCA Civ 1889; [2003] 1 WLR 1511; *Phillips v Symes* [2004] EWHC 1887; *Bailey v Warren* [2006] EWCA Civ 51; The Times, 20 February 2006.

[124] See generally A Zuckerman, *Zuckerman on Civil Procedure: Principles of Practice*, 2nd edn (London, Sweet & Maxwell, 2006) 70–72.

[125] Comparisons of tort law with the criminal law tend to focus on differences in their liability rules and responses to liability. Regrettably, virtually nothing has been said about how these areas of law part company in terms of the role of the trial.

8.5.1.2. The party autonomy argument

Withholding a defence of unfitness to plead is consistent with the principle of party autonomy.[126] Adrian Zuckerman describes this principle, which is a cornerstone of our system of civil procedure, as follows: 'The parties to a dispute are autonomous in procedure. They are free to choose whether to litigate, what to litigate and what evidence to call in support of their respective allegations.'[127] In accordance with this principle, defendants in the civil arena cannot be compelled to appear in court. This goes to show that the civil law, unlike the criminal law, does not think it essential for the defendant to be present during the proceedings.[128] (Indeed, not infrequently, the defendant will not even know that the proceedings are afoot – they will be conducted by his insurer.[129]) Given that this is the case, it would be bizarre if tort law recognised a rule that enabled the defendant to escape from liability on the basis that, due to a want of basic responsibility, he was not mentally present in court.

8.5.2. The Case for Recognition

It is worth considering why unfitness to plead is a bar to criminal proceedings, to see if any of the arguments that support its presence in the criminal sphere can be applied *mutatis mutandis* in the tort context. Several reasons for the existence of this defence have been offered.[130] Two of these reasons are worth mentioning (the others are either so weak as not to merit discussion, or are merely variations of these arguments). The first is that the defence is necessary to ensure that trials are fair (the 'fairness argument'). To expose a defendant who is not responsible in the basic sense to a process that is designed to assess the adequacy of his behaviour and that has the imposition of punishment as one of its potential outcomes is manifestly unjust. The second is that the defence tends to promote accurate verdicts (the 'decisional rectitude argument'). A defendant who is unfit to plead cannot give evidence of facts that might reveal his innocence. Do these arguments also support the recognition of the defence of unfitness to plead in the tort setting?

---

[126] This principle was encountered earlier in 1.8.2 and 6.9.

[127] Zuckerman (n 124) 397.

[128] In the case of criminal proceedings on indictment, the defendant must be present in court. This is unnecessary in the case of summary trials: J Sprack, *A Practical Approach to Criminal Procedure*, 14th edn (Oxford, Oxford University Press, 2012) 171 [10.32], 337–38 [20.71]–[20.73].

[129] Professor Harry Street, the author of *Street on Torts*, revealed that he was once a defendant in a personal injury case arising out of a motor vehicle accident and did not discover that the matter had been heard by the Court of Appeal until he read about it in a newspaper: DW Elliott and H Street, *Road Accidents* (Harmondsworth, Penguin Books, 1968) 209–10.

[130] RA Duff, *Trials and Punishments* (Cambridge, Cambridge University Press, 1986) 119–22; RJ Bonnie, 'The Competence of Criminal Defendants: Beyond *Dusky* and *Drope*' (1993) 47 *University of Miami Law Review* 539; RD Mackay, *Mental Condition Defences in the Criminal Law* (Oxford, Clarendon Press, 1995) 216–19.

8.5.2.1. The fairness argument

Like criminal trials, tort trials involve an assessment of the adequacy of the defendant's behaviour and the possibility of sanctions being visited upon him in the event that it is found to be inadequate. There is, therefore, some unfairness in subjecting to tort trials those who lack basic responsibility. One might respond that the potential for unfairness in this respect is tolerable since such defendants will have their interests protected by a litigation friend. Clearly, this answer would not be an effective riposte to the fairness argument as a rationale for the defence of unfitness to plead in the criminal setting. Few would not think it acceptable to put a defendant who is not responsible in the basic sense through a criminal trial so long as he is legally represented, no matter how competently. However, in the tort environment, this response seems to pack more of a punch, owing to the fact that the sanctions meted out by tort law are generally not as censorious as those imposed by the criminal law. In short, whereas provision for a litigation friend would not render it just to put a defendant who is unfit to plead through a criminal trial, such provision may substantially ameliorate any unfairness that would be caused by putting such a defendant through a tort trial.

It should be noted that the fairness argument focuses exclusively on the injustice likely to be caused to defendants by withholding a defence of unfitness to plead. But it is also necessary to consider claimants. Clearly, admitting a defence of unfitness to plead would involve some injustice to claimants, since it would prevent, in a certain number of cases, the recovery of redress when redress is warranted. It is arguable that the best way of minimising the collective injustice caused to the parties is to withhold the defence of unfitness to plead and insist that the defendant be provided with a litigation friend. This solution would not stand in the way of claimants who have been wronged obtaining a remedy in tort law, and it would do something to reduce the unfairness involved in subjecting to tort trials defendants who lack basic responsibility.

8.5.2.2. The decisional rectitude argument

It is doubtful whether the decisional rectitude argument, taken alone, justifies the retention of the defence of unfitness to plead in the criminal domain as the defence is presently formulated. For instance, it does not support the defence's application where all concerned are confident of the defendant's guilt notwithstanding the absence of evidence from him. Neither does it support the defence's existence in so far as the defence can apply when the defendant, after having given evidence, becomes unfit to participate further in the trial. Deployed in the tort setting, the decisional rectitude argument is even less persuasive. This is because tort law has a considerably higher tolerance for fact-finding errors than the criminal law, as is exemplified by the fact that tort law requires proof only to the civil standard.

8.5.3. Conclusion

Unlike the criminal law, tort law does not provide for a defence of unfitness to plead. The argument in this part of the chapter attempted to support this difference between these areas of law. The justifications for recognising the defence of unfitness to plead in the criminal sphere are much less powerful when applied in the tort context. Moreover, there are reasons not to welcome this defence into tort law. Recognising it would seem to entail that tort trials should not be conducted if the claimant is unfit to participate in them. This would be unacceptable. Additionally, admitting a defence of unfitness to plead would conflict with the principle of party autonomy.[131]

8.6. Further Questions

Were insanity and infancy to be recognised as tort defences, as has been argued in this chapter, the bipartite taxonomy of defences promoted in this book would need to be expanded since insanity and infancy are neither justifications nor public policy defences. A new category – denials of responsibility – would be required to accommodate them. Admitting a third category to the taxonomy would raise at least two important questions.

8.6.1. Implications of a Defence being a Denial of Responsibility

In chapter six it was argued that classifying a given defence as either a justification or a public policy defence has a wide range of important implications. Were tort law to recognise denial of responsibility defences, it would be necessary to revisit the analysis in chapter six in order to ascertain to what extent the ramifications discussed in it are relevant to such defences. This will not be done comprehensively given that tort law does not, at present, recognise any denial of responsibility defences. However, a few brief comments will be made about what implications would attend any denial of responsibility defences if and when such defences join the ranks of tort law defences.

First, the burdens of pleading and proving denial of responsibility defences should rest with the defendant, in accordance with the usual rule regarding the allocation of these burdens in tort law.

Secondly, vagueness in the scope of denial of responsibility defences would be unproblematic for the purposes of the rule of law (although such vagueness may

---

[131] The conclusion that tort law should not recognise a defence of unfitness to plead may have implications for whether defendants who are unfit to plead should ever be liable for punitive damages. Unfortunately, it is not possible to discuss this interesting issue here.

of course be objectionable for other reasons). If denial of responsibility defences existed in the law of torts, one would hope that they would not cause those who might be eligible for them to modify their behaviour so as to bring themselves within their ambit. Indeed, a defendant who attempts to bring himself within the reach of a denial of responsibility defence would probably be ineligible for it, since planning to capitalise on a defence reveals that the defendant in fact enjoyed responsibility in the basic sense at a relevant point in time.

Thirdly, as is the case with public policy defences, but in contrast with justification defences, it is obvious that the availability of denial of responsibility defences ought not to be contingent upon the defendant being aware of any particular facts. For instance, the defence of insanity, if added to tort law's repertoire of defences, should not require any appreciation by the defendant of the fact that he was not responsible in the basic sense. It would be inconsistent with the nature of denial of responsibility defences for them to insist on the defendant being aware of certain facts. Just as the defendant's knowledge ought to be immaterial to the applicability of denial of responsibility defences, these defences should be insensitive to the defendant's motive.

Fourthly, denial of responsibility defences should not be amenable to being shared with other defendants. The fact that D1 is granted a denial of responsibility defence does not mean that D2, who helps D1 to commit a tort, should be entitled to that defence too. Any denial of basic responsibility defences that are admitted into tort law should be personal to the defendants who are entitled to them.

Fifthly, it is doubtful whether denial of responsibility defences, if they are ushered into law of torts, should be susceptible to being invoked by the court. Because of the doctrine of party autonomy,[132] defences should not in principle be raised other than by the parties. The courts depart from this doctrine, and raise defences *proprio motu*, only where some significant public interest would be jeopardised if a defence, despite being applicable, was not introduced into the proceedings.

8.6.2. The Priority Thesis

If defences that are triggered by a lack of basic responsibility are welcomed into tort law, the taxonomy of defences promoted in this book would need to be expanded to accommodate them, as has already been noted. The addition of a category for denials of responsibility would raise the possibility that certain types of defences might be superior to others. This possibility will be called the 'priority thesis'. The thesis holds as follows. The ideal outcome for a defendant is for him to be found not to have committed a tort. If it is determined that the defendant committed no tort, the defendant will have achieved perfect success in his life so far as tort law is concerned. But if the defendant has committed a tort, it is best if he did so with justification. This is because justifications are available only to those defendants

---

[132] See 1.8.2, 6.9.

who act in accordance with the balance of reasons. Denials of responsibility are inferior to justifications because defendants who need to deny their responsibility to avoid liability do not even operate within the realm of reason. Put differently, denials of responsibility reflect less favourably on the defendant as a rational being than justifications. The priority thesis does not make any claims about public policy defences. Public policy defences cannot be said to be superior or inferior to other types of defences since they are unconcerned with the rational defensibility of the defendant's behaviour.

The idea that some defences might be superior to others in terms of how highly they speak of the defendant as a rational being is not new. The priority thesis has been strongly supported by criminal law theorists.[133] It uncovers a basis for ordering justifications and denials of responsibility, even though both types of defences result in the same outcome in terms of the court's verdict.

8.7. Conclusion

In this chapter it has been argued that insanity and infancy should be admitted as tort defences. In contrast, it was suggested that tort law should not provide for a defence of unfitness to plead. The recognition of defences of insanity and infancy would call for the taxonomy of tort law defences which has been developed in this book to be enlarged. This is because these defences are *sui generis*. Unlike justifications and excuses, they require a lack of basic responsibility on the part of the defendant.

---

[133] See, especially Gardner (n 2) 87–88, whose analysis shaped the discussion here. For further analysis of the priority thesis, see DN Husak, 'The Serial View of Criminal Law Defenses' (1992) 3 *Criminal Law Forum* 369; DN Husak, *The Philosophy of Criminal Law* (Oxford, Oxford University Press, 2010) ch 11.

9

Future Directions

The argument presented in this book to this point has been summarised at the end of each chapter. This exercise is not repeated here. Rather, by way of conclusion, this chapter discusses a selection of issues regarding tort law defences that are important to their future.

9.1. Statutes and Defences

At the outset of this book, it was observed[1] that whereas most of the law concerning the elements of torts is judge-made, a far greater proportion of the law regarding defences is statutory in origin.[2] This significant fact about the law of torts has hitherto passed unnoticed. This is a convenient place in which to analyse the 'statutorification'[3] of defences, since it raises several important issues that are relevant to the future of defences.

9.1.1. Legislative Techniques

Some general remarks need to be made about the way in which legislatures have tended to legislate with respect to tort law defences. Two tendencies in this regard stand out. First, by and large, the changes to the law of defences made by legislatures, while very numerous, have generally been relatively narrow in scope. Sweeping changes, covering multiple torts, or several contextual settings, are uncommon. For example, no legislature in a common law jurisdiction has created a generalised defence of 'justification' that would apply whenever a defendant acts reasonably in committing a tort.[4] Rather, legislatures have tended to create a host of justificatory defences with limited spheres of application. Justificatory defences created by the

---

[1] See 1.3.

[2] This claim is developed in J Goudkamp, 'Statutes and Tort Defences' in TT Arvind and J Steele (eds), *Tort Law and the Legislature: Common Law, Statute and the Dynamics of Legal Change* (Oxford, Hart Publishing, 2013).

[3] The term is Guido Calabresi's: G Calabresi, *A Common Law for the Age of Statutes* (Cambridge, Mass, Harvard University Press, 1982) 1.

[4] Cf the generalised 'lesser evils' defence in the Model Penal Code, § 3.02.

Parliament at Westminster include those such as prevention of crime,[5] the many law-and-order defences granted to constables and sometimes to private citizens,[6] and the defences that facilitate the provision of medical treatment.[7]

The legislative preference to enact defences with tightly-controlled ambits is readily explicable. In the first place, there will usually be less resistance to tweaks being made to the law than to across-the-board changes, all other things being equal. Proposals for extensive reform will normally affect many more stakeholders. This greater interest will often create sufficient resistance to prevent them from coming to fruition. Hence, it is normally easier for governments to enact legislation that makes small-scale changes to the law. Secondly, legislatures may prefer to make relatively modest adjustments to the law, all other things being equal, as it might be thought that such changes are less likely than more major modifications to have unanticipated and possibly unwelcome side-effects.

The other noteworthy tendency of legislatures is to supplement rather than to replace common law defences. For example, the numerous special heads of qualified privilege created by the Defamation Act 1996 (UK)[8] and the Defamation Act 2013 (UK)[9] exist alongside the general common law defence of qualified privilege, the statutory illegality defence in section 329 of the Criminal Justice Act 2003 (UK)[10] is available concurrently with its common law counterpart,[11] and the medical treatment defences in the Mental Health Act 1983 (UK) and the Mental Capacity Act 2005 (UK)[12] run together with the common law defence of public necessity. This trend is also easily explained. Usually, it seems, the creation of a statutory defence is a response to complaints by a pressure group that liability is too extensive in some respect. If a relevant common law defence is replaced instead of left to operate in tandem with a statutory defence, it is possible that the circumstances in which liability arises might unwittingly be widened in some respect. Such a situation would be embarrassing for lawmakers. It would obviously not reflect favourably on them if, in endeavouring to restrict a given net of liability, they actually enlarged it in some way. Lawmakers are keenly aware that the safer way in which to proceed is to add to the number of defences. This ensures that the zone of liability will not be accidentally increased. An unfortunate consequence of this state of affairs, however, is that it has contributed to tort law becoming increasingly complex. In some contexts, such as defamation and trespass to the person, the pool of defences has become exceedingly large.

---

[5] Criminal Law Act 1967 (UK), s 3(1). This defence is mentioned in passing in ch 5, n 93.

[6] See, in particular, the Police and Criminal Evidence Act 1984 (UK), pts 1–2; Criminal Justice and Police Act 2001 (UK), pt 2. These statutes are also touched upon in ch 5, n 93.

[7] See 5.2.2.7.

[8] See s 15 and sch 1.

[9] See s 6.

[10] See 5.3.1.11.

[11] Criminal Justice Act 2003 (UK), s 329(6).

[12] See 5.2.2.7.

9.1.2. Reasons for the Focus of Legislatures on Defences

Why have legislatures concentrated on defences when legislating with respect to tort law? In the previous section it was observed that it is usually significantly easier, all other things being equal, for a government to enact legislation that tweaks the law than statutes that make far-reaching changes to it. It was suggested that this explains the preference of legislatures to make relatively limited changes to the law of defences. It also would seem to go some way towards explaining the focus of legislatures on defences. Since statutory intervention in the defence context affects what are, in a sense, supplementary rules, whereas changes to the definitional elements of torts alter the core rules themselves, legislative modification of the law governing defences is less likely to excite controversy than alterations of the definitional elements of torts, all other things being equal.

Another explanation for legislatures' concentration on defences, which is closely related to the first, concerns the fact that legislation is not infrequently enacted in response to calls for reform by pressure groups. If a government is sympathetic to the complaints of stakeholders that their exposure to liability is too great, it will normally want to tailor its response to those complaints. Why should political capital be spent making changes that are more extensive than have been sought? The easiest way in which to ensure a proportionate response will usually be (or will usually be perceived to be) to alter the law concerning defences. Specific stakeholders can be given a defence of their own. Conversely, it may sometimes be more difficult (or be perceived to be more difficult) to address stakeholders' complaints about the law by modifying the definitional elements of torts without the changes being more extensive than is necessary to alleviate a given stakeholder's anxieties about the law.

9.1.3. The Balkanisation of the Law of Defences

The tendency of legislatures to concentrate on the law of defences when legislating with respect to tort law has not been confined to any single jurisdiction or a few jurisdictions. It is a phenomenon that transcends jurisdictional borders. It is particularly obvious in the case of those countries that have undergone extensive 'tort reform'. For example, the waves of tort reform that washed across Australia[13]

---

[13] Overviews of the Australian reforms are offered in P Cane, 'Reforming Tort Law in Australia: A Personal Perspective' (2003) 27 *Melbourne University Law Review* 649; H Luntz, 'The Australian Picture' (2004) 35 *Victoria University of Wellington Law Review* 879; P Underwood, 'Is Ms Donoghue's Snail in Mortal Peril?' (2004) 12 *Torts Law Journal* 39; B McDonald, 'Legislative Intervention in the Law of Negligence: The Common Law, Statutory Interpretation and Tort Reform in Australia' (2005) 27 *Sydney Law Review* 443; B McDonald, 'The Impact of the Civil Liability Legislation on the Fundamental Policies and Principles of the Common Law of Negligence' (2006) 14 *Torts Law Journal* 268; J Goudkamp, 'The Young Report: An Australian Perspective on the Latest Response to Britain's "Compensation Culture"' (2012) 28 *Journal of Professional Negligence* 4.

and the United States[14] deposited numerous eclectic statutory defences[15] while making comparatively minor changes to the elements of torts. The important point to note for present purposes is that the law governing tort law defences is now highly jurisdiction-specific. This situation has severely diminished the ability of the courts in a given jurisdiction to draw upon case law pertaining to defences emanating from other jurisdictions. The hypertrophication of statutory law in the context of defences means that local factors will often render it inappropriate to have recourse to foreign authorities in circumstances where recourse otherwise might usefully have been had.

9.1.4. Challenges Created by the Statutorification of Defences

The ubiquity of statutory modification of law governing tort law defences presents several challenges for the future. First, there is the problem of relevant statutory provisions being overlooked. The vast number of statutory provisions concerning defences has severely diminished the accessibility of tort law. This problem has been aggravated by the tendency of legislatures to scatter provisions creating or modifying defences across countless Acts. It has also been compounded by the fact that relevant provisions are not infrequently deposited in Acts that, on the whole, have little to do with tort law. Consider the statutory defences of illegality[16] and prevention of crime[17] in England. The provisions creating these defences are contained in statutes that are concerned predominantly with the criminal law. The titles of the Acts in issue do not suggest that they have anything to do with tort law. It is little wonder that tort lawyers have often failed to notice them.[18] The difficulty in identifying statutory provisions relevant to defences is so great that it is inevitable that material provisions will be overlooked by judges and litigants with some regularity. Legislatures may also fail to notice provisions that they enacted, with the result that duplicate provisions are created.[19]

Secondly, the frenzy of statute-making concerning defences presents difficult questions regarding the permissibility of judicial development of common law defences. Does the extensive intervention by the legislature in the defence setting

---

[14] For synopses, see DB Dobbs, *The Law of Torts* (St Paul, Minn, West Publishing Co, 2000) 1093–95; SD Sugarman, 'United States Tort Reform Wars' (2002) 25 *University of New South Wales Law Journal* 849.

[15] The details of these statutory defences cannot be given here. They are discussed at length elsewhere. In the case of Australia, see Goudkamp (n 2).

[16] Criminal Justice Act 2003 (UK), s 329.

[17] Criminal Law Act 1967 (UK), s 3(1).

[18] Eg, neither is mentioned in T Weir, *An Introduction to Tort Law*, 2nd edn (Oxford, Clarendon Press, 2006).

[19] This recently occurred in Queensland. The Queensland legislature enacted an illegality defence in 2003: Civil Liability Act 2003 (Qld), s 45. However, it had already created such a defence in 1997: Criminal Law Amendment Act 1997 (Qld), s 4(2), amending s 6 of the Criminal Code Act 1899 (Qld). An inspection of the relevant Parliamentary *Hansard*, and the fact that the 1997 defence is significantly wider in certain respects than the 2003 defence, puts it beyond doubt that the Queensland lawmakers failed to notice the 1997 defence when they created the 2003 defence.

mean that the courts should be especially cautious about changing the law in this area? Because the legislature has shown that it is attentive to the law on defences, it might be said that the courts can be reasonably confident that the legislature approves of the remaining common law. On the other hand, it can be argued strongly that the fact that the legislature regularly enacts laws in the defence setting should have no bearing on how the courts should discharge their law-making function in this field. On this view, simply because the legislature has left a given corner of the law of defences untouched does not mean that it is satisfied with it. There may be many other possible reasons for legislative inactivity, such as a lack of consensus as to how the law should be reformed or because other projects are regarded as more pressing.[20]

Thirdly, the influence of statutes in relation to defences, which is likely to continue to grow exponentially in the future, raises many complex issues of statutory interpretation. For example, to what extent should the courts remain committed to the presumption that the legislature does not intend to authorise tortious conduct?[21] This principle seems to be farcical considering the prodigious number of statutory defences that have been created. Similar remarks can be made about the related presumption that the legislature does not intend to restrict liberty.[22] This presumption has an air of unreality about it in view of, for instance, the many defences afforded to constables.[23]

Fourthly, the dominance of statutory law in the context of defences gives rise to the spectre of obsolescence. The classic treatment of the problem of anachronistic statutes is Guido Calabresi's book *A Common Law for the Age of Statutes.*[24] Calabresi argued that the 'orgy of statute-making' in the twentieth century in the United States, coupled with the general neglect of statutes once they have been enacted, meant that America was being governed by laws that were seriously outdated. He suggested that the courts had developed numerous *ad hoc* strategies in order to address anachronistic statutes. In these strategies, he saw the seeds of a new doctrine that would enable the courts to ensure that the law remains in phase with the modern world. This is not the place to engage with Calabresi's work or that of others who have addressed the same issue. The important point to note here is that statutory obsolescence in the tort defence context is a cause for concern, and is a problem that is likely to become increasingly troubling. Consider, for example, the defence of prior private prosecution,[25] which was enacted almost 150 years ago. The Court of Appeal, in a recent case, regarded it as a relic of an earlier time.[26] It is difficult to believe that it fits perfectly the needs of contemporary society.

---

[20] Support for this analysis can be found in A Burrows, 'The Relationship between Common Law and Statute in the Law of Obligations' (2012) 128 *Law Quarterly Review* 232, 247–48.

[21] For discussion of this presumption, see FAR Bennion, *Bennion on Statutory Interpretation: A Code*, 5th edn (London, LexisNexis, 2008) 1074–75.

[22] This presumption is addressed *ibid*, 836–40.

[23] See n 6 above.

[24] Calabresi (n 3).

[25] See 5.3.2.7.

[26] *Wong v Parkside Health NHS Trust* [2001] EWCA Civ 1721, [2003] 3 All ER 932, 938 [16].

Lastly, there is the issue of the analogical use of statutes to develop the common law. In a speech delivered in 1984, Patrick Atiyah famously queried whether the analogical use of statutes is permissible. He asked:[27]

> [Is it possible] for the courts to take account of statute law . . . in the very development of the common law itself? Can the courts, for instance, use statutes as analogies for the purpose of developing the common law? Can they justify jettisoning obsolete cases, not because they have been actually reversed by some statutory provision, but because a statute suggests that they are based on outdated values? Could the courts legitimately draw some general principle from a limited statutory provision, and apply that principle as a matter of common law?

In view of both the proliferation of statutory defences and the tendency of the legislature to supplement rather than to replace common law defences,[28] the courts will need to think about these questions in the defence context in the near future more seriously than they have to date. The constitutional arrangements of the legal system in which they are asked may be relevant in this connection. For instance, it is hard to see how the common law of Australia could be developed by analogy to statute unless at least several states and territories had legislated in unison.[29]

9.2. Reforming the Law of Tort Defences

The law of tort defences is one of the more dynamic parts of tort law. The legal landscape in this regard has changed very dramatically since the Industrial Revolution,[30] and it is unlikely that forces of change have been spent. Accordingly, it is worth discussing how the reform of defences ought to proceed.

9.2.1. Coherent Development

This book is the first occasion on which tort law defences have been examined systematically. It has endeavoured to identify a coherent basis for categorising defences. The analysis has demonstrated, it is hoped, the utility of looking at the defence empire as a whole. Unfortunately, this is not how defences have generally been approached. For example, whenever consideration is given to reforming a given defence, it is relatively rare for the defence concerned to be analysed other than in isolation. At most, particular defences are examined in conjunction only with other defences with which they are typically raised. This approach is a recipe

---

[27] PS Atiyah, 'Common Law and Statute Law' (1985) 48 *Modern Law Review* 1, 6.
[28] See 9.1.1.
[29] *Esso Australia Resources Ltd v Commissioner of Taxation* [1999] HCA 67; (1999) 201 CLR 49, 59–63 [18]–[28].
[30] Some of the changes in this regard are recounted in 1.3.

for an incoherent law of defences. Whenever the future of a defence is in issue, the defence in question should be considered not only in view of other defences that tend to be pleaded concurrently with it, but also alongside *all* of the defences that fall into the same defence category. The reform of defences ought to proceed in this fashion because there ought to be a degree of consistency among defences of the same class. For example, it is important to ask questions about the proper scope of the defence of responsible journalism with an eye to other justificatory defences, including justificatory defences that are unavailable in defamation actions. This is because all justifications should be consistent with each other in terms of how the onuses of pleading and proof are assigned in respect of them, whether they can be raised by the court *proprio motu*, the extent to which they are sensitive to the defendant's motive and so on. The same goes for public policy defences. In short, a logical system of tort defences cannot be achieved so long as defences are treated individually. An understanding of the importance of maintaining consistency between cognate defences is required.

9.2.2. Certainty in Classification

Suppose that a law-making body decides that liability in tort law is too extensive in some respect and creates a rule in order to reduce the zone of liability. It is crucial that the law-making body concerned makes it abundantly clear whether the new rule is an addition to the elements of a tort or a defence. This is because much turns, as has been stressed throughout this book,[31] on whether a defendant seeks to avoid liability via a denial of an element of the tort in which he is sued or a defence. If it is specified that the new rule relates to the elements of a tort, the rule concerned will automatically assume a wide range of attributes. Conversely, if it is a defence, it will possess many quite different features. The laborious chore of detailing the qualities of every new liability rule individually consequently can be avoided if it is stated whether each new rule creates room for a denial by augmenting the elements of a tort or is a defence. If a law-making body attends to the issue of classification when creating liability rules, numerous attributes of freshly-minted rules will be known from the outset. It is vital, for the same reasons, for a law-making body that ushers a new defence into the world to indicate whether it is a justification or a public policy defence. Law-making bodies have no excuse for ignoring how the liability rules they create should be classified. It is a simple matter to specify whether a given rule relates to the elements of a tort or constitutes a defence. Likewise, if a defence is inserted into tort law it is straightforward for the legislature to say whether it is a justification or a public policy defence. Neglecting the task of classification will inevitably result in uncertainty as to the parameters of new liability rules. This outcome will, in turn, provoke litigation that could have been easily avoided.

---

[31] See, especially, 2.3.9.2 and ch 6.

9.2.3. Creation of Defences versus Abolition of Defences

Legislatures and the courts stand in fundamentally different positions in so far as their capacity to change the law is concerned. One major difference which is relevant for present purposes relates to their ability to change the law only prospectively. Legislatures can (and frequently do) confine changes that they make to the law to events that occur in the future. In contrast, judicial law-making alters the law both retrospectively and prospectively.[32] The retrospective effect of judicial law-making is a reason for judges to tread carefully when they are invited to recognise a new tort.[33] This is because, when a judge creates a cause of action in tort, he renders unlawful conduct that previously might have been lawful. This is, of course, inconsistent with the principle of fair warning, a principle that, for obvious reasons, tends to be mentioned mostly in relation to the criminal law[34] but which is certainly not unimportant in the tort context. The same problem does not arise when judges are requested to abolish a tort.

What is the situation in this regard in relation to the judicial creation (and extension) and abolition (and restriction) of tort defences?[35] The creation of defences will be taken first. The effect of recognising defences is to reduce the size of the net of liability cast by the torts to which they pertain. In other words, admitting new defences narrows the circumstances in which liability arises. Considerations of fair warning do not, as a result, argue against judicial law-making on this point. But the position is different in relation to the abolition of defences. Judicial removal of defences, like judicial creation of torts, retrospectively casts the net of liability more widely in contravention of the fair warning principle.

It is sometimes claimed that the fact that judges created a given defence means that they should also have the power to abolish it and that the task of abolition should not be left for parliament.[36] This position may need to be rethought if the argument in the previous paragraph is correct. Because abolishing a defence is not the inverse of forging a new defence in so far as the principle of fair warning is

---

[32] It is generally true throughout the Commonwealth that the courts cannot make purely prospective changes to the law. For strong statements to this effect see *Edward v Edward Estate* (1987) 57 Sask R 67, 73–76 [18]–[32]; (1987) 39 DLR (4th) 654, 661–64 (CA); *Ha v New South Wales* (1997) 189 CLR 465, 503–04 (HCA). However, in the United Kingdom, the House of Lords has left the door to prospective overruling ajar: *In Re Spectrum Plus Ltd* [2005] UKHL 41; [2005] 2 AC 680. It is unclear whether the New Zealand courts can make wholly prospective changes: *Lai v Chamberlains* [2006] NZSC 70; [2007] 2 NZLR 7, 48 [95].

[33] Note that it is primarily because of the retrospective nature of judicial law-making that judges have renounced the ability to invent new criminal law offences. For a clear judicial statement of the abdication of the power to fashion new offences, see *R v Rimmington* [2005] UKHL 63; [2006] 1 AC 459, 480–83 [33]–[35] (Lord Bingham of Cornhill).

[34] For discussion, see A Ashworth, *Principles of Criminal Law*, 6th edn (Oxford, Oxford University Press, 2009) 57–74.

[35] The discussion here has been influenced by GP Fletcher, *Rethinking Criminal Law* (Boston, Mass, Little, Brown & Co, 1978) 573–74; G Williams, 'Necessity' [1978] *Criminal Law Review* 128, 128–31.

[36] See, eg, *Arthur J S Hall & Co v Simons* [2002] 1 AC 615, 704–05 [23] (HL) (Lord Hoffmann); *D'Orta-Ekenaike v Victoria Legal Aid* [2005] HCA 12; (2005) 223 CLR 1, 107–08 [343] (Kirby J).

concerned, there is reason to suppose that the power to create does not necessarily entail a correspondingly broad power to terminate. This is not to suggest, of course, that judges should have free rein to invent defences. That is not the point that has been made.

9.3. Interactional Effects

Principles of law are not freestanding. They all form part of a web. Tugging on any one part of the web can cause other parts of it to move too. This section considers a range of interactional issues concerning defences.

9.3.1. Interactions Between the Elements of Torts and Defences

Judges have sometimes argued that liability should not be imposed in a given tort because the claimant would have been entitled to relief in another tort but for the fact that the defendant had a defence to the latter tort. This reasoning was embraced in *Sullivan v Moody*.[37] The claimants in this case were suspected by the authorities of molesting children. The investigating healthcare authorities concluded that the children concerned had been sexually assaulted and notified the police. The claimants, who were never tried, subsequently sued the authorities, asserting that the authorities negligently diagnosed sexual abuse and caused them damage as a result. The High Court of Australia held that no duty of care was owed to the claimants. One of the reasons given by the Court in support of this conclusion was the fact that the claimants could not have succeeded in actions in defamation since the authorities' statements to the police were published on a privileged occasion.[38] *Sullivan* is, therefore, an instance where a defence to one tort affected the scope of an element of another tort.[39]

It is very doubtful whether defences should interact with the elements of torts in this way.[40] The decision in *Sullivan* implies that instances where one person has said something defamatory about another to a third party should be dealt with by the tort of defamation rather than the tort of negligence. Why, however, should not the actions in negligence and defamation overlap? The High Court did not say. It simply asserted that no duty of care should be recognised because doing so 'would allow recovery of damages for publishing statements to the discredit of a

---

[37] [2001] HCA 59; (2001) 207 CLR 562.

[38] *Ibid*, 580–81 [53]–[54].

[39] The same reasoning featured in Lord Keith of Kinkel's dissenting speech in *Spring v Guardian Assurance Plc* [1995] 2 AC 296, 309–15 (HL).

[40] For a searing indictment of the logic offered in *Sullivan*, see J Stapleton, 'Duty of Care Factors: a Selection from the Judicial Menus' in P Cane and J Stapleton (eds), *The Law of Obligations: Essays in Celebration of John Fleming* (Oxford, Clarendon Press, 1998) 71.

person where the law of defamation would not'.[41] This reasoning is unpersuasive given that concurrent liability in tort law is far from exceptional. A single set of facts not infrequently generates liability in multiple torts.

9.3.2. Interactions Between Defences

It has occasionally been contended that a given defence should not be recognised or expanded because it would result in other defences becoming otiose. This reasoning was adopted by Lord Cooke of Thorndon in *Reynolds v Times Newspapers Ltd*.[42] The defendants in this case argued for the creation of a 'generic privilege' to publish defamatory statements to the public at large on governmental and political matters affecting people of the United Kingdom. Lord Cooke rejected this contention for several reasons, including the following:[43]

> A new, generic qualified privilege ... would do violence to the present pattern of the law ... As regards discussion of government and political matters, the defences of justification, fair comment, and privilege for fair and accurate reports of certain proceedings would all, at one stroke, be rendered virtually obsolete.

This passage, which raises the issue of interactions within the law of defences, identifies no justification for preserving the existing pattern of defences to liability arising in the tort of defamation. Why should not a series of defences be brought within the net of a wider defence? Why should it be thought that it is a problem for one defence to render another defence or several defences nugatory in the defamation context given that the history of tort law is littered with instances where new defences have reduced the significance of existing defences?[44] Unless satisfactory answers are given to these questions, Lord Cooke's logic is unconvincing. This is not to say, of course, that the generic privilege for which the defendants in *Reynolds* argued should be recognised. That is not the point that has been made. Rather, the contention has simply been that the reason offered by Lord Cooke for declining to welcome the postulated generic privilege into tort law is, as it stands, unpersuasive.

9.3.3. Interaction with the Apportionment Legislation

9.3.3.1. Oblique impact

The introduction of the apportionment legislation[45] is a landmark in the history of the law of torts. Arguably, it was the most significant development in tort law in

---

[41] [2001] HCA 59; (2001) 207 CLR 562, 580–81 [53]–[54].

[42] [2001] 2 AC 127 (HL).

[43] *Ibid*, 220.

[44] Eg, the statutory law-and-order defences extended to constables (see ch 5, n 93) eclipsed the ill-defined protection that the common law afforded to constables.

[45] Law Reform (Contributory Negligence) Act 1945 (UK), s 1.

the twentieth century, the decision in *Donoghue v Stevenson*[46] notwithstanding.[47] Its direct effect was to abolish the defence of contributory negligence and to install in its place the apportionment regime. When legal writers consider the apportionment legislation, they usually limit their attention to these changes that it made.[48] However, the legislation has had a range of very significant indirect ramifications.[49] It is explained elsewhere how it has impacted upon the circumstances in which a duty of care will arise, the willingness of the courts to treat the claimant's conduct as an intervening act and the preparedness of the courts to accept the plea that, because the claimant's voluntarily assumed a risk of injury, an element of the tort in which he sues is absent.[50]

The legislation has also indirectly affected defences. Consider the defence of illegality in Canada. The leading authority in this area is *Hall v Hebert*.[51] In that landmark case, the Supreme Court severely curtailed the defence's scope. It confined it to situations where, were the claimant able to recover damages, tort law would stultify the operation of the criminal law.[52] Cory J, in a concurring opinion, argued that the enactment of the apportionment legislation weighed strongly in favour of hobbling the illegality defence. His Honour asserted that 'There is in my view a great deal to be said for the position that apportionment legislation goes far towards removing [illegality] as a defence.'[53] Cory J adopted this view on the ground that the apportionment legislation, which will often be engaged where the claimant was injured while committing a crime, enables the courts to award partial damages and therefore to deliver more sensitive justice than the illegality defence, which operates in an all-or-nothing way.[54]

---

[46] [1932] AC 562 (HL).

[47] Guido Calabresi and Jeffrey Cooper state that the enactment of apportionment legislation 'is as important for tort law as was the coming of insurance': G Calabresi and JO Cooper, 'New Directions in Tort Law' (1996) 30 *Valparaiso University Law Review* 859, 868. Robert Rabin identifies the introduction of apportionment as among the five most crucial developments in tort law in the 20th century: RL Rabin, 'Past as Prelude: The Legacy of Five Landmarks of Twentieth-Century Injury Law for the Future of Torts' in MS Madden (ed), *Exploring Tort Law* (Cambridge, Cambridge University Press, 2005) 70–72.

[48] An exception is MD Green, 'The Unanticipated Ripples of Comparative Negligence: Superseding Cause in Products Liability and Beyond' (2002) 53 *South Carolina Law Review* 1103.

[49] This seems to be what Denning LJ meant in *Davies v Swan Motor Co (Swansea) Ltd* (1949) 2 KB 291, 322 (CA) when he said that 'the practical effect of the [apportionment legislation] is wider than its legal effect'.

[50] J Goudkamp, 'Rethinking Contributory Negligence' in SGA Pitel, JW Neyers and E Chamberlain (eds), *Tort Law: Challenging Orthodoxy* (Oxford, Hart Publishing, 2013) 338–44.

[51] [1993] 2 SCR 159. See also *British Columbia v Zastowny* [2008] 1 SCR 27.

[52] See further J Goudkamp, 'Can Tort Law be Used to Deflect the Impact of Criminal Sanctions? The Role of the Illegality Defence' (2006) 14 *Torts Law Journal* 20; J Goudkamp, 'The Defence of Joint Illegal Enterprise' (2010) 34 *Melbourne University Law Review* 425.

[53] [1993] 2 SCR 159, 206. This logic was also embraced by Sedley LJ in his dissent in *Vellino v Chief Constable of Greater Manchester* [2001] EWCA Civ 1249; [2002] 3 All ER 78, 87–88 [46]–[48]; [2002] 1 WLR 218, 228–29, and by Murphy J in *Jackson v Harrison* (1978) 138 CLR 438, 465 (HCA).

[54] Cf *Miller v Miller* [2011] HCA 9; (2011) 242 CLR 446, 480–81 [97]–[99]; *Stones & Rolls Ltd v Moore Stephens* [2009] UKHL 39; [2009] AC 1391, 1499 [185].

9.3.3.2. *Are complete defences anomalous?*

In addition to bringing pressure to bear on certain individual defences, the apportionment legislation may be pregnant with the potential to affect defences in a far more widespread way, including, possibly, defences to actions to which the apportionment legislation does not apply. In *Crocker v Sundance Northwest Resorts Ltd*, Wilson J wrote that 'complete bar[s] to recovery [are] ... anomalous in an age of apportionment'.[55] This short passage lays bare the enormous potential of the apportionment provision radically to restructure the law of defences. However, brief reflection reveals that it is quite incorrect to say that the apportionment legislation has rendered defences generally anomalous. This claim is manifestly incorrect, even if attention is confined to the tort of negligence. The only defence that was abolished by the apportionment legislation was the common law rule that contributory negligence is fatal to the claimant's cause of action. All other defences to negligence liability were left intact, such as the descent of a limitation bar, *res judicata*, abuse of process and various immunities. Accordingly, it is patently wrong to say that defences are 'anomalous'. Judges should not limit defences on this basis.

9.3.4. Interaction with Criminal Law Defences

A topical issue is the extent to which the law concerning defences in tort law should be consistent with that governing criminal law defences. A spotlight had been shone on this question by the recent decision of the House of Lords in *Ashley v Chief Constable of Sussex Police*.[56] In this case, a police officer, while executing a warrant to search premises for drugs, shot and killed a man because he mistakenly thought that he was reaching for a gun. Proceedings in battery were brought against the Chief Constable by the man's dependants and on behalf of his estate.[57] The Chief Constable resisted the action on the ground that the police officer, despite his mistake, was entitled to the defence of self-defence. The House of Lords was called upon to determine the test for self-defence in the tort context. The Chief Constable argued that the test should be the same as in the criminal law, which grants the defence even if the mistake as to the need for self-defence was unreasonable.[58] The claimants, in contrast, supported the Court of Appeal's view[59] that only a reasonable mistake will suffice. The House of Lords, by a narrow majority,[60] sided with the claimants and, in doing so, took the law of self-defence in tort law in a different direction from the law in this regard in the criminal context. The majority placed their decision on the

---

[55] [1988] 1 SCR 1186, 1202.

[56] [2008] UKHL 25; [2008] 1 AC 962.

[57] The Chief Constable was also sued in negligence, but this action is not of interest for present purposes.

[58] *R v Martin* [2001] EWCA Crim 2245; [2003] QB 1.

[59] *Ashley v Chief Constable of Sussex Police* [2006] EWCA Civ 1085; [2007] 1 WLR 398.

[60] Lord Scott of Foscote, Lord Rodger of Earlsferry and Lord Neuberger of Abbotsbury; Lord Bingham of Cornhill and Lord Carswell dissenting.

basis of the different functions of the criminal law and tort law. The following passage from Lord Scott of Foscote's speech captures the majority's logic in this regard:[61]

> The function of the civil law of tort is different [from that of the criminal law. Tort law's] main function is to identify and protect the rights that every person is entitled to assert against, and require to be respected by, others. The rights of one person, however, often run counter to the rights of others and the civil law, in particular the law of tort, must then strike a balance between the conflicting rights . . . [E]very person has the right in principle not to be subjected to physical harm by the intentional actions of another person. But every person has the right also to protect himself by using reasonable force to repel an attack or to prevent an imminent attack. The rules and principles defining what does constitute legitimate self-defence must strike the balance between these conflicting rights. The balance struck is serving a quite different purpose from that served by the criminal law when answering the question whether the infliction of physical injury on another in consequence of a mistaken belief by the assailant of a need for self-defence should be categorised as a criminal offence and attract penal sanctions. To hold, in a civil case, that a mistaken and unreasonably held belief by A that he was about to be attacked by B justified a pre-emptive attack in believed self-defence by A on B would, in my opinion, constitute a wholly unacceptable striking of the balance. It is one thing to say that if A's mistaken belief was honestly held he should not be punished by the criminal law. It would be quite another to say that A's unreasonably held mistaken belief would be sufficient to justify the law in setting aside B's right not to be subjected to physical violence by A. I would have no hesitation whatever in holding that for civil law purposes an excuse of self-defence based on non-existent facts that are honestly but unreasonably believed to exist must fail.

It is strongly arguable that *Ashley* is authority not only for the proposition that mistakes of fact must be reasonable in order for the defence of self-defence to be available in tort law, but also for the more general principle that justificatory defences in tort law will not be granted if the defendant acted as he did because he made an unreasonable mistake of fact. But the significance of *Ashley* is wider still. The main reason why it is important is that it sets the stage for debate about the extent to which tort law defences and criminal law defences should march together.[62] This debate, which raises many challenging questions about the relationship between tort law and the criminal law, was recently addressed by Graham Virgo in a provocative contribution. Virgo argues that the default position ought to be that there should be no discrepancy between criminal law defences and tort law defences, unless a compelling reason is identified for them to come apart at particular points.[63] He points, by way of illustration, to the defence of defence of

---

[61] [2008] UKHL 25; [2008] AC 962, 973–74 [18]. See also at 984 [53], 989–90 [76], 992–93 [85]–[88].

[62] See also *R v Wacker* [2002] EWCA Crim 1944; [2003] QB 1207; and *R v Willoughby* [2004] EWCA Crim 3365; [2005] 1 WLR 1880, concerning whether the criminal law should embrace the defence of illegality as it applies in tort law.

[63] G Virgo, '"We do this in the Criminal Law and that in Tort Law": A New Fusion Debate' in SGA Pitel, JW Neyers and E Chamberlain (eds), *Tort Law: Challenging Orthodoxy* (Oxford, Hart Publishing, 2013) 338–44.

one's property. It seems that this defence is denied in the criminal law context if force is used to eject a person who was originally an invitee, at least in certain circumstances.[64] Tort law is different in this connection. In tort law, the defence allows reasonable force to be used to eject a person from property if consent for that person to remain on the property has been withdrawn.[65] Virgo complains that it indefensible that different stances are taken by the criminal law and tort law in relation to this defence. The courts have not, he notes, offered any reason for the dissonance in approach.

Virgo's thesis, while interesting and deserving of attention, is arguably misconceived. It is based on the fact that tort law and the criminal law have many concepts in common. He claims that these similarities mean that the law would be inconsistent to the extent that tort law and the criminal law deviate from each other, and that any such inconsistencies must either be justified or, if they are incapable of justification, removed. It is unclear whether this argument sustains the default rule that he supports. Why should it not be accepted instead that there should be no presumption that tort law and the criminal law should be aligned with each other given the very many respects in which tort law and the criminal law depart from each other? In other words, why should the focus be on the similarities between tort law and the criminal law rather on than the differences? Virgo does not say. Even if Virgo's thesis is correct, many difficult questions would remain about how consistency should be achieved. For example, should the tort law fall into line with the criminal law or vice versa (or should some middle ground be found)? Are there any situations where a certain amount of inconsistency might be tolerated in order to advance some other goal?

9.3.5. Interaction with the European Convention on Human Rights

The Human Rights Act 1998 (UK) entered into force on 2 October 2000.[66] It incorporates the European Convention on Human Rights (the 'Convention') into domestic law[67] and provides that it is unlawful for public bodies, which includes the courts,[68] to act incompatibly with the Convention.[69] As a result, the Convention has influenced many aspects of the common law of England, including that relating to tort defences. This section traces some of the ways in which the common law in this regard has responded to the Convention. It also mentions several ways

---

[64] *R v Burns* [2010] EWCA Crim 1023; [2010] 1 WLR 2694, 2698 [14]. The Court of Appeal mistakenly thought that it was discussing the defence of recapture of chattels, but it was in fact dealing with the defence of property defence. Virgo, in his treatment of this case, commits the same error.

[65] *Jordan House Ltd v Menow* [1974] SCR 239.

[66] The Human Rights Act 1998 (Commencement No 2) Order 2000, SI 2000/1851 (UK). Some of the Act's provisions came into force earlier.

[67] Section 1(2).

[68] Section 6(3)(a).

[69] Section 6(1).

in which the common law might in the future be adjusted in the light of the Convention.

9.3.5.1. *Impact to date*

Probably the most significant influence of the Convention on tort law defences has been in relation to the tort of defamation. In an earlier chapter,[70] it was explained that the House of Lords gave birth to the defence of responsible journalism in *Reynolds v Times Newspapers Ltd*,[71] and what this defence entails. Anticipating the entry into force of the Human Rights Act, the House recognised the defence primarily because of fears that, previously, the law of defamation did not comply with the requirements of article 10 of the Convention, which guarantees freedom of expression.[72] In particular, there was concern about the fact that media defendants might be exposed to liability for publishing an untrue defamatory statement of fact even if, in the circumstances, it was reasonable to publish the statement in question.

Arguably, the abolition of the immunity of advocates[73] by a majority of the House of Lords in *Arthur J S Hall & Co v Simons*[74] was motivated, at least in part, by article 6 of the Convention, which enshrines the right to a fair trial. Although the Human Rights Act was not then in force, the House proceeded on the footing that it would soon come into effect. Lord Millett, who formed part of the majority, said that were the immunity not abolished, the House would undoubtedly be called upon, following the entry into force of the Act, to determine its compatibility with article 6.[75] His Lordship saw no reason to postpone the removal of the immunity.

Also worth mentioning is the withdrawal of the defence of discipline from teachers who administer corporal punishment to their pupils.[76] Parliament progressively legislated to eliminate the defence in this setting.[77] The process began with the Education (No 2) Act 1986 (UK),[78] which denied the defence in the context of publicly-funded schools. It culminated with the enactment of the School Standards and Framework Act 1998 (UK),[79] which extended the denial of the defence to schools of all types.[80] This intervention was precipitated primarily by

---

[70] See 5.2.2.6.

[71] [2001] 2 AC 127 (HL).

[72] See also Human Rights Act 1998 (UK), s 12.

[73] The demise of the immunity is mentioned in 5.3.1.12.

[74] [2002] 1 AC 615 (HL).

[75] *Ibid*, 753.

[76] Education Act 1996 (UK), s 548.

[77] The material events are eloquently summarised in *R v Secretary of State for Education and Employment, ex p Williamson* [2005] UKHL 15; [2005] 2 AC 246, 253–54 [2]–[7].

[78] Section 47.

[79] Section 131.

[80] Note also the Day Care and Child Minding (National Standards) (England) Regulations 2003, SI 2003/1996 (UK), reg 5.

decisions of the European Court of Human Rights[81] in which it was held that the United Kingdom, prior to the enactment of the aforementioned legislation, was in breach of its obligation to secure certain Convention rights, including 'the right of parents to ensure . . . education and teaching in conformity with their own religions and philosophical convictions'.[82]

A final change is that wrought by section 58(3) of the Children Act 2004 (UK). This provision provides that the defence of discipline is inapplicable where actual bodily harm is inflicted against a child. This provision was prompted by the decision of the Strasbourg Court in *A v United Kingdom (Human Rights: Punishment of a Child)*.[83] The applicant in this case was a child who had been beaten by his step-father. The step-father was acquitted by a jury on a charge of assault occasionally actual bodily harm, apparently on the ground of the defence of discipline. The Strasbourg Court held that the United Kingdom, in granting the step-father this defence, breached the applicant's right under article 3 to be free from 'inhuman or degrading treatment or punishment'.

9.3.5.2. Potential future impact

The Convention has the potential to affect the law of tort defences in two ways. In the first place, it may place pressure on law-making bodies to create fresh defences or to liberalise existing defences. It is extremely difficult to predict with any reasonable degree of accuracy the changes to the law that the Convention may provoke in this regard. Arguably, despite the birth of the responsible journalism defence, existing defences to liability in defamation need to be made more robust, or additional defences need to be created, in order sufficiently to protect the right to freedom of expression, as expressed in article 10.[84] Empirical evidence that the defence of responsible journalism rarely succeeds might suggest that the creation of this defence has not reduced adequately the chilling effect of the law of defamation.[85] It is worth bearing in mind that English law still imposes liability in defamation far more readily than the law in the United States. The Supreme Court of the United States, motivated by the First Amendment, has developed a raft of restrictions on defamation liability that are unknown to the law of England.[86] It is certainly not beyond the power of judges to recognise new

---

[81] Eg, *Campbell and Cosans v United Kingdom* (1982) 4 EHRR 293 (ECtHR).

[82] European Convention on Human Rights, Protocol 1, art 2.

[83] (1998) 27 EHRR 611 (ECtHR).

[84] Cf the view of the editors of *Gatley on Libel and Slander*, who write: 'The current judicial view in England is that the combination of the defences of justification, qualified privilege (as extended by *Reynolds v Times Newspapers Ltd*) and fair comment sufficiently meet the requirements of the Convention': P Milmo and WVH Rogers (eds), *Gatley on Libel and Slander*, 11th edn (London, Sweet & Maxwell, 2008) 866 [25.18] (footnote omitted). This text, in view of the changes made to the law by the Defamation Act 2013, does not feature in the twelfth edition of this work

[85] This argument is developed at length by D Milo, *Defamation and Freedom of Speech* (Oxford, Oxford University Press, 2008) ch 5.

[86] See, especially, *New York Times v Sullivan* 376 US 254 (1964); *Gertz v Robert Welch, Inc* 418 US 323 (1974).

defamation defences. Existing defences to liability in defamation do not constitute a *numerous clausus*.[87]

The second way in which the Convention might affect the law concerning tort defences is by placing stress on existing defences. Consider article 2, which guarantees the right to life, and the defence of self-defence. Had the House of Lords, in *Ashley v Chief Constable of Sussex Police*,[88] not denied that defence to defendants who proceeded on the basis of an unreasonable mistake as to the need for defensive force, it would have been strongly arguable that the defence would have been incompatible with article 2. Many criminal law scholars contend that there are serious doubts about whether the criminal law is compliant with article 2 in this regard, given that it grants the defence of self-defence even to defendants who defend themselves on the basis of an unreasonable mistake.[89]

Of more general relevance is article 6 of the Convention. It is obvious that a claimant cannot justifiably complain that his right to a fair trial secured by article 6 has been violated simply because he cannot sue the defendant. The European Court of Human Rights has made it clear that the right in article 6 extends only to rights and obligations 'which can be said, at least on arguable grounds, to be recognised under domestic law'.[90] That article 'does not in itself guarantee any particular content for (civil) "rights and obligations" in the substantive law of the Contracting States'.[91] It follows that those defences that constitute part of the 'substantive law' are not incompatible with article 6. However, a claimant who is unable to maintain an action in tort due to the application of a 'procedural bar' may have cause for complaint. As the Strasbourg Court explained in *Fayed v United Kingdom*:[92]

> Whether a person has an actionable domestic claim may depend not only on the substantive content, properly speaking, of the relevant civil right as defined under national law but also on the existence of procedural bars preventing or limiting the possibilities of bringing potential claims to court. In the latter kind of case Article 6(1) may have a degree of applicability. ... [I]t would not be consistent with the rule of law in a democratic society or with the basic principle underlying Article 6(1) – namely that civil claims must be capable of being submitted to a judge for adjudication – if, for example, a State could, without restraint or control by the Convention enforcement bodies, remove from the jurisdiction of the courts a whole range of civil claims or confer immunities from civil liability on large groups or categories of persons.

Hence, those defences that amount to 'procedural bars' will be subject to article 6. Such defences will be inconsistent with that article 'if [they do] not pursue a legitimate aim and if there is no reasonable relationship of proportionality between the means employed and the aim sought to be achieved'.[93] The relevant issues, then, are

---

[87] *National Media Ltd v Bogoshi* (1998) 4 SA 1196, 1204.

[88] [2008] UKHL 25; [2008] 1 AC 962.

[89] Eg, Ashworth (n 34) 124–25; F Leverick, *Killing in Self-Defence* (Oxford, Oxford University Press, 2006) 183–90.

[90] *James v United Kingdom* (1986) 8 EHRR 123, 157 [81] (ECtHR).

[91] *Ibid*, 157–58. See also *Matthews v Ministry of Defence* [2003] UKHL 4; [2003] 1 AC 1163.

[92] (1994) 18 EHRR 393, 429–30 [65] (ECtHR).

[93] *Fogarty v United Kingdom* (2002) 34 EHRR 302, 313 [33] (ECtHR) (footnote omitted).

what defences are 'procedural bars' and which 'procedural bars' might unjustifiably interfere with the right to a fair trial? Pinning down the distinction between substance and procedure is not a simple task. In *Fayed*, the Court remarked:[94]

> It is not always an easy matter to trace the dividing line between procedural and substantive limitations of a given entitlement under domestic law. It may sometimes be no more than a question of legislative technique whether the limitation is expressed in terms of the right or its remedy.

It has been suggested that the defence of illegality may fall foul of article 6.[95] It is questionable, however, whether this defence is a procedural limitation.[96] It does not seem to be implausible to say that it is concerned with the merits of the claimant's action and is hence a substantive rule. Even if the defence is a procedural bar, it might be thought that it serves a legitimate purpose and advances that purpose in a proportionate way given that it is not engaged by trivial offending.[97]

Limitation bars are procedural defences. However, it would be difficult to argue convincingly that any limitation bar in English law disproportionately interferes with the right to a fair trial. The Strasbourg Court has accepted that even the short limitation period applicable to defamation actions (one year[98]) is a legitimate restriction on the right protected by article 6. That Court has indicated that limitation periods serve legitimate aims[99] and that '[i]t is, in principle, for contracting states, in the exercise of their margin of appreciation, to set a limitation period which is appropriate'.[100] However, it is conceivable that a particularly short limitation period, or a limitation bar that made no allowances for, say, special circumstances that might dissuade a potential claimant from bringing proceedings promptly, might infringe article 6.[101]

A final defence that is worth mentioning in this connection, since it is plainly a procedural bar, is that of abuse of process. It would be difficult to impugn this defence on the ground that it is not compliant with article 6. It serves the legitimate aims of ensuring that the integrity of the judicial system is not undermined and that litigants are protected from unfair practices. Because its application turns on a consideration of all of the relevant circumstances and will not be engaged except by 'a use of the court process for a purpose or in a way which is significantly different from the ordinary and proper use of the court process',[102] it cannot plausibly be contended that it is a disproportionate restriction on the right to a fair trial.

---

[94] (1994) 18 EHRR 393, 430 [67] (ECtHR).

[95] Law Commission, *The Illegality Defence in Tort* (Law Com No 160, 2001) 2–3 [1.5]–[1.8]; Law Commission, *The Illegality Defence* (Law Com CP No 189, 2009) 45–47 [3.90]–[3.95]; H Beale and N Pittam, 'The Impact of the Human Rights Act 1998 on English Tort and Contract Law' in D Friedmann and D Barak-Erez (eds), *Human Rights in Private Law* (Oxford, Hart Publishing, 2001) 153.

[96] In *Soteriou v Ultrachem Ltd* [2004] EWHC 983 (QB); [2004] IRLR 870, 887–82 [43]–[75], it was held that the defence of illegality in the contractual context is a substantive rather than procedural bar.

[97] Consider *ibid*, 882–83 [76]–[81].

[98] Limitation Act 1980 (UK), s 4A.

[99] *Stubbings v United Kingdom* (1997) 23 EHRR 213, 227 [54]–[55] (ECtHR).

[100] *Times Newspapers Ltd v United Kingdom* [2009] EMLR 254, 267 [46] (ECtHR).

[101] Consider the facts in *Pérez de Rada Cavanilles v Spain* (2000) 29 EHRR 109 (ECtHR).

[102] *Attorney General v Barker* [2000] 2 FCR 1, 6 [19] (QBD) (Lord Bingham of Cornhill CJ).

9.4. A Taxonomy of Defences to Civil Liability

This book has been limited to tort law defences. It has not addressed defences to liability arising in other causes of action. Only a subset of defences to civil liability has, therefore, been examined. Perhaps the most obvious way in which the analysis undertaken here may be extended is to determine to what extent the propositions advanced in it apply to defences to civil liability arising other than in tort.[103] In particular, the creation of a map of defences to civil liability generally is a target on which private lawyers should set their sights. It would complement the significant progress that has been made in recent decades charting the relations between the different forms of civil wrongs.

---

[103] For an attempt to extend it to defences to liability arising in unjust enrichment, see J Goudkamp and C Mitchell, 'Denials and Defences in the Law of Unjust Enrichment' in C Mitchell and W Swadling (eds), *The Restatement Third, Restitution and Unjust Enrichment: Comparative and Critical Essays* (Oxford, Hart Publishing, 2013).

INDEX OF AUTHORS

INDEX

Lightning Source UK Ltd.
Milton Keynes UK
UKOW01f1252040717
304624UK00003B/108/P